European Literary Theory and Practice

*From Existential Phenomenology
to Structuralism*

EDITED WITH INTRODUCTION BY

VERNON W. GRAS

A DELTA BOOK

ACKNOWLEDGMENTS

"Hölderlin and the Essence of Poetry" from *Existence and Being* by Martin Heidegger. Reprinted by permission of the publisher, Henry Regnery Company.

"Heidegger's Analytic of Existence and Its Meaning for Psychiatry" from *Being-in-the-world* by Ludwig Binswanger, translated by Jacob Needleman. Copyright © 1963 by Basic Books, Inc., Publishers, New York. Reprinted by permission of the publisher.

"Consciousness and Imagination" from *The Psychology of the Imagination* by Jean-Paul Sartre. Copyright © 1948 by Philosophical Library, Inc. Reprinted by permission of the publisher.

"What Is Phenomenology?" from *Phenomenology of Perception* by Maurice Merleau-Ponty. Reprinted by permission of the publishers, Humanities Press Inc. and Routledge and Kegan Paul, Ltd.

"Hermeneutics: The Approach to Symbol" from *Freud and Philosophy* by Paul Ricoeur, translated by Denis Savage. Copyright © 1970 by Yale University. Reprinted by permission of the publisher, Yale University Press.

"Two Aspects of Language: Metaphor and Metonymy" by Roman Jakobson from *Fundamentals of Language* by Roman Jakobson and Morris Halle. Reprinted by permission of the author.

"The Science of the Concrete" from *The Savage Mind* by Claude Levi-Strauss. Copyright © 1962 by Librairie Plon. Copyright

To the memory of
O. M. Jolles,
a humanist and teacher extraordinary.

Contents

INTRODUCTION   1

THEORY   26

EXISTENTIAL PHENOMENOLOGY   27

Hölderlin and the Essence of Poetry   27
Martin Heidegger

Heidegger's Analytic of Existence and
    Its Meaning for Psychiatry   43
Ludwig Binswanger

Consciousness and Imagination   61
Jean-Paul Sartre

What Is Phenomenology?   69
Maurice Merleau-Ponty

Hermeneutics: The Approaches to Symbol   87
Paul Ricoeur

STRUCTURALISM   119

Two Aspects of Language: Metaphor and Metonymy   119
Roman Jakobson

The Science of the Concrete   133
Claude Levi-Strauss

The Structuralist Activity   157
Roland Barthes

PRACTICE   165

EXISTENTIAL PHENOMENOLOGY   167

Hölderlin's "Nature and Art or Saturn and Jupiter"   167
Emil Staiger

Ibsen's *The Masterbuilder*   185
Ludwig Binswanger

Goethe's *Faust* (excerpt)   217
Johannes Pfeiffer

Saint Genet: "My Victory Is Verbal"   243
Jean-Paul Sartre

The Phenomenology of Roundness   263
Gaston Bachelard

Notes on Racinian Time   273
Georges Poulet

STRUCTURALISM   289

The Structural Study of Myth   289
Claude Levi-Strauss

Genesis as Myth   317
Edmund R. Leach

Racinian Man (excerpt)   331
Roland Barthes

On Fairy Tales   349
Michel Butor

APPENDIX   363

The Mirror of Enigmas   365
Jorge Luis Borges

Introduction

The central tenet of the existential phenomenologists, the basis of all their philosophizing, is that the essential nature of man must be understood as being-in-the-world. Very simply stated, this phrase, which is Heidegger's, defines man as the meaning-giver. All existing things come "to be," that is to have meaning, through him. This is a Kantian conception but with some differences. Where Kant's transcendental categories were immanent, static, and cognitive, Heidegger views man not as a thinking subject with fixed properties or categories, but as *Dasein*, as a function more than as an object. Borrowing Husserl's notion that consciousness is an *intentionality*, that consciousness is always a consciousness *of* something, Heidegger enlarges the concept to incorporate the whole existence of man in its various modes. Rather than beginning with Descartes' fully reflective consciousness, man as ego, Heidegger makes of this intentionality a pre-reflective structure of consciousness. Intentional consciousness precedes the fully self-aware and cognitive individual and the emergence of the world as a system of meanings. It includes and underlies them both. As Merleau-Ponty put it: "What distinguishes intentionality from the Kantian relation to a possible object is that the unity of the world, before being posited by knowledge in a specific act of identification, is 'lived' as ready-made or already there." (See "What Is Phenomenology," p. 69.) Merleau-Ponty goes on to point out that in his last writings Husserl had also broadened his earlier and too narrow intellectualistic notion of intentionality to include this pre-reflective "lived" experience. His distinction between intentionality of act (the kind Kant discusses in his *Critique of Pure Reason*) and operative intentionality ("that which produces the natural and antepredicative unity of the world and of our life . . . furnishing the text which our knowledge tries to translate into precise language") parallels Heidegger's view of man as that temporal horizon within which the things of the world appear and thereby come "to be" in time and history. Thus, man is not so much an object as a process whereby meaning comes into being. True enough, man needs matter or body to exist, but human "existence" consists precisely in the creation of meaning. Being-in-the-world is first and foremost a creative intentionality, a turning to the things-that-are in order to express and articulate them. Without human "care," without the exercise of human freedom as the "being who raises the question of being," neither self nor world would exist. If Dasein is the ontological ground of the emergence of both the world as it is commonly meant and of the ego or self, then, as the fundamental truth about man, it can serve as a norm for psychotherapy and ethics (in terms of authentic and inauthentic functioning) and also provide guidelines for a new approach to literature. In short, *being-in-the-world* can found a philosophical anthropology with fruitful applications in many fields, including literary criticism.

Of the theoretical offerings presented here, most were selected for the light they cast on human existence viewed as *being-in-the-world*. Of these, Ludwig Binswanger's essay on Heidegger is certainly a most brilliant extension of the latter's insight to the field of psychotherapy. Binswanger appropriates Heidegger's ontological *existentials* and uses them as the actual *existential a prioris* of a particular individual.[1] Thus, the various possible modes of the *Dasein* find expression in actual case histories. The modes of temporality (possibility, fallenness, facticity); spatiality; materiality; tone, etc., become meaning matrices which include in their purview the whole man, his unique historical aspects as well as his organic substrate. If a person is viewed as an intentional structure—as the projection and disclosure of the world—rather than the *homo natura* of the behaviorists or Freud, then such mental disturbances as schizophrenia must be considered primarily a dysfunction of the Dasein's ontological potentialities. As Binswanger says, ". . . from the perspective of Heidegger's analytic of existence, (we) must conceive of both mental disease . . . and neurosis as a disturbance of *koinonia*, of the functional *unity* of the Dasein's ontological potentialities" (*Heidegger's Analytic of Existence*). Human existence needs a different explanatory paradigm than Freud's *homo natura* because man is more than an instinctuality driven by mechanical necessity. Freud's doctrine, unlike Goethe's or Nietzsche's, does not include the concept of genuine change. The Freudian "instinct" underlying all anthropological metamorphoses or transformations remains the indestructible and controlling *operational* factor. Sublimation, displacement, and condensation are all techniques of change, but for psychoanalysis they are mere transitory effects, facades or illusions that must be stripped away to reveal the permanent and causally determining instincts. A truly human anthropology, says Binswanger, must include freedom as well as necessity, the historically developing person as well as the physiological organism.[2] Thus, in his psychotherapy, Binswanger dispenses with the naturalistic schema which reduces to an absolute mechanism all the unique problems of self-creating individuals. To get at this man no longer viewed as a machine but as *being-in-the-world*, as a structure of intentional meanings, Binswanger employed phenomenological analysis. He desired through empathy (*Einfühlung*) to come to understand his patient's inner world of experience. Each person has his own way of experiencing temporality, spatiality, materiality, and causality, but every one of these *existential* coordinates must be interrelated with the others to get at the patient's total world design (*Weltbild*). This "world design" provides the key whereby the patient becomes accessible. "For the *what* of the world-design always furnishes information about the *how* of the being-in-the-world and the *how* of being oneself" ("Existential Analytical School of Thought," in Rollo May (ed.), *Existence*, p. 195). As most of the world-design of the patient is expressed through language, the clinical procedure becomes a veritable hermeneutics—a movement from the words uttered to their meaning in terms of the speaker's intentional project. That such a hermeneutic is admirably suited to literary interpretation and analysis comes as no surprise; like psychoanalysis it may be applied either to the work separately, or to the author and work together. Binswanger has done the latter in his monograph *Henrik Ibsen* (1949), which ends with a "Daseinanalyse" of *The Masterbuilder* illustrating that "disturbance of koinonia" which Binswanger labels "*Verstiegenheit*" (extravagance) and which expresses its disproportions primarily through human spatiality. Translated by the editor, this fascinating analysis is to be found in the second part of the present volume.

The early Heidegger of *Being and Time* had an enormous influence on existential psychology by providing it with new coordinates for human existence—the existential a prioris of understanding, facticity, falling, and discourse. With his notion of death terminating the Dasein's future projects and thereby making it possible for the Dasein to take over his life responsibly, Heidegger provided a norm (authenticity) for psychotherapists, religionists (who adapted it), and ethical philosophers like Sartre. As stated earlier, human nature could no longer be described or understood in terms of substance. The very etymology of the word *ek-sistence* repudiates any attempt to convert man into a thing. The fundamental structure of human Dasein is process, a temporality of action and decision. Whereas a thing has an external relation to time, merely enduring time as a series of "nows" without past or future, human Dasein, or existence, projects into the future, while as "thrown" always finds itself with a past. To quote Heidegger, Dasein represents "the unity of a future which makes present in the process of having been; we designate it as temporality" (*Being and Time*, p. 374). Only by unifying properly his future and past in the present does Dasein live authentically. Because man is fundamentally a temporality, his existence is not a static entity but an emerging, unfolding development. In and through temporality, human Dasein discloses the things that are while simultaneously creating his own identity. Human existence becomes world disclosure and can best be described as the place (or "there") where particular beings appear and take on meaning. The motion of Dasein extending itself through the future, past, and present "ecstasies" of temporality constitutes the historicity whereby Being becomes accessible as meaning via human consciousness. Historicity thus reveals itself both as the inescapable mode of understanding Being and as the characteristic of Dasein and culture in general. Accordingly, literature as well as other cultural products should be studied existentially. True enough, literature becomes accessible only as a concrete document in need of scientific empirical investigation (e.g., establishing texts), but its historical significance lies in its tie to human existence. It is a precipitate of the meaning-giving function and must be approached as the product of consciousness "speaking" Being. It is through language that the phenomenon arising from the subject-object polarity finds articulation. This speech or discourse is viewed as a primordial *existential* of Dasein by Heidegger. Through discourse the meaning of Being stands revealed. Genuine discourse (the *dichten* and *denken* of the later Heidegger) becomes a "letting-be" of Being, an unveiling of the hiddenness of things. "Primordial" thinking or poetizing differs from scientific "calculative" thinking in that the former thinks of Being while the latter is concerned with beings and technological mastery. Calculative thinking is busy, distracted, and activistic. It lacks the wise passivity, the listening *Gelassenheit* of the poet or philosopher who speaks and mediates Being through language. In his essay on Hölderlin, Heidegger describes it thus: ". . . poetry is the inaugural naming of Being and of the essence of all things—not just any speech, but that particular kind which for the first time brings into the open all that which we then discuss and deal with in everyday language." All other kinds of thinking are derivative from this originative revealing of the truth, which Heidegger names *aletheia*. The poet is the mediator between the gods (Being) and the people. But it is precisely in his role of mediator that the poet is the most human of men and reveals man's true occupation and destiny: "poetically dwells man on this earth." In writing poetry about the essence of poetry, Hölderlin understood its meaning-giving function and thus anticipated our own time. He was a predecessor of such modern writers as Jorge Luis Borges and John Barth, who also make art the subject of their art and as tenants of the new time announced by Hölderlin make do without past comforts. Heidegger describes their plight thus: "It is the time of the gods that have fled *and* of the god that is coming. It is the time of need, because it lies under a double lack and a double Not: the No-more of the gods that have fled and the Not-yet of the god that is coming."

A more concrete working out of Heidegger's "being-in-the-world" is the philosophy of Merleau-Ponty. In his preface to *The Phenomenology of Perception*, Merleau-Ponty writes that phenomenology wishes to move beyond the explanatory impasses of idealism and empiricism. By putting out of play the naïve objectivity of a world-in-itself as well as the belief in some absolute mind, phenomenology concentrates "upon re-achieving a direct and primitive contact with the world." For Merleau-Ponty this primitive contact is established through the body (*corps propre*), not my body as an empirical object or as viewed from outside, but as phenomenal body, as the means of situating me in a world. Through it I perceive and simultaneously am part of the world. Because the body functions as both object and subject, as a physical being and as a mode of consciousness turning back on being, it can mediate the extremes of idealism and materialism. The body as incarnate subject is the world-opening horizon through which Being reveals itself, not in the Sartrian manner by an absolute negativity but as the result of a *pli*, or fold, of Being turning back on itself. Incarnated consciousness is a formation of Being brought about by Being itself so that body turning to the world creates a field or gestalt which acts as the underlying schema of all experience. This "lived experience" provides the raw data that the various sciences and humanities attempt to render in conceptual language. Essentially, all knowledge is conscious reflection on pre-reflective experience constituted by the "perceptual" body-world relationship. Furthermore, says Merleau-Ponty, "the perceptual synthesis is a temporal synthesis, and subjectivity, at the level of perception, is nothing but temporality, and this is what enables us to leave to the subject of perception his opacity and historicity" (*Phenomenology of Perception*, p. 239). Like Heidegger, Merleau-Ponty sees time not as an object of our knowledge, but as a dimension of our being. The historical coming to be of perception and all ensuing dependent reflections are opaque because perception, first of all, is not transparently clear, as intellectual conceptions are. It is "lived experience" that needs reflection to clarify itself. But this pursuit of meaning can never reach total completion because every conceptualization takes its sense from its figure-background relation to the horizons of the prior "lived world." Meaning, thus, becomes a dialectical movement of bringing to explicit foreground what is only potentially and latently present to the tacit incarnated cogito. This expressive activity or symbolization is the mode of authentic human existence, and culture is but the sedimentation and accumulation of man's past acts of signification. Both culture and the constitution of self-consciousness create themselves on the active-passive relationship existing between subjectivity and the historical situation. At the level of language, for example, new meanings come to be when our speech (subjectivity) recenters the language that encompasses us (situation) through a " 'coherent deformation' (Malraux) of available significations which arranges them in a new sense and takes not only the hearers but the *speaking subject as well* through a decisive *step*" (*Signs*, p. 91). Such a decentering and recentering of the entire language incarnates "the excess of what I have lived over what has been said." For a literary critic, it is mandatory that he understand this gesture by taking up the author's style and living through the excess of the author's experience over what has been said already. In this way he comes to understand the author's original project and shares in his world. This notion underlies the methods of the French "critics of consciousness." Like Heidegger, Merleau-Ponty also posits inauthentic modes of human existence but he describes them as failures in expression. *Activism* and *fascination*, the two kinds of failures, occur whenever the meaning-giving process absolutizes itself around one or the other pole of the perceptual field. Instead of "sense," man then promulgates "non-sense."

Gaston Bachelard's outlook, superficially quite different from Merleau-Ponty's, has much in common with the latter's in respect to underlying concerns, problems, and solutions. Both men had scientific backgrounds, were interested in psychology, and focused their philosophy on the meaning-giving process. Whereas Merleau-Ponty diversified his fundamental notion of "gesture" by extending it analogously to varied cultural expressions (see, e.g., *Signs*), Bachelard restricted his investigation to the image, which he regarded as the originative moment in the creative process. Even so, Bachelard's distinction between soul and mind, given in his introduction to *The Poetics of Space*, resembles Merleau-Ponty's pre-reflective-reflective dichotomy. Like the *corps propre*, the soul has affinities with the unconscious in being prior, originative, and immediate, while the fully conscious and reflective mind constructs derivatively. Because the soul (unconscious) has an inner light which speaks through the imagination, poetry becomes "a soul inaugurating a form." The poetic image "places us at the origin of the speaking being." The reader must take the image not as a representation but as a creative reality. It is neither an object nor a substitute for one but has an ontology all its own. The fact that an image communicates, that it is transsubjective even though new, finds its explanation in the reader's echoing "reverberation" to that interior light which has created the "being" of that expression. Bachelard's imagination acts as the center of the equilibrium between self and world just as the *corps propre* and his image is equivalent to that moment of *dehiscence de l'Etre* in which sense is born. The image combines interiority with exteriority, and matter with spirit, and overcomes the Cartesian bifurcation of reality into subject and object. Because of his interest in the "originative moment" Bachelard restricts himself to explicating images. Whole poems or art works require participation of the reflective consciousness and for that reason become combinations of genuine creativity and derived representations. Thus, Bachelard's technique, illustrated here in "The Phenomenology of Roundness," is to "reverberate" phenomenologically to a series of detached though related images while ignoring their context. In our example, images of roundness taken from various sources confirm the intuition often given in propositional form that "being is round." In their iridescence, these images of "dreaming consciousness" reveal being in its cosmic dimension.

Without doubt, Jean-Paul Sartre is the most famous of the existential phenomenologists. Philosopher, psychologist, novelist, dramatist, and critic—he performs all his roles brilliantly. Plainly visible in these diverse pursuits, however, is a unifying ethical concern. Sartre believes that as giver of meanings, man creates his norms and values. They are not ready-made but emerge as the product of man's freedom. Man's essence is to create both himself and "world" through his intentional freedom, which Sartre defines as a wholly transcendental, spontaneous activity never coincidental with the originating self but always ahead of it. Like Merleau-Ponty, Satre posits two levels of self-consciousness: the fully reflective consciousness of self in which the ego is the object of consciousness and a pre-reflective consciousness which, unlike Merleau-Ponty's, is pure negation. Man's essential freedom is the intentionality of this latter transparent consciousness which, in contrast to *being*, can best be defined as a *nothing*, as a lack or negation of all that is. Completely empty of being, a void, or hole in being, this intentional consciousness yearns for the condition of a thing-in-itself. The paradox of being "condemned to be free" consists in the vain attempt of this freedom, the for-itself, to achieve the status of a thing, the in-itself. Man "is a useless passion" because he will never achieve the unification of the *pour soi* (a free and dynamically "ek-sisting" transcendence) and the *en soi* (a static entity completely determined and self-contained). The *en soi* always is what it is. But human existence remains ambiguously unstable because consciousness separates and opposes itself to all that is, making it impossible that man can ever *be* what he *is*. He can never exist as being because he exists always apart as consciousness of being. He is separated from what he is precisely by *nothing*, by a consciousness defined as a free transcending negativity always ahead of itself and beyond the given present. Ultimately, this freedom consists in being a function or insubstantial process existing only in and through its dialectical opposition to the positivity of being. Most of Sartre's writings revolve around the loving hatred of these two poles of human existence. He either exposes the deep yearning of man to escape from the anguish and abandonment of dreadful freedom into the security of *mauvaise foi*, as in *The Respectful Prostitute*, or reveals the violence and rupture occasioned by freedom's *depassement* (going beyond) of all dead formulas (moral, political, or otherwise) as exemplified in *The Devil and the Good Lord*.

At this point, let me offer a critique in order to explain my choice of the two Sartre essays included here. That Sartre insists on the difference between things and consciousness is acceptable enough, but consciousness as the opposite of things is more than nothing, or negation. Consciousness must first be consciousness *of* something. As Merleau-Ponty points out, consciousness makes the world appear. There is no in-itself outside of a perceiving consciousness. Sartre has a tendency to absolutize the in-itself as the opposite of the for-itself, as well as to make the latter an absolute freedom. Such an interpretation of human existence becomes an ontology of being viewed as nothingness. This ontology of nothingness we can forget about—it is mistaken and Sartre himself no longer holds to it— but the phenomenologist who described the operation of this freedom did say important things about creativity and about the way the imagination functions. As phenomenological studies of the workings of the imagination and its illustration in the creative work of a single writer, *The Psychology of Imagination* and *Saint Genet*, respectively, may well belong among Sartre's most lasting contributions.

In the concluding chapter of *The Psychology of Imagination* (from which we excerpt), Sartre lays bare the nihilating quality of imagination and its virtual identity with the power of consciousness to transcend any and every situation. He affirms that "imagination is not an empirical and superadded power of consciousness, it is the whole of consciousness as it realizes its freedom; every concrete and real situation of consciousness in the world is big with imagination inasmuch as it always presents itself as a withdrawing from the real" (p. 270). Further phenomenological description of this imagination at work is provided in the excerpt from *Saint Genet*, "My Victory Is Verbal." Genet's project of martyrdom to the "morality of the possessors" resembles in its inversion the stance of the Negro grandfather in Ralph Ellison's *The Invisible Man* who made his weakness over against southern whites into a defense by "yes(ing) them to death." Genet's blatant espousal of evil forms an authentic record of human freedom asserting itself in adversity— through thievery and the imagination of an artist.

Our two German language critics, Emil Staiger and Johannes Pfeiffer, are very Heideggerian in their approach. Pfeiffer interprets Faust's quest as a form of activism deficient in necessary patience. Faust's tragedy runs its course between the polarities of egoistic self-seeking linked to mastery of the other and a receptive openness to Being—the wise passivity of Heidegger's *Gelassenheit*. Faust seeks the unconditional, but to achieve it he must learn submission to the fullness of Being. His freedom has too much defiance to admit the needed receptivity to that Being which "remains superior to all thought." Only trusting patience "with believing surmise" can read finitude as the "hieroglyphics of Being." Every time Faust appears to be on the verge of achieving the proper attitude, he rushes into another excess of "world consumption and possession." In Pfeiffer's interpretation, Faust never unambiguously gains the necessary patience which finite man needs to open himself to the infinite. This is his tragedy. The second part of the essay, not included here, takes up the problem of Faust's salvation and purification which occurs in the frame or outer action and which seems to contradict the tragic inner action.

According to Staiger, a similar activism is attacked in Hölderlin's ode. Jupiter, whose emergence and displacement of Saturn is synonymous with the emergence of art and language, must resist the hubris inherent in language. He must not make himself the sole source and center of meaning nor allow utility and calculative reason to be the subjugating norms. Art must articulate and express nature, for this is the service the poet renders unto nature. Despite the advent of Jupiter (or art) ending the mute prehistory of Saturn's golden age, new Saturn days may return. For though language and temporality differentiate the earlier Primal Unity, "language that makes love known differentiates but no longer separates. It differentiates only in order to unite more intimately." Thus, the poet under Jupiter's aegis reveals "drunken Saturn as Unity and Unifying Power" behind the manifold appearances of things. Saturn is nature viewed as love. In all this, however, the poet must guard himself because language has a dangerous inherent tendency toward abstraction—to separate itself from the living temporal process into some dead formula or another. Thus, the greatest danger for the artist in giving utterance to mute nature would be to feel himself the center and origin of life rather than merely the agency through which it stands revealed. Both our critics understand the problem posed by Goethe and Hölderlin, respectively, as the difficulty to exist authentically, and both view their authors' resolutions as supporting the Heideggerian ontology.

So far, George Poulet has written three volumes of Studies of Human Time. The last was *Le Point de depart* (1964).[3] In these critical studies he writes about literature as the "history of the human consciousness." Literature is viewed as the "expression" of that ongoing experiential process by which a creative consciousness simultaneously establishes both the world and its own self. In his preface to Jean Richard's *Littérature et sensation*, he writes: "Criticism cannot be contented with thinking a thought. It must work its way farther back, from image to image to feelings. It must reach the act by which the mind . . . united itself to an object to invent itself as subject" (quoted in Lawall, p. 79). Like Bachelard, Poulet often uses individual lines, images, or words to bring to the surface the central mediating moment, the starting point of a writer's sensibility. In his earlier studies, Poulet abstracted the *existentials* of temporality and spatiality as generic universals through which work and artist could be treated. In addition, somewhat in Lovejoy's manner, he places his writers into historical epochs that may be characterized by shared viewpoints or ideas. For Poulet, these are especially the periodic conceptualizations of time and space. Thus, in the seventeenth century, the idea of continued creation inherited from the medieval period was no longer identical in its duration with personal existence. Continued creation "instead of continually conferring upon man an existence which is a duration, . . . now confers upon him an existence which is confined to the instant, and which therefore needs perpetually to be prolonged from instant to instant. . . . An intimate awareness of an ever actual existence, an acute sense of the discontinuity of duration, and a total dependence upon a creation continually reiterated—these are indeed the essential traits of human time in the seventeenth century" (*Studies in Human Time* [1956], p. 14). For Racine, however, "the continued creation of the world implies the creation of a being which is prolonged backward, whose existence consists not only in living, but in having lived, and lived badly." His tragedies depict existence as a problem because God's continuous creation inevitably brings with it the past with all its evils. The time sense of Racine's tragedies is dominated by the past and the subject of almost every tragedy "consists in the repetition and the ineluctable continuation of the past into the present." The Racinian tragedy is essentially "an action *in the past*." Its characters are overwhelmed by a feeling of past guilt, "of what stains and destroys" them. In *Phaedra*, however, a change occurs so that "past cause and past evil is exorcised by the recognition of a cause which transcends all duration." In the plays that follow, *Esther* and *Athalie*, the divine acts of Providence are then set forth in human durations. In contrast to Binswanger, who uses the *existentials* to psychoanalyze both the characters of *The Masterbuilder* and Ibsen himself—Poulet, in "Notes on Racinian Time," uses the *existential* of temporality to link Racine to the broader concerns of literary history. The work of these two writers strikingly illustrates the power, flexibility, and scope in the methods of phenomenological criticism.

Of all the phenomenological essays, Paul Ricoeur's excerpt from *Freud and Philosophy* (1970) is the most recent and constitutes an answer to the structuralist theory of language. Actually, Ricoeur is fighting on two fronts. He opposes his hermeneutics and theory of symbolization to Freud's while simultaneously subordinating the structural semiology of sign-signified to a creative semantics of the speech act. As a phenomenologist, Ricoeur could not allow meaning to reside self-containedly within a system of signs having no reference to the outside world nor particularly needing a subject to originate them. For the structuralists, language is an autonomous system whose signs derive their meaning from inner relationships and not by designating things. Intelligibility is a function of the relationships and oppositions of terms in a system. Changes are kept separate from the state of the system, and history becomes the juxtaposing of one state of the system (or intelligibility) to another. Ricoeur's phenomenology of language unifies semiology and semantics by subordinating signs with their duality of signifier-signified to the symbolic function. The inner systematic relationship between signifier and signified is not possible, Ricoeur affirms, without the prior "designating" relationship between sign and thing. This latter dialectical relationship is the creative living substrate of symbolism which founds the conditions of language as code.

However, a symbol is an equivocal expression whose double meaning not only discloses creative intentionality, but also includes the "interference of desire with intentionality, upon which desire inflicts an invincible obscurity" (p. 458). Disguise and disclosure operate in all symbolism; that is why art and dreams are "physical expressions of the same nature." They merely differ in their emphasis: dream is the indirect language of desire which seeks to disguise itself through displacement and substitution while staying riveted to the past and childhood; art emphasizes disclosure and is a mediation or sublimation which binds desire (the "matter" of dreams) to the aims and intentions of the spirit. Thus, "works of art tend to be prospective symbols of one's personal synthesis and of man's future and not merely a regressive symptom of the artist's unresolved conflicts." Balancing the regressive archaeology of Freudian psychoanalysis with the progressive teleology of a Hegelian intentionality, Ricoeur emerges with a comprehensive theory of symbolization holding within its parameters the central tension of human existence. Having in an earlier work described this tension between nature and freedom as *the* problem of our time, he formulated his own mediating principle as "nature makes freedom actual while freedom makes nature meaningful." Translated onto the level of language and symbolization this reciprocal principle now becomes "the return of freedom to nature through the recapture of desire in the works of culture." Hermeneutics or symbolic exegesis must always reveal the dialectical structure of this opposition and reciprocity. Thus, in his own example of interpretation, Ricoeur can allow the presence of the Oedipal dream as background for Sophocles' *Oedipus Rex*. But contrary to Freud's reductive interpretation, he views the tragedy as a conflict between that regressive childhood complex and an adult movement toward truth and light. "By reason of this impure passion with respect to the truth, (Oedipus') hubris rejoins that of Prometheus: what leads him to disaster is the passion for non-knowing. His guilt is no longer in the sphere of the libido, but in that of self-consciousness: it is man's anger as the power of nontruth." Keeping in mind that for Ricoeur truth is viewed in a rather broad fashion as "fulfillment," the aesthetic pleasure given by an art work such as *Oedipus Rex* is "the pleasure of sharing in the work of truth that comes about through the hero." Symbolization is then a derivation of energy from nature but simultaneously a transformation or sublimation of this energy into innovative meaning. By reflecting on the cultural products of this sublimation, phenomenology through hermeneutics may recover the incarnated Ego's effort to exist.

II

The controversy over the "death of the subject" raging in France between phenomenologists and structuralists in recent years might well raise doubts over their intellectual kinship. So before taking up the divisive issue, perhaps we should briefly sketch in their affiliation. Structuralism, like phenomenology, remains in the critical idealist stream of continental philosophy. Unlike traditional Anglo-American science and philosophy, which begin with observable behavior and proceed to inductive generalizations, structuralism assumes the categorical primacy of the human mind and approaches cultural phenomena in order to illustrate the workings of this universal mind. Thus, structuralism, like phenomenology, focuses on the meaning-giving process and emphasizes the active constituting role of the human participant in that process. Because epistemological "conditionals" have a way of becoming ontological, we are not surprised to hear of "structural man" replacing the earlier slogan of "existential man." Furthermore, as Roland Barthes stresses in his article, structuralism is an ongoing repetitive *activity*. It has no body of beliefs to affirm aside from its structuralist premises and is just as empty of content as Sartrean existentialism. Process and "structural function" dominate over semantic considerations so that substantialists with their essentialistic thinking (whether religious, ethical, or scientific) remain the common enemy for both existential phenomenologists and structuralists.

The parting of ways occurs in the description of the meaning-giving activity. Here the two methods could not be more radically opposed. Whereas existential phenomenology takes the high road on which the fully conscious subject exercising his freedom brings meaning into existence, structuralism takes the low road, on which a universal but latent and unconscious human mind inscribes its deterministic architecture everywhere. Levi-Strauss puts it this way:

> In anthropology as in linguistics, therefore, it is not comparison that supports generalization, but the other way around. If . . . the unconscious activity of the mind consists in imposing forms upon content, and if these forms are fundamentally the same for all minds—ancient and modern, primitive and civilized . . . —it is necessary and sufficient to grasp the unconscious structure underlying each institution and each custom, in order to obtain a principle of interpretation valid for other institutions and other customs . . . (*Structural Anthropology:* Anchor edition, p. 21).

The issue is clear-cut. Structuralism must view existential temporality and transcendence as illusory as long as it affirms the priority of the mind's unconscious patterning. Having articulated the unconscious and given it a function and pre-eminence, structuralism opposes the freedom of the fully conscious subject, making of him a product rather than an originator. The conscious subject is always the object of the structuring system which has its true initiating agent in the unconscious. So man is fundamentally heteronomous or non-identical with himself. But though this phrase seems to echo the existential cliché, the valuation of its dichotomy is exactly reversed. The subject, no longer constituting but constituted, merely participates as one of the terms in a set of functions.

Having so neatly separated the structuralists from the phenomenologists, we now have to blur this demarcation somewhat. The above orientation applies pre-eminently to Levi-Strauss and Jacques Lacan as the fathers of the structuralist movement, but it applies to a lesser degree to Roland Barthes and those other structuralists interested in literary matters. Levi-Strauss approaches the study of myth from a scientific anthropological viewpoint. He is a new breed of positivist who substitutes the functioning of the human mind for nineteenth-century materialism. When studying primitive man and his relatively unsophisticated and naïve understanding of the world as reflected in his myths, rituals, and tribal organization, Levi-Strauss takes these cultural manifestations—often enough in the case of myths literally absurd and nonsensical to us in their content—and indicates their underlying sense by revealing the latent problem or contradiction they mediate. A structural analysis of myths reveals that primitive man thought just as logically as modern man and that the human brain has always operated in the same logical fashion. The only change lies in the materials with which the mind operates. Structuralism thus brings clarification and intellectual order to an area of human activity that previously had allowed only irrational or patronizing theories of explanation. Ultimately, the structuralist hypothesis desires the status of a universal natural law. Roland Barthes, on the other hand, accepts the structural theory more as method than as some absolute truth. He remains a historical relativist who acknowledges that structural theory participates in history like other ideologies and so cannot hope to escape becoming the object of some metalanguage of the future which in turn will "speak" it. Meantime, he feels the need to institute a criticism of signification, i.e., to make us aware of the structural activity—or *how* meaning comes into being no matter how diverse the ideology or semantic content of the language systems investigated. Historical perspective shows us the shortcomings and ephemerality of past beliefs and the necessity to subordinate content to the unconscious structural activity whereby man brings himself into equilibrium with his world. As we will point out later, this kind of criticism often becomes a negative critique or demythologization of past ideologies. On its positive side, however, structural analysis concerns itself with the meaning-giving process. Barthes is actually pursuing the same goal as the phenomenologists. He wants to focus on the creative process which he, however, defines as an unconscious structural activity.

But how does the human mind unconsciously operate? Roland Barthes in "The Structuralist Activity" gives a coherent and economical description of how to uncover this structuring process. He begins by emphasizing that "the goal of all structuralist activity is to reconstruct an 'object' in such a way as to manifest thereby the rules of functioning (the 'functions') of the object." Structuralism is basically an *intellectual activity*. The artist when he creates and the critic when he analyzes really engage in a comparable procedure, for the intellectual processes are the same in both cases. Both are imitations (what Levi-Strauss calls homologies) of a more general ordering process underlying all cultural phenomena. It is this intellectual technique rather than any material content that a structuralist (artist or critic) believes primary. "We recompose the object *in order* to make certain functions appear, and it is, so to speak, the way that makes the work . . ." To the structuralist, meaning does not ever appear in the guise of a simple denotation (sign/referent). Empiricism and naïve realism believe that language derives its meaning by referring to an "object" in the world. The structuralists (following Saussure) affirm that meaning is diacritical, emanating from terms relating to each other within a system; in themselves, the terms carry no meaning. Fundamentally, it is through combination and selection that terms interrelate and establish meaning.[4]

How this works can be illustrated in Levi-Strauss' *Totemism* (1963) and "The Structural Study of Myth." The diacritical principle of differential elements establishes that meaning results from two or more terms in relation within a system. Just as phonemes have no meaning in themselves but through *their differences* articulate a meaningful sound (word) so in turn do totemic classifications and myths establish meanings out of binary oppositions or differences. Thus, totemic species differ between themselves in the same manner as human groups do. The resemblance exists *between these two systems of difference*. For example, primitive man ordered his social life by the use of a "science of the concrete." He used names of animals and birds in his classificatory schemes rather than our logical "p's" and "q's." Animal species were "translated into terms of friendship and conflict, solidarity and opposition." It was possible to classify and use natural species as pairs of opposites if first a common characteristic permitted them to be compared. Accordingly, the bird totems, crow and eaglehawk—used by natives to relate two social groups—both eat meat, but one is a hunter while the other is a scavenger. Meat-eating also provides the point of comparison with human beings so that totemic classifications stand revealed as a metaphoric nomenclature by which human social correlations and oppositions have been formalized. As Levi-Strauss sees it, totemism, a social ordering process, is a particular expression of the more general problem "how to make opposition, instead of being an obstacle to integration, serve rather to produce it." Myth is more complex but functions quite similarly. Its oppositions are not between natural species like birds, animals, or plants standing metaphorically for human relations. Mythemes emerge from bundles of sentences which already have two terms in relationship, e.g., Oedipus kills Laius. Though more complex than phonemes, the constituting sentences function analogously to create the mytheme just as phonemic discriminations articulate a word. Certain sentences whose two terms are similar in their relationship to "Oedipus kills Laïus" find themselves opposed by other sentences grouped with "Oedipus marries Jocasta." The meaning of the myth emerges only from the opposition of these two groups of sentences which, by endlessly replicating like musical motifs, create the mythemes. The units or sentences themselves have no further importance except as posing the contradiction to be mediated.

For Levi-Strauss, all cultural phenomena reduce to codes built on binary oppositions which then are mediated. All of these codes must be understood as systems. For a structuralist, an individual cultural element receives its meaning only from its relationship

to all the other elements constituting its particular system. Totemism, myth, exchange of women, religion, art, economics, are all
systems of communication from the structuralist viewpoint. They
may be analyzed as so many separate "languages" or investigated
metalinguistically as homologues of each other emanating from the
same depth model or "symbolic order" which makes all these different languages possible. Edmund Leach describes these two levels
of investigation thus: "The structure of relations which can be
discovered by analyzing materials drawn from any one culture is an
algebraic transformation of other possible structures belonging to a
common set, and this common set constitutes a pattern which
reflects an attribute of the mechanism of all human brains" (E.
Leach, *Claude Levi-Strauss*, p. 52).

From such a point of view aesthetic pleasure or emotion could
never function as a cause or end-in-itself. It is derivative—the consequence or result of the ordering process. The basic opposition reconciled in art (and science), according to Levi-Strauss, is that
between structure (necessity) and event (contingency) with the
contingent appearing in three modes: occasion, execution, purpose.
The laws which govern this dialectic between structure and event
are borrowed from linguistics: metaphor and metonymy. In *The
Fundamentals of Language* (1954) Roman Jakobson already indicated that these linguistic categories undoubtedly extend beyond
language to more basic thought processes. But most original of all,
he pointed out that the workings of the Freudian unconscious,
which operate through condensation and displacement, could be
assimilated to the linguistic categories of metaphor and metonymy.
Much of the interest and excitement generated by structuralism
comes from this transposition of the Freudian unconscious into a
linguistically structured unconscious. The entire domain of human
conduct and expression mapped out by psychoanalysis finds itself
suddenly under new management. It is a breathtaking, fascinating
prospect magnetically attractive to artist and scholar alike. At
present, this movement to regroup the human sciences around linguistics has taken on the label of "the sciences of man." [5]

While structuralism can aim at laying bare the unconscious "functioning" of the human mind, it can also open to inspection the

underlying "epistemic models" which in the past have identified themselves as both organizing principle and fundamental reality. This latter kind of "preconstraint"—the historical and contingent semantical charge inherited from past culture—often solidifies and impedes the process of structuring meaning. Analysis then changes from admiration of the "aesthetic" and "totalizing" primitive mind to a criticism or demythologizing of a historical society entangled in myth or ideological bonds. In both cases, structuralist criticism makes structural activity visible. In both ways there is a devaluation of the denotative or empirical content. In the Levi-Strauss mode, empirical content is the necessary material through which structural activity stands revealed but is rarely itself the object of investigation. In the second approach, empirical content is viewed as ideological or mythic, determined by collective attitudes of class or historical period, and then structural analysis becomes a liberation because it demythologizes. It reveals the underlying attitudes controlling the manifest content. Of our structuralist critics, Leach, Butor, and Barthes (in his essay on Racine) take representations from historical societies and demythologize this material in varying degrees. Leach, for example, deliberately cites a theological definition of myth: "the expression of unobservable realities in terms of observable phenomena" in order to completely subvert it (and religious transcendence) to his own system. Genesis, of course, is a combination of pure myth (creation to flood) and some historical facts (the patriarchs). Because the book shifts from cosmogony to history of a single people, Leach's analysis shifts from the more general consideration of "the antinomy of life and death" with its repetitive mediations to the incest/exogamy problem of the Hebrews' first ancestors. The tales of Abraham, Lot, Isaac, Jacob, and Esau repeat the underlying motif of "the virtue of close kin endogamy" to the extent that the relations of Abraham and Sarah, even though incestuous, "stand out as uniquely virtuous."

Michel Butor's "On Fairy Tales" narrows its topic by eliminating the peasant oral folk tale and concentrating on the French written fairy tales of the seventeenth to nineteenth centuries (those of Perrault, Mme. d'Aulnoy, and the Comtesse de Segur). Butor views the *function* of fairy tales just as favorably as Levi-Strauss does myth. Fairy tales invert the world of reality and help the growing child adjust to certain social inequalities or hardships with which accident of birth often confronts him. In counterpoising these inequities, fairy tales promote social survival and thus function positively. For example, tales of kings and shepherds exaggerate the extremes of social status with their attendant disparity between rich and poor, only to overcome them in the end. Eventually, the poor man becomes rich, usually through a marriage. The tale implies that low social status is not a permanent unalterable reality. Again, in a society ruled by primogeniture, the younger son (whose inferior status gives him no prospects) must leave home and seek his fortune. Invariably, he succeeds and displaces his older brother(s) in wealth and social prestige. Other areas of conflict in need of mediation are those between parents and children and between men and women. In many tales the son displaces (kills) the father (ogre) and takes over his function (obtains wealth and power). Girls, on the other hand, must be admonished about the dangers surrounding their transformation to womanhood. The essential episode for heroines is most often a catastrophe (symbolic of the sexual act) which only a public marriage sets right again. Though fairyland is a compensatory world of wishful thinking, Butor finds in fairy tales a critique of ossified reality and veiled suggestions on how to get on in the bourgeois world, e.g., marry well. Ultimately, Butor's intention is to praise the function of fairy tales while disassociating their functional value from any particular content. He concludes that because the difficulties of the growing child of today have changed, we must invent new stories to mediate these new social realities.

Roland Barthes reduces the eleven Racinian plays into one essential tragedy. The paradigmatic model is Freud's primeval horde with its "incest, rivalry among the brothers, murder of the father, overthrow of the sons . . . the fundamental actions of the Racinian theatre." This dissection strips all the characters down to their basic status and relationships in the archaic family while eliminating surface motivations, individual characterization, any subtle development of themes among the plays themselves, and their historical setting at Versailles. The Freudian metalanguage liberates Barthes to depict on a grand scale certain simplified oppositions, resolutions, and failures present in all Racine's work. True to his dictum, Barthes seeks not so much the meaning of any particular work as the discovery of "how meaning is possible and by what means." The entire Racinian theater no longer exists in a historical ambience nor on the level of individuated plot and character; the plays exist only as problems of structure.

> Racinian division is rigorously binary, the possible is never anything but the contrary. This elementary partition doubtless reproduces a Christian idea; but in the profane Racine, there is no Manicheism, division is pure form: it is the dual function that counts, not its terms. Racinian man does not debate between Good and Evil: he debates, that is all; his problem is on the level of structure, not of character.

The tendency of such criticism to become too comprehensive, to employ all-encompassing categories that lose analytical value, and to obliterate the unique flavor of author or work must be admitted. On the other hand, this same grand deployment of unifying oppositions cannot cease to attract, if for no other reasons than the reader's aesthetic joy in the catharsis attendant on such extensive clarification and the fact that "structural man . . . experiences his validity (but not his truth) in his power to speak the old languages of the world in a new way."

NOTES

1. For a clear and full account, see Jacob Needleman's introduction to Ludwig Binswanger, *Being-in-the-world* (New York, 1963).
2. In *Childhood and Society* and other works, Eric Erikson tries also to amalgamate the socio-cultural with the psychobiological level of human existence. For him historic temporality and spatiality need to be integrated with the individual's sexual and somatic maturation. For the similarity between Erikson's and Binswanger's concerns, see William Sadler, *Existence and Love* (New York, 1969).
3. For an excellent presentation and critique of Poulet's theory, see Sarah Lawall, *Critics of Consciousness* (Cambridge, 1968), pp. 74–135.
4. See the essay by Roman Jakobson on "combination" and "selection" which identify with the later "metonymy" and "metaphor."
5. For a sampling of the movement, see Richard Macksey and E. Donato (eds.), *The Language of Criticism and the Sciences of Man* (Baltimore, 1970).

THEORY

Existential Phenomenology

Hölderlin and
the Essence of Poetry

MARTIN HEIDEGGER

THE FIVE POINTERS

1. Writing poetry: "That most innocent of all occupations." (III, 377)

2. "Therefore has language, most dangerous of possessions, been given to man . . . so that he may affirm what he is. . . ." (IV, 246)

3. "Much has man learnt.
   Many of the heavenly ones has he named,
   Since we have been a conversation
   And have been able to hear from one another." (IV, 343)

4. "But that which remains, is established by the poets." (IV, 63)

5. "Full of merit, and yet poetically, dwells Man on this earth." (VI, 25)

Why has Hölderlin's work been chosen for the purpose of showing the essence of poetry? Why not Homer or Sophocles, why not Virgil or Dante, why not Shakespeare or Goethe? The essence of poetry is realized in the works of these poets too, and more richly even, than in the creative work of Hölderlin, which breaks off so early and abruptly.

This may be so. And yet Hölderlin has been chosen, and he alone. But generally speaking is it possible for the universal essence of poetry to be read off from the work of one single poet? Whatever is universal, that is to say, what is valid for many, can only be reached through a process of comparison. For this, one requires a sample containing the greatest possible diversity of poems and kinds of poetry. From this point of view Hölderlin's poetry is only one among many others. By itself it can in no way suffice as a criterion

for determining the essence of poetry. Hence we fail in our purpose at the very outset. Certainly—so long as we take "essence of
poetry" to mean what is gathered together into a universal concept,
which is then valid in the same way for every poem. But this universal which thus applies equally to every particular, is always the
indifferent, that essence which can never become essential.

Yet it is precisely this essential element of the essence that we are
searching for—that which compels use to decide whether we are
going to take poetry seriously and if so how, whether and to what
extent we can bring with us the presuppositions necessary if we are
to come under the sway of poetry.

Hölderlin has not been chosen because his work, one among many,
realizes the universal essence of poetry, but solely because Hölderlin's
poetry was borne on by the poetic vocation to write expressly of the
essence of poetry. For us Hölderlin is in a pre-eminent sense *the poet
of the poet*. That is why he compels a decision.

But—to write about the poet, is this not a symptom of a perverted
narcissism and at the same time a confession of inadequate richness
of vision? To write about the poet, is that not a senseless exaggera-
tion, something decadent and a blind alley?

The answer will be given in what follows. To be sure, the path by
which we reach the answer is one of expediency. We cannot here,
as would have to be done, expound separately each of Hölderlin's
poems one after the other. Instead let us take only five pointers
which the poet gave on the subject of poetry. The necessary order
in these sayings and their inner connectedness ought to bring before
our eyes the essential essence of poetry.

I.

In a letter to his mother in January, 1799, Hölderlin calls the
writing of poetry "that most innocent of all occupations" (III, 377).
To what extent is it the "most innocent"? Writing poetry appears
in the modest guise of *play*. Unfettered, it invents its world of images
and remains immersed in the realm of the imagined. This play thus
avoids the seriousness of decisions, which always in one way or
another create guilt. Hence writing poetry is completely harmless.
And at the same time it is ineffectual, since it remains mere saying

and speaking. It has nothing about it of action, which grasps hold directly of the real and alters it. Poetry is like a dream, and not reality; a playing with words, and not the seriousness of action. Poetry is harmless and ineffectual. For what can be less dangerous than mere speech? But in taking poetry to be the "most innocent of all occupations," we have not yet comprehended its essence. At any rate this gives us an indication of where we must look for it. Poetry creates its works in the realm and out of the "material" of language. What does Hölderlin say about language? Let us hear a second saying of the poet.

2.

In a fragmentary sketch, dating from the same period (1800) as the letter just quoted, the poet says:

> But man dwells in huts and wraps himself in the bashful garment, since he is more fervent and more attentive too in watching over the spirit, as the priestess the divine flame; this is his understanding. And therefore he has been given arbitrariness, and to him, godlike, has been given higher power to command and to accomplish, and therefore has language, most dangerous of possessions, been given to man, so that creating, destroying, and perishing and returning to the everliving, to the mistress and mother, he may affirm what he is—that he has inherited, learned from thee, thy most divine possession, all-preserving love. (IV, 246)

Language, the field of the "most innocent of all occupations," is the "most dangerous of possessions." How can these two be reconciled? Let us put this question aside for the moment and consider the three preliminary questions: 1. Whose possession is language? 2. To what extent is it the most dangerous of possessions? 3. In what sense is it really a possession?

First of all we notice where this saying about language occurs: in the sketch for a poem which is to describe who man is, in contrast to the other beings of nature; mention is made of the rose, the swans, the stag in the forest (IV, 300 and 385). So, distinguishing plants from animals, the fragment begins: "But man dwells in huts."

And who then is man? He who must affirm what he is. To affirm
means to declare; but at the same time it means: to give in the
declaration a guarantee of what is declared. Man is *he* who he *is*,
precisely in the affirmation of his own existence. This affirmation
does not mean here an additional and supplementary expression of
human existence, but it does in the process make plain the existence
of man. But what must man affirm? That he belongs to the earth.
This relation of belonging to consists in the fact that man is heir and
learner in all things. But all these things are in conflict. That which
keeps things apart in opposition and thus at the same time binds them
together, is called by Hölderlin "intimacy." The affirmation of belonging to this intimacy occurs through the creation of a world and
its ascent, and likewise through the destruction of a world and its
decline. The affirmation of human existence and hence its essential
consummation occurs through freedom of decision. This freedom
lays hold of the necessary and places itself in the bonds of a supreme
obligation. This bearing witness of belonging to all that is existent
becomes actual as history. In order that history may be possible,
language has been given to man. It is one of man's possessions.

But to what extent is language the "most dangerous of possessions"? It is the danger of all dangers, because it creates initially the
possibility of a danger. Danger is the threat to existence from what
is existent. But now it is only by virtue of language at all that man
is exposed to something manifest, which, *as* what is existent, afflicts
and enflames man in his existence, and as what is nonexistent deceives
and disappoints. It is language which first creates the manifest conditions for menace and confusion to existence, and thus the possibility
of the loss of existence, that is to say—danger. But language is not
only the danger of dangers, but necessarily conceals in itself a continual danger for itself. Language has the task of making manifest in
its work the existent, and of preserving it as such. In it, what is purest
and what is most concealed, and likewise what is complex and
ordinary, can be expressed in words. Even the essential word, if it
is to be understood and so become a possession in common, must
make itself ordinary. Accordingly it is remarked in another fragment of Hölderlin's: "Thou spokest to the Godhead, but this you
have all forgotten, that the first-fruits are never for mortals, they
belong to the gods. The fruit must become more ordinary, more

everyday, and then it will be mortals' own" (IV, 238). The pure and the ordinary are both equally something said. Hence the word as word never gives any direct guarantee as to whether it is an essential word or a counterfeit. On the contrary—an essential word often looks in its simplicity like an unessential one. And on the other hand that which is dressed up to look like the essential is only something recited by heart or repeated. Therefore language must constantly present itself in an appearance which it itself attests, and hence endanger what is most characteristic of it, the genuine saying.

In what sense however is this most dangerous thing one of man's possessions? Language is his own property. It is at his disposal for the purpose of communicating his experiences, resolutions and moods. Language serves to give information. As a fit instrument for this, it is a "possession." But the essence of language does not consist entirely in being a means of giving information. This definition does not touch its essential essence, but merely indicates an effect of its essence. Language is not a mere tool, one of the many which man possesses; on the contrary, it is only language that affords the very possibility of standing in the openness of the existent. Only where there is language, is there world, i.e., the perpetually altering circuit of decision and production, of action and responsibility, but also of commotion and arbitrariness, of decay and confusion. Only where world predominates, is there history. Language is a possession in a more fundamental sense. It is good for the fact that (i.e., it affords a guarantee that) man can *exist* historically. Language is not a tool at his disposal, rather it is that event which disposes of the supreme possibility of human existence. We must first of all be certain of this essence of language, in order to comprehend truly the sphere of action of poetry and with it poetry itself. How does language become actual? In order to find the answer to this question, let us consider a third saying of Hölderlin's.

3.

We come across this saying in a long and involved sketch for the unfinished poem which begins "Versöhnender, der du nimmergeglaubt . . ." (IV, 162ff. and 339ff):

Much has man learnt.
Many of the heavenly ones has he named,
Since we have been a conversation
And have been able to hear from one another. (IV, 343)

Let us first pick out from these lines the part which has a direct bearing on what we have said so far: "Since we have been a conversation . . ." We—mankind—are a conversation. The being of men is founded in language. But this only becomes actual in *conversation*. Nevertheless the latter is not merely a manner in which language is put into effect, rather it is only as conversation that language is essential. What we usually mean by language, namely, a stock of words and syntactical rules, is only a threshold of language. But now what is meant by "a conversation"? Plainly, the act of speaking with others about something. Then speaking also brings about the process of coming together. But Hölderlin says: "Since we have been a conversation and have been able to hear from one another." Being able to hear is not a mere consequence of speaking with one another, on the contrary it is rather presupposed in the latter process. But even the ability to hear is itself also adapted to the possibility of the word and makes use of it. The ability to speak and the ability to hear are equally fundamental. We are a conversation—and that means: we can hear from one another. We are a conversation, that always means at the same time: we are a *single* conversation. But the unity of a conversation consists in the fact that in the essential word there is always manifest that one and the same thing on which we agree, and on the basis of which we are united and so are essentially ourselves. Conversation and its unity support our existence.

But Hölderlin does not say simply: we are a conversation—but: "Since we have been a conversation . . ." Where the human faculty of speech is present and is exercised, that is not by itself sufficient for the essential actualization of language—conversation. Since when have we been a conversation? Where there is to be a *single* conversation, the essential word must be constantly related to the one and the same. Without this relation an argument too is absolutely impossible. But the one and the same can only be manifest in the light of something perpetual and permanent. Yet permanence and perpetuity only appear when what persists and is present begins to shine.

But that happens in the moment when time opens out and extends. After man has placed himself in the presence of something perpetual, then only can he expose himself to the changeable, to that which comes and goes; for only the persistent is changeable. Only after "ravenous time" has been riven into present, past and future, does the possibility arise of agreeing on something permanent. We have been a single conversation since the time when it "is time." Ever since time arose, we have *existed* historically. Both—existence as a *single* conversation and historical existence—are alike ancient, they belong together and are the same thing.

Since we have been a conversation—man has learnt much and named many of the heavenly ones. Since language really became actual as conversation, the gods have acquired names and a world has appeared. But again it should be noticed: the presence of the gods and the appearance of the world are not merely a consequence of the actualization of language, they are contemporaneous with it. And this to the extent that it is precisely in the naming of the gods, and in the transmutation of the world into word, that the real conversation, which we ourselves are, consists.

But the gods can acquire a name only by addressing and, as it were, claiming us. The word which names the gods is always a response to such a claim. This response always springs from the responsibility of a destiny. It is in the process by which the gods bring our existence to language that we enter the sphere of the decision as to whether we are to yield ourselves to the gods or withhold ourselves from them.

Only now can we appreciate in its entirety what is meant by: "Since we have been a conversation . . ." Since the gods have led us into conversation, since time has been time, ever since then the basis of our existence has been a conversation. The proposition that language is the supreme event of human existence has through it acquired its meaning and foundation.

But the question at once arises: how does this conversation, which we are, begin? Who accomplishes this naming of the gods? Who lays hold of something permanent in ravenous time and fixes it in the word? Hölderlin tells us with the sure simplicity of the poet. Let us hear a fourth saying.

4.

This saying forms the conclusion of the poem "Remembrance" and runs:

> But that which remains, is established by the poets. (IV, 63)

This saying throws light on our question about the essence of poetry. Poetry is the act of establishing by the word and in the word. What is established in this manner? The permanent. But can the permanent be established then? Is it not that which has always been present? No! Even the permanent must be fixed so that it will not be carried away, the simple must be wrested from confusion, proportion must be set before what lacks proportion. That which supports and dominates the existent in its entirety must become manifest. Being must be opened out, so that the existent may appear. But this very permanent is the transitory. "Thus, swiftly passing is everything heavenly; but not in vain" (IV, 163f.). But that this should remain, is "Entrusted to the poets as a care and a service" (IV, 145). The poet names the gods and names all things in that which they are. This naming does not consist merely in something already known being supplied with a name; it is rather that when the poet speaks the essential word, the existent is by this naming nominated as what it is. So it becomes known *as* existent. Poetry is the establishing of being by means of the word. Hence that which remains is never taken from the transitory. The simple can never be picked out immediately from the intricate. Proportion does not lie in what lacks proportion. We never find the foundation in what is bottomless. Being is never an existent. But, because being and essence of things can never be calculated and derived from what is present, they must be freely created, laid down and given. Such a free act of giving is establishment.

But when the gods are named originally and the essence of things receives a name, so that things for the first time shine out, human existence is brought into a firm relation and given a basis. The speech of the poet is establishment not only in the sense of the free act of giving, but at the same time in the sense of the firm basing of human existence on its foundation.

If we conceive this essence of poetry as the establishing of being by means of the word, then we can have some inkling of the truth of that saying which Hölderlin spoke long after he had been received into the protection of the night of lunacy.

5.

We find this fifth pointer in the long and at the same time monstrous poem which begins:

> In the lovely azure there flowers with its
> Metallic roof the church-tower. (VI, 24ff)

Here Hölderlin says (line 32f.):

> Full of merit, and yet poetically, dwells
> Man on this earth.

What man works at and pursues is through his own endeavors earned and deserved. "Yet"—says Hölderlin in sharp antithesis, all this does not touch the essence of his sojourn on this earth, all this does not reach the foundation of human existence. The latter is fundamentally "poetic." But we now understand poetry as the inaugural naming of the gods and of the essence of things. To "dwell poetically" means: to stand in the presence of the gods and to be involved in the proximity of the essence of things. Existence is "poetical" in its fundamental aspect—which means at the same time: in so far as it is established (founded), it is not a recompense, but a gift.

Poetry is not merely an ornament accompanying existence, not merely a temporary enthusiasm or nothing but an interest and amusement. Poetry is the foundation which supports history, and therefore it is not a mere appearance of culture, and absolutely not the mere "expression" of a "culture-soul."

That our existence is fundamentally poetic, this cannot in the last resort mean that it is really only a harmless game. But does not Hölderlin himself, in the first pointer which we quoted, call poetry "That most innocent of all occupations"? How can this be reconciled with the essence of poetry as we are now revealing it? This brings us back to the question which we laid aside in the first instance. In now proceeding to answer this question, we will try at the same time to summarize and bring before the inner eye the essence of poetry and of the poet.

First of all it appeared that the field of action of poetry is language. Hence the essence of poetry must be understood through the essence of language. Afterwards it became clear that poetry is the inaugural naming of being and of the essence of all things—not just any speech, but that particular kind which for the first time brings into the open all that which we then discuss and deal with in everyday language. Hence poetry never takes language as a raw material ready to hand, rather it is poetry which first makes language possible. Poetry is the primitive language of a historical people. Therefore, in just the reverse manner, the essence of language must be understood through the essence of poetry.

The foundation of human existence is conversation, in which language does truly become actual. But primitive language is poetry, in which being is established. Yet language is the "most dangerous of possessions." Thus poetry is the most dangerous work—and at the same time the "most innocent of all occupations."

In fact—it is only if we combine these two definitions and conceive them as one that we fully comprehend the essence of poetry.

But is poetry then truly the most dangerous work? In a letter to a friend, immediately before leaving on his last journey to France, Hölderlin writes: "O Friend! The world lies before me brighter than it was, and more serious. I feel pleasure at how it moves onward, I feel pleasure when in summer 'the ancient holy father with calm hand shakes lightnings of benediction out of the rosy clouds.' For amongst all that I can perceive of God, this sign has become for me the chosen one. I used to be able to exult over a new truth, a better insight into that which is above us and around us, now I am frightened lest in the end it should happen with me as with Tantalus of old, who received more from the gods than he was able to digest" (V, 321).

The poet is exposed to the divine lightnings. This is spoken of in the poem which we must recognize as the purest poetry about the essence of poetry, and which begins:

> When on festive days a countryman goes
> To gaze on his field, in the morning . . .
>
> (IV, 151ff)

There, the last stanza says:

> Yet it behoves us, under the storms of God,
> Ye poets! with uncovered head to stand,
> With our own hand to grasp the very lightning-flash
> Paternal, and to pass, wrapped in song,
> The divine gift to the people.

And a year later, when he had returned to his mother's house, struck down with madness, Hölderlin wrote to the same friend, recalling his stay in France:

"The mighty element, the fire of heaven and the stillness of men, their life amid nature, and their limitation and contentment, have constantly seized me, and, as it is told of the heroes, I can truly say that I have been struck by Apollo" (V, 327). The excessive brightness has driven the poet into the dark. Is any further evidence necessary as to the extreme danger of his "occupation"? The very destiny itself of the poet tells everything. The passage in Hölderlin's "Empedocles" rings like a premonition:

> He, through whom the spirit speaks, must leave
> betimes. (III, 154)

And nevertheless: poetry is the "most innocent of all occupations," Hölderlin writes to this effect in his letter, not only in order to spare his mother, but because he knows that this innocent fringe belongs to the essence of poetry, just as the valley does to the mountain; for how could this most dangerous work be carried on and preserved, if the poet were not "cast out" ("Empedocles" III, 191) from everyday life and protected *against* it by the apparent harmlessness of his occupation?

Poetry looks like a game and yet it is not. A game does indeed bring men together, but in such a way that each forgets himself in the process. In poetry on the other hand, man is reunited on the foundation of his existence. There he comes to rest; not indeed to the seeming rest of inactivity and emptiness of thought, but to that infinite state of rest in which all powers and relations are active (cf. the letter to his brother, dated 1st January, 1799. III, 368f).

Poetry rouses the appearance of the unreal and of dream in the face of the palpable and clamorous reality, in which we believe ourselves at home. And yet in just the reverse manner, what the poet says and undertakes to be, is the real. So Pathea, with the clairvoyance of a friend, declares of "Empedocles" (III, 78):

> That he himself should be, is
> What is life, and the rest of us are dreams of it.

So in the very appearance of its outer fringe the essence of poetry seems to waver and yet stands firm. In fact it is itself essentially establishment—that is to say: an act of firm foundation.

Yet every inaugural act remains a free gift, and Hölderlin hears it said: "Let poets be free as swallows" (IV, 168). But this freedom is not undisciplined arbitrariness and capricious desire, but supreme necessity.

Poetry, as the act of establishing being, is subject to a *twofold* control. In considering these integral laws we first grasp the essence entire.

The writing of poetry is the fundamental naming of the gods. But the poetic word only acquires its power of naming when the gods themselves bring us to language. How do the gods speak?

> . . . . And signs to us from antiquity are the
> language of the gods. (IV, 135)

The speech of the poet is the intercepting of these signs, in order to pass them on to his own people. This intercepting is an act of receiving and yet at the same time a fresh act of giving; for "in the first signs" the poet catches sight already of the completed message and in his word boldly presents what he has glimpsed, so as to tell in advance of the not-yet-fulfilled. So:

> . . . the bold spirit, like an eagle
> Before the tempests, flies prophesying
> In the path of his advancing gods. (IV, 135)

The establishment of being is bound to the signs of the gods. And at the same time the poetic word is only the interpretation of the "voice of the people." This is how Hölderlin names the sayings in which a people remembers that it belongs to the totality of all that exists. But often this voice grows dumb and weary. In general even it is not capable of saying of itself what is true, but has need of those who explain it. The poem which bears the title "Voice of the People," has been handed down to us in two versions. It is above all the concluding stanzas which are different, but the difference is such that they supplement one another. In the first version the ending runs:

> Because it is pious, I honor for love of the
>   heavenly ones
> The people's voice, the tranquil,
> Yet for the sake of gods and men
> May it not always be tranquil too willingly!
>   (IV, 141)

And the second version is:

> . . . and truly
> Sayings are good, for they are a reminder
> Of the Highest, yet something is also needed
> To explain the holy sayings. (IV, 144)

In this way the essence of poetry is joined onto the laws of the signs of the gods and of the voice of the people, laws which tend toward and away from each other. The poet himself stands between the former—the gods, and the latter—the people. He is one who has been cast out—out into that *Between*, between gods and men. But only and for the first time in this Between is it decided, who man is and where he is settling his existence. "Poetically, dwells man on this earth."

Unceasingly and ever more securely, out of the fullness of the images pressing about him and always more simply, did Hölderlin devote his poetic word to this realm of Between. And this compels us to say that he is the poet of the poet.

Can we continue now to suppose that Hölderlin is entangled in an empty and exaggerated narcissism due to inadequate richness of vision? Or must we recognize that this poet, from an excess of impetus, reaches out with poetic thought into the foundation and the midst of being. It is to *Hölderlin himself* that we must apply what he said of Oedipus in the late poem "In the lovely azure there flowers . . .":

> King Oedipus has one
> Eye too many perhaps. (VI, 26)

Hölderlin writes poetry about the essence of poetry—but not in the sense of a timelessly valid concept. This essence of poetry belongs to a determined time. But not in such a way that it merely conforms to this time, as to one which is already in existence. It is that Hölderlin, in the act of establishing the essence of poetry, first determines a new time. It is the time of the gods that have fled *and* of the god that is coming. It is the time *of need*, because it lies under a double lack and a double Not: the No-more of the gods that have fled and the Not-yet of the god that is coming.

The essence of poetry, which Hölderlin establishes, is in the highest degree historical, because it anticipates a historical time; but as a historical essence it is the sole essential essence.

The time is needy and therefore its poet is extremely rich—so rich that he would often like to relax in thoughts of those that have been and in eager waiting for that which is coming and would like only to sleep in this apparent emptiness. But he holds his ground in the Nothing of this night. Whilst the poet remains thus by himself in the supreme isolation of his mission, he fashions truth, vicariously and therefore truly, for his people. The seventh stanza of the elegy "Bread and Wine" (IV, 123f.) tells of this. What it has only been possible to analyze here intellectually, is expressed there poetically.

> "But Friend! we come too late. The gods are alive, it is true,
> But up there above one's head in another world.
> Eternally they work there and seem to pay little heed
> To whether we live, so attentive are the Heavenly Ones.
> For a weak vessel cannot always receive them,

Only now and then does man endure divine abundance.
Life is a dream of them. But madness
Helps, like slumber and strengthens need and night,
Until heroes enough have grown in the iron cradle,
Hearts like, as before, to the Heavenly in power.
Thundering they come. Meanwhile it often seems
Better to sleep than to be thus without companions,
To wait thus, and in the meantime what to do and say
I know not, and what use are poets in a time of need?
But, thou sayest, they are like the wine-god's holy priests,
Who go from land to land in the holy night."

Heidegger's Analytic of Existence and Its Meaning for Psychiatry

LUDWIG BINSWANGER

Translated by *Jacob Needleman*

> *And do you think that you can know the nature of the soul intelligently without knowing the nature of the whole?* PLATO, *Phaedrus*, 270c

Martin Heidegger's analytic of existence is doubly significant for psychiatry. It affords empirical psychopathological research a new methodological and material basis that goes beyond its previous framework, and its treatment of the existential concept of science places *psychiatry in general* in a position to account for the actuality, possibility, and limits of its own scientific world-design or, as we may also call it, transcendental horizon of understanding. These two aspects are quite closely related, and both have their roots in Heidegger's *Sein und Zeit* and *Vom Wesen des Grundes*.

The purpose of *Sein und Zeit* was the "concrete" working out of the question as to the meaning of *Being*. Its preliminary goal was to interpret time as the possible horizon of any understanding of Being. To this end, Heidegger, as we know, gives us the "concrete" working out of the *ontological structure* of the Dasein as being-in-the-world or transcendence. In thus indicating the basic structure of the Dasein as being-in-the-world, Heidegger places in the psychiatrist's hands a key by means of which he can, free of the prejudice of any scientific *theory*, ascertain and describe the *phenomena* he investigates in their full phenomenal content and intrinsic context. It was Edmund Husserl's great achievement to have shown, after Brentano, just what this "phenomenological" method is, and to have indicated what enormous vistas it opened for research in the various sciences. Husserl's doctrine, however, concerns itself solely with the sphere of *intentionality*, considered as the unitary relation between transcendental subjectivity and transcendental objectivity. The shift from the "theoretical" ascertainment and description of psychic processes or events in a "subject" to the ascertainment and description of the forms and structures of "intentional consciousness," consciousness of something or directedness toward something, was a quite decisive shift for psychopathological research. Nevertheless, this consciousness was still suspended in the air, in the thin air of the transcendental ego. The —in the full sense of the word—"fundamental" accomplishment of Heidegger consisted not only in stating the problematic nature of the transcendental possibility of intentional acts. What he did, in addition, was to solve this problem by showing how the intentionality of consciousness is grounded in the temporality of human existence, in the Dasein. Intentionality in general is only possible on the basis of "transcendence" and is thus neither identical with it nor, conversely, does it make transcendence possible. Only by referring intentionality back to the Dasein as transcendence or being-in-the-world and only, therefore, with the inclusion of the transcendental ego in the actual Dasein, was the ("objective-transcendental") question posed as to the *what-ness* of the beings that we ourselves are.[1] We may thus say, with Wilhelm Szilazi, that *Sein und Zeit* is the first inquiry into our existence "with regard to its objective transcendence."

Since, in "The Existential Analysis School of Thought," [2] I have already sketched the path thus taken, we turn our attention now to the second aspect of Heidegger's dual significance for psychiatry—namely, the question as to the actuality, possibility, and limits of the horizon of understanding, or world-design of psychiatry in general. This problem might also be characterized as concerning the awareness by psychiatry of its own essential structure as science, or, again, as the effort of psychiatry *to understand itself as science*. It goes without saying that in this brief space I can only hint at what the answer to this problem might be.

I

A science does not understand itself simply by being clear as to the "object" it studies and the basic concepts and research methods by which it conducts these studies. Rather, a science understands itself only when it—in the full sense of the Greek *lógon didónai*—accounts for its interpretation (expressed in its basic concepts) of its particular region of being upon the background of that region's basic ontological structure. Such an accounting cannot be executed with the methods of the particular science itself, but only with the aid of philosophical methods.

Science is autonomous with regard to what, in its terms, can be *experienced.* Here it justifiably protects itself against any philosophical "encroachment," just as, for its part, any philosophy aware of its own purposes restrains itself from such encroachment. While, as history has shown, science and philosophy share the same roots, this means that whereas science sets the questions by which it approaches that which is, philosophy poses the question as to the nature of proof as ground and foundation—the question, that is, as to the function performed by transcendence, as such, of establishing a ground. This is simply to repeat—in different words—that a science can understand itself only if it accounts for the original formulation of its question within which, *qua* this particular *scientific* mode of grounding, it approaches the things it studies and has them speak to it. To this extent, and only to this extent, is science to be "referred" to philosophy; to the extent, that is, that the self-understanding of a science, considered as the articulation of an actual store of ontological understanding, is possible only on the basis of *philosophical,* i.e., ontological, understanding, in general.

II

Whereas physics and biology and the humanistic sciences as well rest upon their own particular "actual store of ontological understanding," [3] the same cannot be said of psychiatry. In its clinical setting, psychiatry views its object, the "mentally ill human being" from the aspect of nature, and, thus, within the natural-scientific—

mainly biological—horizon of understanding. Here psychiatry's object is—as it is in all of medicine—the "sick" organism. But in psychotherapy, it views its object from the aspect of "the human being," and thus within an (either prescientific or systematic) anthropological horizon of understanding. Here the object of psychiatry is the "mentally ill" Other, the fellow man. The incompatibility of these two conceptual horizons or reality-conceptions is not resolvable within science and leads not only to endless scientific controversy, but, also, as the present situation in psychiatry shows, to a split into two separate psychiatric camps. This fact alone shows how important it is for psychiatry to concern itself with the question as to what we human beings *are*.

In actual practice, these two conceptual orientations of psychiatry usually overlap—as one quick glance at its "praxis" tells us. The clinician, too, first "relates himself to" his patient or seeks "an understanding with him." And precisely from this relating or understanding he attains his initial perspective from which to ascertain the *symptoms* of the disease. It was, in fact, Hönigswald who expressed the view that psychiatric symptoms are primarily disturbances of communication and thus refer [4] to a "meaning given to human intercourse." One of the basic demands of medical psychotherapy, on the other hand, is to view the prospective patient *also* as an organism, the demand, namely, that what must first be ascertained is whether the patient is intact "as" an organism—especially as regards the central nervous system—and whether the possibility of such a disturbance of intactness sets up certain therapeutic limitations from the outset.

To the extent, now, that the psychiatrist views the organism as a natural object, i.e., "physicalistically," to the extent that he thus views the fellow man before him, with whom he tries to come to an understanding and who is his partner in the community of man and is another "human soul"—to that extent will his ontological understanding be clouded, at the outset, by the *psychophysical problem*. For, the mind-body problem is not an ontological problem, but a problem of scientific knowledge, a purely theoretical problem. "Theory," therefore, is called in for help in "solving" this problem. No theory, however, can really "solve" it, but can only seek to bridge mind and body with more or less perfunctory theoretical sham solutions ("auxiliary hypotheses"), or immerse the whole problem in a pseudophilosophical (materialistic, spiritualistic, biologistic, or psychologistic) smoke screen.

The problem of mind and body, though it arises out of urgent practical scientific needs, is incorrectly formulated because science —as it must—fails to see that what is involved are two quite different scientific conceptions of reality which cannot be bridged by any theory nor merged together by any amount of speculation. For as soon as I objectify my fellow man, as soon as I objectify his subjectivity, he is no longer my fellow man; and as soon as I subjectify an organism or make a natural object into a responsible subject, it is no longer an organism in the sense intended by medical science. The situation can be put to rights only if we go *behind* both conceptual horizons or reality-conceptions—that of nature and that of "culture"—and approach man's basic function of understanding Being as the establishing of ground—a transcendental function. Our task, then, is to use philosophical rigor in understanding both the power and the impotence of these two conceptions considered as *scientific*, or even as prescientific or "naïve," modes of transcendental grounding or establishment.

III

Scientific understanding is oriented toward fact and factuality, i.e., toward reality and objectivity. Such a project (or design) separates areas of fact and places the various entities in a factual, real, objective, and systematic interconnection.[5] Heidegger has shown that such a project is not simply a demarcation of regions, but is also the establishing of a ground. That is, in such a project a particular sphere "of being" (beings) are "thematized" and thereby rendered accessible to objective inquiry and determination. If this is so, then such a project must be constantly subjected to a critique that concerns itself with the fundamental issues of all scientific inquiry. It is not *only* philosophy that performs this function of criticism. We find it constantly being effected in the way scientific concepts of themselves break down and undergo transformations—in, that is, the various *crises* of science.

Today psychiatry finds itself in just such a crisis. The "Magna

Charta" [6], or framework, that was its guide up to now has been broken down on the one hand by psychoanalysis and by psychotherapy's generally deepened understanding of its own scientific bases, and on the other hand by ever-increasing insight into the game of psychosomatics, and above all by "structural" [7] and empirical existential-analytic research, which has widened the scope and cast light on psychiatry's horizon of understanding.

Simply as regards this "crisis," Heidegger's phenomenological-philosophical analytic of existence is important for psychiatry. This is so because it does not inquire merely into particular regions of phenomena and fact to be found "in human beings," but, rather, inquires into the *being* of *man as a whole*. Such a question is not answerable by scientific methods alone. The conception of man as a physical-psychological-spiritual unity does not say enough. For, as Heidegger says, the being of man cannot be ascertained by the "summative enumeration" of the rather ambiguous ontological modes of body, mind, and soul. What is needed is the return to (subjective) transcendence, to the Dasein as being-in-the-world, even while constant attention is being accorded its objective transcendence.

It is, of course, true that modern psychiatry also seeks to know the nature of the "soul" by regarding the nature of the whole— as Plato prescribed (see the chapter motto). But psychiatry, as a branch of medicine, primarily views this whole as "life," as a biological whole, and every "consideration" of this whole ordinarily takes place at the level of factual objective "relations." In addition, the soul is understood as something neutrally present (*vorhanden*) in or with the body. But even aside from these considerations, what is meant by the Greek expression *to Holon*—in contrast to *to Pan*—is not the totality of the whole, but—as in Aristotle— wholeness as such. Heidegger's analytic of existence, by inquiring into the being of the whole man, can provide not scientific, but philosophical understanding of this wholeness. Such an understanding can indicate to psychiatry the limits within which it may inquire and expect an answer and can, as well, indicate the general horizon within which answers, as such, are to be found.

It is incorrect to accuse Heidegger's analytic of existence of failing to deal with nature, for it is through this same analytic of existence that the basis for the problem of nature can be obtained —*via* the approach to the Dasein as situationally attuned (*befindlich-gestimmten*) existence *among beings*. It would be equally incorrect to accuse *Daseinsanalyse* of "neglecting the body." Insofar as a world-design is seen as *thrown*—and this means situationally attuned—then, explicitly or not, attention is being directed to the Dasein in its bodiliness.

In practice, whenever the psychiatrist himself tries to look beyond the limitations of his science and seeks to know the ontological grounds of his understanding and treatment of those placed in his care, it is Heidegger's analytic of existence that can broaden his horizon. For it offers the possibility of understanding man as both a creature of nature, and a socially determined or historical being —and this by means of *one* ontological insight, which thus obviates the separation of body, mind, and spirit. Man as a creature of nature is revealed in the thrownness of the Dasein, its "that-it-is," its *facticity*. "Has the Dasein, as such, ever freely decided and will it ever be able to decide as to whether it wants to come into 'existence' or not?" The Dasein, although it exists essentially for its own sake (*umwillen seiner*), has nevertheless not itself laid the ground of its *being*. And also, as a creature "come into existence," it is and remains, *thrown*, determined, i.e., enclosed, possessed, and compelled by beings in general. Consequently it is not "completely free" in its world-design either. The "powerlessness" of the Dasein here shows itself in that certain of its possibilities of being-in-the-world are *withdrawn* because of commitment to and by beings, because of its facticity. But it is also just this withdrawal that lends the Dasein its *power:* for it is this that first brings *before* the Dasein the "real," graspable possibilities of world-design.

Transcendence is thus not only a striding or swinging of the Dasein toward the world, but is, at the same time, withdrawal, limitation—and only *in* this limiting does transcendence gain power "over the world." All this, however, is but a "transcendental document" of the Dasein's *finitude*. The thrownness of the Dasein, its facticity, is the transcendental horizon of all that scientific systematic psychiatry delimits as reality under the name of organism, body (and heredity, climate, milieu, etc.), and also for all that which is delimited, investigated, and researched as psychic *determinateness:* namely, as mood and ill humor, as craziness, compulsive or insane "possessedness," as addiction, instinctuality, as confusion, phantasy determination, as, in general, unconsciousness. Now, whereas the science of psychiatry not only observes and establishes connections *between* these two spheres, but also erects the theoretical bridge of the psychophysical—*Daseinsanalyse*, on the other hand, shows that it is the scientific dichotomization of man's ontological wholeness that gives rise to this postulate in the first place. It shows that this dichotomization results from projecting the whole of human being upon the screen of that which is merely objectively present [*vorhanden*]. It also indicates the general world-design of science as stemming from one and the same Dasein, from, namely, the Dasein's ontological potentiality of scientific being-in-the-world. Here, too, it is true to say that what lends the world-design its (limited) scientific power is obtained only through its powerlessness to understand the being of human existence [Dasein] as a whole.

It is to Heidegger's great credit that he summed up the being of the Dasein under the all too easily misunderstood title of Care (=caring for), and to have phenomenologically explored its basic structures and make-up. Thrownness, in the sense of the facticity of the Dasein's answerability to its that-it-is, is only *one* component ("existential") of this structure, the others, as we know, being existence (project) and fallenness.[8] Thus what in psychiatry is irreversibly separated into discrete realities of fields of study, namely, the finite human Dasein, is presented here in its basic structural unity. (It cannot be emphasized too often that this presentation signifies something quite different from the approach to man under the aegis of one particular *idea*, such as the idea of the will to power, libido, or any idea involving man as, in general, a creature of nature, or even, indeed, the idea of man as a child of God, as *homo aeternus*, etc.) But where there is structure there can be no dissociation of one structural member from the structural whole. Each, rather, remains implicated in the others, and a change in one structural element involves a change in the others. The

Dasein can thus never get "behind" its thrownness and can only project those possibilities into which it is thrown. Only, therefore, as surrendered to its *that*, as thrown, does the Dasein *exist* within the ground of its power-to-be. The self of existence, although it has to lay its own ground, can therefore never have power over this ground. As a being, it has to be "as it is and can be." Its being is a projection of its own power-to-be, and to this extent it is always already in *advance* [9] of itself. This being in advance of itself also concerns the whole of the Dasein's structure. Corresponding to all that we know of its thrownness (as already-being-in-the-world), the being-in-advance-of itself of the Dasein, its futurity, is through and through implicated with its past. Out of both these temporal "ecstasies" the authentic present temporalizes itself. This is what was referred to in the opening pages as the "way" of *Sein und Zeit:* the attempt to understand the basic structure of the Dasein *via* the unitariness of temporality and its ecstasies.

I have elsewhere [10] tried to indicate the significance of this way for psychopathological knowledge and the understanding of the basic forms of human existence. Here, however, we are concerned with pointing out its significance for psychiatry's understanding of itself. The insight into the temporal essence of the Dasein, or transcendence, not only instructs psychiatry as to its "object"—the various modes of "abnormal" human existence—but also instructs it in its understanding of itself in that it compels it to realize that its dissection of human being into various factual regions with their corresponding conceptualizations cannot be the last word. For, as I have already mentioned, it thereby takes *one* level, that of things objectively present [*vorhanden*] "in time and space," here and now, and projects upon that level what makes the understanding of spatialization and temporalization possible in the first place: the Dasein. But if psychiatry realizes—and this is true for all sciences—how provisional its world-designs, its reality-conceptions, are, it will hold on to its basic concepts less rigidly and will find it easier to deepen and change these concepts. It is obvious, after all we have said, that these conceptual changes can be instigated only within scientific research and its particular crises, and therefore only within psychiatry's efforts in its own proper sphere of activity. A "dogmatic" importation of philosophical doctrines as such has almost always been detrimental to science and research.

IV

It is not enough to realize the necessary limitedness of psychiatry's world-design, which, like all world-designs, derives its power from the *elimination* of other possibilities. The analytic of existence can, in addition, show psychiatry *what*, *materially*, must be "withdrawn," must be neglected, when man is dissected into body, mind, and soul.

I have already cited Hönigswald's essay on philosophy and psychiatry. In it, he also remarks that it must essentially be expected of the organism "that it call itself *I*." The analytic of existence indicates the root of this "expectation," namely, the basic anthropological fact that the Dasein is, in its being, concerned essentially with this being itself, in other words, that its whereto and wherefore is always directed toward itself. This being for itself by no means signifies an attitude of the I to itself that gives it the possibility of calling itself *I*. If this potentiality is to be "expected" also of the organism, it is because we realize that if this power to say *I* (and *me* and *mine*) is lost sight of in the reality-conception wherein man is projected, then the splitting of man into organism and Ego, body and soul, physical and psychic, *res extensa* and *res cogitans*, will never be set aright, and that what will be lost sight of is man as he really is. There may be many "factual" grounds for undertaking this separation. But this should not prevent us from seeing that it is undertaken only "for the sake of the matter" and ceases to be valid once we turn our attention from the particular "circumstances" to the being of the Dasein itself. For, the being for itself also concerns the Dasein *qua* organism or body, the Dasein that *is* organism only as mine, yours, or his, and that, under no circumstances, is purely and simply organism and body as such. It is, consequently, naïve to see the psychophysical problem as a riddle of the universe.

For science, this also means that as biologists, or even as physiologists, we ought not to view the organism only as a natural object, but must keep in mind that the concept of organism results from a natural-scientific *reduction* [11] of man to his bodily existence and the further reduction of this bodily existence to a mere neutrally present, "ownerless," object.

One brief example: the conception of remembering, forgetting, and recollection as Mneme and Exphoresis (Semon, E. Bleuler, among others). Here, memory and recollection are conceived purely as brain functions, as "processes in the brain." As opposed to this, however, it is not hard to show that "the brain," like the organism itself, can still only be my, your, or his brain in its "reality." In other words, the mnemonic "brain-function" can be understood only within the perspective of *my Dasein's* power to be-in-the-world as retentive, forgetful, and recollective. This means, in short, that memory cannot be understood solely within physiology. It means, rather, that retention as well as forgetting involves a retreat by the Dasein to its bodily existence and that recollection means a return of the Dasein from its involvement "in the body" to its psychic existence.[12]

The degree to which both modes of human being are interrelated through their "alliance," through what Plato termed *koinonia*, was recently well shown by Wilhelm Szilazi in his Heideggerian interpretation of Plato's *Philebus*.[13] There we find quite clearly stated that the "elements" of the Dasein's power of being stem from the totality of ontological potentialities (the All), but that corporeality only becomes body *via* the *koinonia* that links "the soul" with that which is corporeal.[14] Equally clearly drawn is the way in which the Dasein "distances" itself from its bodily involvement, its thrownness, in order first to be fully *free as* "spirit." Wherever one leaves out the *koinonia* of the Dasein's ontological potentialities and their gradations—which Aristotle characterized as *syntheton*—then an understanding of man is unattainable. For then, instead of the facticity of the Dasein, which, though it is an inner-wordly being, differs basically from the factuality of the neutrally on-hand (the *Vorhanden*), in place of this facticity, the "universal riddle" of the psychophysical problem rears its head.

Turning now to the concept of *disease* in psychiatry, we must consider Paul Häberlin's excellent essay "The Object of Psychiatry." [15] On the basis of anthropology,[16] Häberlin comes to the conclusion that the pathological character of mental diseases is somatically, rather than psychologically, patterned, and that only the so-called neuroses are really psychic diseases and only they should really be called psychoses. The extent to which this view approaches the state of affairs in psychiatry is the extent to which it presupposes a *koinonia* of mind and body that is of a *different kind* than that which we ourselves are presenting here. Häberlin understands the body as the *image* of the mind, and he characterizes man as a "mental nation" governed with relative success by its founder, the mind. These two types of disease are distinguished, according to Häberlin, in that in one case the mind is "at odds" with *itself*, while in the other case (what is usually called mental disease), it is primarily the—*central*—organization of the *body* that is disturbed. *Both kinds* of disease necessarily express themselves mentally *and* physically. In the first case, that of the so-called neuroses, the mind cannot uniformly carry out its functions, among which is the function of governing the body, and we therefore, to a greater or lesser extent, find somatic consequences in neurosis. But in the case of the so-called psychoses, the mind, in turn, suffers from the disturbance in the organism because this disturbance hinders its governance of the body and, in its receptive aspect, presents the mind with a distorted image of the world so that it, the mind, reacts abnormally. Thus, in *both* cases, the normal *relation* between body and mind (*koinonia*) is disturbed. Every disease affects both sides, regardless of where the primary conditioning factors lie.

And *we too*, from the perspective of Heidegger's analytic of existence, must conceive of both mental disease (Häberlin's somatosis) and neurosis (Häberlin's psychosis) as a disturbance of *koinonia*, of the functional *unity* of the Dasein's ontological potentialities. On this basis it is, for example, understandable that the mental disease called melancholia can be conceived as a disturbance of the *koinonia* between the bodily and mental being of the Dasein, which manifests itself on the one hand as a "vegetative" disturbance of the organism, and on the other hand as an "isolated," heightened, and distorted form of the finite Dasein's inherent guilt. It is not surprising, therefore, that melancholia can arise because of family tragedy, loss of power, or concrete guilt on the one hand, or on the other hand, in connection with intestinal diseases or even "for no reason at all." Nor is it surprising, then, that we can "cure" the melancholic with electroshock, or calm him with opium, or comfort him with assurances about his recovery and thus spur him on toward a steadfast endurance of his suffering. In each instance, we seek to restore the *koinonia* of body and mind. That in this case success is easier when the patient is treated from the "physical" side only indicates the nature of the melancholic form of existence that involves the *dominant power* of thrownness as already-being-in-the-world (mood), i.e., pastness (*Gewesenheit*) over existence as being-in-advance-of-itself in the future. It in no way argues against the notion that the mental illness known as melancholia involves the Dasein as a whole. The same, in turn, is true of the "neuroses." No matter how well psychopathology may understand neurosis (in strictly Freudian terms) as "psychic conflict," from the point of view of existential analysis, the neuroses must not *merely* be understood within the perspective of existence. That human beings *can* become "neurotic" at all is *also* a sign of the thrownness of the Dasein and a sign of its potentiality of fallenness —a sign, in short, of its finitude, its transcendental limitedness or unfreedom.

Only he who scorns these limits, who—Kierkegaard's terms —is at odds with the fundamental conditions of existence, can become "neurotic," whereas only he who "knows" of the unfreedom of finite human existence and who obtains "power" over his existence within this very powerlessness is unneurotic or "free." The *sole task* of "psychotherapy" lies in assisting man toward · this "power." It is only the *ways* to this goal that are *various*.

Naturally, the philosophical analytic of existence neither will nor can intrude upon psychiatry's conception of reality, nor doubt its empirically established "psycho-physical" connections. However, what it can do and what it seeks to do is simply to show that what we have cited as psychiatry's dual reality-conception owes its power and meaning to its being limited to particular scientific world-designs and not the being of those beings that it thematizes. All those issues, therefore, that extend beyond the field of this "thematization," i.e., questions as to human freedom, "time and space," relation of "mind and matter," questions of philosophy, art, religion, questions as to the nature of genius, etc.—such questions are not to be answered by the science of psychiatry.

A word, in conclusion, about the psychiatric problem of the *unconscious*. While psychoanalysis, as we know, interprets the unconscious from the perspective of consciousness,[17] it is clear that a doctrine that does not proceed from the intentionality of consciousness, but that, rather, shows how this intentionality is grounded in the temporality of human existence, must interpret the difference between consciousness and unconsciousness temporally and existentially. The point of departure for this interpretation cannot, therefore, be consciousness. It can, instead, only be the "unconscious," the thrownness and determinateness of the Dasein. A closer examination of this issue would, however, require a separate paper.

From the perspective of psychiatry's transcendental understanding of itself as a science—and only from that perspective—we may now interpret the being of the psychiatrist.[18] Those whose concern is man's physical health know that they must be not only "medical men," but also physicians. To the extent that diagnostic judgment is rooted not in observations of the patient's organism, but in the "coming to an understanding" with him as a human being, as one who also exists humanly—to that extent what is *essentially* involved is not just the attitude of the "medical man" toward his scientific object. What is involved is his *relation* [19] to the patient, a relation rooted equally in "care" and love. It is of the *essence* of being a psychiatrist, *therefore*, that he reaches beyond all factual knowledge and the abilities that go with it, and that he reaches beyond *scientific* knowledge found in the fields of psychology, psychopathology, and psychotherapy. This swinging beyond or transcending the factuality, objectivity, and reality-orientation of psychiatry can be understood only from the point of view of transcendence itself as being-in-the-world and being-beyond-the-world.[20]

Not only at the initial interview or examination, but also during the course of the whole *treatment*, being a psychiatrist goes beyond being a medical man (in the sense of knowing and mastering the field of medicine). The being of a psychiatrist—I mean, of course, a psychiatrist, as such, and not what is called a "good" psychiatrist—involves, therefore, the insight that no whole, and thus no "whole man," can be "grasped" with the methods of science. Now, if the psychiatrist is oriented toward encounter and mutual understanding with his fellow man and is oriented toward understanding human beings in their totality, in the *koinonia* of their ontological potentialities and the *koinonia* of this totality with more universal ontological potentialities, then the being of the psychiatrist reaches beyond the purely "theoretical" ontological potentialities of man and is directed toward transcendence itself.

It follows from this that the psychiatrist in his being summons and lays claim to the whole man. Whereas in other branches of science it may, to a greater or lesser extent, be possible to separate one's vocation and existence and, so to speak, find one's "existential center of gravity" in a hobby or in some other scientific activity, or in philosophy, a religion, or art, it is not so in psychiatry. In a certain sense being a psychiatrist also claims the existence of the psychiatrist. For where meeting and mutual understanding furnish the grounds and basis for everything that can be viewed as symptoms or even as disease and health per se, and where, therefore, there can be nothing human upon which—*in a psychiatric sense*—judgment cannot be passed, then hobby, science, philosophy, art, and religion must be capable of being projected and understood from the perspective of personal existence as ontological potentialities and conceptual projects. Where this is not the case—as the history of psychiatry shows—every psychiatric judgment actually is deprived of a solid basis. Consequently, the being of the psychiatrist cannot be understood without understanding transcendence as "the freedom to establish a ground."

This "freedom" now permits us to understand that the scientific concerns and necessities (basic concepts, research methods) of psychiatry must stand not in a rigid, but in a flexible and vital relation to the Dasein as being-in-the-world and being-beyond-the-world. It also permits us to understand why scientific progress in psychiatry is especially bound up with the interaction between research into matters of fact and transcendental reflection upon its nature as science.

NOTES

1. Here is one juncture where the gap separating Sartre and Heidegger reveals itself. Sartre does not refer back in this manner; indeed, he reproaches Heidegger: "that he has completely avoided any appeal to consciousness in his description of Dasein" (*Being and Nothingness*, p. 85).
2. See Rollo May, Ernest Angel, and Henri F. Ellenberger (eds.), *Existence* (New York, 1958), pp. 191–213.
3. See the (expanded) lecture of W. Szilasi (January 10, 1945) in *Wissenschaft als Philosophie* (Zurich, New York, 1945).
4. See Richard Hönigswald, "Philosophie und Psychiatrie," *Archiv. f. Psychiatrie u. Nervenkrankheiten*, Vol. 87, No. 5 (1929), and Ludwig Binswanger, "Über die manische Lebensform," *Ausg. Vort. u. Aufs.*, Vol. II.
5. See Szilasi, *op. cit.*
6. See "Freud and the Magna Charta of Clinical Psychiatry," in Ludwig Binswanger, *Being-in-the-world* (New York, 1963).
7. This term is meant to include those psychiatric schools of thought attached to the names of E. Minkowski, Erwin Straus, and V. E. von Gebsattel.
8. For the significance of fallenness "toward the world"—and not only the *Mitwelt*—see *Schizophrenie*.
9. Regarding the extent to which the various psychotic forms of manic depression and schizophrenia are rooted in various modes of this being-in-advance-of-itself of the Dasein (be it from the aspect of attunement [*Gestimmtheit*] or "Extravagant" ideal-formation), see my studies *Über Ideenflucht* and *Schizophrenie*.
10. *Grundformen und Erkenntnis menschlichen Daseins.*
11. See my "Über die manische Lebensform," and above all the excellent treatment by René Le Senne of "La dialectique de naturalisation" in *Obstacle et Valeur*. See further, T. Haering, *Philosophie der Naturwissenschaft* (1923).
12. See "Über Psychotherapie."
13. W. Szilasi, *Macht und Ohnmacht des Geistes.*
14. Thus Häberlin (see below) makes no bones about saying that the isolated body ("body without soul") does not exist.
15. P. Häberlin, in *Schweiz. Archiv. f. Psych. u. Neur.*, Vol. 60.
16. *Der Mensch, eine philosophische Anthropologie* (Zurich, 1941).

17. Whereby there obtains the disproportion between the high methodological esteem given to consciousness—indeed, in this respect the best thing that can be said of the workings of the unconscious is that it approaches consciousness or even excels it—and low esteem accorded its material, psychological significance.

18. It goes without saying that what holds true for the physician in general is also true of the psychiatrist, namely: "For him, health is the principle of his profession, and wherever he disregards its recognized limits, he makes himself guilty at every step." See the sharp and unambiguous treatment of "Das Prinzip des Ärztlichen Berufs" by Paul Matussek in *Festschrift für Kurt Schneider* (Heidelberg: 1947).

19. See *Grundformen*, Part II.

20. *Ibid.*

Consciousness and Imagination

JEAN-PAUL SARTRE

We now can see what the essential requisite is in order that a consciousness may be able to imagine; it must have the possibility of
positing an hypothesis of unreality. But we must clarify this requisite. It does not mean that consciousness must cease being consciousness *of* something. It is of the very nature of consciousness to be
intentional and a consciousness that would cease to be consciousness
of something would for that very reason cease to exist. But consciousness should be able to form and posit objects possessing a
certain trait of nothingness in relation to the whole of reality. In
fact, we recall that the imaginary object can be posited as nonexistent or as absent or as existing elsewhere or not posited as
existing. We note that the common property of these four theses is
that they include the entire category of negation (nihilation),
though at different degrees. Thus the negative (nihilating) act is
constitutive of the image. We have already mentioned, in fact, that
the theme is not added to the image but that it is its most intimate
structure. But in relation to what is the negation carried out? To
answer this question we need but consider for a moment what
happens when I grasp the portrait of Charles VIII as *an* image of
Charles VIII. At one stroke I stop to consider the picture as forming
a part of a real world. It is no longer possible that the perceived
object *on* the picture can be changed by the changes of the milieu
surrounding it. The picture itself, as a *real thing*, can be more or less
brightened, its colors can peel off, it can burn. This is because it
possesses—due to lack of a "being-in-the-world" which is restricted
to consciousness—a "being-in-the-midst-of-the-world." Its objective
nature depends upon reality grasped as a spatio-temporal whole.
But if, on the contrary, I grasp Charles VIII as an image on the
picture, the object apprehended can no longer be subjected for

instance to changes in brightness. It is not true that I can more or less brighten the *cheek* of Charles VIII.

The brightening of that cheek has been, in fact, once and for all, established in the unreal by the painter. It is the unreal sun—or the unreal candle placed by the painter at this or that distance from the face being painted—which determines the degree of the brightness of the cheek. All that a real projector can do is to brighten the part of the real picture that corresponds to the cheek of Charles VIII. Likewise, if the picture burns—it is not Charles VIII as an image who is burning but only the material object which serves as analogue for the manifestation of the imagined object. Thus the unreal object appears at one stroke to be beyond the reach of reality. We therefore see that in order to produce the object "Charles VIII" as an image, consciousness must be able to deny the reality of the picture and that it could deny that reality only by retreating from reality grasped in its totality. To posit an image is to construct an object on the fringe of the whole of reality, which means therefore to hold the real at a distance, to free oneself from it, in a word, to deny it. Or, in other words, to deny that an object belongs to the real is to deny the real in positing the object; the two negations are complementary, the former being the condition for the latter. We know, besides, that the totality of the real, so long as it is grasped by consciousness as a synthetic *situation* for that consciousness, is the world. There is then a twofold requisite if consciousness is to imagine: it must be able to posit the world in its synthetic totality, and, it must be able to posit the imagined object as being out of reach of this synthetic totality, that is, posit the world as a nothingness in relation to the image. From this it follows clearly that all creation of the imaginary would be completely impossible to a consciousness whose nature it would be precisely to be "in-the-midst-of-the-world." If we assume a consciousness placed in the very bosom of the world as one existence among others, we must conceive it hypothetically as completely subjected to the action of a variety of realities—without its being able to avoid the detail of these realities by an intuition which would embrace their totality. This consciousness could therefore contain only real modifications aroused by real actions and all imagination would be prohibited to it, exactly in the degree to which it would be engulfed in the real.

This conception of an imagination enmired in the world is not unknown to us since it is precisely that of psychological determinism. We can affirm fearlessly that if consciousness is a succession of determined psychical facts it is entirely impossible for it ever to produce anything but the real. For a consciousness to be able to imagine, it must be able to escape from the world by its very nature, it must be able by its own efforts to withdraw from the world. In a word, it must be free. Thus the thesis of unreality has yielded us the possibility of negation (nihilation) as its condition. Now, the latter is possible only by the "negation" ("nihilation") of the world as a whole, and this negation has revealed itself to us as being the reverse of the very freedom of consciousness. But at this point several comments force themselves to the fore: first of all we must bear in mind that the act of positing the world as a synthetic totality and the act of "taking perspective" from the world are both one and the same. If we may use a comparison, it is precisely by placing oneself at a convenient distance from the picture that the impressionist painter disengages the whole "forest" or the "white water lilies" from the multitude of small strokes he has placed on the canvas. But, reciprocally, the possibility of constructing a whole is given as the primary structure of the act of taking perspective. It is therefore enough to be able to posit reality as a synthetic whole in order to posit oneself as free from it and this going-beyond is freedom itself since it could not happen if consciousness were not free. Thus to posit the world as a world or to "negate" it is one and the same thing. In this sense Heidegger can say that nothingness is the constitutive structure of the existent. To be able to imagine, it is enough that consciousness be able to surpass the real in constituting it as a world, since the negating of the real is always implied by its constitution in the world. But this surpassing cannot be brought about by any means whatever, and the freedom of consciousness must not be confused with the arbitrary. For an image is not purely and simply the *world-negated*, it is always *the world negated from a certain point of view*, namely, the one that permits the positing of the absence or the nonexistence of the object presented "as an image." The arbitrary position of the real as a world will not of itself cause the appearance of the centaur as an unreal object. For the centaur to emerge as unreal the world must be grasped as a world-where-the-centaur-is-not, and this can only happen if consciousness is led by different motivations to grasp the world as being exactly the sort in which the centaur has no place. Likewise, if my friend Peter is to be given me as absent I must be led to grasp the world as that sort of a whole in which Peter cannot *actually exist* and *be present to me*. (He can actually be present for others—in Berlin, for instance.) What motivates the appearance of the unreal is not necessarily nor most often the *representative* intuition of the world from some point of view. Consciousness as a fact has many other ways of *surpassing the real in order to make a world of it:* the surpassing can and should happen at first by affectivity or by action. The appearance of a dead friend as unreal, for instance, is built on the foundation of affective expectation of the real as an *empty world* from this point of view.

We shall give the name of "situations" to the different immediate ways of apprehending the real as a world. We can therefore say that the essential prerequisite that enables consciousness to imagine is that it be "situated in the world" or, more briefly, that it "be-in-the-world." It is the situation-in-the-world, grasped as a concrete and individual reality of consciousness, which is the motivation for the construction of any unreal object whatever and the nature of that unreal object is circumscribed by this motivation. Thus the *situation* of consciousness does not need to appear as a pure and abstract condition of possibility for all imagination but as the concrete and exact motivation for the appearance of a certain particular imagination.

From this point of view we finally grasp the relation between the unreal and the real. At first, even if an image is not produced at this moment, every apprehension of the real as a world tends of its own accord to end up with the production of unreal objects because it is always, in one sense, a free negation of the world and that always *from a particular point of view*. Thus, if consciousness is free, the noematic correlative of its freedom should be the *world* which carries in itself its possibility of negation, at each moment and from each point of view, by means of an image, even while the image must as yet be constructed by a particular intention of consciousness. But, reciprocally, an image, being a negation of the world from a particular point of view, can never appear excepting *on the foundation of the world* and in connection with the foundation. Naturally the appearance of the image demands that the particular perceptions should be diluted in the syncretic wholeness *world* and that this wholeness should withdraw. But it is exactly the withdrawal of the wholeness which turns it into a foundation, the foundation on which the unreal form must detach itself. Thus, although as a result of producing the unreal, consciousness can appear momentarily delivered from "being-in-the-world," it is just this "being-in-the-world" which is the necessary condition for the imagination.

Thus the critical analysis of the conditions that made all imagination possible has led us to the following discoveries: in order to imagine, consciousness must be free from all specific reality and this freedom must be able to define itself by a "being-in-the-world" which is at once the constitution and the negation of the world; the concrete situation of the consciousness in the world must at each moment serve as the singular motivation for the constitution of the unreal. Thus the unreal—which is always a twofold nothingness: nothingness of itself in relation to the world, nothingness of the world in relation to itself—must always be constituted on the foundation of the world which it denies, it being well understood, moreover, that the world does not present itself only to a representative intuition and that this synthetic foundation simply demands to be lived as a situation. If these are the conditions that make imagination possible, do they correspond to a specification, to an enrichment contingent upon the essence "consciousness" or are they nothing else than the very essence of that consciousness considered from a particular point of view? It seems that the answer lies in the question. Indeed, what is this free consciousness whose nature is to be the consciousness *of* something, but which, for this very reason, constructs itself before the real and which surpasses it at each moment because it can exist only by "being-in-the-world," that is, by living its relation to the real as *situation*, what is it, indeed, if not simply consciousness such as it reveals itself to itself in the cogito?

Is not doubt the very primary condition of the cogito, that is, at once the constitution of the real as a world and its negation from this same point of view and does not reflective grasp of the doubt as doubt coincide with the apodictic intuition of freedom?

We may therefore conclude that imagination is not an empirical and superadded power of consciousness, it is the whole of consciousness as it realizes its freedom; every concrete and real situation of consciousness in the world is big with imagination inasmuch as it always presents itself as a withdrawing from the real. It does not follow that all perception of the real must reverse itself in imagination, but as consciousness is always "in a situation" because it is always free, it always and at each moment has the concrete possibility of producing the unreal. These are the various motivations which decide at each moment whether consciousness will only be realized or whether it will imagine. The unreal is produced outside of the world by a consciousness which *stays in the world* and it is because he is transcendentally free that man can imagine.

But, in its turn, the imagination, which has become a psychological and empirical function, is the necessary condition for the freedom of empirical man in the midst of the world. For, if the negating function belonging to consciousness—which Heidegger calls surpassing—is what makes the act of imagination possible, it must be added on the other hand that this function can manifest itself only in an imaginative act. There can be no intuition of nothingness just because nothingness is nothing and because all consciousness intuitive or not is consciousness of something. Nothingness can present itself only as an infra-structure of something. The experience of nothingness is not, strictly speaking, an indirect one, it is an experience which is in principle given "with" and "in." The analyses of Bergson are pertinent in this connection: any attempt to directly conceive death or the nothingness of existence is by nature bound to fail.

The gliding of the world into the bosom of nothingness and the emergence of human reality in this very nothingness can happen only through the position of *something* which is nothingness in relation to the world and in relation to which the world is nothing. By this we evidently define the structure of the imagination. It is the appearance of the imaginary before consciousness which permits the grasping of the process of turning the world into nothingness as its essential condition and as its primary structure. If it were possible to conceive for a moment a consciousness which does not imagine it would have to be conceived as completely engulfed in the existent and without the possibility of grasping anything but the existent. But it is exactly that which cannot be nor could be: all existence as soon as it is posited is surpassed by itself. But it must retreat *toward something*. The imaginary is in every case the "something" concrete toward which the existent is surpassed. When the imaginary is not posited as a fact, the surpassing and the nullifying of the existent are swallowed up in the existent; the surpassing and the freedom *are there* but are not revealed; the person is crushed in the world, run through by the real, he is closest to the thing. However, as soon as he apprehends in one way or another (most of the time without representation) the whole as a *situation*, he retreats from it toward that in relation to which he is *a lack*, an *empty space*, etc. In a word, the concrete motivation of the imaginative consciousness itself presupposes the imaginative structure of consciousness; the realizing consciousness always includes a retreat toward a particular imaginative consciousness which is like the reverse of the situation and in relation to which the situation is defined. For instance, if I desire to see my friend Peter who is not here now, the situation defines itself as a "being in the world" such as Peter is not now given, and Peter is this because the whole of the real is surpassed in order to make a world. But it is not at all the real Peter who, on the contrary, if he were given as present or as envisioned on the basis of the real by empty and presentifying intentions (for instance, if I heard his steps outside the door), would be a part of the situation: this Peter in relation to whom the situation becomes defined is exactly the *absent* Peter.

The imaginary thus represents at each moment the implicit meaning of the real. The imaginative act itself consists in positing the imaginary for itself, that is, in making that meaning explicit—as when Peter as an image rises suddenly before me—but this specific position of the imaginary will be accompanied by a collapsing of the world which is then no more than the negated foundation of the unreal. And if the negation is the unconditioned principle of all imagination, it itself can never be realized excepting in and by an act of imagination. That which is denied must be imagined. In fact, the object of a negation cannot be *real* because that would be affirming what is being denied—but neither can it be a complete nothing, since it is *something* that is being denied. So the object of a negation must be posited as imaginary. And this is true for the logical forms of negation (doubt, restriction, etc.) as it is for its active and affective forms (defense, consciousness of impotence, of deprivation, etc.).

Now we are at the point of understanding the meaning and the value of the imaginary. The imaginary appears "on the foundation of the world," but reciprocally all apprehension of the real as world implies a hidden surpassing toward the imaginary. All imaginative consciousness uses the world as the negated (nihilated) foundation of the imaginary and reciprocally all consciousness of the world calls forth and motivates an imaginative consciousness as grasped from the particular *meaning* of the situation. The apprehension of nothingness could not occur by an immediate unveiling, it develops in and by the free succession of acts of consciousness, the nothingness is the material of the surpassing of the world toward the imaginary. It is as such that it is *lived*, without ever being posited for itself. There could be no developing consciousness without an imaginative consciousness, and vice versa. So imagination, far from appearing as an *actual* characteristic of consciousness turns out to be an essential and transcendental condition of consciousness. It is as absurd to conceive of a consciousness which would not imagine as it would be to conceive of a consciousness which could not realize the cogito.

What Is Phenomenology?

MAURICE MERLEAU-PONTY

TRANSLATED BY *Colin Smith*

What is phenomenology? It may seem strange that this question has still to be asked half a century after the first works of Husserl. The fact remains that it has by no means been answered. Phenomenology is the study of essences; and according to it, all problems amount to finding definitions of essences: the essence of perception, or the essence of consciousness, for example. But phenomenology is also a philosophy which puts essences back into existence, and does not expect to arrive at an understanding of man and the world from any starting point other than that of their "facticity." It is transcendental philosophy which places in abeyance the assertions arising out of the natural attitude, the better to understand them; but it is also a philosophy for which the world is always "already there" before reflection begins—as an inalienable presence; and all its efforts are concentrated upon re-achieving a direct and primitive contact with the world, and endowing that contact with a philosophical status. It is the search for a philosophy which shall be a "rigorous science," but it also offers an account of space, time, and the world as we "live" them. It tries to give a direct description of our experience as it is, without taking account of its psychological origin and the causal explanations which the scientist, the historian, or the sociologist may be able to provide. Yet Husserl in his last works mentions a "genetic phenomenology," [1] and even a "constructive phenomenology." [2] One may try to do away with these contradictions by making a distinction between Husserl's and Heidegger's phenomenologies; yet the whole of *Sein und Zeit* springs from an indication given by Husserl and amounts to no more than an explicit account of the "natürlicher Weltbegriff" or the "Lebenswelt" which Husserl, toward the end of his life, identified as the central theme of phenomenology, with the result that the contradiction re-appears in Husserl's own philosophy. The reader pressed for time will be inclined to give up the idea of covering a doctrine which says everything, and will wonder whether a philosophy which cannot define its scope deserves all the discussion which has gone on around it, and whether he is not faced rather by a myth or a fashion.

Even if this were the case, there would still be a need to understand the prestige of the myth and the origin of the fashion, and the opinion of the responsible philosopher must be that *phenomenology can be practiced and identified as a manner or style of thinking, that it existed as a movement before arriving at complete awareness of itself as a philosophy*. It has been long on the way, and its adherents have discovered it in every quarter, certainly in Hegel and Kierkegaard, but equally in Marx, Nietzsche, and Freud. A purely linguistic examination of the texts in question would yield no proof; we find in texts only what we put into them, and if ever any kind of history has suggested the interpretations which should be put on it, it is the history of philosophy. We shall find in ourselves, and nowhere else, the unity and true meaning of phenomenology. It is less a question of counting up quotations than of determining and expressing in concrete form this *phenomenology for ourselves* which has given a number of present-day readers the impression, on reading Husserl or Heidegger, not so much of encountering a new philosophy as of recognizing what they had been waiting for. Phenomenology is accessible only through a phenomenological method. Let us, therefore, try systematically to bring together the celebrated phenomenological themes as they have grown spontaneously together in life. Perhaps we shall then understand why phenomenology has for so long remained at an initial stage, as a problem to be solved and a hope to be realized.

It is a matter of describing, not of explaining or analyzing. Husserl's first directive to phenomenology, in its early stages, to be a "descriptive psychology," or to return to the "things themselves," is from the start a rejection of science. I am not the outcome or the meeting-point of numerous causal agencies which determine my bodily or psychological makeup. I cannot conceive myself as nothing but a bit of the world, a mere object of biological, psychological, or sociological investigation. I cannot shut myself up within the realm of science. All my knowledge of the world, even my scientific knowledge, is gained from my own particular point of view, or from some experience of the world without which the symbols of science would be meaningless. The whole universe of science is built upon the world as directly experienced, and if we want to subject science itself to rigorous scrutiny and arrive at a precise assessment of its meaning and scope, we must begin by re-awakening the basic experience of the world of which science is the second-order expression. Science has not and never will have, by its nature, the same significance *qua* form of being as the world which we perceive, for the simple reason that it is a rationale or explanation of that world. I am, not a "living creature" nor even a "man," nor again even "a consciousness" endowed with all the characteristics which zoology, social anatomy, or inductive psychology recognize in these various products of the natural or historical process—I am the absolute source, my existence does not stem from my antecedents, from my physical and social environment; instead it moves out toward them and sustains them, for I alone bring into being for myself (and therefore into being in the only sense that the word can have for me) the tradition which I elect to carry on, or the horizon whose distance from me would be abolished—since that distance is not one of its properties—if I were not there to scan it with my gaze. Scientific points of view, according to which my existence is a moment of the world's, are always both naïve and at the same time dishonest, because they take for granted, without explicitly mentioning it, the other point of view, namely that of consciousness, through which from the outset a world forms itself round me and begins to exist for me. To return to things themselves is to return to that world which precedes knowledge, of which knowledge always *speaks,* and in relation to which every scientific schematization is an abstract and derivative sign-language, as is geography in relation to the countryside in which we have learnt beforehand what a forest, a prairie, or a river is.

This move is absolutely distinct from the idealist return to consciousness, and the demand for a pure description excludes equally the procedure of analytical reflection on the one hand, and that of scientific explanation on the other. Descartes and particularly Kant *detached* the subject, or consciousness, by showing that I could not possibly apprehend anything as existing unless I first of all experienced myself as existing in the act of apprehending it. They presented consciousness, the absolute certainty of my existence for myself, as the condition of there being anything at all; and the act of relating as the basis of relatedness. It is true that the act of relating is nothing if divorced from the spectacle of the world in which relations are found; the unity of consciousness in Kant is achieved simultaneously with that of the world. And in Descartes methodical doubt does not deprive us of anything, since the whole world, at least insofar as we experience it, is reinstated in the *Cogito*, enjoying equal certainty, and simply labeled "thought about. . . ." But the relations between subject and world are not strictly bilateral: if they were, the certainty of the world would, in Descartes, be immediately given with that of the *Cogito*, and Kant would not have talked about his "Copernican revolution." Analytical reflection starts from our experience of the world and goes back to the subject as to a condition of possibility distinct from that experience, revealing the all-embracing synthesis as that without which there would be no world. To this extent it ceases to remain part of our experience and offers, in place of an account, a reconstruction. It is understandable, in view of this, that Husserl, having accused Kant of adopting a "faculty psychologism," [3] should have urged, in place of a noetic analysis which bases the world on the synthesizing activity of the subject, his own "*noematic reflection*" which remains within the object and, instead of begetting it, brings to light its fundamental unity.

The world is there before any possible analysis of mine, and it would be artificial to make it the outcome of a series of syntheses which link, in the first place sensations, then aspects of the object corresponding to different perspectives, when both are nothing but products of analysis, with no sort of prior reality. Analytical reflection believes that it can trace back the course followed by a prior constituting act and arrive, in the "inner man"—to use Saint Augustine's expression—at a constituting power which has always been identical with that inner self. Thus reflection itself is carried away and transplanted in an impregnable subjectivity, as yet untouched by being and time. But this is very ingenuous, or at least it is an incomplete form of reflection which loses sight of its own beginning. When I begin to reflect, my reflection bears upon an unreflective experience; moreover my reflection cannot be unaware of itself as an event, and so it appears to itself in the light of a truly creative act, of a changed structure of consciousness, and yet it has to recognize, as having priority over its own operations, the world which is given to the subject, because the subject is given to himself. The real has to be described, not constructed or formed. Which means that I cannot put perception into the same category as the syntheses represented by judgments, acts, or predications. My field of perception is constantly filled with a play of colors, noises, and fleeting tactile sensations which I cannot relate precisely to the context of my clearly perceived world, yet which I nevertheless immediately "place" in the world, without ever confusing them with my daydreams. Equally constantly I weave dreams round things. I imagine people and things whose presence is not incompatible with the context, yet who are not in fact involved in it: they are ahead of reality, in the realm of the imaginary. If the reality of my perception were based solely on the intrinsic coherence of "representations," it ought to be for ever hesitant and, being wrapped up in my conjectures on probabilities, I ought to be ceaselessly taking apart misleading syntheses, and reinstating in reality stray phenomena which I had excluded in the first place. But this does not happen. The real is a closely woven fabric. It does not await our judgment before incorporating the most surprising phenomena, or before rejecting the most plausible figments of our imagination. Perception is not a science of the world, it is not even an act, a deliberate taking up of a position; it is the background from which all acts stand out, and is presupposed by them. The world is not an object such that I have in my possession the law of its making; it is the natural setting of, and field for, all my thoughts and all my explicit perceptions. Truth does not "inhabit" only "the inner man," [4] or more accurately, there is no inner man, man is in the world, and only in the world does he know himself. When I return to myself from an excursion into the realm of dogmatic common sense or of science, I find, not a source of intrinsic truth, but a subject destined to be in the world.

All of which reveals the true meaning of the famous phenomenological reduction. There is probably no question over which Husserl has spent more time—or to which he has more often returned, since the "problematic of reduction" occupies an important place in his unpublished work. For a long time, and even in recent texts, the reduction is presented as the return to a transcendental consciousness before which the world is spread out and completely transparent, quickened through and through by a series of apperceptions which it is the philosopher's task to reconstitute on the basis of their outcome. Thus my sensation of redness is *perceived as* the manifestation of a certain redness experienced, this in turn as the manifestation of a red surface, which is the manifestation of a piece of red cardboard, and this finally is the manifestation or outline of a red thing, namely this book. We are to understand, then, that it is the apprehension of a certain *hylè*, as indicating a phenomenon of a higher degree, the *Sinngebung*, or active meaning-giving operation which may be said to define consciousness, so that the world is nothing but "world-as-meaning," and the phenomenological reduction is idealistic, in the sense that there is here a transcendental idealism which treats the world as an indivisible unity of value shared by Peter and Paul, in which their perspectives blend. "Peter's consciousness" and "Paul's consciousness" are in communication, the perception of the world "by Peter" is not Peter's doing any more than its perception "by Paul" is Paul's doing; in each case it is the doing of pre-personal forms of consciousness, whose communication raises no problem, since it is demanded by the very definition of consciousness, meaning, or truth. Insofar as I am a consciousness, that is, insofar as something has meaning for me, I am neither here nor there, neither Peter nor Paul; I am in no way distinguishable from an "other" consciousness, since we are immediately in touch with the world and since the world is, by definition, unique, being the system in which all truths cohere. A logically consistent transcendental idealism rids the world of its opacity and its transcendence. The world is precisely that thing of which we form a representation, not as men or as empirical subjects, but insofar as we are all one light and participate in the One without destroying its unity. Analytical reflection knows nothing of the problem of other minds, or of that of the world, because it insists that with the first glimmer of consciousness there appears in me theoretically the power of reaching some universal truth, and that the other person, being equally without thisness, location, or body, the Alter and the Ego are one and the same in the true world which is the unifier of minds. There is no difficulty in understanding how *I* can conceive the Other, because the I and consequently the Other are not conceived as part of the woven stuff of phenomena; they have validity rather than existence. There is nothing hidden behind these faces and gestures, no domain to which I have no access, merely a little shadow which owes its very existence to the light. For Husserl, on the contrary, it is well known that there is a problem of other people, and the *alter ego* is a paradox. If the other is truly for himself alone, beyond his being for me, and if we are for each other and not both for God, we must necessarily have some appearance for each other. He must and I must have an outer appearance, and there must be, besides the perspective of the For Oneself—my view of myself and the other's of himself—a perspective of For Others—my view of others and theirs of me. Of course, these two perspectives, in each one of us, cannot be simply juxtaposed, *for in that case it is not I that the other would see, nor he that I should see.* I must be the exterior that I present to others, and the body of the other must be the other himself. This paradox and the dialectic of the Ego and the Alter are possible only provided that the Ego and the Alter Ego are defined by their situation and are not freed from all inherence; that is, provided that philosophy does not culminate in a return to the self, and that I discover by reflection not only my presence to myself, but also the possibility of an "outside spectator"; that is, again, provided that at the very moment when I experience my existence—at the ultimate extremity of reflection—I fall short of the ultimate density which would place me outside time, and that I discover within myself a kind of internal weakness standing in the way of my being totally individualized: a weakness which exposes me to the gaze of others as a man among men or at least as a consciousness among consciousnesses. Hitherto the *Cogito* depreciated the perception of others, teaching me as it did that the I is accessible only to itself, since it defined *me* as the thought which I have of myself, and which clearly I am alone in having, at least in this ultimate sense. For the "other" to be more than an empty word, it is necessary that my existence should never be reduced to my bare awareness of existing, but that it should take in also the awareness that *one* may have of it, and thus include my incarnation in some nature and the possibility, at least, of a historical situation. The *Cogito* must reveal me in a situation, and it is on this condition alone that transcendental subjectivity can, as Husserl puts it,[5] *be* an intersubjectivity. As a meditating Ego, I can clearly distinguish from myself the world and things, since I certainly do not exist in the way in which things exist. I must even set aside from myself my body understood as a thing among things, as a collection of physico-chemical processes. But even if the *cogitatio*, which I thus discover, is without location in objective time and space, it is not without place in the phenomenological world. The world, which I distinguished from myself as the totality of things or of processes linked by causal relationships, I rediscover "in me" as the permanent horizon of all my *cogitationes* and as a dimension in relation to which I am constantly situating myself. The true *Cogito* does not define the subject's existence in terms of the thought he has of existing, and furthermore does not convert the indubitability of the world into the indubitability of thought about the world, nor finally does it replace the world itself by the world as meaning. On the contrary it recognizes my thought itself as an inalienable fact, and does away with any kind of idealism in revealing me as "being-in-the-world."

It is because we are through and through compounded of relationships with the world that for us the only way to become aware of the fact is to suspend the resultant activity, to refuse it our complicity (to look at it *ohne mitzumachen*, as Husserl often says), or yet again, to put it "out of play." Not because we reject the certainties of common sense and a natural attitude to things—they are, on the contrary, the constant theme of philosophy—but because, being the presupposed basis of any thought, they are taken for granted, and go unnoticed, and because in order to arouse them and bring them to view, we have to suspend for a moment our recognition of them. The best formulation of the reduction is probably that given by Eugen Fink, Husserl's assistant, when he spoke of "wonder" in the face of the world.[6] Reflection does not withdraw from the world toward the unity of consciousness as the world's basis; it steps back to watch the forms of transcendence fly up like sparks from a fire; it slackens the intentional threads which attach us to the world and thus brings them to our notice; it alone is consciousness of the world because it reveals that world as strange and paradoxical. Husserl's transcendental is not Kant's and Husserl accuses Kant's philosophy of being "worldly," because it *makes use* of our relation to the world, which is the motive force of the transcendental deduction, and makes the world immanent in the subject, instead of *being filled with wonder* at it and conceiving the subject as a process of transcendence toward the world. All the misunderstandings with his interpreters, with the existentialist "dissidents" and finally with himself, have arisen from the fact that in order to see the world and grasp it as paradoxical, we must break with our familiar acceptance of it and, also, from the fact that from this break we can learn nothing but the unmotivated upsurge of the world. The most important lesson which the reduction teaches us is the impossibility of a complete reduction. This is why Husserl is constantly reexamining the possibility of the reduction. If we were absolute mind, the reduction would present no problem. But since, on the contrary, we are in the world, since indeed our reflections are carried out in the temporal flux onto which we are trying to seize (since they *sich einströmen*, as Husserl says), there is no thought which embraces all our thought. The philosopher, as the unpublished works declare, is a perpetual beginner, which means that he takes for granted nothing that men, learned or otherwise, believe they know. It means also that philosophy itself must not take itself for granted, insofar as it may have managed to say something true; that it is an ever-renewed experiment in making its own beginning; that it consists wholly in the description of this beginning, and finally, that radical reflection amounts to a consciousness of its own dependence on an unreflective life which is its initial situation, unchanging, given once and for all. Far from being, as has been thought, a procedure of idealistic philosophy, phenomenological reduction belongs to existential philosophy: Heidegger's "being-in-the-world" appears only against the background of the phenomenological reduction.

A misunderstanding of a similar kind confuses the notion of the "essences" in Husserl. Every reduction, says Husserl, as well as being transcendental is necessarily eidetic. That means that we cannot subject our perception of the world to philosophical scrutiny without ceasing to be identified with that act of positing the world, with that interest in it which delimits us, without drawing back from our commitment which is itself thus made to appear as a spectacle, without passing from the *fact* of our existence to its *nature*, from the Dasein to the Wesen. But it is clear that the essence is here not the end, but a means, that our effective involvement in the world is precisely what has to be understood and made amenable to conceptualization, for it is what polarizes all our conceptual particularizations. The need to proceed by way of essences does not mean that philosophy takes them as its object, but, on the contrary, that our existence is too tightly held in the world to be able to know itself as such at the moment of its involvement, and that it requires the field of ideality in order to become acquainted with and to prevail over its facticity. The Vienna Circle, as is well known, lays it down categorically that we can enter into relations only with meanings. For example, "consciousness" is not for the Vienna Circle identifiable with what we are. It is a complex meaning which has developed late in time, which should be handled with care, and only after the many meanings which have contributed, throughout the word's semantic development, to the formation of its present one have been made explicit. Logical positivism of this kind is the antithesis of Husserl's thought. Whatever the subtle changes of meaning which have ultimately brought us, as a linguistic acquisition, the word and concept of consciousness, we enjoy direct access to what it designates. For we have the experience of ourselves, of that consciousness which we are, and it is on the basis of this experience that all linguistic connotations are assessed, and precisely through it that language comes to have any meaning at all for us. "It is that as yet dumb experience . . . which we are concerned to lead to the pure expression of its own meaning." [7] Husserl's essences are destined to bring back all the living relationships of experience, as the fisherman's net draws up from the depths of the ocean quivering fish and seaweed. Jean Wahl is therefore wrong in saying that "Husserl separates essences from existence." [8] The separated essences are those of language. It is the office of language to cause essences to exist in a state of separation which is in fact merely apparent, since through language they still rest upon the ante-predicative life of consciousness. In the silence of primary consciousness can be seen appearing not only what words mean, but also what things mean: the core of primary meaning round which the acts of naming and expression take shape.

Seeking the essence of consciousness will therefore not consist in developing the *Wortbedeutung* of consciousness and escaping from existence into the universe of things said; it will consist in rediscovering my actual presence to myself, the fact of my consciousness which is in the last resort what the word and the concept of consciousness mean. Looking for the world's essence is not looking for what it is as an idea once it has been reduced to a theme of discourse; it is looking for what it is as a fact for us, before any thematization. Sensationalism "reduces" the world by noticing that after all we never experience anything but states of ourselves. Transcendental idealism too "reduces" the world since, insofar as it guarantees the world, it does so by regarding it as thought or consciousness of the world, and as the mere correlative of our knowledge, with the result that it becomes immanent in consciousness and the "aseity" of things is thereby done away with. The eidetic reduction is, on the other hand, the determination to bring the world to light as it is before any falling back on ourselves has occurred, it is the ambition to make reflection emulate the unreflective life of consciousness. I aim at and perceive a world. If I said, as do the sensationalists, that we have here only "states of consciousness," and if I tried to distinguish my perceptions from my dreams with the aid of "criteria," I should overlook the phenomenon of the world. For if I am able to talk about "dreams" and "reality," to bother my head about the distinction between imaginary and real, and cast doubt upon the "real," it is because this distinction is already made by me before any analysis; it is because I have an experience of the real as of the imaginary, and the problem then becomes one not of asking how critical thought can provide for itself secondary equivalents of this distinction, but of making explicit our primordial knowledge of the "real," of describing our perception of the world as that upon which our idea of truth is forever based. We must not, therefore, wonder whether we really perceive a world, we must instead say: the world is what we perceive. In more general terms we must not wonder whether our self-evident truths are real truths, or whether, through some perversity inherent in our minds, that which is self-evident for us might not be illusory in relation to some truth in itself. For insofar as we talk about illusion, it is because we have identified illusions, and done so solely in the light of some perception which at the same time gave assurance of its own truth. It follows that doubt, or the fear of being mistaken, testifies as soon as it arises to our power of unmasking error, and that it could never finally tear us away from truth. We are in the realm of truth and it is "the experience of truth" which is self-evident.[9] To seek the essence of perception is to declare that perception is, not presumed true, but defined as access to truth. So, if I now wanted, according to idealistic principles, to base this *de facto* self-evident truth, this irresistible belief, on some absolute self-evident truth, that is, on the absolute clarity which my thoughts have for me; if I tried to find in myself a creative thought which bodied forth the framework of the world or illumined it through and through, I should once more prove unfaithful to my experience of the world, and should be looking for what makes that experience possible instead of looking for what it is. The self-evidence of perception is not adequate thought or apodeictic self-evidence.[10] The world is not what I think, but what I live through. I am open to the world, I have no doubt that I am in communication with it, but I do not possess it; it is inexhaustible. "There is a world," or rather: "There is the world"; I can never completely account for this ever-reiterated assertion in my life. This facticity of the world is what constitutes the *Weltlichkeit der Welt*, what causes the world to be the world; just as the facticity of the *cogito* is not an imperfection in itself, but rather what assures me of my existence. The eidetic method is the method of a phenomenological positivism which bases the possible on the real.

We can now consider the notion of intentionality, too often cited as the main discovery of phenomonology, whereas it is understandable only through the reduction. "All consciousness is consciousness of something"; there is nothing new in that. Kant showed, in the *Refutation of Idealism*, that inner perception is impossible without outer perception, that the world, as a collection of connected phenomena, is anticipated in the consciousness of my unity, and is the means whereby I come into being as a consciousness. What distinguishes intentionality from the Kantian relation to a possible object is that the unity of the world, before being posited by knowledge in a specific act of identification, is "lived" as ready-made or already there. Kant himself shows in the *Critique of Judgment* that there exists a unity of the imagination and the understanding and a unity of subjects *before the object*, and that, in experiencing the beautiful, for example, I am aware of a harmony between sensation and concept, between myself and others, which is itself without any concept. Here the subject is no longer the universal thinker of a system of objects rigorously interrelated, the positing power who subjects the manifold to the law of the understanding, insofar as he is to be able to put together a world—he discovers and enjoys his own nature as spontaneously in harmony with the law of the understanding. But if the subject has a nature, then the hidden art of the imagination must condition the categorial activity. It is no longer merely the aesthetic judgment, but knowledge too which rests upon this art, an art which forms the basis of the unity of consciousness and of consciousnesses.

Husserl takes up again the *Critique of Judgment* when he talks about a teleology of consciousness. It is not a matter of duplicating human consciousness with some absolute thought which, from outside, is imagined as assigning to it its aims. It is a question of recognizing consciousness itself as a project of the world, meant for a world which it neither embraces nor possesses, but toward which it is perpetually directed—and the world as this pre-objective individual whose imperious unity decrees what knowledge shall take as its goal. This is why Husserl distinguishes between intentionality of act, which is that of our judgments and of those occasions when we voluntarily take up a position—the only intentionality discussed in the *Critique of Pure Reason*—and operative intentionality (*fungierende Intentionalität*), or that which produces the natural and antepredicative unity of the world and of our life, being apparent in our desires, our evaluations, and in the landscape we see, more clearly than in objective knowledge, and furnishing the text which our knowledge tries to translate into precise language. Our relationship to the world, as it is untiringly enunciated within us, is not a thing which can be any further clarified by analysis; philosophy can only place it once more before our eyes and present it for our ratification.

Through this broadened notion of intentionality, phenomenological "comprehension" is distinguished from traditional "intellection," which is confined to "true and immutable natures," and so phenomenology can become a phenomenology of origins. Whether we are concerned with a thing perceived, a historical event or a doctrine, to "understand" is to take in the total intention—not only what these things are for representation (the "properties" of the thing perceived, the mass of "historical facts," the "ideas" introduced by the doctrine) —but the unique mode of existing expressed in the properties of the pebble, the glass or the piece of wax, in all the events of a revolution, in all the thoughts of a philosopher. It is a matter, in the case of each civilization, of finding the Idea in the Hegelian sense, that is, not a law of the physico-mathematical type, discoverable by objective thought, but that formula which sums up some unique manner of behavior toward others, toward Nature, time, and death: a certain way of patterning the world which the historian should be capable of seizing upon and making his own. These are the *dimensions* of history. In this context there is not a human word, not a gesture, even one which is the outcome of habit or absentmindedness, which has not some meaning. For example, I may have been under the impression that I lapsed into silence through weariness, or some minister may have thought he had uttered merely an appropriate platitude, yet my silence or his words immediately take on a significance, because my fatigue or his falling back upon a ready-made formula are not accidental, for they express a certain lack of interest, and hence some degree of adoption of a definite position in relation to the situation.

When an event is considered at close quarters, at the moment when it is lived through, everything seems subject to chance: one man's ambition, some lucky encounter, some local circumstance or other appears to have been decisive. But chance happenings offset each other, and facts in their multiplicity coalesce and show up a certain way of taking a stand in relation to the human situation, reveal in fact an *event* which has its definite outline and about which we can talk. Should the starting-point for the understanding of history be ideology, or politics, or religion, or economics? Should we try to understand a doctrine from its overt content, or from the psychological makeup and the biography of its author? We must seek an understanding from all these angles simultaneously, everything has meaning, and we shall find this same structure of being underlying all relationships. All these views are true provided that they are not isolated, that we delve deeply into history and reach the unique core of existential meaning which emerges in each perspective. It is true, as Marx says, that history does not walk on its head, but it is also true that it does not think with its feet. Or one should say rather that it is neither its "head" nor its "feet" that we have to worry about, but its body. All economic and psychological explanations of a doctrine are true, since the thinker never thinks from any starting-point but the one constituted by what he is. Reflection even on a doctrine will be complete only if it succeeds in linking up with the doctrine's history and the extraneous explanations of it, and in putting back the causes and meaning of the doctrine in an existential structure. There is, as Husserl says, a "genesis of meaning" (*Sinngenesis*),[11] which alone, in the last resort, teaches us what the doctrine "means." Like understanding, criticism must be pursued at all levels, and naturally, it will be insufficient, for the refutation of a doctrine, to relate it to some accidental event in the author's life: its significance goes beyond, and there is no pure accident in existence or in coexistence, since both absorb random events and transmute them into the rational.

Finally, as it is indivisible in the present, history is equally so in its sequences. Considered in the light of its fundamental dimensions, all periods of history appear as manifestations of a single existence, or as episodes in a single drama—without our knowing whether it has an ending. Because we are in the world, we are *condemned to meaning*, and we cannot do or say anything without its acquiring a name in history.

Probably the chief gain from phenomenology is to have united extreme subjectivism and extreme objectivism in its notion of the world or of rationality. Rationality is precisely measured by the experiences in which it is disclosed. To say that there exists rationality is to say that perspectives blend, perceptions confirm each other, a meaning emerges. But it should not be set in a realm apart, transposed into absolute Spirit, or into a world in the realist sense. The phenomenological world is not pure being, but the sense which is revealed where the paths of my various experiences intersect, and also where my own and other people's intersect and engage each other like gears. It is thus inseparable from subjectivity and intersubjectivity, which find their unity when I either take up my past experiences in those of the present, or other people's in my own. For the first time the philosopher's thinking is sufficiently conscious not to anticipate itself and endow its own results with reified form in the world. The philosopher tries to conceive the world, others and himself and their interrelations. But the meditating Ego, the "impartial spectator" (*uninteressierter Zuschauer*)[12] do not rediscover an already given rationality, they "establish themselves," [13] and establish it, by an act of initiative which has no guarantee in being, its justification resting entirely on the effective power which it confers on us for taking our own history upon ourselves.

The phenomenological world is not the bringing to explicit expression of a preexisting being, but the laying down of being. Philosophy is not the reflection of a preexisting truth, but, like art, the act of bringing truth into being. One may well ask how this creation is *possible*, and if it does not recapture in things a preexisting Reason. The answer is that the only preexistent Logos is the world itself, and that the philosophy which brings it into visible existence does not begin by being *possible*; it is actual or real like the world of which it is a part, and no explanatory hypothesis is clearer than the act whereby we take up this unfinished world in an effort to complete and conceive it. Rationality is not a *problem*. There is behind it no unknown quantity which has to be determined by deduction, or, beginning with it, demonstrated inductively. We witness every minute the miracle of related experiences, and yet nobody knows better than we do how this miracle is worked, for we are ourselves this network of relationships. The world and reason are not problematical. We may say, if we wish, that they are mysterious, but their mystery defines them: there can be no question of dispelling it by some "solution," it is on the hither side of all solutions. True philosophy consists in re-learning to look at the world, and in this sense a historical account can give meaning to the world quite as "deeply" as a philosophical treatise. We take our fate in our hands, we become responsible for our history through reflection, but equally by a decision on which we stake our life, and in both cases what is involved is a violent act which is validated by being performed.

Phenomenology, as a disclosure of the world, rests on itself, or rather provides its own foundation.[14] All knowledge is sustained by a "ground" of postulates and finally by our communication with the world as primary embodiment of rationality. Philosophy, as radical reflection, dispenses in principle with this resource. As, however, it too is in history, it too exploits the world and constituted reason. It must therefore put to itself the question which it puts to all branches of knowledge, and so duplicate itself infinitely, being, as Husserl says, a dialogue or infinite meditation, and, insofar as it remains faithful to its intention, never knowing where it is going. The unfinished nature of phenomenology and the inchoative atmosphere which has surrounded it are not to be taken as a sign of failure, they were inevitable because phenomenology's task was to reveal the mystery of the world and of reason.[15] If phenomenology was a movement before becoming a doctrine or a philosophical system, this was attributable neither to accident, nor to fraudulent intent. It is as painstaking as the works of Balzac, Proust, Valéry, or Cézanne—by reason of the same kind of attentiveness and wonder, the same demand for awareness, the same will to seize the meaning of the world or of history as that meaning comes into being. In this way it merges into the general effort of modern thought.

NOTES

1. *Méditations cartésiennes*, pp. 120 ff.
2. See the unpublished *6th Méditation cartésienne*, edited by Eugen Fink, to which G. Berger has kindly referred us.
3. *Logische Untersuchungen, Prolegomena zur reinen Logik*, p. 93.
4. *In te redi; in interiore homine habitat veritas* (Saint Augustine).
5. *Die Krisis der europäischen Wissenschaften und die transzendentale Phänomenologie*, III (unpublished).
6. *Die phänomenologische Philosophie Edmund Husserls in der gegenwärtigen Kritik*, pp. 331 and ff.
7. *Méditations cartésiennes*, p. 33.
8. *Réalisme, dialectique et mystère*, l'Arbalète, Autumn, 1942, unpaginated.
9. *Das Erlebnis der Wahrheit (Logische Untersuchungen, Prolegomena zur reinen Logik)*, p. 190.
10. There is no apodeictic self-evidence, the *Formale und transzendentale Logik* (p. 142) says in effect.
11. The usual term in the unpublished writings. The idea is already to be found in the *Formale und transzendentale Logik*, pp. 184 and ff.
12. *6th Méditation cartésienne* (unpublished).
13. *Ibid.*
14. "*Rückbeziehung der Phänomenologie auf sich selbst*," say the unpublished writings.
15. We are indebted for this last expression to G. Gusdorf, who may well have used it in another sense.

Hermeneutics:
The Approaches to Symbol

PAUL RICOEUR

Translated by *Denis Savage*

It is only now that we reach the level of the most ambitious interrogations of our "Problematic"; and it is only now that we can glimpse a solution—no longer eclectic, but dialectical—of the hermeneutic conflict. We now know that the key to the solution lies in the dialectic between archaeology and teleology. It remains to find the *concrete* "mixed texture" in which we see the archaeology and teleology. This concrete mixed texture is *symbol*. I propose to show, at my own risk, that what psychoanalysis describes as overdetermination finds its full meaning in a dialectic of interpretation, whose opposed poles are constituted by archaeology and teleology.

It was impossible to understand the overdetermination of symbols without making a long and involved detour; we could not appeal to such overdetermination as our starting-point, nor is it certain that we truly can attain to it; that is why I speak of the *approaches to symbol*. As I said in the "Problematic," a general hermeneutics does not yet lie within our scope; this book is no more than a propaedeutic to that extensive work. The task we set ourselves was to integrate into reflection the opposition between conflicting hermeneutics. Now that we have made such a long detour we are simply at the threshold of our enterprise. Let us turn back and consider the path we have taken.

First, it was necessary to pass through the stage of dispossession —the dispossession of consciousness as the place and origin of meaning. Freudian psychoanalysis appeared to us as the discipline best equipped to instigate and carry through this ascesis of reflection: its topography and its economic help displace the locus of meaning toward the unconscious, that is, toward an origin over which we have no control. This first stage terminates in an archaeology of reflection.

Next, it was necessary to traverse an antithetic of reflection. Here the archaeological interpretation appeared as the counterpart of a progressive genesis of meaning through successive figures, where the meaning of each figure is dependent upon the meaning of the subsequent figures.

Finally, Hegel served as an inverse model and helped us form a dialectic, not *between* Freud and Hegel, but in each one of them. It is only when each interpretation is seen to be contained in the other that the antithetic is no longer simply the clash of opposites but the passage of each into the other. Only then is reflection truly in the archaeology and the archaeology in the teleology: reflection, teleology, and archaeology pass over into one another.

Now that we have thought through in the abstract the reconciliation of these two lines of interpretation, the possibility arises of seeking their point of intersection in the meaningful texture of symbols.

In this sense, symbols are the *concrete* moment of the dialectic, but they are not its *immediate* moment. The concrete is always the fullness or peak of mediation. The return to the simple attitude of listening to symbols is the "reward consequent upon thought." The concreteness of language which we border upon through painstaking approximation is the second naïveté of which we have merely a frontier or threshold knowledge.

The danger for the philosopher (for the philosopher, I say, and not for the poet) is to arrive too quickly, to lose the tension, to become dissipated in the symbolic richness, in the abundance of meaning. I do not retract the descriptions of the problematic; I continue to state that symbols call for interpretation because of their peculiar signifying structure in which meaning inherently refers beyond itself. But the explanation of this structure requires the threefold discipline of dispossession, antithetic, and dialectic. In order to think in accord with symbols one must subject them to a dialectic; only then is it possible to set the dialectic within interpretation itself and come back to living speech. This last stage of reappropriation constitutes the transition to concrete reflection. In returning to the attitude of listening to language, reflection passes into the fullness of speech simply heard and understood.

Let us not be mistaken about the meaning of this last stage: this return to the immediate is not a return to silence, but rather to the spoken word, to the fullness of language. Nor is it a return to the dense enigma of initial, immediate speech, but to speech that has been instructed by the whole process of meaning. Hence this concrete reflection does not imply any concession to irrationality or effusiveness. In its return to the spoken word, reflection continues to be reflection, that is, the understanding of meaning; reflection becomes hermeneutic; this is the only way in which it can become concrete and still remain reflection. The second naïveté is not the first naïveté; it is postcritical and not precritical; it is an informed naïveté.

THE OVERDETERMINATION OF SYMBOLS

The thesis I am proposing is this: what psychoanalysis calls overdetermination cannot be understood apart from a dialectic between two functions which are thought to be opposed to one another but which symbols coordinate in a concrete unity. Thus the ambiguity of symbolism is not a lack of univocity but is rather the possibility of carrying and engendering opposed interpretations, each of which is self-consistent.

The two hermeneutics, one turned toward the revival of archaic meanings belonging to the infancy of mankind, the other toward the emergence of figures that anticipate our spiritual adventure, develop, in opposite directions, the beginnings of meaning contained in language—a language richly endowed with the enigmas that men have invented and received in order to express their fears and hopes. Thus we should say that symbols carry two vectors. On the one hand, symbols repeat our childhood in all the senses, chronological and nonchronological, of that childhood. On the other hand, they explore our adult life: "O my prophetic soul," says Hamlet. But these two functions are not external to one another; they constitute the overdetermination of authentic symbols. By probing our infancy and making it live again in the oneiric mode, symbols represent the projection of our human possibilities onto the area of imagination. These authentic symbols are truly regressive-progressive; remembrance gives rise to anticipation; archaism gives rise to prophecy.

Pursuing this analysis of the intentional structure of symbols more deeply, I would say that the opposition between regression and progression, which we have struggled to establish and to overcome at the same time, throws light on the paradoxical texture described as the unity of concealing and showing. True symbols are at the crossroads of the two functions which we have by turns opposed to and grounded in one another. Such symbols both disguise and reveal. While they conceal the aims of our instincts, they disclose the process of self-consciousness. Disguise, reveal; conceal, show; these two functions are no longer external to one another; they express the two sides of a single symbolic function. Because of their overdetermination symbols realize the concrete identity between the progression of the figures of spirit or mind and the regression to the key signifiers of the unconscious. Advancement of meaning occurs only in the sphere of the projections of desire, of the derivatives of the unconscious, of the revivals of archaism. We nourish our least carnal symbols with desires that have been checked, deviated, transformed. We represent our ideals with images issuing from cleansed desire. Thus symbols represent in a concrete unity what reflection in its antithetic stage is forced to split into opposed interpretations; the opposed hermeneutics disjoin and decompose what concrete reflection recomposes through a return to speech simply heard and understood. If my analysis is correct, sublimation is not a supplementary procedure that could be accounted for by an economics of desire. It is not a mechanism that could be put on the same plane as the other instinctual vicissitudes, alongside reversal, turning round upon the self, and repression. Insofar as revealing and disguising coincide in it, we might say that sublimation is the symbolic function itself. Reflection's initial approach to this function is necessarily divisive. An economics isolates the element of disguise in the symbolic function, insofar as dreams distort the secret intentions of our forbidden desires. The economics must then be counterbalanced by a phenomenology of mind or spirit in order to preserve the other dimension and to show that symbols involve a development of the self that opens up to what the symbols disclose. But one must go beyond this dichotomy which always keeps recurring within symbols; one must see that this second function of symbols runs through and takes into itself the projective function in order to raise it up and, in the proper sense of the term, sublimate it. By means of disguise and projection something further transpires—a function of dis-covery, of dis-closure, which sublimates the oneirism of man.

To what extent does this conception of the dialectical structure of symbols retain a connection with orthodox Freudian doctrine? I do not deny that Freud would reject our interpretation of overdetermination.[1] But the treatment of symbols in *The Interpretation of Dreams* and the *Introductory Lectures* is less unfavorable to our position, because of the ambiguities and unsolved difficulties Freud encounters in that treatment. Let us now relate these difficulties to those of sublimation.

Freud's theory of symbolism is indeed quite disconcerting.[2] On the one hand, symbolism in the mechanism of dreams is very narrowly restricted to the sterotypes that resist the piecemeal method of deciphering dreams through the dreamer's free associations. In this sense there is no strictly symbolic function that might stand as a distinct procedure alongside condensation, displacement, and pictorial representation. Nor does symbolization constitute a peculiar problem from the point of view of dream interpretation, for the symbols used in dreams have been formed elsewhere. Symbols have a permanently fixed meaning in dreams, like the grammalogues in shorthand. Consequently their interpretation can be direct and does not require a long and difficult work of deciphering.

Lecture X of the *Introductory Lectures on Psychoanalysis* confirms this first aspect of the problem: the comparisons at the basis of dream-symbols "lie ready to hand and are complete, once and for all."[3] More than fifteen years after *The Interpretation of Dreams*, the question of symbolism is still set within the context of the failure of the method of free association. Symbols are subject to fixed or constant translations—"just as popular 'dream-books' provide [translations] for *everything* that appears in dreams."[4] And Freud expressly states: "A constant relation of this kind between a dream-element and its translation is described by us as a 'symbolic' one, and the dream-element itself as a 'symbol' of the unconscious dream-thought."[5] Thus the symbolic relation becomes a "fourth" relation in addition to condensation, displacement, and pictorial representation.[6] The interpretation of symbols by means of "stable translations" forms a *supplement* to interpretation based on association. As in *The Interpretation of Dreams*, Freud again refers to Scherner as being the first to recognize that symbolism is essentially a fantasying of the body. What is symbolically represented is the human body. The sexual etiology of the neuroses enabled Freud to center this symbolization on sexuality and to link the fantasying of the body with the general finality of dreams, that is, with their function of substitute satisfaction.

If the reader considers only the content this symbolism *thematizes*, he might hastily conclude that Lecture X has nothing interesting to offer. From the standpoint of what is thematized one can only say that, first, the "contents" discovered are monotonous —they are always the same things: the genitals, sexual processes, sexual intercourse; and second, the representations symbolizing them are extremely numerous—the same subject matter can be symbolized by almost anything. This curious fact raises the question of the common element, the *tertium comparationis*, of the supposed comparison.[7] It is precisely the *disproportion* [8] between the number of symbols and the monotony of the contents, especially when "the common element is not understood," [9] that directly poses the problem of the constitution of the symbolic relation. Dreams do not institute this relation; they find it ready-made and they make use of it. Hence the elaboration of a dream does not involve any work of symbolization comparable to what was described as the work of condensation, displacement, and pictorial representation. But how then do we "come to know the meaning of these dream-symbols"? The answer is that

> we learn it from very different sources—from fairy tales and myths, from buffoonery and jokes, from folklore (that is, from knowledge about popular manners and customs, sayings and songs) and from poetic and colloquial linguistic usage. In all these directions we come upon the same symbolism, and in some of them we can understand it without further instruction. If we go into these sources in detail, we shall find so many parallels to dream-symbolism that we cannot fail to be convinced of our interpretations.[10]

Thus it is not the dream-work that constructs the symbolic relation, but the work of culture. This means that the symbolic relation is formed within language. But Freud does not draw any consequences from this discovery; the analogy between myths and dreams simply verifies and confirms our dream interpretations. Thus Otto Rank's study of "the birth of the hero" simply furnishes parallels to the symbolic representations of birth that occur in dreams. The confirmation of the sexual symbolism of dreams by the symbolism of myths is equivalent to a reduction of the mythical to the oneiric—even though myths supply the element of speech in which the semantics of symbolism has actually been built up.

The puzzling thing about symbols is not that ships stand for women but that women are signified and, in order to be signified on the level of images, verbalized. It is the spoken woman that becomes the dreamed woman; it is the mythicized woman that becomes the oneiric woman. But how is one to examine myths without also examining rituals and cults, emblems and heraldic devices (Freud mentions the French fleur-de-lis and the *triskeles* of Sicily and the Isle of Man)? Freud is well aware that there is more in myths, fairy tales, sayings, and poetry than in dreams. He himself emphasizes this fact at the end of his study of symbolism. But the fact itself is simply the occasion for showing that psychoanalysis is a discipline of "general interest," [11] that it establishes links with other disciplines, and that in these links, as he proudly states, "the share of psychoanalysis is in the first instance that of giver and only to a less extent that of receiver": [12] "it is psychoanalysis which provides the technical methods and the points of view whose application in these other fields should prove fruitful." [13] There is reason to fear that the comparative method is being restricted here to a mere apologetics.

This imperialism was unfortunately reinforced by certain supplementary but disastrous hypotheses concerning language itself. Freud is struck by the fact that the symbolism employed in myths is less exclusively sexual than the symbolism of dreams. He reduces the anomaly in the following way. He supposes a state of language in which all symbols were sexual symbols, a state in which "the original sounds of speech served for communication, and summoned the speaker's sexual partner." Later on, a sexual interest became attached to work; but man accepted this displacement of sexual interest only by treating work as an equivalent of and substitute for sexual activity. The ambiguity of language dates from this period when "words enunciated during work in common thus had two meanings; they denoted sexual acts as well as the working activity equated with them. . . . In this way a number of verbal roots would have been formed, all of which were of sexual origin and had subsequently lost their sexual meaning." [14] If this hypothesis, which Freud borrows from the Scandinavian philologist H. Sperber, were correct, the symbolic relation, which dreams preserve better than myths, "would be the residue of an ancient verbal identity." [15] It is clear why Freud adopted this nonanalytic hypothesis; it gives our dreams an advantage over myths; although myths provide the broadest parallels of sexual symbolism, the fact that dream-symbolism is almost exclusively sexual is justified by this "primitive language" of which dreams would be the privileged witness.

But even if we were to credit this hypothesis with some linguistic value, it casts us adrift: all dream-symbolism is found to be related to an activity of language, but the enigma of this activity is simply disguised by the supposition of an original verbal identity where the same words denote the sexual and the nonsexual. The hypothesis of these ancient ambiguous roots is simply an expedient whereby one solves the problem by projecting it into a "basic language" in which similarity would already be identity.[16]

In my opinion, these speculations close more paths than they open. By assuming everything at the outset, they imply that thereafter we can never encounter anything but residues. When we presented the theory of symbol as given in *The Interpretation of Dreams*, we asked whether Freud was not mistaken in limiting the notion of symbol to common stenographic signs; are symbols merely vestiges, or are they not also the dawn of meaning? We can now take up the question again in the light of our dialectical conception of overdetermination. I suggest that we distinguish various levels of creativity of symbols (before distinguishing, in the following section, various spheres in which symbols actually occur). At the lowest level we come upon sedimented symbolism: here we find various stereotyped and fragmented remains of symbols, symbols so commonplace and worn with use that they have nothing but a past. This is the level of dream-symbolism, and also of fairy tales and legends; here the work of symbolization is no longer operative. At a second level we come upon the symbols that function in everyday life; these are the symbols that are useful and are actually utilized, that have a past and a present, and that in the clockwork of a given society serve as a token for the nexus of social pacts; structural anthropology operates at this level. At a higher level come the prospective symbols; these are creations of meaning that take up the traditional symbols with their multiple significations and serve as the vehicles of new meanings. This creation of meaning reflects the living substrate of symbolism, a substrate that is not the result of social sedimentation. Later in this chapter we will try to state how this creation of meaning is at the same time a recapture of archaic fantasies and a living interpretation of this fantasy substrate. Dreams provide a key only for the symbolism of the first level; the "typical" dreams Freud appeals to in developing his theory of symbolism do not reveal the canonical form of symbols but merely their vestiges on the plane of sedimented expressions. The true task, therefore, is to grasp symbols in their creative moment, and not when they arrive at the end of their course and are revived in dreams, like stenographic grammalogues with their "permanently fixed meaning." Further on, the tragedy of *Oedipus Rex* will enable us to recapture the birth of symbol, at the moment when the symbol is itself the interpretation of a prior legendary substrate. But it is impossible to proceed directly to the center of this creative source. We must make use of all the available mediations.

THE HIERARCHIAL ORDER OF SYMBOL

The dialectical interpretation of the concept of overdetermination, understood as the twofold possibility of a teleological exegesis and a regressive exegesis, must now be brought to bear on certain definite problems. What are we to take as our guide? The *Phenomenology of Spirit?* As I have said, I do not think we can restore, after more than a century, the *Phenomenology of Spirit* in the form in which it was written. I propose to put to the test of reflection a principle of hierarchy that I already used in *Fallible Man* to articulate the notion of feeling.[17] The working hypothesis is plausible: feeling, too, is "mixed"; it is that "mixed texture" explored by Plato in Book IV of the *Republic* under the title of *thumos,* i.e., "spiritedness" or "heart." Spiritedness, Plato said, sometimes fights on the side of reason in the form of indignation and courage, and sometimes sides with desire in the form of aggressiveness, irritation, and anger. Spiritedness, I added, is the restless heart that knows not the surcease of pleasure and the repose of happiness, and I suggested that this ambiguous and fragile heart represents the entire middle region of the affective life between the vital affections and the rational or spiritual affections, that is to say, the entire activity that forms the transition between living and thinking, between Bios and Logos. And I had already noted: "It is in this intermediate region that the *self* is constituted as different from natural beings and other selves. . . . Only with *thumos* does desire assume the character of otherness and subjectivity which constitute a self." [18]

I wish to reexamine this problem of mixed texture in the light of our antithesis between the two hermeneutics. The same feelings that I previously studied under the heading of thumos will now be seen as being subject to two modes of exegesis, one along the lines of the Freudian erotics, the other along the lines of a phenomenology of spirit.

To this effect, I propose to reexamine the trilogy of fundamental feelings that I borrowed from the Kantian anthropology—the trilogy of the passions of having, power, and valuation or worth [*avoir, pouvoir, valoir*]—and to redo the exegesis of the three "quests" that the moralist knows only under the distorted mask of fallen figures—the "passions" of possession, domination, and pretension, or, in another language, of avarice, tyranny, and vanity (*Habsucht, Herrschsucht, Ehrsucht*). What we must discover behind this threefold *Sucht,* with its aberration and violence, is the authentic *Suchen;* "behind this passional pursuit," we must attain to "the 'quest' of humanity, a quest no longer mad and in bondage but constitutive of human praxis and the human self. "[19]

I would like to show that this threefold quest pertains to a phenomenology in the style of Hegel and to an erotics in the style of Freud.

It should be emphasized that the three spheres of meaning through which the trajectory of feeling passes as it moves from having, to power, and to worth, constitute regions of human meanings that are in essence nonlibidinal. Not that they are "spheres free of conflict," as certain neo-Freudians say;[20] no region of human existence escapes the libidinal cathexis of love and hate; but the important point is that, whatever be the secondary cathexis of the inter-human relations formed on the occasions of having, power, and worth, these spheres of meaning are not constituted by the libidinal cathexis.

By what, then, are they constituted? It seems to me this is where the Hegelian method is of help. One way of modernizing the Hegelian enterprise would be to constitute through progressive synthesis the moments of "objectivity" that guide the human feelings as they center on having, power, and worth. Such moments are indeed moments of objectivity: to understand these affective factors, which we name possession, domination, and valuation, is to show that these feelings internalize a series of object-relations that pertain not to a phenomenology of perception, but to an economics, a politics, a theory of culture. The progress of this constitution of objectivity should guide the investigation of the affectivity proper to man.[21] At the same time that they institute a new relationship to things, the properly human quests of having, power, and worth institute new relationships to other persons, through which one can pursue the Hegelian process of the reduplication of consciousness and the advancement of self-consciousness.

Let us examine, from this double point of view, the successive constitution of the three spheres of meaning.

By relations of *having* I understand the relations involved in appropriation and work within a situation of "scarceness." To this day we know of no other condition of human having. In connection with these relations, however, we see new human feelings arise that do not pertain to the biological sphere; these feelings proceed not from life but from the reflection into human affectivity of a new domain of objects, of a specific objectivity that is "economic" objectivity. Man appears here as a being capable of feelings relative to having and of an alienation that in essence is nonlibidinal. This is the alienation Marx described in his theory of the fetishism of money; it is the economic alienation that Marx showed is capable of engendering a "false consciousness," or ideological thinking. Thus man becomes adult and, in the same movement, capable of adult alienation. What is important to note, however, is that the areas in which these feelings, passions, and alienations multiply are new objects, values of exchange, monetary signs, structures, and institutions. We may say, then, that man becomes self-consciousness insofar as he experiences this economic objectivity as a new modality of his subjectivity and thus attains specifically human "feelings" relative to the availability of things as things that have been worked upon and appropriated, while at the same time he becomes an expropriated appropriator. This new objectivity gives rise to a specific group of impulses, ideas, and affects.

The sphere of *power* should be examined in the same way, that is to say, from the point of view of objectivity and the feelings and alienations this objectivity engenders. The sphere of power is likewise constituted in an objective structure. Thus Hegel used the term "objective spirit" to designate the structures and institutions in which the relation of commanding-obeying, essential to political power, actualizes and engenders itself; as we see at the beginning of the *Principles of the Philosophy of Right*, man engenders himself as spiritual will by entering into the relation of commanding-obeying. Here too the development of self-consciousness is bound up with a development of "objectivity." The "feelings" centering around this "object," which is power, are specifically human feelings, such as intrigue, ambition, submission, responsibility; so too the alienations are specifically human alienations. The ancients already described these alienations in the figure of the tyrant. Plato clearly shows how the maladies of the soul, which are exhibited in the figure of the tyrant, spread out from a center he calls *dunamis*, or power, and even extend into the region of language in the form of "flattery"; thus the tyrant gives rise to the sophist. Hence one can say that man becomes human insofar as he can enter into the political problematic of power, adopt the feelings that center around power, and deliver himself up to the evils accompanying that power. Thus there arises a specifically adult sphere of guilt; power leads to madness, says Alain, following Plato. This second example makes it clear how a psychology of consciousness is simply the projected shadow of this movement of figures that man assumes in engendering economic and then political objectivity.

The same may be said of the third properly human sphere of meaning, the sphere of *valuation* or *worth*. This third moment may be understood as follows: the constitution of the self is not completed in an economics and a politics, but continues on into the region of culture. Here too the psychology of personality grasps only the shadow, that is to say, the aim, present in each man, of being respected, approved, and recognized as a person. My existence for myself is dependent on this constitution of self in the opinion of others; my "self" is shaped by the opinion and acceptance of others. But this constitution of subjects, this mutual constitution through opinion, is guided by new figures which may be said to be "objective" in a new sense. These objects are no longer *things*, as are the objects in the sphere of having; they do not always have corresponding *institutions*, as do the objects in the sphere of power. These new figures of man are to be found in the works and monuments of law, art, and literature. The exploration of man's possibilities extends into this new kind of objectivity, the objectivity of cultural objects properly so-called. Even when Van Gogh sketches a chair, he at the same time portrays man; he projects a figure of man, namely the man who "has" this represented world. Thus, the various modes of cultural expression give these "images" the density of "thingness"; they make these images exist between men and among men, by embodying them in "works." It is through the medium of these works and monuments that a human dignity and self-regard are formed. Finally, this is the level at which man can become alienated from himself, degrade himself, make a fool of himself, destroy himself.

Such is, it seems to me, the exegesis that may be made of consciousness according to a method that is not a psychology of consciousness, but a reflective method that has its starting point in the objective movement of the figures of man. This objective movement is what Hegel calls spirit. Reflection is the means for deriving from this movement the subjectivity that constitutes itself at the same time that the objectivity engenders itself.

It is clear that this indirect, mediate approach to consciousness has nothing to do with an immediate self-presence of consciousness, an immediate self-certainty.

But no sooner have we noted the specificity of economic, political, and cultural objectivity, and the specificity of the related human feelings, than we have to take the reverse path and point out the gradual cathexis or investment of these regions of meaning by what Freud calls the "derivatives from the unconscious." The three spheres we have examined, like the whole life of civilization, are involved in a history of instinct; none of the figures of the phenomenology of spirit escapes the libidinal investment, and consequently the possibilities of regression inherent in the instinctual situation. We shall outline briefly the dialectic of the two hermeneutics at the levels of having and power, and reserve a more extensive analysis for the symbolism of the strictly cultural sphere.

Freud presents a libidinal interpretation of having that is thoroughly compatible with an interpretation that allows the economic sphere, in the sense of political economy, its own specificity. Well known are the attempts made by Freud and his followers to derive the apparently nonlibidinal relations to things and men from the successive phases through which the libido passes: oral phase, anal phase, phallic phase, genital phase. Freud uses the term "transformation" [22] (*Umsetzung*) to designate this displacement of instinctual emotions from certain erotogenic zones onto seemingly quite different objects. Thus Freud borrows the notion from Abraham that after a person's excrement has lost its value for him,

> this instinctual interest . . . passes over onto objects that can be presented as *gifts*. . . . After this, corresponding exactly to analogous changes of meaning that occur in linguistic development, this ancient interest in feces is transformed into the high valuation of *gold* and *money* but also makes a contribution to the affective cathexis of *baby* and *penis*. . . . If one is not aware of these profound connections, it is impossible to find one's way about in the fantasies of human beings, in their associations, influenced as they are by the unconscious, and in their symptomatic language. Feces—money—gift—baby—penis are

treated there as though they meant the same thing, and they are represented too by the same symbols.

Freud uses the same terms in speaking of the "formation of character" that begins in the pregenital phases of the libido; he believes that the triad of orderliness, thrift, and obstinacy is connected with anal erotism: "We therefore speak of an 'anal character' in which we find this remarkable combination and we draw a contrast to some extent between the anal character and unmodified anal erotism." [23]

In this example we can see both the validity and the limits of this type of interpretation. The Freudian interpretation functions as a kind of hyletic of affects (here I take *hylê* or "matter" in the Husserlian sense of the term).[24] It enables us to set forth the genealogy of the main human affects and to establish the table of their derivatives; it verifies Kant's insight that there is only one "faculty of desiring"; in Freudian terms, our love of money is the same love we had as infants for our feces. But at the same time we realize that this kind of exploration into the substructures of our affects does not substitute for a constitution of the economic object. The regressive genesis of our desires does not replace a progressive genesis concerned with meanings, values, symbols. That is why Freud speaks of "transformations of instinct." But a dynamics of affective cathexes cannot account for the innovation or advancement of meaning that is inherent in this transformation.

The same may be said of the political sphere, which constitutes, as we have seen, a specific region of interhuman relationships and an original class of human objects. It is perfectly possible to erect two interpretations upon this single affective complex, an interpretation according to the figures of the phenomenology of spirit and an interpretation of the type that Freud elaborated in 1921 in *Group Psychology and the Analysis of the Ego*. Freud regards the concept of "suggestion," espoused by the social psychology of the beginning of the century, as a screen for the libido: it is Eros, he states, "which holds together everything in the world." [25] And he confidently proceeds to write a chapter on the libidinal structure of the army and the church. We should not be surprised that an enterprise of this kind never attains to the level of a structural analysis of groups. The key notions here are the concrete tie with the leader and homosexual object-cathexis. The various ideas or causes that might hold a group or society together are regarded as derived from interpersonal ties that ultimately are rooted in the invisible leader. Freud admits that "we are concerned here with love instincts which have been diverted from their original aims, though they do not operate with less energy on that account." [26] This inability on the part of a mere psychoanalysis of the leader to attain to the fundamental constitution of social ties does not prevent the interpretation from being extremely penetrating.

Such an investigation inevitably brings us back to the concept of identification; indeed, Chapter 7 of *Group Psychology* is Freud's most important study of identification. "*A primary group of this kind is a number of individuals who have put one and the same object in the place of their ego ideal and have consequently identified themselves with one another in their ego.*" [27] But Freud himself points out the limits of his enterprise. Ultimately, his investigation is concerned less with the formation and development of social groups than with the regressive characteristics of groups as described by Le Bon at the turn of the century: namely, "the lack of independence and initiative in their members, the similarity in the reactions of all of them, their reduction so to speak, to the level of group individuals"; and at the level of the group as a whole, "the weakness of intellectual activity, the lack of emotional restraint, the incapacity for moderation and delay, the inclination to exceed every limit in the expression of emotion and to work it off completely in the form of action." [28]

Even when he extends his investigation to what he calls "artificial groups"—army or church—the explanation is still in terms of the libidinal ties holding a group or the hypothetical primal horde together:

> The uncanny and coercive characteristics of group formations, which are shown in the phenomena of suggestion that accompany them, may therefore with justice be traced back to the fact of their origin from the primal horde. The leader of the group is still the dreaded primal father; the group still wishes to be

governed by unrestricted force; it has an extreme passion for authority; in Le Bon's phrase, it has a thirst for obedience. The primal father is the group ideal, which governs the ego in the place of the ego ideal.[29]

In conclusion, Freud states: "We are aware that what we have been able to contribute towards the explanation of the libidinal structure of groups leads back to the distinction between the ego and the ego ideal and to the double kind of tie which this makes possible— identification, and putting the [external libidinal] object in the place of the ego ideal." [30] But if we ask psychoanalysis what constitutes the specificity of the political tie, its only answer is to invoke the notion of a "diversion of aim."

In the same text Freud admits that "there is some difficulty in giving a description of such a diversion of aim which will conform to the requirements of metapsychology." [31] And he adds: "If we choose, we may recognize in this diversion of aim a beginning of the *sublimation* of the sexual instincts, or on the other hand we may fix the limits of sublimation at some more distant point." [32] Is this not rather the sign that sublimation is a mixed concept, which designates both a derivation of energy and an innovation of meaning? The derivation of energy shows that there is but one libido and merely various vicissitudes of that one libido, but the innovation of meaning requires another hermeneutics.

A DIALECTICAL REEXAMINATION OF THE PROBLEM OF SUBLIMATION AND THE CULTURAL OBJECT

I now wish to show, in a very precise example, how a dialectical exegesis may be applied to symbols belonging to the third cycle of man's *Suchen*. I will take this example from the aesthetic sphere, where Freud's interpretation is less reductive than it is in the sphere of religious symbolism. It is here that the profound identity of the two hermeneutics, regressive and progressive, may be shown most clearly and forcefully. It is here that the teleology of consciousness will appear in the detailed structure of the archaeology itself, and the telos of the human adventure will be foreshadowed in the endless exegesis of the myths and hidden secrets of our childhood and birth.

This privileged example, this prototypic example, will be Sophocles' *Oedipus Rex*. The tragedy is built around a fantasy well known to the interpretation of dreams, the fantasy in which we live through the childhood drama that we call Oedipal. In this sense, we may say with Freud that there is nothing more behind the work of art created by Sophocles than a dream. From the start Freud rejects the classical interpretation of the *Oedipus Rex* as a tragedy of destiny, whose effect lies in the contrast between the omnipotence of the gods and the vain efforts of mankind to escape the evil that threatens them. This type of conflict, he thinks, no longer affects a modern audience, whereas spectators are still moved by *Oedipus Rex*. What moves us is not the conflict between destiny and human will, but the particular nature of this destiny, which we recognize without knowing it: "His destiny moves us only because it might have been ours—because the oracle laid the same curse upon us before our birth as upon him." [33] Freud compares the legend and the drama with dreams of incest and parricide.

> King Oedipus, who slew his father Laïus and married his mother Jocasta, merely shows us the fulfillment of our own childhood wishes. . . . Here is one in whom these primeval wishes of our childhood have been fulfilled, and we shrink back from him with the whole force of the repression by which those wishes have since that time been held down within us.[34]

Just as these typical dreams are accompanied by feelings of repulsion whereby we comply with the censorship and make the dream content admissible to consciousness, "so too," says Freud, "the legend must include horror and self-punishment." [35] Thus the famous tragic *phobos* would express merely the violence of our own repression against the revival of those childhood wishes. As for the theological interpretation concerning the conflict between Providence and human freedom, Freud casually attributes it to "a misconceived secondary revision of the material." [36]

At this point I would like to counter with a second interpretation, which is in fact contained in the preceding one by reason of the overdetermination of the Oedipus symbol. This interpretation no longer concerns the drama of incest and parricide, a drama that has already taken place when the tragedy begins, but rather the tragedy of truth. It appears that Sophocles' creation does not aim at reviving the Oedipus complex in the minds of the spectators; on the basis of a first drama, the drama of incest and parricide, Sophocles has created a second, the tragedy of self-consciousness, of self-recognition. Thus Oedipus enter into a second guilt, an adult guilt, expressed in the hero's arrogance and anger. At the beginning of the play Oedipus calls down curses upon the unknown person responsible for the plague, but he excludes the possibility that that person might in fact be himself. The entire drama consists in the resistance and ultimate collapse of this presumption. Oedipus must be broken in his pride through suffering; this presumption is no longer the culpable desire of the child, but the pride of the king; the tragedy is not the tragedy of Oedipus the child, but of Oedipus Rex. By reason of this impure passion with respect to the truth, his hubris rejoins that of Prometheus: what leads him to disaster is the passion for nonknowing. His guilt is no longer in the sphere of the libido, but in that of self-consciousness: it is man's anger as the power of nontruth. Thus Oedipus becomes guilty precisely because of his pretension to exonerate himself from a crime that, ethically speaking, he is not in fact guilty of.

It is therefore possible to apply to Sophocles' drama what we have called an antithetic of reflection. One might illustrate this opposition between the two dramas and between the two kinds of guilt by saying that the initial drama, which comes within the province of psychoanalysis, has its antagonist in the sphinx, which represents the enigma of birth—the source, according to Freud, of all the strange events of childhood; whereas the second order drama, which Freud seems to reduce to the status of a secondary revision, and even of a misconception—although it actually constitutes the true tragedy—has its antagonist in Tiresias the seer. In the language of our antithetic, the sphinx represents the side of the unconscious, the seer the side of spirit or mind. As in the Hegelian dialectic, Oedipus is not the center from which the truth proceeds; a first mastery, which is only pretension and pride, must be broken; the figure from which truth proceeds is that of the seer, which Sophocles describes as the "force of truth." [37] This figure is no longer a tragic one; it represents and manifests the vision of the totality. The seer, akin to the fool of Elizabethan tragedy, is the figure of comedy at the heart of tragedy, a figure Oedipus will rejoin only through suffering and pain. The underlying link between the anger of Oedipus and the power of truth is thus the core of the veritable tragedy. This core is not the problem of sex, but the problem of light. The seer is blind with respect to the eyes of the body, but he sees the truth in the light of the mind. That is why Oedipus, who sees the light of day but is blind with regard to himself, will achieve self-consciousness only by becoming the blind seer: night of the senses, night of the understanding, night of the will; nothing more to see, nothing more to love, nothing more to enjoy. "Cease being a master," Creon says harshly; "you won the mastery but could not keep it to the end."

Such is the antithetic reading of *Oedipus Rex;* but we must now combine the two readings in the unity of the symbol and its power to disguise and reveal. I will start with a remark of Freud's which we have omitted and which concerns not the matter of the drama, which we are told is identical with the dream material,[38] but the manner in which the drama unfolds. "The action of the play," he says, "consists in nothing other than the process of revealing, with cunning delays and ever-mounting excitement—a process that can be likened to the work of a psychoanalysis—that Oedipus himself is the murderer of Laïus, but further that he is the son of the murdered man and of Jocasta." [39] But we have already seen that psychoanalysis as a therapeutic activity, as a process of reduplicated consciousness, revives the whole history of master and slave. Thus the analytic interpretation, inasmuch as it is itself a struggle for recognition and hence a struggle for truth, a movement of self-consciousness, suggests the other drama, that of anger and non-truth. That is why Freud himself is not content with saying that Oedipus "shows us the fulfillment of our own childhood wishes"; this is the drama's oneiric function. He adds:

> While the poet, as he unravels the past, brings to light the guilt of Oedipus, he is at the same time compelling us to recognize our own inner minds, in which those same impulses, though

suppressed, are still to be found. The contrast with which the
closing Chorus leaves us confronted—

> . . . *Fix on Oedipus your eyes,*
> *Who resolved the dark enigma, noblest champion and most*
> *wise.*
> *Like a star his envied fortune mounted beaming far and*
> *wide:*
> *Now he sinks in seas of anguish, whelmed beneath a raging*
> *tide . . .*

—strikes as a warning at ourselves and our pride, at us who
since our childhood have grown so wise and so mighty in our
own eyes.[40]

Freud did not clearly distinguish between the mere revival of childhood wishes in dreams and the "warning," addressed to the adult in
us, upon which the drama of truth ends. An antithetic method was
required to bring this double function of Sophocles' drama to the
fore. It is only then that we can see the necessity of going beyond
the duality.

In this connection, what is particularly striking about the symbol
created by Sophocles is the fact that the drama of truth centers
precisely around the mystery of birth. The Oedipal situation contains all the "spiritual" overtones developed by the process of truth:
curiosity, resistance, pride, distress, wisdom. Between the question
of the father and the question of truth a secret alliance is formed
that resides in the overdetermination of the symbol itself. The
father is much more than the father, and the question of the father
is much more than an inquiry about my own father. The father,
after all, is never *seen* in his fatherhood, but only conjectured. The
whole power of questioning is contained in the fantasies of this conjecture. The symbolism of engendering embraces all the questions
concerning generation, genesis, origin, development. But if the
childhood Oedipus drama is already potentially the tragedy of
truth, Sophocles' tragedy of truth is not superimposed upon the
drama of origin, for the material of that tragedy, as Freud says, is
the same as the dream material. The second order tragedy belongs
to the primary tragedy, as is clear from the play's ambiguous and
overdetermined ending. The crime of Oedipus culminates in the

punishment of mutilation inflicted by the anger of nontruth. What is punishment in the tragedy of sex is the dark night of the senses in the final tragedy of truth. And if we return to an earlier part of the play, we see that the king's anger toward the seer derives its energy from the resistance stemming from the Oedipal situation and the dissolution of the childhood complex.

The exegesis of Sophocles' *Oedipus Rex* enables us now to complete the parallel analysis of sublimation and cultural objects, which are in a sense the noematic correlates of sublimation.

We began the dialectical interpretation of sublimation in the spheres of having and power, where we saw the profoundly antithetical nature of sublimation. As we said before, it is on the basis of affects belonging to different libidinal stages that we form the feelings and corresponding meanings that establish us in an economic and a political order. But the example of such an exceptional creation as Sophocles' tragedy reveals more than an antithetic; it reveals, *in the work of art itself,* the profound unity of disguise and disclosure, inherent in the very structure of symbols that have become cultural objects.

It thus becomes possible to locate the oneiric and the poetic on the same symbolic scale. The production of dreams and the creation of works of art represent the two ends of this scale, according to whether the predominant emphasis in the symbolism is disguise or disclosure, distortion or revelation. By this formula I attempt to account both for the functional unity existing between dreams and creativity and for the difference in value that separates a mere product of our dreams from the lasting works that become a part of the cultural heritage of mankind. Between dreams and artistic creativity there is a functional continuity, in the sense that disguise and disclosure are operative in both of them, but in an inverse proportion. That is why Freud is justified in moving from one to the other by a series of imperceptible transitions, as he does in "Creative Writers and Daydreaming." [41] Passing from night dreams to daydreams, from daydreams to play and humor, then to folklore and legends, and finally to works of art, he attests, by this species of increasingly closer analogy, that all creativity is involved in the same economic function and brings about the same substitution of satisfaction as the compromise formations of dreams and the neuroses.

But the question remains: Can an economics account for the in-creasing prevalence, through the functional analogy, of a mytho-poetic power that places the oneiric in the area of creations of speech, themselves rooted in the hierophanies of the sacred and in the symbolism of the cosmic elements? Of this other function Freud recognizes only a very partial aspect, which he describes in terms of an "aesthetic incentive" and which comes down to the purely formal pleasure produced by the artist's technique in presenting his mate-rial. This "incentive" or "allurement" is incorporated into the econ-omy of desire as a type of forepleasure: "We give the name of an *incentive bonus*, or a *forepleasure*, to a yield of pleasure such as this, which is offered to us so as to make possible the release of still greater pleasure arising from deeper psychical sources." [42] Thus the economic framework of the explanation would reduce the entire Kantian analysis of the "judgment of taste" to a "hedonics." Freud accounts very well for the functional unity of dreams and artistic creation, but the qualitative difference, the difference in "aim" which renders instincts dialectical, escapes him; this is why the ques-tion of sublimation remains unsolved.

We thus see in what sense it is true, and in what sense it is not true, that works of art, the lasting and memorable creations of our days, and dreams, the fleeting and sterile products of our nights, are psychical expressions of the same nature. Their unity is assured by the fact that they share the same "hyletic," the same "matter" of de-sire. But their difference, which Freud himself describes as a "trans-formation of aim," a "diversion of aim," "sublimation," is bound up with the process of the figures of spirit. We thus relate Freud to Plato, the Plato of the *Ion* and the *Symposium*, who posited the underlying unity of the poetic and the erotic, and who regarded the philosophic mania or madness as belonging to the manifold unity of all forms of enthusiasm and exaltation. Within their intentional structure symbols have both the unity of a hyletic matter and the qualitative diversity of aims and intentions, with the emphasis either upon the disguising of the hylê or upon the revealing of a further, spiritual meaning. If dreams remain a private expression lost in the solitude of sleep, it is because they lack the mediation of the arti-san's work that embodies the fantasy in a solid material and com-municates it to a public. This mediation of the artisan's work and this communication accrue only to those dreams that at the same time carry values capable of advancing consciousness toward a new understanding of itself. If Michelangelo's *Moses*, Sophocles' *Oedipus Rex*, and Shakespeare's *Hamlet* are creations, they are so in proportion as they are not mere projections of the artist's conflicts, but also the sketch of their solution. Because of their emphasis on disguise, dreams look more to the past, to childhood. But in works of art the emphasis is on disclosure; thus works of art tend to be prospective symbols of one's personal synthesis and of man's future and not merely a regressive symptom of the artist's unresolved conflicts. The same emphasis upon disclosure is the reason our pleasure as viewers of art is not the simple revival, even accompanied by an incentive bonus, of our own conflicts, but the pleasure of sharing in the work of truth that comes about through the hero.

This approach to the intentional unity of symbols has enabled us to overcome the remaining distance between regression and progression. From now on regression and progression do not represent two truly opposed processes; they are rather the abstract terms employed to designate the two end limits of a single scale of symbolization. Are not dreams a compromise fluctuating between these two functions, according as the neurotic aspect inclines dreams toward repetition and archaism, or as they themselves are on the way to a therapeutic action exercised by the self upon itself? Inversely, are there any great symbols created by art or literature that are not rooted in the archaism of the conflicts and dramas of our individual or collective childhood? The most innovative figures that the artist, writer, or thinker can produce call forth ancient energies originally invested in archaic figures; but in activating these figures, comparable to oneiric and neurotic symptoms, the creator reveals man's most open and fundamental possibilities and erects them into new symbols of the suffering of self-consciousness.

But just as there is a scale or gradation in the oneiric, perhaps there is also a scale in the poetic. Surrealism shows quite well how the poetic can return to the oneiric, or even tend to copy neurosis when aesthetic creativity gives free rein to the fantasies of obsession, organizes itself around themes of repetition, or even regresses to automatic writing. Thus, not only would works of art and dreams be located at the two ends of a single scale of symbolization, but each of these kinds of production would reconcile, according to an inverse pattern, the oneiric and the poetic.

To overcome what remains abstract in the opposition between regression and progression would require a study of these concrete relations, shifts of emphasis, and inversion of roles between the functions of disguise and disclosure. At least we have shown that the area in which this concrete dialectic must be worked out is that of language and its symbolic function.

Corresponding to this dialectical structure of sublimation is a similar structure of the "cultural objects" that are the correlates of sublimation. These objects pertain to the third sphere of feelings, which we have described as the sphere of worth or valuation. These feelings appeared to us to form a region of meaning irreducible to a political economy and a politics. The process in which man achieves consciousness is not restricted to relationships between the ego and possessions, to relations of appropriation and mutual expropriation, or of exchange, sharing, and giving; nor is it restricted to the relations of dominance and obedience, of hierarchy and sharing of influence. The quest for recognition also extends into a quest for mutual esteem and approval. My existence for myself is thus dependent on the way I am regarded by other people; the self is shaped by the opinion and acceptance of others. This mutual constitution through opinion is still guided by objects, but these objects are no longer "things" in the sense of the goods, commodities, and services of the sphere of having, nor do they have corresponding institutions as in the sphere of power; these objects are the monuments and works of law, art, literature, philosophy. The exploration of man's possibilities extends into this new kind of objectivity, the objectivity of works or cultural objects properly so-called. Painted, sculptured, or written works give these "images of man" the density of thingness, the stability of reality; they make these images exist between men and among men by embodying them in the material of stone, color, musical score, or the written word. It is through the medium of these works or monuments that a certain dignity of man is formed, which is the instrument and trace of a process of reduplicated consciousness, of recognition of the self in another self.

These works or cultural objects, however, cannot be accounted for by a simple antithetic that would see a split between the creative process along which man's human development lies and the affective material upon which the history of spirit works. The only thing that can do justice to both an economics of culture and a phenomenology of spirit is a dialectic based on the overdetermination of symbols. I propose therefore that cultural phenomena should be interpreted as the objective media in which the great enterprise of sublimation with its double value of disguise and disclosure becomes sedimented. Such an interpretation opens up to us the meaning of certain synonymous expressions. Thus the term "education" designates the movement by which man is led out of his childhood; this movement is, in the proper sense, an "erudition" whereby man is lifted out of his archaic past; but it is also a *Bildung*, in the twofold sense of an edification and an emergence of the *Bilder* or "images of man" which mark off the development of self-consciousness and open man to what they disclose. And this education, this erudition, this Bildung function as a second nature, for they remodel man's first nature. In them is realized the movement so well described by Ravaisson in the limited example of habit; this movement is at the same time the return of freedom to nature through the recapture of desire in the works of culture.[43] Because of the overdetermination of symbols, these works are closely tied in with the world of our experience: it is indeed where id was that the ego comes to be. By mobilizing all our childhood stages, all our archaisms, by embodying itself in the oneiric, the poetic keeps man's cultural existence from being simply a huge artifice, a futile "artifact," a Leviathan without a nature and against nature.

NOTES

1. It is true that the distinction between overdetermination and over-interpretation is to be found in Freud: GW, 2/3, 253 (1), 270 (1), 272, 528; SE, 4, 248, n. 1, 263, n. 2 (an addition of 1914 concerning the interpretation of the Oedipus myth), 266, and SE, 5, 523. But this overinterpretation does not denote interpretations that differ from that of psychoanalysis; cf. above, "Analytic," Part II, Chap. 2, p. 193, n. 25.

2. Besides the works of J. Lacan, which have been already cited, see S. Nacht and P. C. Racamier, "La Théorie psychanalytique du délire." *Rev. fr. de psychan.*, *22* (1958), 418–574; R. Diatkine and M. Benassy, "Ontogénèse du fantasme," *Rev. fr. de psychan.*, *28* (1964), 217–34; J. Laplanche and J. B. Pontalis, "Fantasme originaire, fantasme des origines, origine du fantasme," *Les Temps modernes*, *19* (1964), 1833–68.

3. *GW*, *11*, 168; *SE*, *15*, 165.

4. *GW*, *11*, 151–152; *SE*, *15*, 150.

5. *Ibid.*

6. *Ibid.*

7. *GW*, *11*, 153–154; *SE*, *15*, 152.

8. *GW*, *11*, 154; *SE*, *15*, 153.

9. *GW*, *11*, 159; *SE*, *15*, 157.

10. *GW*, *11*, 160–161; *SE*, *15*, 158–159.

11. *GW*, *11*, 170–171; *SE*, *15*, 167–168.

12. *Ibid.*

13. *Ibid.*

14. *Ibid.*

15. *Ibid.*

16. Ernest Jones' essay on symbolism ("The Theory of Symbolism" [1916], in *Papers on Psychoanalysis* [5th ed. London, Baillière, Tindall and Cox, 1948], Chap. 3, pp. 87–144) is no doubt the most remarkable work of the Freudian school that is based on Lecture X of the *Introductory Lectures*. It is of great interest from three points of view: descriptive, genetic, and critical.

   Descriptively, the author places symbols, in the psychoanalytic sense, in the general class of indirect representations commonly called symbolic and characterized by the role of double meaning, by the analogy between primary meaning and secondary meaning, by the attributes of concreteness and primitiveness, by the fact that symbols represent hidden or secret ideas, and by the fact that they are made spontaneously. To specify the characteristics of "true symbolism," Jones comments on and modifies the criteria proposed by Rank and Sachs in their *Die Bedeutung der Psychoanalyse für die Geisteswissenschaften* (1913): (1) true symbols always represent repressed unconscious themes; (2) they have a constant meaning, or very limited scope for variation in meaning; (3) they are not dependent on individual factors only; this is not to say that they are archetypes in the Jungian sense, but rather that they are stereotypes that betray the limited and uniform character of the primordial interests of mankind; (4) they are archaic; (5) they have linguistic connections, strikingly revealed by etymology; (6) they have parallels in the fields of myth, folklore, poetry. Thus the range of symbolism is candidly restricted to the substitute figures that arise from a compromise between the unconscious and the censorship; moreover, all symbols represent themes relating to the bodily self, immediate blood relatives, or the phenomena of birth, love, and death. This is so because these themes correspond to the earliest repressed functions which were held in such high esteem in primitive civilizations.

Jones then goes on to explain why sexuality, the invariant theme of symbolism, has invested such varied regions of language, and why association operates from the sexual to the nonsexual and never in the reverse direction. It is here that the switch is made from the descriptive point of view to the genetic explanation. As for the origin of the associative connection which is the basis of symbolism, it is not enough to call attention to an incapacity for discrimination (an "apperceptive insufficiency") in primitive minds, which in other respects are so gifted in making distinctions and classifications. Following Freud, Jones adopts the theory of the Swedish philologist Sperber of a primal identity of sexual language and the language of work, the same words having originally served the purpose of calling the sexual mate and of providing rhythmic accompaniment during work; since that time weapons and tools, seed and plowed land symbolically express sexual things. In my opinion, Jones' paper underscores the expediency of this explanation, which assumes everything by making identity prior to similarity. More seriously still, the explanation glosses over the *prior difficulty concerning the elevation of erotic impulses to language and the fact that such impulses are capable of being indefinitely symbolized.* It is not sufficient simply to invoke "the call of the mate"; one must proceed to reflect on what makes desire speak—namely, the *absence* inherent in instincts and the connection between *lost* objects and symbolization. In answer to the second question concerning the origin of symbolism—why symbolism should take place in one direction only—Jones posits that symbolism has a single function, that of disguising prohibited themes: "Only what is repressed is symbolized; only what is repressed needs to be symbolized. This conclusion is the touchstone of the psychoanalytic theory of symbolism" (p. 116).

This answer, which excludes any doctrinal compromise, leads to the critical part of Jones' paper, the part that directly concerns my own enterprise. The criticism is aimed primarily at Silberer, who, starting in 1909, had developed in a half dozen essays a very detailed theory of the formation of symbols. For Silberer, the production of symbols includes other procedures besides the disguising of sexual themes that have been repressed by the censorship; thus symbols may be formed of the modes or ways in which the mind is working (slowly, quickly, lightly, heavily, cheerfully, successfully, etc.). Repression would simply be one of these modes of mental functioning. Jones' main objection to this "functional symbolism" is that it has "proceeded, by rejecting the hardly won knowledge of the unconscious, to reinterpret the psychoanalytical findings back again into the surface meanings characteristic of pre-Freudian experience" (p. 117). Thus Jones rejects any attempt to make sexual symbols the *symbols of something else;* in our terminology, the sexual is always *signified,* and never *signifier.* Why this intransigence? The reason, Jones states, is that repression is the sole cause of the distortion operative in the formation of true symbols. The passing of *material* symbolism (mainly representing sexual things) over into *functional* symbolism (representing the modes of mental functioning) is itself a ruse employed by the unconscious and a manifestation of our resistance to the only true interpretation of symbolism. Thus Silberer's interpretation is a defensive or "reactionary" interpretation. Jones grants that any nonsexual idea may indeed be symbolized, but only if it has first had some symbolic connection with a sexual theme; it is precisely the function of metaphor to replace symbolism, which is always grounded in forbidden impulses, by a harmless presentation of the abstract in terms of the concrete; thus the serpent, a sexual symbol, will become the metaphor of wisdom, the wedding ring, a symbol of the female organ, the emblem of fidelity, etc. Every replacement of material symbolism by functional symbolism is an instance of this type of reinterpretation of the repressed in harmless terms.

However great the force of this argumentation may be, it seems to me that Jones' intransigence is not justified; *psychoanalysis has no way of proving that repressed impulses are the only sources of what can be symbolized.* Thus the view that in Eastern religions the phallus became the symbol of a creative power cannot be dismissed for psychoanalytic reasons, but for philosophical reasons which must be debated on other grounds. Jones' disdainful rejection of the view that symbols may have an "anagogic" meaning (Silberer), a "programmatic" meaning (Adler), or a "prospective" meaning (Jung) is characteristic: according to Jones, these authors abandon "the methods and canons of science, particularly the conceptions of causality and determinism" (p. 136). The argument is not psychoanalytical, but philosophical. But that is not the root of the matter; every one-sided theory of symbolism seems to me to break down at a precise point: such theories account for the substitutive or compromise aspect of symbols, but not for their power of denying and overcoming their own origin. Symbolism in the Freudian sense expresses the failure of sublimation and not its advancement, as Jones readily admits: "The affect investing the symbolized ideas has not, insofar as the symbolism is concerned, proved capable of that modification in quality denoted by the term 'sublimation'" (p. 139). Moreover, Jones himself introduces a second pole of the symbolic function when he considers symbolism in terms of the reality principle and not simply in terms of the pleasure principle (pp. 132 ff.) and quite correctly points out that "every step in progress in the line of the reality principle connotes, not only a use of this primordial association [between a new percept and some unconscious complex], but also a partial renunciation of it" (p. 133). However, in the one-sided conception of symbolism, this renunciation can only be a weakening of true symbolism, as in the case where primitive symbols serve to facilitate the formation of objective concepts or scientific generalizations. Such a conception does not account for the immense symbolic domain explored by Western thought since Plato and Origen, but only for the pale metaphors of ordinary language and its rhetoric.

17. Ricoeur, *L'Homme faillible* (Paris, 1960), Chap. 4, Section 3; trans. by Charles Kelbley, *Fallible Man* (Chicago, 1965).

18. *Ibid.*, p. 123; Eng. trans., p. 163.

19. *Ibid.*, 127; Eng. trans., pp. 169–170.

20. Heinz Hartmann, *Ego Psychology and the Problem of Adaptation*, Chap. 1.

21. As in *Fallible Man*, I adopt Alfred Stern's idea that feeling internalizes

man's relationship to the world; thus new aspects of objectivity are internalized in the feelings of possession, power, and worth.

22. *New Introductory Lectures, GW, 15,* 106–107; *SE, 22,* 100–101.
23. *GW, 15,* 107; SE, *22,* 102.
24. Husserl, *Ideen* I, §§ 85, 97. It is to be noted that in Husserl the words *Formung, Meinung,* and *Deutung* designate the relationship of the intentional act to the matter; the intention "interprets" the matter, just as in Aristotle discourse is the interpretation (*hermêneia*) of the affections (*pathê*) of the soul. The comparison is all the more striking in that for Husserl, the *hylê* includes both affections or feelings and sensations.
25. *Group Psychology and the Analysis of the* Ego, *GW, 13,* 100; *SE, 18,* 92.
26. *GW, 13,* 113; *SE, 18,* 103.
27. *GW, 13,* 128; *SE, 18,* 116.
28. *GW, 13,* 129; *SE, 18,* 117.
29. *GW, 13,* 142; *SE, 18,* 127.
30. *GW, 13,* 145; *SE, 18,* 130.
31. *GW, 13,* 155 (*Zielablenkung*); *SE, 18,* 138.
32. *GW, 13,* 155; *SE, 18,* 139.
33. *The Interpretation of Dreams, GW, 2/3,* 269; *SE, 4,* 262.
34. *GW, 2/3,* 269; *SE, 4,* 262–263.
35. *GW, 2/3,* 270; *SE, 4,* 264.
36. *Ibid.*
37. Sophocles, *Oedipus Rex*, verse 356.
38. *GW, 2/3,* 269; *SE 4,* 263.
39. *GW, 2/3,* 268; *SE, 4,* 261–262.
40. *GW, 2/3,* 269; *SE, 4,* 263. On the Oedipus of fantasy, myth, and tragedy, see C. Stein, "Notes sur la mort d'Oedipe: Préliminaire à une anthropologie psychanalytique," *Rev. fr. de psychan., 23* (1959), 735–756; C. Lévi-Strauss, *Anthropologie structurale* (Paris, Plon, 1958), Chap. 11.
41. Cf. above, "Analytic," Part II, Chap. 1, pp. 165–167. On the relationship between the oneiric and the poetic, see P. Luquet, "Ouvertures sur l'artiste et la psychanalyse; la fonction esthétique du moi," *Rev. fr. de psychan., 27* (1963), 585–618; also the work of La Décade de Cerisy, *Art et psychanalyse,* soon to be published.
42. *GW, 7,* 223; *SE, 9,* 153.
43. Paul Ricoeur, "Nature et liberté," *Études philosophiques* (1962).

Structuralism

Two Aspects of Language: Metaphor and Metonymy

ROMAN JAKOBSON

Speech implies a selection of certain linguistic entities and their combination into linguistic units of a higher degree of complexity. At the lexical level this is readily apparent: the speaker selects words and combines them into sentences according to the syntactic system of the language he is using; sentences are in their turn combined into utterances. But the speaker is by no means a completely free agent in his choice of words: his selection (except for the rare case of actual neology) must be made from the lexical storehouse which he and his addressee possess in common. The communication engineer most properly approaches the essence of the speech event when he assumes that in the optimal exchange of information the speaker and the listener have at their disposal more or less the same "filing cabinet of *prefabricated* representations": the addresser of a verbal message selects one of these "preconceived possibilities" and the addressee is supposed to make an identical choice from the same assembly of "possibilities already foreseen and provided for." [1] Thus the efficiency of a speech event demands the use of a common code by its participants.

" 'Did you say *pig* or *fig?*,' said the Cat. 'I said *pig*,' replied Alice." [2] In this peculiar utterance the feline addressee attempts to recapture a linguistic choice made by the addresser. In the common code of the Cat and Alice, i.e., in spoken English, the difference between a stop and a continuant, other things being equal, may change the meaning of the message. Alice had used the distinctive feature "stop *vs.* continuant," rejecting the latter and choosing the former of the two opposites; and in the same act of speech she combined this solution with certain other simultaneous features, using the gravity and the tenseness of /p/ in contradistinction to the acuteness of /t/ and to the laxness of /b/. Thus all these attributes have been combined into a bundle of distinctive features, the so-called phoneme. The phoneme /p/ was then followed by the phonemes /i/ and /g/, themselves bundles of simultaneously produced distinctive features. Hence the concurrence of simultaneous entities and the concatenation of successive entities are the two ways in which we speakers combine linguistic constituents.

Neither such bundles as /p/ or /f/ nor such sequences of bundles as /pig/ or /fig/ are invented by the speaker who uses them. Neither can the distinctive feature "stop *versus* continuant" nor the phoneme /p/ occur out of a context. The stop feature appears in combination with certain other concurrent features, and the repertory of combinations of these features into phonemes such as /p/, /b/, /t/, /d/, /k/, /g/, etc., is limited by the code of the given language. The code sets limitations on the possible combinations of the phoneme /p/ with other following and/or preceding phonemes; and only a part of the permissible phoneme-sequences are actually utilized in the lexical stock of a given language. Even when other combinations of phonemes are theoretically possible, the speaker, as a rule, is only a word-user, not a word-coiner. When facing with individual words, we expect them to be coded units. In order to grasp the word *nylon* one must know the meaning assigned to this vocable in the lexical code of modern English.

In any language, there exist also coded word-groups called phrase-words. The meaning of the idiom *how do you do* cannot be derived by adding together the meanings of its lexical constituents; the whole is not equal to the sum of its parts. Those word-groups, which in this respect behave like single words, are a common but nonetheless only marginal case. In order to comprehend the overwhelming majority of word-groups, we must be familiar only with the constituent words and with the syntactical rules of their combination. Within these limitations we are free to set words in new contexts. Of course, this freedom is relative, and the pressure of current clichés upon our choice of combinations is considerable. But the freedom to compose quite new contexts is undeniable, despite the relatively low statistical probability of their occurrence.

Thus in the combination of linguistic units there is an ascending scale of freedom. In the combination of distinctive features into phonemes, the freedom of the individual speaker is zero; the code has already established all the possibilities which may be utilized in the given language. Freedom to combine phonemes into words is circumscribed, it is limited to the marginal situation of word-coinage. In the forming of sentences out of words the speaker is less constrained. And finally, in the combination of sentences into utterances, the action of compulsory syntactical rules ceases and the freedom of any individual speaker to create novel contexts increases substantially, although again the numerous stereotyped utterances are not to be overlooked.

Any linguistic sign involves two modes of arrangement.

(1) Combination. Any sign is made up of constituent signs and/or occurs only in combination with other signs. This means that any linguistic unit at one and the same time serves as a context for simpler units and/or finds its own context in a more complex linguistic unit. Hence any actual grouping of linguistic units binds them into a superior unit: combination and contexture are two faces of the same operation.

(2) Selection. A selection between alternatives implies the possibility of substituting one for the other, equivalent to the former in one respect and different from it in another. Actually, selection and substitution are two faces of the same operation.

The fundamental role which these two operations play in language was clearly realized by Ferdinand de Saussure. Yet from the two varieties of combination—concurrence and concatenation—it was only the latter, the temporal sequence, which was recognized by the Geneva linguist. Despite his own insight into the phoneme as a set of concurrent distinctive features (*éléments différentiels des phonèmes*), the scholar succumbed to the traditional belief in the linear character of language "*qui exclut la possibilité de prononcer deux éléments à la fois.*" [3]

In order to delimit the two modes of arrangement which we have described as combination and selection, F. de Saussure states that the former "is *in presentia:* it is based on two or several terms jointly present in an actual series," whereas the latter "connects terms *in absentia* as members of a virtual mnemonic series." That is to say, selection (and, correspondingly, substitution) deals with entities conjoined in the code but not in the given message, whereas, in the case of combination, the entities are conjoined in both or only in the actual message. The addressee perceives that the given utterance (message) is a combination of constituent parts (sentences, words, phonemes, etc.) selected from the repository of all possible constituent parts (code). The constituents of a context are in a status of contiguity, while in a substitution set signs are linked by various degrees of similarity which fluctuate between the equivalence of synonyms and the common core of antonyms.

These two operations provide each linguistic sign with two sets of interpretants, to utilize the effective concept introduced by Charles Sanders Peirce: [4] there are two references which serve to interpret the sign—one to the code, and the other to the context, whether coded or free; and in each of these ways the sign is related to another set of linguistic signs, through an alternation in the former case and through an alignment in the latter. A given significative unit may be replaced by other, more explicit signs of the same code, whereby its general meaning is revealed, while its contextual meaning is determined by its connection with other signs within the same sequence.

The constituents of any message are necessarily linked with the code by an internal relation and with the message by an external relation. Language in its various aspects deals with both modes of relation. Whether messages are exchanged or communication proceeds unilaterally from the addresser to the addressee, there must be some kind of contiguity between the participants of any speech event to assure the transmission of the message. The separation in space, and often in time, between two individuals, the addresser and the addressee, is bridged by an internal relation: there must be a certain equivalence between the symbols used by the addresser and those known and interpreted by the addressee. Without such an equivalence the message is fruitless—even when it reaches the receiver it does not affect him. . . .

The varieties of aphasia are numerous and diverse, but all of them oscillate between the two polar types just described. Every form of aphasic disturbance consists in some impairment, more or less severe, either of the faculty for selection and substitution or for combination and contexture. The former affliction involves a deterioration of metalinguistic operations, while the latter damages the capacity for maintaining the hierarchy of linguistic units. The relation of similarity is suppressed in the former, the relation of contiguity in the latter type of aphasia. Metaphor is alien to the similarity disorder, and metonymy to the contiguity disorder.

The development of a discourse may take place along two different semantic lines: one topic may lead to another either through their similarity or through their contiguity. The metaphoric way would be the most appropriate term for the first case and the metonymic way for the second, since they find their most condensed expression in metaphor and metonymy respectively. In aphasia one or the other of these two processes is restricted or totally blocked—an effect which makes the study of aphasia particularly illuminating for the linguist. In normal verbal behavior both processes are continually operative, but careful observation will reveal that under the influence of a cultural pattern, personality, and verbal style, preference is given to one of the two processes over the other.

In a well-known psychological test, children are confronted with some noun and told to utter the first verbal response that comes into their heads. In this experiment two opposite linguistic predilections are invariably exhibited: the response is intended either as a substitute for, or as a complement to the stimulus. In the latter case the stimulus and the response together form a proper syntactic construction, most usually a sentence. These two types of reaction have been labeled substitutive and predicative.

To the stimulus *hut* one response was *burnt out*; another, *is a poor little house*. Both reactions are predicative; but the first creates a purely narrative context, while in the second there is a double connection with the subject *hut*: on the one hand, a positional (namely, syntactic) contiguity, and on the other a semantic similarity.

The same stimulus produced the following substitutive reactions: the tautology *hut*; the synonyms *cabin* and *hovel*; the antonym *palace*, and the metaphors *den* and *burrow*. The capacity of two words to replace one another is an instance of positional similarity, and, in addition, all these responses are linked to the stimulus by semantic similarity (or contrast). Metonymical responses to the same stimulus, such as *thatch*, *litter*, or *poverty*, combine and contrast the positional similarity with semantic contiguity.

In manipulating these two kinds of connection (similarity and contiguity) in both their aspects (positional and semantic)—

selecting, combining, and ranking them—an individual exhibits his personal style, his verbal predilections and preferences.

In verbal art the interaction of these two elements is especially pronounced. Rich material for the study of this relationship is to be found in verse patterns which require a compulsory parallelism between adjacent lines, for example in Biblical poetry or in the West Finnic and, to some extent, the Russian oral traditions. This provides an objective criterion of what in the given speech community acts as a correspondence. Since on any verbal level—morphemic, lexical syntactic, and phraseological—either of these two relations (similarity and contiguity) can appear—and each in either of two aspects—an impressive range of possible configurations is created. Either of the two gravitational poles may prevail. In Russian lyrical songs, for example, metaphoric constructions predominate, while in the heroic epics the metonymic way is preponderant.

In poetry there are various motives which determine the choice between these alternants. The primacy of the metaphoric process in the literary schools of romanticism and symbolism has been repeatedly acknowledged, but it is still insufficiently realized that it is the predominance of metonymy which underlies and actually predetermines the so-called realistic trend, which belongs to an intermediary stage between the decline of romanticism and the rise of symbolism and is opposed to both. Following the path of contiguous relationships, the realistic author metonymically digresses from the plot to the atmosphere and from the characters to the setting in space and time. He is fond of synecdochic details. In the scene of Anna Karenina's suicide Tolstoy's artistic attention is focused on the heroine's handbag; and in *War and Peace* the synecdoches "hair on the upper lip" or "bare shoulders" are used by the same writer to stand for the female characters to whom these features belong.

The alternative predominance of one or the other of these two processes is by no means confined to verbal art. The same oscillation occurs in sign systems other than language.[5] A salient example from the history of painting is the manifestly metonymical orientation of cubism, where the object is transformed into a set of synecdoches; the surrealist painters responded with a patently metaphorical attitude. Ever since the productions of D. W. Griffith, the art of the cinema, with its highly developed capacity for changing the angle, perspective and focus of "shots," has broken with the tradition of the theater and ranged an unprecedented variety of synecdochic "close-ups" and metonymic "set-ups" in general. In such pictures as those of Charlie Chaplin, these devices in turn were superseded by a novel, metaphoric "montage" with its "lap dissolves"—the filmic similes.[6]

The bipolar structure of language (or other semiotic systems), and, in aphasia, the fixation on one of these poles to the exclusion of the other require systematic comparative study. The retention of either of these alternatives in the two types of aphasia must be confronted with the predominance of the same pole in certain styles, personal habits, current fashions, etc. A careful analysis and comparison of these phenomena with the whole syndrome of the corresponding type of aphasia is an imperative task for joint research by experts in psychopathology, psychology, linguistics, poetics, and semiotic, the general science of signs. The dichotomy here discussed appears to be of primal significance and consequence for all verbal behavior and for human behavior in general.[7]

To indicate the possibilities of the projected comparative research, we choose an example from a Russian folk tale which employs parallelism as a comic device: "Thomas is a bachelor; Jeremiah is unmarried" (*Fomá xólost; Erjóma neženát*). Here the predicates in the two parallel clauses are associated by similarity: they are in fact synonymous. The subjects of both clauses are masculine proper names and hence morphologically similar, while on the other hand they denote two contiguous heroes of the same tale, created to perform identical actions and thus to justify the use of synonymous pairs of predicates. A somewhat modified version of the same construction occurs in a familiar wedding song in which each of the wedding guests is addressed in turn by his first name and patronymic: "Gleb is a bachelor; Ivanovič is unmarried." While both predicates here are again synonyms, the relationship between the two subjects is changed: both are proper names denoting the same man and are normally used contiguously as a mode of polite address.

In the quotation from the folk tale the two parallel clauses refer to two separate facts, the marital status of Thomas and the similar status of Jeremiah. In the verse from the wedding song, however, the two clauses are synonymous: they redundantly reiterate the celibacy of the same hero, splitting him into two verbal hypostases.

The Russian novelist Gleb Ivanovič Uspenskij (1840-1902) in the last years of his life suffered from a mental illness involving a speech disorder. His first name and patronymic, *Gleb Ivanovič*, traditionally combined in polite intercourse, for him split into two distinct names designating two separate beings: Gleb was endowed with all his virtues, while Ivanovič, the name relating the son to the father, became the incarnation of all Uspenskij's vices. The linguistic aspect of this split personality is the patient's inability to use two symbols for the same thing, and it is thus a similarity disorder. Since the similarity disorder is bound up with the metonymical bent, an examination of the literary manner Uspenskij had employed as a young writer takes on particular interest. And the study of Anatolij Kamegulov, who analyzed Uspenskij's style, bears out our theoretical expectations. He shows that Uspenskij had a particular penchant for metonymy, and especially for synecdoche, and that he carried it so far that "the reader is crushed by the multiplicity of detail unloaded on him in a limited verbal space, and is physically unable to grasp the whole, so that the portrait is often lost." [8]

To be sure, the metonymical style in Uspenskij is obviously prompted by the prevailing literary canon of his time, late nineteenth-century "realism"; but the personal stamp of Gleb Ivanovič made his pen particularly suitable for this artistic trend in its extreme manifestations and finally left its mark upon the verbal aspect of his mental illnes.

A competition between both devices, metonymic and metaphoric, is manifest in any symbolic process, either intrapersonal or social. Thus in an inquiry into the structure of dreams, the decisive question is whether the symbols and the temporal sequences used are based on contiguity (Freud's metonymic "displacement" and synecdochic "condensation") or on similarity (Freud's "identification and symbolism"). [9] The principles underlying magic rites have been resolved by Frazer into two types: charms based on the law of similarity and those founded on association by contiguity. The first of these two great branches of sympathetic magic has been called "homoeopathic" or "imitative," and the second, "contagious magic." [10] This bipartition is indeed illuminating. Nonetheless, for the most part, the question of the two poles is still neglected, despite its wide scope and importance for the study of any symbolic behavior, especially verbal, and of its impairments. What is the main reason for this neglect?

Similarity in meaning connects the symbols of a metalanguage with the symbols of the language referred to. Similarity connects a metaphorical term with the term for which it is substituted. Consequently, when constructing a metalanguage to interpret tropes, the researcher possesses more homogeneous means to handle metaphor, whereas metonymy, based on a different principle, easily defies interpretation. Therefore nothing comparable to the rich literature on metaphor[11] can be cited for the theory of metonymy. For the same reason, it is generally realized that romanticism is closely linked with metaphor, whereas the equally intimate ties of realism with metonymy usually remain unnoticed. Not only the tool of the observer but also the object of observation is responsible for the preponderance of metaphor over metonymy in scholarship. Since poetry is focused upon sign, and pragmatical prose primarily upon referent, tropes and figures were studied mainly as poetical devices. The principle of similarity underlies poetry; the metrical parallelism of lines or the phonic equivalence of rhyming words prompts the question of semantic similarity and contrast; there exist, for instance, grammatical and anti-grammatical but never agrammatical rhymes. Prose, on the contrary, is forwarded essentially by contiguity. Thus, for poetry, metaphor, and for prose, metonymy is the line of least resistance and, consequently, the study of poetical tropes is directed chiefly toward metaphor. The actual bipolarity has been artificially replaced in these studies by an amputated, unipolar scheme which, strikingly enough, coincides with one of the two aphasic patterns, namely with the contiguity disorder.[12]

NOTES

1. D. M. MacKay, "In Search of Basic Symbols," *Cybernetics*, Transactions of the Eighth Conference (New York, 1952), p. 183.
2. Lewis Carroll, *Alice's Adventures in Wonderland*, Chap. VI.
3. F. de Saussure, *Cours de linguistique générale*, 2nd ed. (Paris, 1922), pp. 68f and 170f.
4. C. S. Peirce, *Collected Papers*, II and IV (Cambridge, Mass., 1932, 1934)—see Index of subjects.
5. I ventured a few sketchy remarks on the metonymical turn in verbal art ("Pro realizm u mystectvi," *Vaplite*, Kharkov, 1927 No. 2; "Randbemerkungen zur Prosa des Dichters Pasternak," *Slavische Rundschau*, VII, 1935), in painting ("Futurizm," *Iskusstvo*, Moscow, Aug. 2, 1919) and in motion pictures ("Upadek filmu," *Listy pro umění a kritiku*, I, Prague, 1933), but the crucial problem of the two polar processes awaits a detailed investigation.
6. Cf. B. Balazs, *Theory of the Film* (London, 1952).
7. For the psychological and sociological aspects of this dichotomy see Bateson's views on "progressional" and "selective integration" and Parsons' on the "conjunction-disjunction dichotomy" in children's development: J. Ruesch and G. Bateson, *Communication, the Social Matrix of Psychiatry* (New York, 1951), pp. 183ff; T. Parsons and R. F. Bales, *Family, Socialization and Interaction Process* (Glencoe, 1955), pp. 119f.
8. A. Kamegulov, *Stil' Gleba Uspenskogo* (Leningrad, 1930), pp. 65, 145. One of such disintegrated portraits cited by the monograph: "From underneath an ancient straw cap with a black spot on its shield, there peeked two braids resembling the tusks of a wild boar; a chin grown fat and pendulous definitively spread over the greasy collars of the calico dicky and in thick layer lay on the coarse collar of the canvas coat, firmly buttoned on the neck. From below this coat to the eyes of the observer there protruded massive hands with a ring, which had eaten into the fat finger, a cane with a copper top, a significant bulge of the stomach and the presence of very broad pants, almost of muslin quality, in the broad ends of which hid the toes of the boots."
9. S. Freud, *Die Traumdeutung*, 9th ed. (Vienna, 1950).
10. J. G. Frazer, *The Golden Bough: A Study in Magic and Religion*, Part I, 3rd ed. (Vienna, 1950), Chap. III.

11. C. F. P. Stutterheim, *Het begrip metaphoor* (Amsterdam, 1941).
12. Thanks are due to Hugh McLean for his valuable assistance and to Justinia Besharov for her original observations on tropes and figures.

1. François Clouet. Portrait of Elizabeth of Austria.

[COURTESY OF THE *Musée du Louvre*]

2. *Club used for killing fish.*

[COURTESY OF *Claude Levi-Strauss*]

The Science of the Concrete

CLAUDE LEVI-STRAUSS

It may be objected that science of this kind can scarcely be of much practical effect. The answer to this is that its main purpose is not a practical one. It meets intellectual requirements rather than or instead of satisfying needs.

The real question is not whether the touch of a woodpecker's beak does in fact cure toothache. It is rather whether there is a point of view from which a woodpecker's beak and a man's tooth can be seen as "going together" (the use of this congruity for therapeutic purposes being only one of its possible uses), and whether some initial order can be introduced into the universe by means of these groupings. Classifying, as opposed to not classifying, has a value of its own, whatever form the classification may take. As a recent theorist of taxonomy writes:

> Scientists do tolerate uncertainty and frustration, because they must. The one thing that they do not and must not tolerate is disorder. The whole aim of theoretical science is to carry to the highest possible and conscious degree the perceptual reduction of chaos that began in so lowly and (in all probability) unconscious a way with the origin of life. In specific instances it can well be questioned whether the order so achieved is an objective characteristic of the phenomena or is an artifact constructed by the scientist. That question comes up time after time in animal taxonomy . . . Nevertheless, the most basic postulate of science is that nature itself is orderly. . . . All theoretical science is ordering and if systematics is equated with ordering, then systematics is synonymous with theoretical science (Simpson, p. 5).

The thought we call primitive is founded on this demand for order.

This is equally true of all thought but it is through the properties common to all thought that we can most easily begin to understand forms of thought which seem very strange to us.

A native thinker makes the penetrating comment that "All sacred things must have their place" (Fletcher 2, p. 34). It could even be said that being in their place is what makes them sacred, for if they were taken out of their place, even in thought, the entire order of the universe would be destroyed. Sacred objects therefore contribute to the maintenance of order in the universe by occupying the places allocated to them. Examined superficially and from the outside, the refinements of ritual can appear pointless. They are explicable by a concern for what one might call "micro-adjustment" —the concern to assign every single creature, object or feature to a place within a class. The ceremony of the Hako among the Pawnee is particularly illuminating in this respect, although only because it has been so well analyzed. The invocation which accompanies the crossing of a stream of water is divided into several parts, which correspond, respectively, to the moment when the travelers put their feet in water, the moment when they move them and the moment when the water completely covers their feet. The invocation to the wind separates the moment when only the wet parts of the body feel cool: "Now, we are ready to move forward in safety" (id., pp. 77–78). As the informant explains: "We must address with song every object we meet, because Tira'wa (the supreme spirit) is in all things, everything we come to as we travel can give us help . . . " (id., pp. 73, 81).

This preoccupation with exhaustive observation and the systematic cataloguing of relations and connections can sometimes lead to scientifically valid results. The Blackfoot Indians, for instance, were able to prognosticate the approach of spring by the state of development of the fetus of bison which they took from the uterus of females killed in hunting. These successes cannot of course be isolated from the numerous other associations of the same kind which science condemns as illusory. It may however be the case that magical thought, that "gigantic variation on the theme of the principle of Causality" as Hubert and Mauss called it (2, p. 61), can be distinguished from science not so much by any ignorance or contempt of determinism but by a more imperious and uncompromising demand for it which can at the most be regarded as unreasonable and precipitate from the scientific point of view.

As a natural philosophy it (witchcraft) reveals a theory of causation. Misfortune is due to witchcraft cooperating with natural forces. If a buffalo gores a man, or the supports of a granary are undermined by termites so that it falls on his head, or he is infected with cerebrospinal meningitis, Azande say that the buffalo, the granary, and the disease are causes which combine with witchcraft to kill a man. Witchcraft does not create the buffalo and the granary and the disease, for these exist in their own right, but it is responsible for the particular situation in which they are brought into lethal relations with a particular man. The granary would have fallen in any case, but since there was witchcraft present it fell at the particular moment when a certain man was resting beneath it. Of these causes the only one which permits intervention is witchcraft, for witchcraft emanates from a person. The buffalo and the granary do not allow of intervention and are, therefore, whilst recognized as causes, not considered the socially relevant ones (Evans-Pritchard *1*, p. 418–419).

Seen in this way, the first difference between magic and science is therefore that magic postulates a complete and all-embracing determinism. Science, on the other hand, is based on a distinction between levels: only some of these admit forms of determinism; on others the same forms of determinism are held not to apply. One can go further and think of the rigorous precision of magical thought and ritual practices as an expression of the unconscious apprehension of the *truth of determinism*, the mode in which scientific phenomena exist. In this view, the operations of determinism are divined and made use of in an all-embracing fashion before being known and properly applied, and magical rites and beliefs appear as so many expressions of an act of faith in a science yet to be born.

The nature of these anticipations is such that they may sometimes succeed. Moreover they may anticipate not only science itself but even methods or results which scientific procedure does not incorporate until an advanced stage of its development. For it seems to be the case that man began by applying himself to the most difficult task, that of systematizing what is immediately presented to the senses, on which science for a long time turned its back and which it is only beginning to bring back into its purview. In the history of scientific thought this "anticipation-effect" has, incidentally, occurred repeatedly. As Simpson (pp. 84–85) has shown with the help of an example drawn from nineteenth-century biology, it is due to the fact that, since scientific explanation is always the discovery of an "arrangement," any attempt of this type, even one inspired by nonscientific principles, can hit on true arrangements. This is even to be foreseen if one grants that the number of structures is by definition finite: the "structuring" has an intrinsic effectiveness of its own whatever the principles and methods which suggested it.

Modern chemistry reduces the variety of tastes and smells to different combinations of five elements: carbon, hydrogen, oxygen, sulfur and nitrogen. By means of tables of the presence and absence of the elements and estimates of proportions and minimum amounts necessary for them to be perceptible, it succeeds in accounting for differences and resemblances which were previously excluded from its field on account of their "secondary" character. These connections and distinctions are, however, no surprise to our aesthetic sense. On the contrary they increase its scope and understanding by supplying a basis for the associations it already divined; and at the same time one is better able to understand why and in what conditions it should have been possible to discover such associations solely by the systematic use of intuitive methods. Thus to a logic of sensations tobacco smoke might be the intersection of two groups, one also containing broiled meat and brown crusts of bread (which are like it in being composed of nitrogen) and the other one to which cheese, beer, and honey belong on account of the presence of diacetyl. Wild cherries, cinnamon, vanilla, and sherry are grouped together by the intellect as well as the senses, because they all contain aldehyde, while the closely related smells of wintergreen, lavender, and bananas are to be explained by the presence of ester. On intuitive grounds alone we might group onions, garlic, cabbage, turnips, radishes, and mustard together even though botany separates lilaceae and crucifers. In confirmation of the evidence of the senses, chemistry shows that these different families are united on another plane: they contain sulfur (W.K.). A primitive philosopher or a poet could have effected these regroupings on the basis of considerations foreign to chemistry or any other form of science. Ethnographic literature reveals many of equal empirical and aesthetic value. And this is not just the result of some associative madness destined sometimes to succeed simply by the law of chance. Simpson advances this interpretation in the passage quoted above; but he displays more insight when he shows that the demand for organization is a need common to art and science and that in consequence "taxonomy, which is ordering par excellence, has eminent aesthetic value" (loc. cit., p. 4). Given this, it seems less surprising that the aesthetic sense can by itself open the way to taxonomy and even anticipate some of its results.

I am not, however, commending a return to the popular belief (although it has some validity in its own narrow context) according to which magic is a timid and stuttering form of science. One deprives oneself of all means of understanding magical thought if one tries to reduce it to a moment or stage in technical and scientific evolution. Like a shadow moving ahead of its owner it is in a sense complete in itself, and as finished and coherent in its immateriality as the substantial being which it precedes. Magical thought is not to be regarded as a beginning, a rudiment, a sketch, a part of a whole which has not yet materialized. It forms a well-articulated system, and is in this respect independent of that other system which constitutes science, except for the purely formal analogy which brings them together and makes the former a sort of metaphorical expression of the latter. It is therefore better, instead of contrasting magic and science, to compare them as two parallel modes of acquiring knowledge. Their theoretical and practical results differ in value, for it is true that science is more successful than magic from this point of view, although magic foreshadows science in that it is sometimes also successful. Both science and magic, however, require the same sort of mental operations and they differ not so much in kind as in the different types of phenomena to which they are applied.

These relations are a consequence of the objective conditions in which magic and scientific knowledge appeared. The history of the latter is short enough for us to know a good deal about it. But the fact that modern science dates back only a few centuries raises a problem which ethnologists have not sufficiently pondered. The Neolithic Paradox would be a suitable name for it.

It was in neolithic times that man's mastery of the great arts of civilization—of pottery, weaving, agriculture and the domestication of animals—became firmly established. No one today would any longer think of attributing these enormous advances to the fortuitous accumulation of a series of chance discoveries or believe them to have been revealed by the passive perception of certain natural phenomena.[1]

Each of these techniques assumes centuries of active and methodical observation, of bold hypotheses tested by means of endlessly repeated experiments. A biologist remarks on the rapidity with which plants from the New World have been acclimatized in the Philippines and adopted and named by the natives. In many cases they seem even to have rediscovered their medicinal uses, uses identical with those traditional in Mexico. Fox's interpretation is this:

> . . . plants with bitter leaves or stems are commonly used in the Philippines for stomach disorders. If an introduced plant is found to have this characteristic, it will be quickly utilized. The fact that many Philippine groups, such as the Pinatubo Negritos, constantly experiment with plants hastens the process of the recognition of the potential usefulness, as defined by the culture, of the introduced flora (R. B. Fox, pp. 212–213).

To transform a weed into a cultivated plant, a wild beast into a domestic animal, to produce, in either of these, nutritious or technologically useful properties which were originally completely absent or could only be guessed at; to make stout, watertight pottery out of clay which is friable and unstable, liable to pulverize or crack (which, however, is possible only if from a large number of organic and inorganic materials, the one most suitable for refining it is selected, and also the appropriate fuel, the temperature and duration of firing and the effective degree of oxidation); to work out techniques, often long and complex, which permit cultivation without soil or alternatively without water; to change toxic roots or seeds into foodstuffs or again to use their poison for hunting, war, or ritual—there is no doubt that all these achievements required a genuinely scientific attitude, sustained and watchful interest, and a desire for knowledge for its own sake. For only a small proportion of observations and experiments (which must be assumed to have been primarily inspired by a desire for knowledge) could have yielded practical and immediately useful results. There is no need to dwell on the working of bronze and iron and of precious metals or even the simple working of copper ore by hammering which preceded metallurgy by several thousand years, and even at that stage they all demand a very high level of technical proficiency.

Neolithic, or early historical, man was therefore the heir of a long scientific tradition. However, had he, as well as all his predecessors, been inspired by exactly the same spirit as that of our own time, it would be impossible to understand how he could have come to a halt and how several thousand years of stagnation have intervened between the neolithic revolution and modern science like a level plain between ascents. There is only one solution to the paradox, namely, that there are two distinct modes of scientific thought. These are certainly not a function of different stages of development of the human mind but rather of two strategic levels at which nature is accessible to scientific inquiry: one roughly adapted to that of perception and the imagination: the other at a remove from it. It is as if the necessary connections which are the object of all science, neolithic or modern, could be arrived at by two different routes, one very close to, and the other more remote from, sensible intuition.

Any classification is superior to chaos and even a classification at the level of sensible properties is a step toward rational ordering. It is legitimate, in classifying fruits into relatively heavy and relatively light, to begin by separating the apples from the pears even though shape, color, and taste are unconnected with weight and volume. This is because the larger apples are easier to distinguish from the smaller if the apples are not still mixed with fruit of different features. This example already shows that classification has its advantages even at the level of aesthetic perception.

For the rest, and in spite of the fact there is no necessary connection between sensible qualities and properties, there is very often at least an empirical connection between them, and the generalization of this relation may be rewarding from the theoretical and practical point of view for a very long time even if it has no foundation in reason. Not all poisonous juices are burning or bitter, nor is everything which is burning and bitter poisonous. Nevertheless, nature is so constituted that it is more advantageous if thought and action proceed as though this aesthetically satisfying equivalence also corresponded to objective reality. It seems probable, for reasons which are not relevant here, that species possessing some remarkable characteristics, say, of shape, color, or smell give the observer what might be called a "right pending disproof" to postulate that these visible characteristics are the sign of equally singular, but concealed, properties. To treat the relation between the two as itself sensible (regarding a seed in the form of a tooth as a safeguard against snake bites, yellow juices as a cure for bilious troubles, etc.) is of more value provisionally than indifference to any connection. For even a heterogeneous and arbitrary classification preserves the richness and diversity of the collection of facts it makes. The decision that everything must be taken account of facilitates the creation of a "memory bank."

It is moreover a fact that particular results, to the achievement of which methods of this kind were able to lead, were essential to enable man to assail nature from a different angle. Myths and rites are far from being, as has often been held, the product of man's "myth-making faculty," [2] turning its back on reality. Their principal value is indeed to preserve until the present time the remains of methods of observation and reflection which were (and no doubt still are) precisely adapted to discoveries of a certain type: those which nature authorized from the starting point of a speculative organization and exploitation of the sensible world in sensible terms. This science of the concrete was necessarily restricted by its essence to results other than those destined to be achieved by the exact natural sciences but it was no less scientific and its results no less genuine. They were secured ten thousand years earlier and still remain at the basis of our own civilization.

There still exists among ourselves an activity which on the technical plane gives us quite a good understanding of what a science we prefer to call "prior" rather than "primitive," could have been on the plane of speculation. This is what is commonly called "*bricolage*" in French. In its old sense the verb "*bricoler*" applied to ball games and billiards, to hunting, shooting and riding. It was, however, always used with reference to some extraneous movement: a ball rebounding, a dog straying or a horse swerving from its direct course to avoid an obstacle. And in our own time the "*bricoleur*" is still someone who works with his hands and uses devious means compared to those of a craftsman.[3] The characteristic feature of mythical thought is that it expresses itself by means of a heterogeneous repertoire which, even if extensive, is nevertheless limited. It has to use this repertoire, however, whatever the task in hand because it has nothing else at its disposal. Mythical thought is therefore a kind of intellectual "*bricolage*"—which explains the relation which can be perceived between the two.

Like "*bricolage*" on the technical plane, mythical reflection can reach brilliant unforeseen results on the intellectual plane. Conversely, attention has often been drawn to the mytho-poetical nature of "*bricolage*" on the plane of so-called raw or naïve art, in architectural follies like the villa of Cheval the postman or the stage sets of Georges Méliès, or, again, in the case immortalized by Dickens in *Great Expectations* but no doubt originally inspired by observation, of Mr. Wemmick's suburban "castle" with its miniature drawbridge, its cannon firing at nine o'clock, its bed of salad and cucumbers, thanks to which its occupants could withstand a siege if necessary. . . .

The analogy is worth pursuing since it helps us to see the real relations between the two types of scientific knowledge we have distinguished. The "*bricoleur*" is adept at performing a large number of diverse tasks; but, unlike the engineer, he does not subordinate each of them to the availability of raw materials and tools conceived and procured for the purpose of the project. His universe of instruments is closed and the rules of his game are always to make do with "whatever is at hand," that is to say, with a set of tools and materials which is always finite and is also heterogeneous because what it contains bears no relation to the current project, or indeed to any particular project, but is the contingent result of all the occasions there have been to renew or enrich the stock or to maintain it with the remains of previous constructions or destructions. The set of the *"bricoleur's"* means cannot therefore be defined in terms of a project (which would presuppose besides, that, as in the case of the engineer, there were, at least in theory, as many sets of tools and materials or "instrumental sets," as there are different kinds of projects). It is to be defined only by its potential use or, putting this another way and in the language of the *"bricoleur"* himself, because the elements are collected or retained on the principle that "they may always come in handy." Such elements are specialized up to a point, sufficiently for the *"bricoleur"* not to need the equipment and knowledge of all trades and professions, but not enough for each of them to have only one definite and determinate use. They each represent a set of actual and possible relations; they are "operators" but they can be used for any operations of the same type.

The elements of mythical thought similarly lie halfway between percepts and concepts. It would be impossible to separate percepts from the concrete situations in which they appeared, while recourse to concepts would require that thought could, at least provisionally, put its projects (to use Husserl's expression) "in brackets." Now, there is an intermediary between images and concepts, namely signs. For signs can always be defined in the way introduced by Saussure in the case of the particular category of linguistic signs, that is, as a link between images and concepts. In the union thus brought about, images and concepts play the part of the signifying and signified respectively.

Signs resemble images in being concrete entities but they resemble concepts in their powers of reference. Neither concepts nor signs relate exclusively to themselves; either may be substituted for something else. Concepts, however, have an unlimited capacity in this respect, while signs have not. The example of the *"bricoleur"* helps to bring out the differences and similarities. Consider him at work and excited by his project. His first practical step is retrospective. He has to turn back to an already existent set made up of tools and materials, to consider or reconsider what it contains and, finally and above all, to engage in a sort of dialogue with it and, before choosing between them, to index the possible answers which the whole set can offer to his problem. He interrogates all the heterogeneous objects of which his treasury [4] is composed to discover what each of them could "signify" and so contribute to the definition of a set which has yet to materialize but which will ultimately differ from the instrumental set only in the internal disposition of its parts. A particular cube of oak could be a wedge to make up for the inadequate length of a plank of pine or it could be a pedestal—which would allow the grain and polish of the old wood to show to advantage. In one case it will serve as extension, in the other as material. But the possibilities always remain limited by the particular history of each piece and by those of its features which are already determined by the use for which it was originally intended or the modifications it has undergone for other purposes. The elements which the *"bricoleur"* collects and uses are "pre-constrained" like the constitutive units of myth, the possible combinations of which are restricted by the fact that they are drawn from the language where they already possess a sense which sets a limit on their freedom of maneuver (Levi-Strauss, 5, p. 35). And the decision as to what to put in each place also depends on the possibility of putting a different element there instead, so that each choice which is made will involve a complete reorganization of the structure, which will never be the same as one vaguely imagined nor as some other which might have been preferred to it.

The engineer no doubt also cross-examines his resources. The existence of an "interlocutor" is in his case due to the fact that his means, power, and knowledge are never unlimited and that in this negative form he meets resistance with which he has to come to terms. It might be said that the engineer questions the universe, while the *"bricoleur"* addresses himself to a collection of oddments left over from human endeavors, that is, only a sub-set of the culture. Again, Information Theory shows that it is possible, and often useful, to reduce the physicists' approaches to a sort of dialogue with nature. This would make the distinction we are trying to draw less clear-cut. There remains however a difference even if one takes into account the fact that the scientist never carries on a dialogue with nature pure and simple but rather with a particular relationship between nature and culture definable in terms of his particular period and civilization and the material means at his disposal. He is no more able than the *"bricoleur"* to do whatever he wishes when he is presented with a given task. He too has to begin by making a catalogue of a previously determined set consisting of theoretical and practical knowledge, of technical means, which restrict the possible solutions.

The difference is therefore less absolute than it might appear. It remains a real one, however, in that the engineer is always trying to make his way out of and go beyond the constraints imposed by a particular state of civilization, while the *"bricoleur"* by inclination or necessity always remains within them. This is another way of saying that the engineer works by means of concepts and the *"bricoleur"* by means of signs. The sets which each employs are at different distances from the poles on the axis of opposition between nature and culture. One way indeed in which signs can be opposed to concepts is that whereas concepts aim to be wholly transparent with respect to reality, signs allow and even require the interposing and incorporation of a certain amount of human culture into reality. Signs, in Peirce's vigorous phrase, "address somebody."

Both the scientist and *"bricoleur"* might therefore be said to be constantly on the look out for "messages." Those which the *"bricoleur"* collects are, however, ones which have to some extent been transmitted in advance—like the commercial codes which are summaries of the past experience of the trade and so allow any new situation to be met economically, provided that it belongs to the same class as some earlier one. The scientist, on the other hand, whether he is an engineer or a physicist, is always on the lookout for *that other message* which might be wrested from an interlocutor in spite of his reticence in pronouncing on questions whose answers have not been rehearsed. Concepts thus appear like operators *opening up* the set being worked with and signification like the operator of its *reorganization*, which neither extends nor renews it and limits itself to obtaining the group of its transformations.

Images cannot be ideas but they can play the part of signs or, to be more precise, co-exist with ideas in signs and, if ideas are not yet present, they can keep their future place open for them and make its contours apparent negatively. Images are fixed, linked in a single way to the mental act which accompanies them. Signs, and images which have acquired significance, may still lack comprehension; unlike concepts, they do not yet possess simultaneous and theoretically unlimited relations with other entities of the same kind. They are, however, already *permutable*, that is, capable of standing in successive relations with other entities—although with only a limited number and, as we have seen, only on the condition that they always form a system in which an alteration which affects one element automatically affects all the others. On this plane logicians' "extension" and "intension" are not two distinct and complementary aspects but one and the same thing. One understands then how mythical thought can be capable of generalizing and so be scientific, even though it is still entangled in imagery. It too works by analogies and comparisons even though its creations, like those of the *"bri-coleur,"* always really consist of a new arrangement of elements, the nature of which is unaffected by whether they figure in the instrumental set or in the final arrangement (these being the same, apart from the internal disposition of their parts): "it would seem that mythological worlds have been built up, only to be shattered again, and that new worlds were built from the fragments" (Boas I, p. 18). Penetrating as this comment is, it nevertheless fails to take into account that in the continual reconstruction from the same materials, it is always earlier ends which are called upon to play the part of means: the signified changes into the signifying, and vice versa.

This formula, which could serve as a definition of *"bricolage,"* explains how an implicit inventory or conception of the total means available must be made in the case of mythical thought also, so that a result can be defined which will always be a compromise between the structure of the instrumental set and that of the project. Once it materializes, the project will therefore inevitably be at a remove from the initial aim (which was moreover a mere sketch), a phenomenon which the surrealists have felicitously called "objective hazard." Further, the "*bricoleur*" also, and indeed principally, derives his poetry from the fact that he does not confine himself to accomplishment and execution: he "speaks" not only *with* things, as we have already seen, but also through the medium of things: giving an account of his personality and life by the choices he makes between the limited possibilities. The "*bricoleur*" may not ever complete his purpose but he always puts something of himself into it.

Mythical thought appears to be an intellectual form of "*bricolage*" in this sense also. Science as a whole is based on the distinction between the contingent and the necessary, this being also what distinguishes event and structure. The qualities it claimed at its outset as peculiarly scientific were precisely those which formed no part of living experience and remained outside and, as it were, unrelated to events. This is the significance of the notion of primary qualities. Now, the characteristic feature of mythical thought, as of "*bricolage*" on the practical plane, is that it builds up structured sets, not directly with other structured sets [5] but by using the remains and debris of events: in French "*des bribes et des morceaux*" or odds and ends in English, fossilized evidence of the history of an individual or a society. The relation between the diachronic and the synchronic is therefore in a sense reversed. Mythical thought, that "*bricoleur*," builds up structures by fitting together events, or rather the remains of events,[6] while science, "in operation" simply by virtue of coming into being, creates its means and results in the form of events, thanks to the structures which it is constantly elaborating and which are its hypotheses and theories. But it is important not to make the mistake of thinking that these are two stages or phases in the evolution of knowledge. Both approaches are equally valid. Physics and chemistry are already striving to become qualitative again, that is, to account also for secondary qualities which when they have been explained will in their turn become means of explanation. And biology may perhaps be marking time waiting for this before it can itself explain life. Mythical thought for its part is imprisoned in the events and experiences which it never tires of ordering and re-ordering in its search to find them a meaning. But it also acts as a liberator by its protest against the idea that anything can be meaningless with which science at first resigned itself to a compromise.

The problem of art has been touched on several times in the foregoing discussion, and it is worth showing briefly how, from this point of view, art lies halfway between scientific knowledge and mythical or magical thought. It is common knowledge that the artist is both something of a scientist and of a "*bricoleur*." By his craftsmanship he constructs a material object which is also an object of knowledge. We have already distinguished the scientist and the "*bricoleur*" by the inverse functions which they assign to events and structures as ends and means, the scientist creating events (changing the world) by means of structures and the "*bricoleur*" creating structures by means of events. This is imprecise in this crude form but our analysis makes it possible for us to refine it. Let us now look at this portrait of a woman by Clouet and consider the reason for the very profound aesthetic emotion which is, apparently inexplicably, aroused by the highly realistic, thread by thread, reproduction of a lace collar (Plate 1).

The choice of this example is not accidental. Clouet is known to have liked to paint at less than life-size. His paintings are therefore, like Japanese gardens, miniature vehicles and ships in bottles, what in the "*bricoleur's*" language are called "small-scale models" or "miniatures." Now, the question arises whether the small-scale model or miniature, which is also the "masterpiece" of the journeyman, may not in fact be the universal type of the work of art. All miniatures seem to have intrinsic aesthetic quality—and from what should they draw this constant virtue if not from the dimensions themselves?—and conversely the vast majority of works of art are small-scale. It might be thought that this characteristic is principally a matter of economy in materials and means, and one might appeal in support of this theory to works which are incontestably artistic but also on a grand scale. We have to be clear about definitions. The paintings of the Sistine Chapel are a small-scale model in spite of their imposing dimensions, since the theme which they depict is the End of Time. The same is true of the cosmic symbolism of religious monuments. Further, we may ask whether the aesthetic effect, say, of an equestrian statue which is larger than life derives from its enlargement of a man to the size of a rock or whether it is not rather due to the fact that it restores what is at first from a distance seen as a rock to the proportions of a man. Finally even "natural size" implies a reduction of scale since graphic or plastic transposition always involves giving up certain dimensions of the object: volume in painting, color, smell, tactile impressions in sculpture and the temporal dimension in both cases since the whole work represented is apprehended at a single moment in time.

What is the virtue of reduction either of scale or in the number of properties? It seems to result from a sort of reversal in the process of understanding. To understand a real object in its totality we always tend to work from its parts. The resistance it offers us is overcome by dividing it. Reduction in scale reverses this situation. Being smaller, the object as a whole seems less formidable. By being quantitatively diminished, it seems to us qualitatively simplified. More exactly, this quantitative transposition extends and diversifies our power over a homologue of the thing, and by means of it the latter can be grasped, assessed, and apprehended at a glance. A child's doll is no longer an enemy, a rival, or even an interlocutor. In it and through it a person is made into a subject. In the case of miniatures, in contrast to what happens when we try to understand an object or living creature of real dimensions, knowledge of the whole precedes knowledge of the parts. And even if this is an illusion, the point of the procedure is to create or sustain the illusion, which gratifies the intelligence and gives rise to a sense of pleasure which can already be called aesthetic on these grounds alone.

I have so far only considered matters of scale which, as we have just seen, imply a dialectical relation between size (i.e., quantity) and quality. But miniatures have a further feature. They are "man-made" and, what is more, made by hand. They are therefore not just projections or passive homologues of the object: they constitute a real experiment with it. Now the model being an artefact, it is possible to understand how it is made and this understanding of the method of construction adds a supplementary dimension. As we have already seen in the case of *"bricolage,"* and the example of "styles" of painters shows that the same is true in art, there are several solutions to the same problem. The choice of one solution involves a modification of the result to which another solution would have led, and the observer is in effect presented with the general picture of these permutations at the same time as the particular solution offered. He is thereby transformed into an active participant without even being aware of it. Merely by contemplating it he is, as it were, put in possession of other possible forms of the same work; and in a confused way, he feels himself to be their creator with more right than the creator himself because the latter abandoned them in excluding them from his creation. And these forms are so many further perspectives opening out on to the work which has been realized. In other words, the intrinsic value of a small-scale model is that it compensates for the renunciation of sensible dimensions by the acquisition of intelligible dimensions.

Let us now return to the lace collar in Clouet's picture. Everything that has been said applies in this case, for the procedure necessary to represent it as a projection, in a particular space, of properties whose sensible dimensions are fewer and smaller than that of the object is exactly the reverse of that which science would have employed had it proposed, in accordance with its function, to produce (instead of reproducing) not only a new, instead of an already known, piece of lace but also real lace instead of a picture of lace. Science would have worked on the real scale but by means of inventing a loom, while art works on a diminished scale to produce an image homologous with the object. The former approach is of a metonymical order, it replaces one thing by another thing, an effect by its cause, while the latter is of a metaphorical order.

This is not all. For if it is true that the relation of priority between structure and event is exactly the opposite in science and "*bricolage*," then it is clear that art has an intermediate position from this point of view as well. Even if, as we have shown, the depiction of a lace collar in miniature demands an intimate knowledge of its morphology and technique of manufacture (and had it been a question of the representation of people or animals we should have said: of anatomy and physical attitudes), it is not just a diagram or blueprint. It manages to synthesize these intrinsic properties with properties which depend on a spatial and temporal context. The final product is the lace collar exactly as it is but so that at the same time its appearance is affected by the particular perspective. This accentuates some parts and conceals others, whose existence however still influences the rest through the contrast between its whiteness and the color of the other clothes, the reflection of the pearly neck it encircles and that of the sky on a particular day and at a particular time of day. The appearance of the lace collar is also affected by whether it indicates casual or formal dress, is worn, either new or previously used, either freshly ironed or creased, by an ordinary woman or a queen, whose physiognomy confirms, contradicts, or qualifies her status in a particular social class, society, part of the world and period of history. . . . The painter is always midway between design and anecdote, and his genius consists in uniting internal and external knowledge, a "being" and a "becoming," in producing with his brush an object which does not exist as such and which he is nevertheless able to create on his canvas. This is a nicely balanced synthesis of one or more artificial and natural structures and one or more natural and social events. The aesthetic emotion is the result of this union between the structural order and the order of events, which is brought about within a thing created by man and so also in effect by the observer who discovers the possibility of such a union through the work of art.

Several points are suggested by this analysis. In the first place, the analysis helps us to see why we are inclined to think of myths both as systems of abstract relations and as objects of aesthetic contemplation. The creative act which gives rise to myths is in fact exactly the reverse of that which gives rise to works of art. In the case of works of art, the starting point is a set of one or more objects and one or more events which aesthetic creation unifies by revealing a common structure. Myths travel the same road but start from the other end. They use a structure to produce what is itself an object consisting of a set of events (for all myths tell a story). Art thus proceeds from a set (object + event) to the *discovery* of its structure. Myth starts from a structure by means of which it *constructs* a set (object + event).

The first point tempts one to generalize the theory. The second might seem to lead to a restriction of it. For we may ask whether it is in fact the case that works of art are always an integration of structure and event. This does not on the face of it seem to be true for instance of the cedarwood Haida club, used to kill fish, which I have in front of me on my bookshelf (Plate 2). The artist who carved it in the form of a sea monster intended the body of the implement to be fused with the body of the animal and the handle with its tail, and that the anatomical proportions, taken from a fabulous creature, should be such that the object could *be* the cruel animal slaying helpless victims, at the same time as an easily handled, balanced and efficient fishing utensil. Everything about this implement—which is also a superb work of art—seems to be a matter of structure: its mythical symbolism as well as its practical function. More accurately, the object, its function, and its symbolism seem to be inextricably bound up with each other and to form a closed system in which there is no place for events. The monster's position, appearance, and expression owe nothing to the historical circumstances in which the artist saw it, in the flesh or in a dream, or conceived the idea of it. It is rather as if its immutable being were finally fixed in the wood whose fine grain allows the reproduction of all its aspects and in the use for which its empirical form seems to predetermine it. And all this applies equally to the other products of primitive art: an African statue or a Melanesian mask. . . . So it looks as if we have defined only one local and historical form of aesthetic creation and not its fundamental properties or those by means of which its intelligible relations with other forms of creation can be described.

We have only to widen our explanation to overcome this difficulty. What, with reference to a picture of Clouet's, was provisionally defined as an event or set of events now appears under a broader heading: events in this sense are only one mode of the contingent whose integration (perceived as necessary) into a structure gives rise to the aesthetic emotion. This is so whatever the type of art in question. Depending on the style, place, and period the contingent plays a part in three different ways or at three distinct points in artistic creation (or in all of them). It may play a part in the occasion for the work or in the execution of the work or in the purpose for which it is intended. It is only in the first case that it takes the form of an event properly speaking, that is, of contingency exterior and prior to the creative act. The artist perceives it from without as an attitude, an expression, a light effect or a situation, whose sensible and intellectual relations to the structure of the object affected by these modalities he grasps and incorporates in his work. But the contingent can also play an intrinsic part in the course of execution itself, in the size or shape of the piece of wood the sculptor lays hands on, in the direction and quality of its grain, in the imperfections of his tools, in the resistance which his materials or project offer to the work in the course of its accomplishment, in the unforeseeable incidents arising during work. Finally, the contingent can be extrinsic as in the first case but posterior, instead of anterior, to the act of creation. This is the case whenever the work is destined for a specific end, since the artist will construct it with a view to its potential condition and successive uses in the future and so will put himself, consciously or unconsciously, in the place of the person for whose use it is intended.

The process of artistic creation therefore consists in trying to communicate (within the immutable framework of a mutual confrontation of structure and accident) either with the *model* or with the *materials* or with the future *user* as the case may be, according to which of these the artist particularly looks to for his directions while he is at work. Each case roughly corresponds to a readily identifiable form of art: the first to the plastic arts of the West, the second to so-called primitive or early art and the third to the applied arts. But it would be an oversimplification to take these identifications very strictly. All forms of art allow all three aspects and they are only distinguished from one another by the relative proportion of each. Even the most academic of painters comes up against problems of execution, for example. All the so-called primitive arts can be called applied in a double sense: first, because many of their productions are technical objects and, secondly, because even those which seem most divorced from practical preoccupations have a definite purpose. Finally, as we know, implements lend themselves to disinterested contemplation even among ourselves.

With these reservations, it is easy to show that the three aspects are functionally related and that the predominance of any one of them leaves less or no place for the others. So-called professional painting is, or believes itself to be, quite free so far as both execution and purpose are concerned. Its best examples display a complete mastery of technical difficulties—which, indeed, can be considered to have been completely overcome since Van der Weyden; the problems which painters have set themselves since then amount to little more than a game of technical refinement. In the extreme case it is as though, given his canvas, paints, and brushes, the painter were able to do exactly what he pleased. On the other hand, he also tries to make his work into an object independent of anything contingent, of value in itself and for itself. This is indeed what the formula of the "easel picture" implies. Freed from the contingent both with regard to execution and purpose professional paining can, then, bring it to bear upon the occasion of the work, and indeed if this account is correct it is bound to do so. Professional painting can therefore be defined as "genre" painting if the sense of this expression is considerably widened. For, from the very general viewpoint we are taking, the attempt of a portrait painter—even of a Rembrandt—to recapture on his canvas his model's most revealing expression or secret thoughts belongs to the same genre as that of a painter like Detaille, whose compositions reproduce the hour and order of battle and the number and disposition of the buttons distinguishing the uniforms of each Arm. To use a disrespectful analogy, "opportunity makes the thief" [7] in either case. The relative proportions of the three aspects are reversed in the applied arts. In these, first place is given to purpose and execution, contingent factors playing an approximately equal part in each, in the examples we consider the most "pure," at the same time the occasion of the work plays no part. This can be seen from the fact that a wine cup or goblet, a piece of basketwork or a fabric seems to us perfect when its practical value manifestly transcends time and corresponds wholly to its functions for men of different periods and civilizations. If the difficulties of execution are entirely mastered, as is the case when it is entrusted to machines, the purpose can become more and more precise and specific and applied art is transformed into industrial art. We call it peasant or folk art if the reverse is the case. Finally, primitive art is the opposite of professional or academic art. Professional or academic art internalizes execution (which it has, or believes itself to have, mastered) and purpose ("art for art's sake" being an end in itself). As a result, it is impelled to externalize the occasion (which it requires the model to provide) and the latter thus becomes a part of the signified. Primitive art, on the other hand, internalizes the occasion (since the supernatural beings which it delights in representing have a reality which is timeless and independent of circumstances) and it externalizes execution and purpose which thus become a part of the signifying.

On a different plane we therefore find once more this dialogue with the materials and means of execution by which we defined "*bricolage*." The essential problem for the philosophy of art is to know whether the artist regards them as interlocutors or not. No doubt they are always regarded as such, although least of all in art which is too professional and most of all in the raw or naïve art which verges on "*bricolage*," to the detriment of structure in both cases. No form of art is, however, worthy of the name if it allows itself to come entirely under the sway of extraneous contingencies, whether of occasion or purpose. If it did so it would rate as an icon (supplementary to the model) or as an implement (complementary with the material worked). Even the most professional art succeeds in moving us only if it arrests in time this dissipation of the contingent in favor of the pretext and incorporates it in the work, thereby investing it with the dignity of being an object in its own right. Insofar as early art, primitive art, and the "primitive" periods of professional painting are the only ones which do not date, they owe it to this dedication of the accidental to the service of execution and so to the use, which they try to make complete, of the raw datum as the empirical material of something meaningful.[8]

It is necessary to add that the balance between structure and event, necessity and contingency, the internal and external, is a precarious one. It is constantly threatened by forces which act in one direction or the other according to fluctuations in fashion, style, or general social conditions. From this point of view, it would seem that impressionism and cubism are not so much two successive stages in the development of painting as partners in the same enterprise, which, although not exact contemporaries, nevertheless collaborated by complementary distortions to prolong a mode of expression whose very existence, as we are better able to appreciate today, was seriously threatened. The intermittent fashion for "collages," originating when craftsmanship was dying, could not for its part be anything but the transposition of "*bricolage*" into the realms of contemplation. Finally, the stress on the event can also break away at certain times through greater emphasis either on transient social phenomena (as in the case of Greuze at the end of the eighteenth century or with socialist realism) or on transient natural, or even

meteorological, phenomena (impressionism) at the expense of structure, "structure" here being understood as "structure of the same
level," for the possibility of the structural aspect being reestablished
elsewhere on a new plane is not ruled out.

NOTES

1. An attempt has been made to discover what would happen if copper ore had accidently found its way into a furnace: complex and varied experiments have shown that nothing happens at all. The simplest method of obtaining metallic copper which could be discovered consisted in subjecting finely ground malachite to intense heat in a pottery dish crowned with an inverted clay pot. This, the sole result, restricts the play of chance to the confines of the kiln of some potter specializing in glazed ware (Coghlan).

2. The phrase is from Bergson, *op. cit., "fonction fabulatrice."* (Translator's note.)

3. The *"bricoleur"* has no precise equivalent in English. He is a man who undertakes odd jobs and is a jack-of-all-trades or a kind of professional do-it-yourself man, but, as the text makes clear, he is of a different standing from, for instance, the English "odd-job man" or handyman. (Translator's note.)

4. Cf. "Treasury of ideas," as Hubert and Mauss so aptly described magic.

5. Mythical thought builds structured sets by means of a structured set, namely, language. But it is not at the structural level that it makes use of it: it builds ideological castles out of the debris of what was once a social discourse.

6. *"Bricolage"* also works with "secondary" qualities, i.e., "secondhand."

7. In the original: *"l'occasion fait le larron."* (Translator's note.)

8. Pursuing this analysis, one might define nonrepresentational painting by two features. One, which it has in common with "easel" painting, consists in a total rejection of the contingency of purpose: the picture is not made for a particular use. The other feature characteristic of nonrepresentational painting is its methodical exploitation of the contingency of execution, which is claimed to afford the external pretext or occasion of the picture. Nonrepresentational painting adopts "styles" as "subjects." It claims to give a concrete representation of the formal conditions of all painting. Paradoxically the result is that nonrepresentational painting does not, as it thinks, create works which are as real as, if not more real than, the objects of the physical world, but rather realistic imitations of nonexistent models. It is a school of academic painting in which each artist strives to represent the manner in which he would execute his pictures if by chance he were to paint any.

The Structuralist Activity

ROLAND BARTHES

What is structuralism? Not a school, nor even a movement (at least, not yet), for most of the authors ordinarily labeled with this word are unaware of being united by any solidarity of doctrine or commitment. Nor is it a vocabulary. *Structure* is already an old word (of anatomical and grammatical provenance), today quite overworked: all the social sciences resort to it abundantly, and the word's use can distinguish no one, except to engage in polemics about the content assigned to it; *functions, forms, signs,* and *significations* are scarcely more pertinent; they are, today, words of common usage, from which one asks (and obtains) whatever one wants, notably the camouflage of the old determinist schema of cause and product; we must doubtless go back to pairings like those of *significans/significatum* and *synchronic/diachronic* in order to approach what distinguishes structuralism from other modes of thought: the first because it refers to the linguistic model as originated by Saussure, and because along with economics, linguistics is, in the present state of affairs, the true science of structure; the second, more decisively, because it seems to imply a certain revision of the notion of history, insofar as the notion of the synchronic (although in Saussure this is a preeminently *operational* concept) accredits a certain immobilization of time, and insofar as that of the diachronic tends to represent the historical process as a pure succession of forms. This second pairing is all the more distinctive in that the chief resistance to structuralism today seems to be of Marxist origin and that it focuses on the notion of history (and not of structure); whatever the case, it is probably the serious recourse to the nomenclature of signification (and not to the word itself, which is, paradoxically, not at all distinctive) which we must ultimately take as structuralism's *spoken sign*: watch who uses *signifier* and *signified*, *synchronic* and *diachronic*, and you will know whether the structuralist vision is constituted.

This is valid for the intellectual metalanguage, which explicitly employs methodological concepts. But since structuralism is neither a school nor a movement, there is no reason to reduce it a priori, even in a problematical way, to the activity of philosophers; it would be better to try and find its broadest description (if not its definition) on another level than that of reflexive language. We can in fact presume that there exist certain writers, painters, musicians, in whose eyes a certain *exercise* of structure (and not only its thought) represents a distinctive experience, and that both analysts and creators must be placed under the common sign of what we might call *structural man*, defined not by his ideas or his languages, but by his imagination—in other words, by the way in which he mentally experiences structure.

Hence the first thing to be said is that in relation to *all* its users, structuralism is essentially an *activity*, i.e., the controlled succession of a certain number of mental operations: we might speak of structuralist activity as we once spoke of surrealist activity (surrealism, moreover, may well have produced the first experience of structural literature, a possibility which must some day be explored). But before seeing what these operations are, we must say a word about their goal.

The goal of all structuralist activity, whether reflexive or poetic, is to reconstruct an "object" in such a way as to manifest thereby the rules of functioning (the "functions") of this object. Structure is therefore actually a *simulacrum* of the object, but a directed, *interested* simulacrum, since the imitated object makes something appear which remained invisible, or if one prefers, unintelligible in the natural object. Structural man takes the real, decomposes it, then recomposes it; this appears to be little enough (which makes some say that the structuralist enterprise is "meaningless," "uninteresting," "useless," etc.). Yet, from another point of view, this "little enough" is decisive: for between the two objects, or the two tenses, of structuralist activity, there occurs *something new*, and what is new is nothing less than the generally intelligible: the simulacrum is intellect added to object, and this addition has an anthropological value, in that it is man himself, his history, his situation, his freedom, and the very resistance which nature offers to his mind.

We see, then, why we must speak of a structuralist *activity*: creation or reflection are not, here, an original "impression" of the world, but a veritable fabrication of a world which resembles the first one, not in order to copy it but to render it intelligible. Hence one might say that structuralism is essentially *an activity of imitation*, which is also why there is, strictly speaking, no *technical* difference between structuralism as an intellectual activity on the one hand and literature in particular, art in general on the other: both derive from a *mimesis*, based not on the analogy of substances (as in so-called realist art), but on the analogy of functions (what Levi-Strauss calls *homology*). When Troubetskoy reconstructs the phonetic object as a system of variations; when Dumézil elaborates a functional mythology; when Propp constructs a folk tale resulting by structuration from all the Slavic tales he has previously decomposed; when Levi-Strauss discovers the homologic functioning of the totemic imagination, or Granger the formal rules of economic thought, or Gardin the pertinent features of prehistoric bronzes; when Richard decomposes a poem by Mallarmé into its distinctive vibrations—they are all doing nothing different from what Mondrian, Boulez, or Butor are doing when they articulate a certain object—what will be called, precisely, a *composition*—by the controlled manifestation of certain units and certain associations of these units. It is of little consequence whether the initial object liable to the simulacrum-activity is given by the world in an already assembled fashion (in the case of the structural analysis made of a constituted language or society or work) or is still scattered (in the case of the structural "composition"); whether this initial object is drawn from a social reality or an imaginary reality. It is not the nature of the copied object which defines an art (though this is a tenacious prejudice in all realism), it is the fact that man adds to it in reconstructing it: technique is the very being of all creation. It is therefore to the degree that the goals of structuralist activity are indissolubly linked to a certain technique that structuralism exists in a distinctive fashion in relation to other modes of analysis or creation: we recompose the object *in order* to make certain functions appear, and it is, so to speak, the way that makes the work; this is why we must speak of the structuralist activity rather than the structuralist work.

The structuralist activity involves two typical operations: dissection and articulation. To dissect the first object, the one which is given to the simulacrum-activity, is to find in it certain mobile fragments whose differential situation engenders a certain meaning; the fragment has no meaning in itself, but it is nonetheless such that the slightest variation wrought in its configuration produces a change in the whole; a *square* by Mondrian, a *series* by Pousseur, a *versicle* of Butor's *Mobile*, the "mytheme" in Levi-Strauss, the phoneme in the work of the phonologists, the "theme" in certain literary criticism— all these units (whatever their inner structure and their extent, quite different according to cases) have no significant existence except by their frontiers: those which separate them from other actual units of the discourse (but this is a problem of articulation) and also those which distinguish them from other virtual units, with which they form a certain class (which linguistics calls a *paradigm*); this notion of a paradigm is essential, apparently, if we are to understand the structuralist vision: the paradigm is a group, a reservoir—as limited as possible—of objects (of units) from which one summons, by an act of citation, the object or unit one wishes to endow with an actual meaning; what characterizes the paradigmatic object is that it is, vis-à-vis other objects of its class, in a certain relation of affinity and dissimilarity: two units of the same paradigm must resemble each other somewhat *in order* that the difference which separates them be indeed evident: *s* and *z* must have both a common feature (dentality) and a distinctive feature (presence or absence of sonority) so that we cannot, in French, attribute the same meaning to *poisson* and *poison;* Mondrian's squares must have both certain affinities by their shape as squares, and certain dissimilarities by their proportion and color; the American automobiles (in Butor's *Mobile*) must be constantly regarded in the same way, yet they must differ each time by both their make and color; the episodes of the Oedipus myth (in Levi-Strauss's analysis) must be both identical and varied—in order that all these languages, these works may be intelligible. The dissection-operation thus produces an initial dispersed state of the simulacrum, but the units of the structure are not at all anarchic: before being distributed and fixed in the continuity of the composition, each one forms with its own virtual group or reservoir an intelligent organism, subject to a sovereign motor principle: that of the smallest difference.

Once the units are posited, structural man must discover in them or establish for them certain rules of association: this is the activity of articulation, which succeeds the summoning activity. The syntax of the arts and of discourse is, as we know, extremely varied; but what we discover in every work of structural enterprise is the submission to regular constraints whose formalism, improperly indicated, is much less important than their stability; for what is happening, at this second stage of the simulacrum-activity, is a kind of battle against chance; this is why the constraint of recurrence of the units has an almost demiurgic value: it is by the regular return of the units and of the associations of units that the work appears constructed, i.e., endowed with meaning; linguistics calls these rules of combination *forms*, and it would be advantageous to retain this rigorous sense of an overtaxed word: form, it has been said, is what keeps the contiguity of units from appearing as a pure effect of chance: the work of art is what man wrests from chance. This perhaps allows us to understand on the one hand why so-called nonfigurative works are nonetheless to the highest degree works of art, human thought being established not on the analogy of copies and models but with the regularity of assemblages; and on the other hand why these same works appear, precisely, fortuitous and thereby useless to those who discern in them no *form*: in front of an abstract painting, Khrushchev was certainly wrong to see only the traces of a donkey's tail whisked across the canvas; at least he knew in his way, though, that art is a certain conquest of chance (he simply forgot that every rule must be learned, whether one wants to apply or interpret it).

The simulacrum, thus constructed, does not render the world as it has found it, and it is here that structuralism is important. First of all, it manifests a new category of the object, which is neither the real nor the rational, but the *functional*, thereby joining a whole scientific complex which is being developed around information theory and research. Subsequently and especially, it highlights the strictly human process by which men give meaning to things. Is this new? To a certain degree, yes; of course the world has never stopped looking for the meaning of what is given it and of what it produces; what is new is a mode of thought (or a "poetics") which seeks less to assign completed meanings to the objects it discovers than to know how meaning is possible, at what cost and by what means. Ultimately, one might say that the object of structuralism is not man endowed with meanings, but man fabricating meanings, as if it could not be the *content* of meanings which exhausted the semantic goals of humanity, but only the act by which these meanings, historical and contingent variables, are produced. *Homo significans*: such would be the new man of structural inquiry.

According to Hegel, the ancient Greek was amazed by the *natural* in nature; he constantly listened to it, questioned the meaning of mountains, springs, forests, storms; without knowing what all these objects were telling him by name, he perceived in the vegetal or cosmic order a tremendous *shudder* of meaning, to which he gave the name of a god: Pan. Subsequently, nature has changed, has become social: everything that is given to man is *already* human, down to the forest and the river which we cross when we travel. But confronted with this social nature, which is quite simply culture, structural man is no different from the ancient Greek: he too listens for the natural in culture, and constantly perceives in it not so much stable, finite, "true" meanings as the shudder of an enormous machine which is humanity tirelessly undertaking to create meaning, without which it would no longer be human. And it is because this fabrication of meaning is more important, to its view, than the meanings themselves, it is because the function is extensive with the works, that structuralism constitutes itself as an activity, and refers the exercise of the work and the work itself to a single identity: a serial composition or an analysis by Levi-Strauss are not objects except insofar as they have been *made*: their present being *is* their past act: they are *having-been-mades;* the artist, the analyst recreates the course taken by meaning, he need not designate it: his function, to return to Hegel's example, is a *manteia;* like the ancient soothsayer, he *speaks* the locus of meaning but does not name it. And it is because literature, in particular, is a mantic activity that it is both intelligible and interrogating, speaking and silent, engaged in the world by the course of meaning which it remakes with the world, but disengaged from the contingent meanings which the world elaborates: an answer to the man who consumes it yet always a question to nature, an answer which questions and a question which answers.

How then does structural man deal with the accusation of unreality which is sometimes flung at him? Are not forms in the world, are not forms responsible? Was it really his Marxism that was revolutionary in Brecht? Was it not rather the decision to link to Marxism, in the theater, the placing of a spotlight or the deliberate fraying of a costume? Structuralism does not withdraw history from the world: it seeks to link to history not only certain contents (this has been done a thousand times) but also certain forms, not only the material but also the intelligible, not only the ideological but also the aesthetic. And precisely because all thought about the historically intelligible is also a participation in that intelligibility, structural man is scarcely concerned to *last;* he knows that structuralism, too, is a certain *form* of the world, which will change with the world; and just as he experiences his validity (but not his truth) in his power to speak the old languages of the world in a new way, so he knows that it will suffice that a new language rise out of history, a new language which speaks him in his turn, for his task to be done.

PRACTICE

Existential Phenomenology

Hölderlin's "Nature and Art or Saturn and Jupiter"

EMIL STAIGER

TRANSLATED BY *Vernon W. Gras*

High up in day you govern, your law prevails,
You hold the scales of judgment, O Saturn's son,
Hand out our lots and well-contented
Rest on the fame of immortal kingship.

Yet, singers know it, down the abyss you hurled
The holy father once, your own parent, who
Long now has lain lamenting where the
Wild ones before you more justly languish,

Quite guiltless he, the god of the golden age:
Once effortless and greater than you, although
He uttered no commandment, and no
Mortal on earth ever named his presence.

So down with you! Or cease to withhold your thanks!
And if you'll stay, defer to the older god
And grant him that above all others,
Gods and great mortals, the singer name him!

For as from clouds your lightning, from him has come
What you call yours. And, look, the commands you speak
To him bear witness, and from Saturn's
Primitive peace every power developed.

And once my heart can feel and contain that life
Most living, his, and things that you shaped grow dim,
And in his cradle changing Time has
Fallen asleep and sweet quiet lulls me—

I'll know you then, Kronion, and hear you then,
The one wise master who, like ourselves, a son

Of Time, gives laws to us, uncovers
That which lies hidden in holy twilight.[1]

During work on "Empedokles," Hölderlin felt compelled to make crucial to his thinking and poetry the question of the relationship of nature and art. Already in the early stages of the drama, it is touched on repeatedly. The philosophical study *Grund zum Empedokles*, which prepares for "The Death of Empedokles," conceives the tragic process as a disruption and reinstatement of the balance between nature and art. And the ode "Nature and Art or Saturn and Jupiter" finds in the myth of the older and younger world ruler an image for the being and history of man. Among those written at the turn of the century, this ode seems to have the least lyrical charm. It speaks with a sharp abstract quality about what normally remains silent and implied. For that very reason, it is especially suited to clarify the meaning consciously held to by the poet even in his most rapturous verses and which instills in us that intense lyrical delight unique to his work.

The first stanza in broad outline sketches the character of Jupiter. In this delineation Hölderlin follows ancient mythology; yet overall the particulars take on a new meaning. Jupiter is the god of the heights and the god of the day. The "high up in day" momentarily recalls shining Helios and seems to say that Jupiter's power has arrived at the dividing point, as though it were abiding at its zenith. As long as this continues, his laws "prevail"; not *his* laws in contrast to the laws of other gods, but law in itself which first came into being through him. He "hold(s) the scales"; he compares and "measures" the things of this world; and "hand(s) out our lots," dividing what will make up our good or bad fortune. All order thus is placed into his strong hand. His might is a governance. Moreover, in the last stanza, he is called the "wise master." A student is able to learn from a master, and what he learns are the rules or technique of an art. Furthermore, Jupiter is designated there as a "son of Time," whereas the first stanza introduced him as "Saturn's son." That does not mean that the poet, following the example of Cicero who equated Kronos with kronos, conceives Saturn to be the God of Time. Just the opposite! Time came into being with Jupiter's rule. He is son of Time "like us." Time belongs to him as it belongs now to mankind who are subject to Jupiter's reign. Thus, he is called with equal or perhaps more justification "Master of Time" in "Empedokles." [2] Only because time exists with the beginning of his rule can he and must he ordain laws—is he able (and this word honors him most) to "uncover" or make known.

Saturn is the god of the Golden Age. The "Golden Age," *aetas aurea*, means the world as it existed before *our* time, or rather—as soon to be made evident—before time existed *at all*. Saturn's realm is the "cradle" in which time slept before its transformation and into which it still fades away for the sensitive heart of the poet. An earlier version reads: "*Hab ich am Herzen das Leben erst das Leben der Liebe erfahren, und dämmern und schwinden in Wonne die Gestalten, kehrt die Zeit in ihre Wiege zurück*" [3] (Have I once experienced deep in my life the life of love, and forms in rapture grow dim and vanish, Time returns to its cradle). "Love," "rapture," "happy memories"—these all resemble the older god, whose power had not yet been a governance, who "uttered no commandment," who "effortless(ly)," and because he needed no effort, reigned more greatly. In his realm, the light to distinguish earth's many objects does not shine. "Holy twilight" covers everything, dissolving contours and merging one object unnoticeably into another. Yet no mortal has ever called him by name. By contrasting this with the "uncover" or make known of the last stanza, we discover that language did not exist in the golden age, that language first came into existence in our time with Jupiter. Accordingly, the two powers now stand clearly demarcated: on one side, Jupiter, law, day, master, ruler, language, time; on the other, Saturn, beyond time, mute, effortless, a god of love and holy twilight. The title of the ode ascribes to the older god "nature" and to the younger, Jupiter, "art." This allows us to be even more exact. If we investigate the opposition of nature and art in the study *Grund zum Empedokles*,[4] pursuing it through all its multiple shaded nuances, we find standing for "art" the concepts: organic, spontaneity, reflection, educate, cultivate, discriminate, think, compare, language; for "nature": *aorgisch*,[5] not understandable, not tangible, not perceivable, unlimited, unconscious, speechless, love, element—and furthermore, in regard to the fate of Agrigent and Empedokles, on the side of "art": free-spirited audacity, a hyperpolitical, litigative, and calculating bearing; on the side of nature: anarchic wildness, burning latitudes, luxuriant Sicilian countryside. From these words we may conclude that this realm of Saturn, this nature, must not be confused with that first condition of the world described by Kant and Schiller. Undoubtedly, "The Probable Origin of Human History" influenced Hölderlin as much as Schiller's essay "On Naïve and Sentimental Poetry." But what he means when he says "nature" has as little to do with those essays as with the Gessnerian idyll possibly recalled by the Arcadian phrase "Golden Age." "Nature" is extreme inwardness, a Dasein which knows no separation nor discrimination, the Εν in π∝v, the *o n e* life that penetrates the whole world. The gentle ether as well as the fire seething in Aetna may serve to indicate it as evanescent, dissolving, lacking determinate form and fixity. Because nature is everywhere, it is never met in the here and now; and whosoever directs his eye on the many, never comes to experience it. The heart only makes contact with it at twilight—Hölderlin chose this word *"dämmert"* frequently—"when the green of the earth dims," [6] "when old love grows dim," [7] "when the heart dims the soul," [8] when in uncertainty self and other lose themselves and everything trembles in drunken surmise, nature is encountered by a love forgetting itself through displacement into the infinite, by an ecstasy consuming all earthly things with incandescent passion.

The concept of the "undifferentiated" gathers together what the poet says about nature as does "differentiating" what is said about Jupiter, or art. Governance differentiates between subjects and ruler. Laws derive from the necessity of holding together the multeity that has fallen apart; their unity is not the "effortless" one of nature, but a mediation between warring factions. Such also is the unity created by the "wise master" in his craft. Mastery with its reliable rules becomes necessary only when the beautiful no longer emanates spontaneously from the soul, only when matter lies estranged from the spirit of form and in need of the latter's coercion. More generally, differentiating appears with language. Language fixates the difference of all things. While doing so, it admittedly promotes understanding. But understanding becomes a requirement only when mankind no longer lives in unity with itself and the things of this world. Time abolishes this primal unity,

separating an enduring permanence from the transient in which fare-
wells and expectations, a "nevermore" and a "not yet" find place,
instead of the "simultaneity" which once existed in the realm of
Saturn.

However, the poet clearly states that Jupiter, or art, must remain
instructed by nature.

> For as from clouds your lightning, from him has come
> What you call yours. And, look, the commands you speak
> To him bear witness, and from Saturn's
> Primitive peace every power developed.

A similar statement appears in the first version of the drama. Panthea
describes Empedokles:

> *Ihm schweigt die Welt und aus sich selber wächst*
> *In steigendem Vergnügen die Begeistrung*
> *Ihm auf, bis aus der Nacht des schöpfrischen*
> *Entzückens, wie ein Funke, der Gedanke springt . . ."* [9]

> (The world falls silent and out of itself
> In mounting joy enthusiasm grows within him
> Until out of the night of creative
> Rapture, like a spark flames the thought . . .)

From the clouds, from the night of creative rapture, from the love-
dark of nature, darts the lightning of thought. Thought is not
self-creative. It only illuminates what has always been. The spirit
must ever receive what it desires to clarify, order, form, and cultivate. Knowledge grounds itself in experience. The poet lives upon
the fullness of the heart. And the richness of experience, the fullness
of the heart, is nature's gift. Without nature, art can do nothing.
Jupiter attests and makes known. But though he is able to attest
and make known, what he declares is always primal being resting
independently within itself.

Nevertheless, we are told that Jupiter dared to banish his father
into the abyss with the "intractable ones." How is this possible?
Hölderlin depicts the Titans as "intractable" and the context indi-

cates a freer handling of the ancient legend. Of course, he still keeps the Titans within the realm of Saturn. Indeed, nothing hinders us from viewing them still as his brothers. But while the Titans revolted against the rule of Jupiter, Saturn is called "guiltless." He did not enter the battle. We dare to conjecture that he would have been ready to recognize the new ruler. The appearance of Jupiter has forced nature into two different possibilities. The Titans are lawless, nature viewed as anarchy. Saturn, on the other hand, is without law, nature viewed as love, as that which endures but does not resist. Jupiter had a "right" to hurl the Titans downward. Order exists only by excluding anarchy. But that he had thrown Saturn down into the abyss with the Titans appears so heavy a trespass to the poet that he doesn't hesitate to address Jupiter in that half-forgotten Schiller and Schubert mode of youthful indignation, "*Herab denn!*" (So down with you!)—Jupiter, that highest god, who distributes fortune and determines the laws of human existence! What does it signify, anyhow, that Jupiter banishes Saturn into the abyss, that art banishes nature? The earlier description of the Agrigentines already provided a hint: "Free-spirited audacity, hyperpolitical, litigative, and calculating bearing." Free-spirited is the man who recognizes nothing outside of himself, whose self-certainty draws from ideas their widest conclusions, and who then falls into enormity. Hyperpolitical is the citizen who views the state as an end in itself and forgets order has meaning only when it serves the community. The litigator exists only for "due process," whereas law was written for the sake of life. The calculator dispenses with love and arranges things to serve his special purposes. Over all this Jupiter holds sway, having rid himself of Saturn. But even Empedokles, infused and besouled by nature, accuses himself of the same fault because he had ascribed to his own powers all that had been bestowed on him and said "I" rather than "nature."

> *Ich kannt' es ja,*
> *Das Leben der Natur, wie sollt' es mir*
> *Noch heilig sein, wie einst! Die Götter waren*
> *Mir dienstbar nun geworden, ich allein*
> *War Gott und sprachs im frechen Stolz heraus.*[10]

(I knew it,
The life of nature, how should it remain
Holy to me, as formerly! The gods had
Become serviceable to me, I alone
Was God and proclaimed it with insolent pride.)

In the second version of "Empedokles" he uses the same image found in the ode.

O Geist,
Geist, der mich gross gemacht! du hast
Dir deinen Herrn, hast, alter Saturn!
Dir einen neuen Jupiter
Gezogen, einen schwächern nur und frechern.[11]

(O Spirit,
Spirit who has brought me up! You have
Raised your master, old Saturn!
You have raised a new Jupiter
For yourself, only weaker, and more insolent.)

Jupiter's repeated temptation to such hubris is grounded in his very nature. The danger inheres already in language. Words separate a permanence from the transiency of things. The idea relates itself to the many which it unifies; indeed, it lives only in this relationship. It is precisely because the many and transient are preserved and find permanence in the idea, that the permanent can separate itself from the transient and become independent. Reason can then deal with words independently, joining them together unconcerned whether the things represented by them also fit together. Nothing remains of language now but the dead letter which has no life nor can it instill any. Now the gods can be named without knowing anything about them. The door opens to hypocrisy, error, and betrayal.

And just as words separate from their objects, so does the general separate from the temporal and passing, from the eternal stream of being-there (Dasein): Law, form, and self become fixated; that which should encompass and preserve life does violence to it, misuses it, or excludes it. In Hegel's youthful writings, this fixation is called "positivity" (*Postivität*). Hegel's description matches in detail the condition of the Agrigentians in Hölderlin's presentation. For Hölderlin, however, Agrigent is a picture of his own time. As stated in *Grund zum Empedokles*, "the tragedy . . . includes a third of the poet's own disposition and various strange material from his own world which he chose because he found them analogous enough to allow transporting his total feelings into them and preserving them there as if in a vessel, indeed, all the more securely because of the strangeness of the material." [12]   .

The analogy extends to the whole contemporary world, but especially to the rationalism of the enlightenment as Hölderlin, Hegel, and Schelling had interpreted it already at Tübingen. They had found that all things were measured to human scale, that even the divine—in theodicy—was subjugated to the measurement of reason. Of living nature only that was admitted which was calculable. The question of utility excluded any inward feelings, just as, in general, the enlightenment (indicated already by its name and bearing) desires light and excludes "holy twilight." Those who merely understand are never those who feel deeply. The spirit erects its kingdom upon the defeat of the heart as the poet declares in "Ermunterung":

> *Echo des Himmels! heiliges Herz! warum,*
> *Warum verstummst du unter den Lebenden?*
> *Schläfst, Freies! von den Götterlosen*
> *Ewig hinab in die Nacht verwiesen?* [13]

> (Echo of heaven! O holy heart! why,
> Why fall you silent though yet living?
> Sleep you, O free one! By the godless
> Banished forever into the downward night?)

Those few, however, who seek to release the heart from its banishment, who feel again the One in the All, they share also in Jupiter's guilt, only in a different manner. As much as Hölderlin, in his awe of Fichte and admiration of Schelling, refuses to offer reproach, it appeared a sacrilege to him to call God the Absolute Ego, to identify the World-spirit with the Ego principle of philosophy. In the "Epicurean Confessions of Heinz Widerporstens," a humorous poetical presentation of the Identity-system, Schelling spoke words which in content if not in mood manifest the exact attitude in which Empedokles accuses himself in a god-forsaken hour:

> *Wusst' auch nicht, wie mir vor der Welt sollt' grausen,*
> *Da ich sie kenne von innen und aussen,*
> *Ist gar ein träg und zahmes Tier,*
> *Das weder dräuet dir noch mir.*
> *Muss sich unter Gesetze schmiegen,*
> *Ruhig zu meinen Füssen liegen . . .*
> *Ich bin der Gott, der sie im Busen hegt,*
> *Der Geist, der sich in allem bewegt . . .*

> (Wouldn't know why I should stand in awe of the world
> For I'm familiar with it inside and out
> It's a tame and placid beast
> Who threatens neither you nor me.
> Quietly it lies at my feet,
> Completely submissive to the rule of law . . .
> I am the god that fosters it in my bosom,
> The spirit that moves in all things . . .)

The greatest danger is that the favored individual in whose "spirit and voice" Nature appears "with all its melodies . . . so intimate, warm, and personal" as if "they shared the same heart" feels himself the center and origin of life and thus offends against the Holy even more than his "enlightened" contemporaries.[14] Thus, even the figure of Empedokles in the middle stages of the drama implies a critique of the times. This critique coincides with the words Hölderlin wrote to his brother from Hauptwil in 1801: "All things in eternal unity, however in this All a *superior* Oneness and Unifying Power that in itself is *no* I but among ourselves—is God." [15]

He longed for this "Oneness and Unifying Power" (in contrast to the differentiated and the differentiating temporal world) in his odes; he praised it in his hymns; he hoped to serve it by awakening the slumbering heart; he hoped to extend the love uniting him with Diotima into the whole world; the language of love was to become the language of the country; its soul was to become the speech of the folk.[16] This "Oneness" forms the tenor of the oration directed to the Agrigentines by Empedokles just before his death and just after he had recognized his own sacrilege:

> O gebt euch der Natur, eh sie euch nimmt!
> Ihr dürstet längst nach Ungewöhnlichem,
> Und wie aus krankem Körper sehnt der Geist
> Von Agrigent sich aus dem alten Gleis.
> So wagt's was ihr geerbt, was ihr erworben,
> Was euch der Väter Mund erzählt, gelehrt,
> Gesetz und Bräuch, der alter Götter Namen,
> Vergesst es kühn, und hebt, wie Neugeborne,
> Die Augen auf zur göttlichen Natur . . .[17]

> (O give yourselves to Nature before she takes you!
> You have thirsted long after the unusual,
> As from a sick body the spirit of Agrigent
> Yearns to escape the old ways.
> So dare it! Forget your inheritance
> And what you have acquired, what from fathers
> Has been told and learned, their law and custom,
> The names of the old gods—and like the newborn
> Raise your eyes to holy Nature . . .)

"Happy Saturndays" will then return.[18] In a scene-sketch for the last version, Saturn is still mentioned in this guise: "The following day on the Feast of Saturn" Manes will "make known the last will of Empedokles." [19] The feast of Saturn will prepare the people's *Gemüt* (disposition) for the message left them by the dead seer.

All of this rests on the conviction that restoration is possible without conflict through entreaty of the loving heart, that Art voluntarily will abdicate its power and kneel before Saturn as Hölderlin yet prophesies in the late hymn "Voice of the People":

Und stille vor den Sternen liegt, den
Betenden gleich, in den Sand geworfen,
Freiwillig überwunden die lange Kunst
Vor jenen Unnachahmbaren da; er selbst,
Der Mensch, mit eigner Hand zerbrach, die
Hohen zu ehren, sein Werk, der Künstler.[20]

(And there beneath the stars, like mortals
Deep in their prayers, quite still, prostrated
On sand, outgrown, and willingly, lies long art
Flung down before the Matchless; and he himself,
The man, the artist with his own two
Hands broke his work for their sake, in homage.) [21]

This will occur when the time is fulfilled according to the counsel of the gods. In the great hymns, the poet acquiesced to await this moment. But in the period clarified and brought to an end by "Saturn and Jupiter" he lacked the patience of maturity. We detect an impatience not quite under control in the Titanic "So down with you." Still, this phrase has its limiting condition:

So down with you! Or cease to withold your thanks!
And if you'll stay, defer to the older god

Only if Jupiter finds gratitude embarrassing, would it be better that he be toppled. But if he will thank and serve the old god, then as the last stanza affirms, the poet will "know" and "hear" him. More clearly stated, the poet will obey and acknowledge him as the "wise master" who, as we do, utters and gives laws. Pondering this final turn-about to Saturn, we see that it is not a matter of redoing history, of doing to Jupiter what he did to Saturn. Nature long ago confirmed, even before art subdued the earth, that it needs art less than art needs nature. Even so, nature would suffer if art were to be lost. Saturn's realm existed without language. No mortal had named the gods yet. Everything *was* god, so nobody *was* *conscious* of him. Indeed, he himself knew nothing of himself and remained mute. For knowledge is possible only through opposition,[22] and language only through differentiation. Nature needs mastery.[23]

And the master it needs—not in order to exist, which it does without him, but the master it desires—is the spirit of Jupiter. Empedokles expresses it thus:

> *Was wäre denn der Himmel und das Meer*
> *Und Inseln und Gestirn und was vor Augen*
> *Den Menschen alles liegt, was wär es auch*
> *Dies tote Saitenspiel, gäb' ich ihm Ton*
> *Und Sprach' und Seele nicht? was sind*
> *Die Götter und ihr Geist, wenn ich sie nicht*
> *Verkündige. Nun! Sage, wer bin ich?* [24]

> (What would heaven be and the sea,
> The islands, stars, and all else
> That lie spread out before man's sight;
> What would all this lifeless music be,
> Received it not my speech, soul, and melody?
> What do gods matter, were I not there
> To make them known. So then! Who am I?)

Of course, a fearsome irony undulates in these words. Who am I, goes the thought, that I dared to measure myself with nature? Nevertheless, the thought hides a truth which is found in Pausanias' reply:

> *Verhöhne nur im Unmut dich und alles,*
> *Was Menschen herrlich macht,*
> *Ihr Wirken und ihr Wort . . .*

> (Only deride in displeasure yourself and all that
> Which gives men their grandeur,
> Their working and their word . . .)

Art, the working and the word, elevates mankind; it elevates man in an obvious and simple sense to which the young disciple with all his gentle piety to nature may confess. "The instinct toward art and culture in all its modifications and subspecies" when practiced correctly, is "actually a service . . . which mankind renders unto nature." [25] Indeed, Hölderlin calls it "human destiny . . . to multiply, to expedite, to particularize, to blend, to separate, to unite the life of nature." [26] Even Empedokles after he has conquered the pain of his sacrilege, knows clearly this is so and obligates his disciple in that noble and stately speech, whose torso in the unfinished second version towers up yet so magnificently at the end,

> *Wirken soll der Mensch,*
> *Der sinnende, soll entfaltend*
> *Das Leben um ihn fördern und heitern.*
>   *Denn hoher Bedeutung voll,*
> *Voll schweigender Kraft umfängt*
> *Den ahnenden, dass er bilde,*
> *Die grosse Natur.*
> *Dass ihren Geist hervor er rufe, tragt*
> *Die Sorg' im Busen und die Hoffnung*
> *Der Mensch. Tiefwurzelnd strebt*
> *Das gewaltige Sehnen in ihm auf.*
> *Und viel vermag er; und herrlich ist*
> *Sein Wort, er Wandelt die Welt,*
> *Und unter den Händen—*" [27]

> (Serenely, true, should men,
> The pondering, act upon
> The life around them, to further and make bright
>   for full of lofty purpose,
> Of power contained, unexpressed,
> Great Nature surrounds their
> Foreknowing minds, to bid them fashion a world,
> Deep-rooted
> Within them a mighty longing leaps up
> So that her spirit will come to light.
> And much he can do, and glorious is
> Man's word, it transforms the world
> And where his hands have— [28])

The new Saturndays which are to arrive will have greater "manly strength" [29] than the first which had no Jupiter. They will be "manlier" to the extent that art does not pay for its sacrilegious presumption with death but is continued and maintained properly as a service to nature. If, for this reason, Hölderlin wishes to broaden human love toward the world, it must remain an uttered or publically spoken love. "Voice of love" and "speech of the folk" we quoted earlier. These phrases already describe the correct relationship. Love becomes perceptible through the language that serves to announce it. Language that makes love known differentiates but no longer separates. It differentiates only in order to unite more intimately. A purified existence is attained wherein art and nature oppose each other harmoniously, wherein nature is elevated by art, and art appears as nature's flowering and completion.[30] "Life's twilight figures" now stand in a "secure light." [31] They have been made secure through a "knowledge" still celebrated in a late stanza written from out the dark twilight of the poet's madness:

> *Als wie der Tag die Menschen hell umscheinet*
> *Und mit dem Lichte, das den Höhn entspringet,*
> *Die dämmernden Erscheinungen vereinet,*
> *Ist Wissen, welches tief der Geistigkeit gelinget.*[32]

> (Like the bright day that shines on human kind
> And with a light of heavenly origin
> All things obscure and various gathers in
> Is knowledge, deeply granted to the mind.[33])

The manifold presents itself. But behind the multiplicity glimmers drunken Saturn as Unity and Unifying Power illustrated, for example, in the landscape of "Heidelberg" where all things remain lovingly interrelated; in "Archipelagus" where the ocean god as the "God of myths" [34] holds togther with his mighty arms as out of a magical inner center the most distant reaches; and in "Stuttgart" where enthusiasm melts and threatens to demolish all rigidities, which yet persist and congruent to the will of the gods "enjoy themselves in the light." [35] Images of such "pure existence" hover in that suspension which satisfies both the feeling heart and the discriminating mind. To glorify this condition is the poet's task. Poets are like the "wine-god's . . . ministers"; [36] wine is "dark light." [37] It unifies the twilight of Saturn and the brightness of Jupiter. Thus it dissolves individual reason while simultaneously enkindling it toward memory and speech as happens to the son in the ode "Das Ahnenbild." [38] Songs "filled with nectar" are the language of love and therefore "give pleasure to the gods." [39] They are the proclamation of holy twilight, to speak in the words of the ode's last stanza, which, after the high god's downfall seemed imminent, and the heart lost itself in living, and Time was put to sleep, enkindled a new light which illuminated the pure artist and the authentic hierarchy of the world.

NOTES

1. Translation by Michael Hamburger in *Friedrich Hölderlin: Poems and Fragments* (Ann Arbor, 1966), p. 165. Unless otherwise indicated, verse translations will be mine (Ed.).
2. Friedrich Hölderlin: *Sämtliche Werke* (historisch-kritische Ausgabe von Hellingrath, Selbass und Pigenot, 2 Aufl. Berlin, 1923) III, 220, 223. All of Staiger's citations will be from this edition, referred to as *SW* (Ed.).
3. *SW* II, IV, 292.
4. *SW* III, 321 ff.
5. Hölderlin's term: the silent, primitive, relatively more general and formless cosmic potencies.
6. *SW* IV, 14.
7. *SW* III, 204.
8. *SW* III, 222, 50, 51.
9. *SW* III, 77–78.
10. *SW* III, 95.
11. *SW* III, 18, 7.
12. *SW* III, 319.
13. *SW* IV, 45.
14. *SW* III, 331.
15. *SW* V, 311.
16. *SW* IV, 21.
17. *SW* III, 146.
18. *SW* III, 150.
19. *SW* III, 227.
20. *SW* IV, 142–143.
21. Hamburger, *op. cit.*, p. 179.
22. *SW* V, 277.
23. *SW* III, 193.
24. *SW* III, 194.
25. *SW* III, 401.
26. *SW* III, 400.
27. *SW* III, 194.
28. Hamburger, *op. cit.*, p. 305.
29. *SW* III, 150.
30. *SW* III, 321.
31. *SW* IV, 9.
32. *SW* VI, 39.

33. Hamburger, *op. cit.*, p. 585.
34. *SW* III, 266.
35. *SW* IV, 140.
36. *SW* IV, 124.
37. *SW* IV, 61.
38. *SW* IV, 115.
39. *SW* IV, 121.

Ibsen's *The Masterbuilder* (1892)

LUDWIG BINSWANGER

TRANSLATED BY *Vernon W. Gras*

All this background information was necessary in order to show
even in a single Ibsen drama that creative writing is truly a *seeing*,
that Ibsen, far ahead of his time, is a *seer of anthropological* forms,
and that these forms in various degrees come to light in his dramatic
production. I take for my purpose *The Masterbuilder*. The fact that
I have never seen this drama on stage is considered an interpretative
advantage by Ibsen. He expressly declared (X, 26of.) [1] that he
viewed it "as a misfortune for a dramatic work to have communicated
to the public initially through the stage. . . . The reception of the
piece becomes intertwined with its performance" which "confuses
two completely disparate things." A play should be "comprehended
and judged purely for itself as poetry." A further wish—this one
from his seventieth year and directed to the reader—seems worth
stating here: "Only by approaching and comprehending my entire
output as a whole—continuous and interrelated—will one truly
absorb the intended and correct impression of the individual parts."
Because this orientation had been ignored, "a break has occurred in
the reader's grasp of the unity of my works" resulting in "the
startling, deficient, and erroneous interpretations and analyses" of
his later works. It is important thus to remember as Ibsen himself
points out to a friend (X, 415) that the series of plays ending with
the Epilogue *When We Dead Awaken* (and including *Little Eyolf*
and *John Gabriel Borkmann*) "actually begins with *The Masterbuilder*. But," he adds with his usual shy reticence, "I do not wish
to express myself further on this point. I will leave all explanations
and commentary to you." It seems obvious to us, speaking generally,
that what the "series" has in common is the depiction of certain
possibilities of passion, especially those of the artist (which, if taken
in a wider sense, could also include *John Gabriel Borkmann*). They

also depict the possibilities of foundering in this passion. What Ibsen presents in this series with deepfelt emotion, perhaps even with his own heart's blood, are not conquerors of passion but its victims. With the single exception of *Little Eyolf*, his heroes are not life's artists but life's dilettantes.[2] The extent of Ibsen's reticence about all this may be gauged by his roguish answer to the question of whether the carpenter, Engstrand, in *Ghosts* had really burnt down the asylum or not: he said he did not know. Thus we are left to ferret out our own interpretation of Ibsen's works. But as we are not chiefly concerned with his purely artistic purposes nor even his secondary social ones but rather with the visible and tangible manifestation of his basic "symbol-idea" *viewed anthropologically*, we don't believe we can go wrong.

FIRST ACT

The "world" into which we are led by *The Masterbuilder* and which enfolds us until its end is Solness' own villa furnished in the style of the late nineteenth century. It lies within a garden hedged around by an old picket fence and with ancient trees branching over the verandah. It forms a picture of middle-class comfort well separated from the poorer neighboring area, whose street beyond the garden fence reveals a group of low, squalid houses. Inside the villa adjoined to the living quarters are located the loveless and austere workrooms of the masterbuilder. An oppressive, sultry, almost storm-laden atmosphere greets us, emanating from a dying old man, a sickly young girl who is infatuated with the masterbuilder, and the old man's son who is the girl's fiancé. Almost immediately their employer, the masterbuilder, comes in. Though a strong and healthy man in the prime of life, he displays from the beginning considerable nervous tension. To the girl he shows a secret tenderness, but otherwise he acts surly, rejecting, and potentially explosive. The old man, the masterbuilder's former employer, soon collides with his chief. Their discussion is about building. The masterbuilder refuses a building contract on the grounds that he doesn't build temporary dwellings, but solid "homes." He does not build "randomly into the blue."[3] The old man now begs that his son obtain the rejected commission and reminds the evasive masterbuilder of his prior youthful inexperience before he had swung himself up to the heights and thereby cut the ground out from under others.

Such "getting ahead" which involves cutting the ground out from under others, no matter how much of a boot-strap operation, is no true ascent. The German language has a fitting expression for this hybrid mounting and being-carried-up which appears also in the German translation of the drama: *in die Höhe kommen* (to make it aloft, i.e., succeed). It takes luck to make it aloft, which Solness himself admits. To dig the ground out from under others in order to get up in the world signifies the removal of the foundations supporting others for the purpose of transferring it to one's own use, i.e., to heighten and broaden one's own base. Already here, the opposition to be continued throughout the play—between a below and above, between foundation and superstructure—becomes noticeable. This opposition governs not only Solness' architectural structures but his life (existential) structures as well. The general congruence in the dramatic description between his work and life as a nagging disproportion between foundation and superstructure fascinates us. First of all, we are struck by the disproportion between an unscrupulously acquired and questionable foundation and the emphatically insisted upon solid superstructure which should not be randomly "built into the blue." [4] The superstructure must not equate with a mere "temporary address" (moving in today, to move out tomorrow), but with a durable, comfortable home.

The unscrupulous, almost brutal lack of concern Solness has toward the old man (Brovik) soon becomes all too evident. His urge to appropriate the possessions of others shows itself both in his suppression of the son's talents and his exploitation of the infatuated girl's love for himself. He has alienated the girl's affections from her fiancé by pretending to love her, solely to keep the young man in his employ and noncompetitive. The whole foundation on which the masterbuilder stands—above all as a masterbuilder—has been constructed and maintained with cunning.

The contradiction inherent in having such a questionable foundation while desiring a comfortable, stable superstructure finds psychological expression in Solness' self-doubts. At first we see only the consequence of his self-doubt, a mistrust, an almost agonizing fear of others. His suspicion is directed especially against the younger generation, against those who could do things better than he, who in their originality could view his work as an outmoded joke. From them he intuitively fears will come revolution and requital. His doctor, who functions somewhat like a Greek Koryphaios, seeks to calm him with the assurance that he who started as a poor boy from the country has succeeded in "soaring aloft" (that phrase again), now holds first position in his profession, and has never stood so securely, "like a tower." [5] But no help! Solness feels retribution fast approaching: "Someone or other will push himself forward with the demand 'Give me a chance.' Then will come the others with shouts and threats of 'Room! Make room!'"

What Solness has done to others he now fears will be done to him. As in dreams where conscience pangs may translate into scenes of violence [6] so even in waking does Solness picture youthful violence whose purpose will be to block him and squeeze him aside. He is incapable of taking a single step forward. He feels displaced, driven into a corner, and cut off from every outlet (and every possible future); "because once the younger generation begin to march, then it's all over with Solness, the masterbuilder," and as he later says, he will be "completely finished." For the masterbuilder, whose element is space, the world appears to reduce itself completely to the spatial category. His world design is laid out on the principle of *ôte-toi que je m'y mette*, of a spatial scarcity in which his living area is preempted by another. His existence (Dasein) already shows the dangerous signs of compression and isolation. Besides this guilt felt toward the younger generation which he projects into his shared or public space (*"mitweltlichen Raum"*), Solness is plagued by another guilt, an imaginary guilt toward his wife. In the one case he stands before a simple obstacle (hindering his "external" success), in the other he stands, by his own estimation, before a measureless and bottomless chasm forming an unconquerable obstacle to his inner (*existential*) progress. For that reason, he considers it a relief, a moment to catch his breath, a "benign act of self-justice" to allow his wife to treat him unjustly, i.e., suspect that he is truly in love with the sickly young girl. We see then: Solness is not only driven into a corner by his guilty fear of the younger generation but he is also dragged down into unfathomable depths by a guilt still unknown to us. His unjust and undeserved treatment by Mrs.

Solness momentarily relieves him from the burden of this latter guilt. His existence feels more peril on the brink of this guilty chasm than from all the constraints and oppression emanating from the younger generation. The menace latent in this guilty abyss finds its psychological manifestation in the suspicion that wife and doctor hold him to be insane.

To that, however, must still be added a third guilt in the finely drawn exposition of this piece. Solness is convinced that the young girl actually "senses" his glance when her back is turned; she trembles and shakes if he merely comes into her vicinity. The doctor, quite rightly, thinks this could be explained; on the other hand he doesn't venture to explain Solness' further report that the young girl had believed he actually spoke to her—what had only been his inner desires and wishes. Over the long run, the situation had become damned irksome because he had now to pretend continually (that he loved her). It was really a fraud done to the poor thing, but he could not do otherwise; she would leave him else and so would her fiancé. We notice that Solness' conscience is not silenced but is held in check and steadily repressed by his acquisitive drive. Whether the sickly and infatuated girl really believed that Solness had *told* her what had been merely a wish, need not concern us. What is important is Solness' credulity and his tremendous agitation that she guessed or heard his secret thoughts. In contrast to the spatial constriction and limitation of his existence, what we have here is a widening out of his existence—but it is a pseudo-existential or imaginary expansion. This motif is to recur throughout the play. It belongs to the realm of the "spirits and trolls" in which Solness lies enthralled—in short, to that demonic and superstitious world so clearly articulated by Paul Häberlin in his recent *Ethik*.[7] Demonic is "what threatens our existence, via the mystery of a transcendental, ungraspable authority." Furthermore, it is *anxiety* (*Angst*) that demonizes this objectified force. Added then to his sense of impending diminution and to the deep impalpable guilt he feels against his wife is this threat of being given over to a self-estranging demonic power. The luck to which Solness credits his success is part of this power, as will shortly become clearer.

Summarizing, we can say that Solness, the masterbuilder, must indeed and does feel threatened by the future (mistrust and doubt), by the past (guilt) as well as by the present (self-loss or disintegration). Not only is the foundation insecure under Solness, the masterbuilder, but the ground of his whole existence vacillates so that only with difficulty does he maintain his equilibrium. This accounts for his restless, tense manner that we popularly describe as being "nervous." He lacks having both feet on the ground and has already overreached himself (*sich verstiegen*). Thus we are made dizzy with our first sight of him; nor do we wonder that he himself suffers from giddiness. Dizziness is fear of the breakthrough of the completely Other, of that self- and life-alienating power of the unexpected, of the sudden turnabout and fall into the abyss.

But it now appears that the catastrophe of reversal and fall will be prevented, surprisingly through the agency of youth itself. But it is not a young man symbolizing masculine competition that knocks at his door; instead a young woman enters in the guise of eroticism. For a time the girl seems to keep the catastrophe at bay, but there remains about her a certain ambiguity; for behind her vigorous life-asserting ways lies hidden the menace of the unexpected. She combines life's forward momentum with its abrupt and precipitous fall. Nowhere else does Ibsen outdo the dramatic artistry with which he presents this tragic irony.

The young girl who had so suddenly knocked on the door of the masterbuilder is Hilda Wangel, already known to us as the *enfant terrible* in *The Sea Woman*. The reversal has arrived wearing fortune's face, but it is incomparably more dangerous than any posed by a young male competitor. Because it is no longer a question of the masterbuilder being able to continue building, it now becomes a question of his ability to continue existing. The vibrant, uninhibited young girl, who knows what she wants and pursues it indefatigably, now meets up with a man "strong and healthy in the prime of life," externally secure in his profession but inwardly keeping himself upright and aloft only with effort.

"A woman," says Nils Lykke in *Lady Inger* (II, 87) "is the most powerful being on earth and it is in her province to lead a man where God wants him to go." This symbolic theme resonates through so many of Ibsen's plays that we may assume that here speaks the playwright, himself. To Hilda Wangel it is also given to lead Solness where God wants him! She has been waiting for

Solness as the only person who can "reveal life's highest joys" to her, as Elina, Ibsen's most charming female creation, expresses it in the above drama. But Hilda belongs to those for whom life's joys are limited to the attainment of their own private and highly idiosyncratic dream worlds. Despite her preference for Vikings, she is a younger sister of Hjordis in *The Warriors at Helgeland* who wants to place her lover on "the throne of heaven" with herself at his side; however, she is not cast in the same mold as her mythological sister who, in pursuit of her plans, knows neither restraint nor consideration of others. Up to the end Hilda remains inwardly divided and lacks confidence to achieve her desires. But we are getting ahead of ourselves.

From her first entry, Hilda serves the function of memory or anamnesis. This complements the fact that the underlying action of the play has already taken place and falls outside the presentation. Hilda's task first of all consists merely in reminding the masterbuilder of that "forgotten" transaction. Step by step she lifts the veil covering the masterbuilder's "past." Ten years ago today had been the first and the last time that Hilda had seen him. At that time he was erecting the tower on the old church in her village. She reminds Solness how, wreath in hand, he had climbed straight up the scaffold "to its pinnacle." For her it had been "breathlessly exciting" to look up at him and to think "what if he should fall." She couldn't imagine another masterbuilder in the whole world who could erect such a tremendously high tower. Only to know, as she instinctively did, that he "wasn't even a little bit dizzy" more than anything caused her to reel. Then, too, he had sung while up on the tower so that it rang like "harps in the air." [8] The masterbuilder protests at first that he has never sung a note in his life but finally concedes to Hilda that it might have happened. Afterwards, she further reminds him, he had come to her father's house, taken her in his arms, kissed her many times, and promised her that he would return in ten years. "Like a troll" he would then carry her away and buy her a kingdom. Solness at first says she must have dreamed all this, but then he believes something deeper lies behind it. "I must have thought all that. I must have willed—have wanted—have longed to do it. And then—doesn't that make sense?" . . . "Oh, all right—the devil take it. Then I *did* do it." And now he admits everything that Hilda has wheedled out of him. For Solness, who is no shrinking violet when it comes to the ladies, this must constitute the workings of a long-standing repression.[9] Noteworthy, however, is that here again he lends a kind of omnipotence to thoughts and wishes that erases the dividing line between wish and reality. When this happens, the demonic, those dark, obscure life-forces, takes on a magical form. We will see how great a role this magic plays in that measureless depth of guilt Solness finds so burdensome.

Because Solness had not kept his promise, Hilda appeared at his home exactly ten years later to the day. To her question whether he still builds such tremendously high church towers, he replies no. He builds neither church towers nor churches anymore—only "homes for human beings." The superstructure of which we spoke above no longer serves to glorify God but serves only the well-being of man. Hilda—whose existence (Dasein), like the masterbuilder's, moves more in space than in time, who had experienced the intervening years simply as a tedious spatiality (as *temps espace* and not as a maturing process), and whose spatial orientation is directed completely toward the dimension of dizzying heights—Hilda would like the masterbuilder to place just "a bit of a church tower" on his homes. "Something that points up—points up free into the air. With the weather vane at a dizzying height." The masterbuilder would like nothing better, but he had to dispense with towers because "the people don't want them." People stick close to the earth, Solness seems to be saying, while Hilda and he encounter one another in the dimension of vertiginous elevation. It is purely for the sake of this dizzying altitude and with no consideration for its support (*Unterbau*) that they are brought together and are bound ever closer to each other. Because of their intimacy, Solness confides to Hilda his terrible fear of the younger generation from whom he has sealed himself off completely. He understands now that youth means retribution and "under a new banner they will herald the turn of fortune." Thus Solness admits that he, himself, has cut off the younger generation. Rather than going along with youth, as Ibsen himself did, granting them the right to critically take up his own work (what the older generation must always concede to the younger and even help facilitate), he has isolated himself in premature "age." Solness views Hilda's arrival as lucky. She helped him not only to bring to mind a vital experience that he had struggled so fruitlessly to recall but helped to free him from his powerlessness and self-imprisonment. She also had arrived under a new banner. So it was "youth against youth," for it was she whom he had missed the most. Here again comes the touch of tragic irony. Certainly Hilda succeeds in returning to the masterbuilder both recall and mastery of a forgotten moment, thereby widening and deepening the support his existence has on the past; but can she succeed on this basis to build up a new future for him? Unrestrained by a "sickly conscience," she has no second thoughts about guilt or the blessing of forgetfulness. She cannot know that forgetfulness sometimes "may be a bandage which one should not tear away." [10] To the degree, however, that she persists in her function of anamnesis, she provides us with a view into that strata which governs and controls the motif of climbing and falling so fundamental to *The Master-builder*. We refer here to the hero's "extravagant" (*verstiegenes*) relationship to God. To the social, artistic, and erotic concerns must be added the religious. But we are still a long way from discussing that. Like the dear Lord, the poet allows his people time.

SECOND ACT

Meanwhile, Hilda had found lodging in one of the three empty nursery rooms in the masterbuilder's house. Mrs. Solness, whose inner emptiness suffers dreadfully from the emptiness of these rooms, finds no joy at the prospect of soon moving into the new house built by her husband. For her there is no possibility of again "building up a real home." After Solness, despairingly, holds up to her that no sunshine, not a single glimmer of light dispels the gloom of their present home, she confesses that she knows the new house will not be a home either; it will be equally empty and bleak. So now—perplexed—they stand before the question of why they built at all—or rather, why they believed that their marriage could be put back together. Desperate, Solness again accuses his wife of thinking him a sick man. Simultaneously, he confesses to her that a burdensome guilt weighs on him. At this moment Hilda walks into the room. The dark pall of guilt disappears and everything becomes light again. Hilda reports—not by happenstance—of dreaming about falling from great heights, one of many proofs to what high level in Ibsen's dramas each detail receives its function from the whole and contributes to it; only in relationship to the dramatic problem of ascent, elevation, and sudden fall does this dream of falling find artistic justification, ignoring momentarily its transparent psychological motivation.

Once again Hilda urges and beckons Solness to the dizzy heights: like a modern Hjördis, she wishes that no other be allowed to build except him. He alone should be allowed to build and should do everything himself. Even this thought her fellow traveler on that precarious ridge to the heights had entertained previously. But he turns away now and shows her the new house. Its height is emphasized because it stands "just above the stone quarry"—i.e., over ground that has been cut away—and, in addition, has a very high tower. The scaffold still stands around the tower.

From this bizarre, scaffolded building, the poet leads us back to its builder, indicating clearly thereby that we must simultaneously direct our gaze on both, on the masterbuilder as well as the building. Building can certainly be a metaphor of the manner and extent of the realization of *self* in the *world*. Just as disproportionately high as is the building, just as jarring as its attempt to unite a cozy dwelling and a tower that "points up," just as new and "unlived in" as it appears (the scaffold), and just as close to the precipice as it stands —just so disproportionately deep is the apparent guilt of the masterbuilder, so disharmoniously is his sense of personal happiness linked to his artistic urge to reach the dizzying heights, so cold and inhospitable appears his wedded happiness, and so dangerously does his existence stand before a bottomless precipice. What until now had sounded the prelude reveals itself herewith to our understanding, thanks to the memory-freeing power of erotic recollection. The themes that till now had found utterance from various voices, one after another, are now sounded with the compact resolution of a fugue: the present house stands where the former house inherited by Mrs. Solness had once stood, surrounded by a large garden. From without, it was an ugly wooden box, but from within it was "cozy and comfortable." It had no trace of a tower! Twelve years ago this house burnt to the ground. "An accident? It all depends . . ." The fire, as Solness himself says, had been the means which helped him succeed, whereby he had "made it aloft." "The fire was the making of me." That the fire provides the central motif for the drama is evidenced by a poem which appeared in March, 1892, the year at whose end the drama was completed. It's entitled "They sat there, both of them" and has the undertitle: "Preliminary work on *The Masterbuilder*" (I, 169). The poem in English translation (Binswanger gives a German translation):

> They sat there both of them in the snug house,
> Watched Autumn and Winter go by.
> The house burnt down, all horror and ruin.
> Naught left but to sift the ashes.
>
> For under the rubble is hidden a jewel
> That no fire can destroy;
> And if they diligently search, perhaps
> He or she will uncover the treasure.
>
> But though they—fire impoverished—
> Recovered that rare stone—
> She will not find the trust that vanished
> Nor he the luck that has gone.

The problem that Ibsen does not resolve in *The Masterbuilder*, the search and failure to find a new happiness, finds its resolution in his following play, *Little Eyolf*. There the marriage is patched up again after an "impoverishment" by a courageous renunciation of earthly satisfaction and a look "upwards to the stars, into the great stillness." Success there, but in *The Masterbuilder* as well as in *The Epilogue* again, breakdown and failure! Only by a true and proper "climbing" aloft, only by an inner transformation, by a subordination to the "law of change" (to use Ibsen's own term) will that jewel allow itself to be discovered in the "horror and ruin" which may lead to reconstruction and ascent. The above poem also reveals that the Hilda–Solness theme plays a secondary role—that of retarding *and* precipitating the catastrophe. That Hilda predominates, despite this, has its reasons. She is the antithesis of Mrs. Solness, who has given her life to joyless duty and to whom the masterbuilder feels "chained as to a dead person." Against Mrs. Solness, who symbolizes death, a life-hostile emptiness, the leaden weight of the past, and a bleak hopelessness—Hilda represents "life," vitality and fullness, glowing hope, and an erotic, upward impulse which, nevertheless, must not be mistaken for the "power of love." In the event of the old home burning down, the earlier and separate motifs of "getting to the top" by cutting the ground out from under others, of feeling guilty and of wishing omnipotently—become united. After the fire, the estate was subdivided into lots. Even though Solness was no architect—he lacked the systematic training (and one surmises that he could have been harder on himself)— he now could build "according to his own taste," giving his artistic talents free reign so that "things really leapt forward." Now he could build what he himself had lost in the fire: "Homes for human beings. Cozy, comfortable, light-filled homes, where father and mother and troops of children could live happily and securely, feeling that it is wonderful to be alive in the world" and above all "to belong to each other in great things and small." But what a price he had to pay for all this! To renounce "for all time" ever to have a home for himself. Ibsen expresses it here as well as in *The Epilogue* and in *Brand* that such renunciation is required from the individual who lives the life of the mind, particularly the artist, who sacrifices personal happiness for a life as *passion* (including both meanings of the word). "That price," says Solness, undoubtedly in agreement here with the poet himself, "that price was demanded of me as an artist." [11] The yearning of the "poor boy from the country" for that "divine happiness" to have a family of his own had to give way to a life dedicated exclusively to art—a situation Ibsen had already applied to himself in the poem "On the Vidda." Certainly we must recognize the artist in Solness. His art, "to build according to his own taste," not *just* ambition, spurs him to the heights. At the time of the fire, Mrs. Solness had been carried outside into the icy cold and caught a fever. That affected her milk and the twins died. Since then the masterbuilder had given up building churches. But the worst consequence, in Solness' opinion, was that his wife's "vocation had been stunted and crushed and shattered." Her vocation had been to build up "children's souls in perfect balance and in noble and beautiful forms . . . enabling them to grow into erect, mature human souls." Plainly, what Solness lacked in respect to his own balance, proportionality, and form: that "elevation" into an erect and noble human being—something for which the visionary artist and creator in him had a clear eye and deep love: these at least he had hoped for his posterity, the twins. And he agrees with Pestalozzi, that this kind of artistic vocation belongs to motherhood.

The young assistant now comes in and begs earnestly that Solness write a few encouraging lines to show his dying father. This interlude acts both to retard and to aggravate the development of the guilt motif. Solness again refuses the request—which Hilda, showing her better nature, castigates as "horribly ugly" and "hard, wicked, and cruel." Only when it is too late does Hilda succeed in getting the masterbuilder to send the dying man a few friendly words. Solness denies Hilda the right to judge him, considering the "price he paid for his position." He had sacrificed not only his domestic comfort but the peace of his soul as well. He alone could judge the matter, not she.

The motif fusion of Solness' guilt with his belief in the magical power of thought, his making it to the top, and the constriction of his existential situation all lead back to a small structural defect— a little dark crack in the chimney of the old house. Ibsen's artistry in presenting essential human truths in visual and tangible forms reaches its consummate level here. It is as if the rift in the chimney began to speak; as if this "heavy-lipped, dead and silent, cinderblock orifice" began to shout, as George Britting puts it in a poem. From out of this inert, fire-mouth speaks the living breath of the masterbuilder. "Through that little, dark crack I could perhaps force my way to the top" was the playful, alluring, and irresistibly enticing thought which he entertained. This was his gamble with fate, his frivolity in self-governance, to use Ibsen's terms. Even though later he was able to ascertain that the crack in the chimney did not cause the fire, his resultant guilt feeling became ineradicable. It hung together with his exaggerated (verstiegenen) notion of belonging to an elect. Did not Hilda agree that "there exist specially chosen people" who had been graced with the power and faculty of desiring something—of craving something— of willing it—so persistently and unshakably—that at last it has to happen? Earlier he had already asked Hilda whether she had not observed the indefinable allure of the impossible. We recall also what Solness said about the relationship between his thoughts and acts toward the child, Hilda (after climbing the church steeple), and what he had confided to the doctor concerning Miss Fosli's guessing his thoughts. Here, however, the omnipotence of thought becomes magic, a conjuration of "the helpers." For Solness points out "nobody achieves such great things alone . . . The helpers and servers also must do their part if something is to come of it." But "they never come of themselves. One has to call on them very persistently—sort of from within." [12] Had that not been the case, the house "would never have burnt down so conveniently." It wouldn't have happend to old Brovik "who doesn't know how to call the helpers, nor for the servers, either." Because he had called on them in his hubris, Solness feels blame for the death of his twins and for his wife never functioning as she was intended. That is what people call "being lucky!" But he experiences this luck as "a great raw place on his breast. And the helpers and servers flay off the skin from others in order to close my sore." But the sore will never heal. "How at times it gnaws and festers!" The contrast of brutality and sensibility in Solness's nature had not escaped the more robust Hilda; penetratingly, she calls it being sent into the world with a sickly conscience, a conscience "so delicate that it can absorb no shocks; it hasn't the strength to lift or bear anything heavy." Hilda sees the fissure very well that extends through Solness' whole existence, the fissure between inconsiderate brutal exploitation of others, including every situation that offers—and the sickly, delicately built conscience which can bear no heavy burden. She perceives that the foundation is too weak to carry the superstructure, i.e., the desire to-make-one's-way-at-any-cost. This delicacy, however, that can bear no weight nor stand any shocks is precisely the agency dragging Solness down into the abyss. Both seek to overcome this downward drag—Hilda pursued and driven thither by the memory and hope of her love (as she says); Solness carried upward by the radiance of her youth and her evanescent spirit. Because she restores his youth and deceives his despondent spirit away, she is the "being he has missed the most." In the exuberance of his love he sees in her "the approaching day," the "view into the sunrise." Instead of gaining from her love a "higher" ordination or direction, he sees in her only the working of the trolls. It is the troll in her as in himself ("the troll in us") which "calls down the external powers," like it or not.

There are two kinds of "willing," says Rebecca West in *Rosmersholm*: one kind pulls and attracts a little at a time; the other decides on the basis of free choice. Such is the only phenomenological description of the "theoretical" difference between instinct (urge) and true *willing*. What we see here is the instinctual willing at work, decked out, to be sure, in magical disguise.

Hilda tries to oppose the sickly conscience with what is robust, strong, and healthy—we are almost tempted to say with the Nietzschean conscience that dares do what it most wants to do. That is *one* method of merging the two into one kind of willing. Hilda, still at odds with herself, succeeds in tempting the masterbuilder to will *in this fashion* and causes his downfall. His own will is irremediably broken. Already he fears that the helpers and servers will no longer obey him because the fight has cost him too much agony. He appears at the end of his strength without possibility of a new ascent. He feels the reversal closing in again, the retaliation of those whose ground he had taken away. By speaking so, he makes Hilda frantic, for he takes from her "what is more than (her) life," namely, to see her beloved great again. She expresses here an ingredient of every mature and genuine feminine love; however, the manner in which she wants to see him great, e.g., "in the heights," is avowedly childish if not overstrained. She wants to see the masterbuilder as previously "with a wreath in hand, high, high up on a church tower." For the present, however, he must write—and this wish is not overstrained but a genuine expression of feminine sympathy—some laudatory words on the young man's designs for the sake of his dying father. His earlier cruelty and hardness was petty, not magnanimous. Once this is accomplished, however, her overstrained wish to see him high up returns immediately. Mrs. Solness' remark, whether she knew how dizzy extreme heights made her husband, gives Hilda's faith in him a severe jolt. Could it be "that *my* masterbuilder *dares* not—cannot—climb as high as he builds?" In other words: Is he *himself* unable to do what he demands of others, and is the situation such that while impossibilities attract and fascinate, he is too *cowardly*—the worst disappointment for an enraptured, feminine heart—to attempt it? No! That couldn't be true: "Don't tell me you ever were dizzy?" With that Hilda deludes herself about his weakness and on her side constructs expectations higher than the masterbuilder can surmount. But he allows himself to be carried into the dizzying heights, imagining himself capable of the deed: "This evening then, we will hang up the wreath— Princess Hilda."

THIRD ACT

Before Hilda experiences the fulfillment of her utmost wish, she has yet to descend into a "tomb" in which she is "chilled to the marrow" and from whose confinement she wants to flee. Once more she has the opportunity to turn back and leave the masterbuilder to himself. The earlier tomblike atmosphere encountered in the workrooms of the "successful" masterbuilder now hits us with even greater force from his living quarters—the dark, unlit rooms of his married life. Hilda discovers with an icy shudder that here are two people chained together, complete strangers to each other, and separated by a void of misunderstanding. She is horror-struck at a marriage built up on mutual falsification of the partner's true being, on a foundation which can support neither genuine existence nor future renewal. It smells of the grave, of that lifeless, decaying odor of a past no longer having a future. Hate does not separate the masterbuilder and his wife—hate is still a sign of life—but, in view of their long life together, their almost unbelievable ignorance of each other's true nature separates them. Their true selves suffer inversion from fantastically exaggerated idealizations. It is relatively harmless, of course, when Mrs. Solness tries to allay Hilda's fears about the masterbuilder's fierce demeanor by saying "in reality he is gentle and kind." True enough, he can be gentle and kind, but he also can be very brutal. Hilda experiences the greatest shock, however, when Mrs. Solness reveals her own true nature. Hilda realizes that what oppresses and darkens the masterbuilder's conscience rests on a self-destructive illusion. It is not the loss of the twins that Mrs. Solness can't forget, so that nothing is more mistaken than Solness' belief that he had destroyed his wife's vocation "to build up children's souls." The twins' death after the fire Mrs.

Solness merely assigns to a "higher Providence" to which one must submit and even give thanks. We should feel joy for the two babies because "they are so happy now." "No, it is the small losses in life that grieves one's heart." These small losses are her nine "lovely" dolls and all the clothes, lacework, jewelry, portraits she had inherited from her mother and grandmother. Nobody thought to save these items during the fire. This constitutes her silent reproach against her husband, even though she has never admitted to him her attachment to the dolls. While she had gone on living with the dolls after her marriage, she had done so only in his absence. In fact, Mrs. Solness views the loss of the twins as a "righteous punishment" for not "having enough fortitude in misfortune" about losing these "trivialities." The real loss had been and remains the dolls. For "in their own way, there was life in them, too. I carried them under my heart—like unborn little children."

That Ibsen has sketched here in highly visible and tangible form the characteristics of introversion, infantilism, narcissism, and mother-fixation, before the studies of Freud and Jung, interests us less than how "unsuitable" he shows this misshapen soul to be for marriage and "the proper building up" of children's souls, and how deep the misunderstanding is on which the Solness marriage rests. The ghastly, deeply immoral experience of having lived together as strangers had been presented in Ibsen's *Doll's House*, "At this moment," says Nora to her husband, "I came to the realization that for eight years I have lived together with a strange man, and that I have had three children with him. I can't think about it. I'd gladly kill myself." (VI, 373). In *The Masterbuilder* this realization is made by neither marriage partner; it comes to consciousness only in a third person, Hilda. But in both plays, however, the doll is a symbol of life-denial, of a fraudulent marriage. In contrast to Nora, who feels herself degraded to a lifeless puppet, Mrs. Solness makes of the dolls living beings, imaginary children, more real, vital, and meaningful to her existence than actual children. Mrs. Solness is a completely different person than what the masterbuilder imagines her to be—she is no real mother except to puppets. She exists separate from him in the realm of an impotent, futureless past, in the realm of death. The fire had actually burnt away her past, her only mode of existence. For her, life had withdrawn, indicated already by her mechanical obedience to the dictates of duty. We perceive that these dummy imitations which the anticipatory imaginings of children can endow with life are still so viewed by Mrs. Solness and even preferred to those given her through painful childbirth. Like Hilda, we are almost overcome with pity for the masterbuilder. We understand ever more clearly how he yearns to lift himself out of the dark tomb which is his home, in which no ray of sunshine, no gleam of light falls. The inexorable tragedy lies in the alternatives from which Solness has to choose—either to crawl around as if entombed, or to soar up in an imaginary dream world. To stand and walk on the firm earth is denied him, particularly as he has dug away the ground from everybody else. His existence (Dasein) can only sink down or soar aloft. That is Solness, the masterbuilder! Imprisoned in the dark past, he can only view his future as terribly dark and empty. Thus he believes the erotically tinged "castle-in-the-air" offers the only means of escape. He has no conception of an actual true "present"—neither through work nor through love. Life's challenge has been botched; the drama of his life has miscarried. We cannot blame Hilda, having obtained an insight into all this, for judging it as foolish, "so very foolish." She has to look on while the masterbuilder remains firmly convinced that his wishes, "those devilish powers and the troll within (him)," have sucked all the life-blood out of his wife so that he recognizes, "I am chained alive to a dead woman. I—who cannot live without joy in life." Solness is certainly right about the fire having sucked out the life-blood of his wife, but he is grotesquely wrong about the nature of the loss. The poet puts it into Hilda's grasp to rectify his error. She is free to show him that his marriage never had been "a true intimacy" but from the beginning only a locus for mistaken trust. After she comes to know a good deal of the masterbuilder's life-history, Ibsen leaves it to her to step in and free him from his marriage by founding a new one, to give his life a truly historical dimension. But she is incapable of doing this, for she, herself, is essentially an "ahistorical" being. Unable to found a new home with the masterbuilder, she merely tempts him with erotic fantasies about castles-in-the-air. A real woman, no child-woman like Hilda, could have succeeded in bringing Solness out of his error into a true, healthy, and whole marriage relationship.

Though it is not our purpose to interpret or evaluate *The Master-builder* artistically, it should be noted how the report of Mrs. Solness about the fire and its effect on her increases the dramatic tension by impeding the action. The play's progress falls into abeyance, a suspension. While suspended, the play opens to new dramatic possibilities from which, however, the tragic fall and catharsis will now be seen to flow inevitably and necessarily. Once again retardation serves to precipitate action. But how much more complicated do we find the situation here than in ancient plays! In them a messenger informed us about external happenings or encounters, here the report concerns a highly complex subjective experience. In the earlier plays, fate carried and decided the action; now freedom must carry and decide it—a freedom, of course, that includes a false freedom.

Let us follow the remaining action. Corresponding to the sole proclivity of her *Dasein* (to ascend into dizzying heights), Hilda neither lingers in that icy tomb into which she briefly and shudderingly glimpsed nor does she pull herself together for any firm commitment. She seems unable to leave the masterbuilder to his own devices nor able to take a strong stand on his marriage. The dramatic tension ebbs away, leaving room for the last wave—the tension-filled relationship of the masterbuilder to God.

Instead of coping with the problem of the masterbuilder's joyless marriage, Hilda merely complains that he is married already, that "one cannot grasp at his own happiness" just because "someone you know stands in the way." At this decisive moment, however, it is Solness who frees Hilda "out of the cage," who reawakens in her the "bird of prey" whose desire is "to hunt in the free air." He reminds her of having "a robust conscience." Once he has achieved this, Hilda returns to being the upward driving force. The moment for decisive action in the realm of the *possible* is irredeemably lost. In its place steps once again the "extravagant wish" (*verstiegener Wunsch*) belonging to the realm of the *impossible*. Her castle will stand "on a very great height," high above "the other people" with a clear outlook on all sides "so that (she) can see far—far around." It will have "a tremendously high tower" and at the top of the tower there will be a balcony on which she will stand and look out over the other people—on those building churches and homes for human beings. Hilda now becomes complete enticement in its most seductive form—that of biting irony: if the masterbuilder desires, he may come up, too, and then the two of them will build "the most lovely thing in all the world—*castles-in-the-air*." They are "so comfortable to take refuge in. And so easy to build, especially for those builders who suffer from a dizzy conscience." Hilda's provoking and whiplike derision recalls the scorn of Hedda Gabler, though the former rests on disappointed love, while the latter on hate and contempt.

Before the turning point or ultimate catastrophe arrives, Hilda's function as anamnesis comes to light once more; for the manifest action can't be closed off prior to closing off the latent action operating at the lowest existential depths. Now for the first time, the abyss before which Solness stands becomes plainly visible. Combined with his social excavating (his cutting the ground out from others—his guilt over against the younger generation) and his existential excavation (his guilt-thoughts concerning his wife) must be placed the religious excavation (his guilt toward God). Now for the first time the masterbuilder's "overreach," his hubris, and anxiety about retaliation become *absolutely clear*. As a "pious lad from the country" he had believed no worthier profession existed than to build churches. But still God was not satisfied with him; otherwise he would not have granted trolls and devils to rage so in him. When God had turned the house into rubble and ashes and had taken away the twins, He did so to give Solness "opportunity to become a master" in his profession, in order "to build for Him even more glorious churches." God had taken his little ones so that he "would be bound by nothing else . . . no such things as love and happiness." [13] Whereas he had never been able "to climb up to a great free height" he did do it one single time—that instance when Hilda gazed up at him enthralled. At that moment, he now clearly remembers he had battled through to his proper relationship to God. "And as I stood up there at that great height and hung the wreath around the weather vane, I spoke to him: Now hear me, Mighty one! From this day forward I will be a free builder—I, too, in *my* sphere—as you in yours. Never again will I build churches for you, but only homes for human beings." Later, however, it all went God's way again—because "building homes for human beings—isn't worth a straw . . . people have no use for these homes of theirs to be happy in." We stand here before the abyss of utter meaning-lessness: "Nothing really built. And no sacrifice made for being able to build. Nothing, nothing—the whole is nothing."

Undoubtedly, we have here an expression of that despair which so often gnawed at Ibsen ferociously—a despair about his art, his own talent, and understanding for his art; a despair about God and about his fellowman. Such despair belongs to passion and in fact escorts it steadfastly as loyal companion!

Despite or, perhaps, because of this nothingness, Solness wants to start over. Until now he had built without loving and without being loved; now he is going to build hand-in-hand with a young woman from whom he demands that she "believe in him uncondi-tionally." [14] Hilda, however, can only believe in him if she sees him "free and high up" again. She wants him to do the *impossible* again. Solness will try it. This time, like the last, he is going to address God and tell him: "Hear me, mighty Lord—you may judge me as you deem fit. But from this day forth I shall build only the loveliest thing in the world . . . build it with a princess with whom I am in love . . . and then go down and throw my arms around her and kiss her." "The princess shall have her castle." "*Our* castle," throws in Hilda. "But," adds Solness, "on a solid foundation." Mrs. Solness enters and pleads with her husband to "stay down below—only down below." Solness answers: "That is what I always do—on everyday occasions."

The joyless work-a-day below or the enchanting castle-in-the-air above; his moldering, gloomy corner of "reality" or the bright, airy reaches of extravagant heights; routine or challenge; being chained to a corpse or enticed by an ebullient spirit; to hide himself from God or demand of Him a decision; to live threatened eternally by retaliation, in a present heavily burdened by the past, or to live governed by a future that is heroic, love-filled and free, and purely artistic! Such are the alternatives facing the master-builder.

Hilda has accomplished her mission. She has fulfilled her role of anamnesis by bringing the masterbuilder to an almost complete breakdown, to an open confrontation with nothingness, thereby freeing him for a new beginning and a new future. Indeed, she has done more. She has freed the masterbuilder from an existence that had become immobilized and *made possible* his return to an existence in real time. The masterbuilder's completely ahistorical life constricted within a spatially conceived time has through its contact with her transformed itself back into the continuity of a life-*history*. Hilda, to some degree at least, has reopened the masterbuilder's historical existence. Once more it is possible for him to make a decision, but once more he falls to temptation.

To be sure, the poet allows us a mixture of hope and fear. Our suspense couldn't be greater. While Mrs. Solness perishes with terror, while the young assistant first sneers that now they can watch how "he who has held us down for so very long" will "keep quietly down below, himself" only to admit his error as in wide-eyed amazement he watches the masterbuilder actually climbing the scaffold —Hilda stares fixedly upward, convinced that he *can* achieve the *impossible*. But hardly has he arrived at the top when vertigo tumbles him into the excavated depths of the stone quarry where he lies crushed. Hilda, meantime, has heard again "harps in the air"; in stillness, she has reached her "inner triumph" to see *her* masterbuilder "mount right to the top." She whirls her shawl upward and screams with wild ardor, "My—my masterbuilder!"

Hilda's *Liebestraum* has reached conclusion, but it cost the masterbuilder his life. The "troll in her" had awakened the "troll in him," but instead of directing it and like a mature adult, building it into his life, Solness allowed the troll to invert the lower in him into the higher so that, contrary to his own stated principle, he built "at random into the blue" without a firm foundation. But Hilda, too, has sinned against the spirit of love, both in its nurture and nature. She has falsified the *we* of love into the *I* of self-love, what should be *ours* into *mine*, into *her* sensation of suspense and triumph. In contrast to a truly loving woman who leads her beloved there where God wants him, Hilda has misled Solness to where she wanted him. But God judged him according to His own yardstick and let him fall.

With that, the four skillfully united levels of action are consummated: the religious, the demonic-superstitious, the erotic, and the existential. God let the masterbuilder fall; the "helpers" let him fall; Hilda—who allowed him to climb up alone while she remained below—let him fall; and—most of all—he let himself fall. Those who did *not* let him fall—significantly enough—were the dead person to whom he is chained and who wishes to keep him down below at all costs, and the male younger generation who disbelieves his ability to climb at all. But it is precisely against his wife and the younger generation that his suspicions were directed (e.g., that she thought him crazy and they wanted his ruination)—evidence that Solness saw his enemies where they weren't and, contrariwise, failed to see in Hilda those qualities that made her a deadly adversary rather than an ally. This double deception is not something peculiar to the masterbuilder but is shared in general by mankind. As long as we have not found ourselves but labor under self-deception, we will also be susceptible to deception practiced on us by others. This sentence has special relevance to the persecution mania Ibsen actually makes visible in the masterbuilder.

The poet leaves no doubt which of the four levels carries the others, and which he considers the decisive one: it is the last—the level of the individual and his self-realization. For God is treated here from the viewpoint of man—not man from God's. Ibsen has no use for a theo-anthropology; he recognizes only an anthropology. For him "the highest value" is not God but—we are quite certain—man as he "realizes" himself in the self-guidance of his life.

Why did Solness botch his life and not attain this highest goal? Why did he *have* to fall, even though Hilda had placed him back into the continuity of his life-history and freed him from his "empty spatial existence"? The answer is obvious: his reawakening had been merely an "erotic" affair, not an awakening in the sense of true love or even a real "existential enlightenment." Solness had as little likelihood of achieving a proper relationship to love or to himself as he did to God. Just as he, a child of pious country folk, confused God with a stern master who wished to force him into His service and to punish him for his disobedience, so he confuses love, Eros, with the merely "erotic." Love alone is able to release an individual from a "spatialized existence" and relate him properly to time and to himself. Nothing of that is visible here. Out of collapse and the confrontation of nothingness comes no remorse or rebirth, no metamorphosis or real change, no true regeneration (Wider-Holung in Kierkegaard's sense) but only a repetition of a single past experience

—mounting the tower and measuring himself with God. What is involved here is a "leap" out of a past "space-time" into a future "space of time." But that moment of destiny, the kairos, cannot be forced and even less so can God. His "beginning" was no real *decision* for a new life, no historical process out of a genuine life-history into a future history, but an erotically conditioned "leap into uncertainty," into impossibility, and "into the blue." The "beginning" signifies no real climbing of the heights, at any rate not just that, but primarily a being-carried-upwards, indeed a being driven by an erotic *wish*. If the masterbuilder now wants to climb as high as he can build, that means he regards the foundation, his own past, as capable of carrying and supporting the superstructure, his future, especially since this superstructure consists of a castle-in-the-air. Even so, he finds it advisable to stress the necessity of "good support masonry" for this castle-in-the-air. He seems oblivious of the entangling contradiction. Quite apart from the architectural mistake of providing solid foundations to an airy superstructure or of setting an airy superstructure on a solid base, the masterbuilder repudiates his early view of building, the principle "not to build randomly into the blue" (see Act I). Though indispensable and necessary for human existence, such "dream castles" built into the blue may serve as temporary quarters but never as permanent dwellings. In contrast to his earlier serious intent about building, the "dream-castle" to which Hilda repeatedly invites him now becomes the loveliest object imaginable. If the masterbuilder stands for the creative individual, the artist, then Ibsen is showing us the danger within all creativity, the danger of "building into the blue."

The castle-in-the-air, that disproportionate and unarchitectural structure, even more disproportionate than that "new home" with its high tower at the edge of the stone quarry, signifies—we reiterate —the faulty relationship between past and future, i.e., the fissure or discontinuity in the masterbuilder's self-realization, in his genuine individualization. His future is not truly absorbed into the present out of the past, but is anticipated "fantastically" as a "fantastic" repetition of a past experience. The masterbuilder desires to *reverse* the ripening of time (which, as Weininger sees it, is *the* problem of life [15]), or at least *invert* it. His is no ascent to the heights but extravagant behavior at its highest. Instead of the temporal "ekstasies" of a true ripening, we find mere repetition and anticipation in space-time "phases." Instead of a true recall of the past with its inward change of "remorse and regeneration" in conformity to the call of conscience, we find a being-carried-upward (which ignores conscience) into an "impossible" future, into a future serving as an empty space for the impossible. The label given to this temporal extravagance in the spatial context, a self-deception in respect to one's own powers and maturity, is *dizziness*. Induced by the ignored conscience, it is fear of a sudden, self-alienating reversal, of an internal and external overthrow, of a catastrophe. Silenced momentarily by Hilda but brought thereby to face its most dangerous ordeal, this fear breaks out again at the top of the tower and also breaks the masterbuilder's neck. Of the many Ibsen characters who desire to climb higher than they are able, Solness, the masterbuilder, is merely the most concrete and visible. Jarl Skule in *Pretender to the Throne*, Emperor Julian, Catilina and Gunnar quite early in *The Warriors at Helgeland*, as well as Peer Gynt and that windy, unprincipled agitator, Stensgard, in *League of Youth*— all wish to mount higher than they are able. But none of these figures express it so palpably as Solness, who could not climb as high as he built. Building is, of course, a quite easily understood symbol for self-realization. When firmly grounded and built, it is symbolic of the *achieved security* of self-in-the-world. For that reason we find building expressions quite frequently in Ibsen's dramas, beginning with site descriptions appearing as "solid ground" or as "precarious swamp-ground," or as "camouflaged abyss." Building itself was already referred to in *Pretender to the Throne*. Moreover, we read in *Brand* (IV, 161):

> A building has already forfeited its right
> Should it desire to reach the stars.

In *Emperor and Galilean*, the brothers Gallos and Julian each build a wing onto a church. Gallos finishes; Julian doesn't, because, as Agathon says, the architect *hadn't faith enough in the cause* which the building was to serve, a motif which in a sense turns up again with Solness, whose new faith in himself had been erected purely on Hilda's (shaken) faith in him. On both occasions, an unfinished building symbolizes the self's uncertainty of belief and trust, the first in religion and the second in oneself. In *League of Youth*, "building" has almost the same meaning as venturing something. "What do you wish to build further?" asks Fjeldbo. To which Stensgard replies: "Build? First, it means tearing down" (VI, 25). In *Pillars of Society* "bygone time with its sham and hollowness" is referred to as a museum (VI, 267); similarly in *The Masterbuilder*, the old house represents the past and the new house the future, albeit a comfortless, bleak future. In like fashion, the three bare rooms in which the action takes place represent the barrenness of the past gutted by fire, and the empty nursery in the new house (VIII, 395) the emptiness of the future. Homes for human beings give "tangible" form to happy family life; churches to religious union with God; and church towers to the faith that points to heaven.

However, Ibsen's genius in the art of making "the essence of things" visible, of giving a Gestalt to the essential Dasein modes is most clearly revealed in modes diametrically opposed to that of the masterbuilder. No longer is it a matter of someone who wishes to mount or to build higher than he can climb, but of someone who quietly and relevantly builds on the earth. We refer to the previously mentioned roadbuilder, Borgheim, in *Little Eyolf*, the drama written immediately after *The Masterbuilder*. It is as if Ibsen deliberately wanted to present in this figure the counterpart of Solness. Borgheim doesn't pursue an impossible happiness; rather, he is a "pathfinder of happiness," one who desires no more than he can achieve and whose achievement, in the words of Ibsen's editor (IX, xvii), "therefore continues to grow: the most joyous character Ibsen created, a person who builds roads and who feels fortunate to be a roadbuilder; a person, who, between completed work and work just starting, views life as a game; a person who bears his hardships and trouble alone but who wants to share his happiness; a person with endurance enough to be a pathmaker; a person who courageously seizes life's blessings, even before he has completely earned it. Over against Allmers, sicklied o'er with the pale cast of thought, the poet deliberately sets Borgheim with his Fortinbras disposition, which desires nothing it can't achieve, and achieves everything it desires—even that reserved girl who really belongs to another." In this presentation, the human type psychiatry labels *syntonic* or the *synchronic* comes to the fore, just as in *The Master-builder* the schizoid type found illustration. But how much more tangibly and visibly does the poet sketch in these two types, the lonely "striver" and he, who is "in tune" and "in time" with society and nature (the *mit- und Umwelt*). On one side, there is a building into the heights with no care given about support or "proportion," an activity always threatened by falling, or sudden collapse; on the other side, a building *upon* the earth not *above* it, thus on firm foundation and in harmony with its ground, with no possibility of collapse. On one side, the heavy spirit of being earth-bound which struggles to rise above itself but is always dragged down again; on the other, a spirit, earth-buoyant and free, which neither seeks to climb the heights nor stays glued to the earth; it moves forward easily. (There is still another "spirit of buoyancy" which, contrary to *earth*-buoyant, is *air-borne* or flighty. Being neither earth-bound nor earth-buoyant, it has no weight at all and is blown where the wind lists.)

Only when we compare the Gestalts of the roadbuilder and the masterbuilder does the meaning of anthropological proportion, of the ratio between the vertical and horizontal become entirely clear. In the roadbuilder, this ratio has equilibrium: the horizontal or, statically expressed, the breadth of the foundation is able to carry the height of the superstructure without strain. The road-builder's breadth of experience, that which he has learned, which he has honestly appropriated, is completely adequate to serve as foundation to his activity; his striving, in turn, goes no higher than his "experience" allows. In Ibsen's terms: the life-conduct of the road-builder has brought possibility and reality, capability and plans, life and learning, into harmony. Contrariwise, the masterbuilder: he made things easy for himself; he failed to learn enough to become an architect; and he dug the ground out from under others to appropriate this alien ground for himself. So now he stands there on an admittedly high but narrow pedestal. In addition, he had dug the ground out from under his wife and his God and taken it for himself. The pedestal soars ever higher and becomes ever narrower. The balance between the horizontal and the vertical is *disturbed* so that not only must the masterbuilder become dizzy but we must, too, who observe with what effort he maintains his equilibrium. How inevitable that we perceived him from the beginning to be tense and anxious. Hilda, whose personality base appears somewhat broader, but who erects her life on a *single* childhood memory of dizzying height and who similarly desires to climb higher than she is able— indicated by her dreams of falling—not only places her beloved on a pedestal as do all lovers but incites him to the very top of a tower scaffolding. Her willful but uncertain belief in him goads him, already overextended for his too-narrow base, to go even higher. We arrive then not at a firm, well-proportioned structure, but at the scaffold of a most ill-proportioned new building. The anthropological proportion so long out of kilter is now strained to the utmost. For that reason we await with anxious suspense the unavoidable fall into the abyss; yet when it occurs, we agree to its "fateful" necessity. What the anthropologist could only express in a labored, awkward description and interpretation, the dramatist with his "higher insight into things" constructs in *visible* and *graspable* form as a dramatic masterpiece.

The Masterbuilder, as so many—even the majority—of Ibsen's plays, portrays the drama of human "extravagance" (*Verstiegenheit*). Nowhere else is the nature of extravagance so clearly presented as here, both in its spatial as well as temporal traits. If the first predominate, it is for the reason that the drama takes place on the "stage of life," in lived space as the essential structure of time. Extravagance, however, is one way of bungling life's potential, of not reaching the mark and of trivializing the conduct of life. It is— as a miscarrying of the Dasein—an immanent possibility to human existence in general. As that being "assigned" to climb the heights, to transcend and "overreach" his condition, not just horizontally but vertically, man by his very nature is threatened by the fall, the drop into the abyss. Nobody experiences this danger more intensely than the artist himself for whom art is transcendence, and who transcends or realizes himself in the art *work*. Ibsen experienced the tragedy and passion of the artist, poetically creating from this experience as very few have done. *The Masterbuilder*, artistically more complete than *The Epilogue* which has the same theme, depicts the artist's tragedy, his threatened, fragile life-style, his career as passion—specifically in the form of its miscarrying and extravagance. If Ibsen once said that every one of his plays was a natural outcome of a particular moment in his life experience,[16] we must assume that the tragedy of being an artist must have affected him deeply, especially in his later years. Though it is peculiar to the work of art (as Simmel says) to pose its problem out of itself as finished product, we need not be deterred from turning our regard from the artwork back to the artist. The problem central to *The Masterbuilder* as artwork is (as we say) that of human extravagance in general. But we must not forget when in the drama the helpers, Hilda, and God let the masterbuilder fall—that in the last analysis it is the dramatist who lets him fall. Transformed into the masterbuilder, the alter ego of the poet must fall as a painfully loosened and shed husk, as a scapegoat for the security of his real "whole" self in the world. Even this sacrifice—it perhaps most of all—belongs to the passion and suffering of the artist, to that bridging of the abyss between the artist taken as "typical" and taken as "whole" man. If Ibsen allows Solness to fall while keeping himself afloat we see in that a "healing" act to secure himself in the world, to realize the whole self through art, specifically in Ibsen's two senses of holding on to the highest as well as purging the bottom sediment: what kind of sediment he purged at that moment in his life when he wrote *The Masterbuilder* we neither know nor need to (though easily surmised from the work). To discover and describe the various relations and correspondences between life and work we leave to biographers and literary historians. For us the fact that Ibsen realized himself in his artwork suffices; for him, dramatic art meant "transcendence," that surpassing which kept him "buoyant" and repeatedly kept him from marring his life-options, from that disproportion between the horizontal and the vertical. Then, too, we find it easy to dispense with the establishment of life and work correspondences because, with Paul Valéry, we are convinced that in regard to artistic creativity "*tout ce que l'histoire peut observer est insignifiant.*" [17] Let us then be content with a comparison in which building once more is the issue but involving that which consecrates such building and gives it its value. In *Pretender to the Throne*, King Hakon says to Duke Skule:

> Don't you see that the kingdom of Norway can only be compared to a church lacking its consecration? The walls rise up on strong pillars, the vault arches spaciously above, the spire

points to heaven like a forest pine; but the edifice has no life; it lacks the beating heart and fresh circulating blood; God's living breath hasn't been breathed into it: it has yet to receive its consecration.—I seek to consecrate it.[18]

Just such a structure are Ibsen's dramatic writings. We could not attend his life's work with the great interest we do, had it not been consecrated by way of the poet's beating heart and the divine breath of his art.

NOTES

1. All of Binswanger's citations are from Henrik Ibsen's *Sämtliche Werke* (Berlin, 1898–1904).

2. Looked at from a technical-dramatic view, what this series has in common is an action (to quote Schiller) "that has already occurred and lies entirely outside the tragedy," so that the play itself becomes almost a tragic analysis (cf. the discussion of *Oedipus Rex* in the letter to Goethe of October 2, 1797). This applies chiefly to *John Gabriel Borkmann* but also to *Little Eyolf* where the child's fall from the table with its causes and consequences lies entirely outside the play. Yet this motif informs the play's ensuing development and denouement.

3. The English version of *The Masterbuilder* is from *Six Great Modern Plays* (New York, 1956).

4. Compare Ibsen's conception of the "individual conflict" as an antagonism between a possessive instinct powering itself from one acquisition to the next and a conservative moral consciousness or conscience (X, 372).

5. The word *"turmfest"* (secure like a tower) contains, as we shall see, the tragic irony of the whole piece.

6. Cf. Dostoevski's *The Eternal Husband*.

7. Paul Häberlin, "Daemonism," in *Ethik im Grundriss* (Zurich, 1946), p. 58f.

8. One can observe already in this dramatic vignette the relationship of immature youth to mature age in the image of a fearful and expectant young girl, looking up and listening to that strong and secure man who, so adventurously, has put the whole world at his feet.

9. Hilda, that shrewd girl, sees through the device of repression (*before* Freud) very well: "Oh, you haven't really forgotten anything: you are only a little ashamed of it all. I am sure one doesn't forget things of that kind."

10. Cf. Julien Green, *Journal 1940–1943* (Paris, 1946), p. 171: *"L'oubli est un pansement qu'il ne faut pas arracher."*

11. Concerning Ibsen's own personal happiness, we know very little. We do know that he took an earnest and lifelong interest in the progress of his son and did not hesitate to put his son's well-being ahead of his own.

12. Ibsen busied himself with this theme throughout his life—from *The Warriors at Helgeland* to *The Epilogue*. It always involves the

abetting or restraining of our wishes and plans by demonic powers or fates, what we call having luck or misfortune and what we can do to achieve the one and avoid the other. In *The Warriors at Helgeland*, however, it is not a matter of calling on these powers but of combatting them. Compare Hjordis: "True enough—wicked Norns rule the world: but small is their power, so long as they find no help in the human heart. Luck belongs to him who is strong enough to challenge the Norns—which I intend to do." (III, 58.)

13. We find here again self-denial and "forgetting" as the necessary requisite to creating artistically, as was illustrated in the poem "On the Vidda." New here is the idea that a *life dedicated to art* is a divine calling. Cf. Ibsen's own statement in a letter to his king from Rome (1866): "I fight here for my life's work, not for some carefree outcome—a work I unshakably know and believe that God has laid upon me—a work I am convinced is the most important and necessary for Norway: to awaken the people and teach them to think nobly." (X 55.)

14. This motif, the search for someone who believes in us in order to win back our self-confidence through this belief, is quite often repeated in Ibsen. For example, Jarl Skule in *Pretender to the Throne*.

15. *Ueber die letzten Dinge*. 9te Auflage, p. 104.

16. Compare the Preface to the second edition of *Festes auf Solhaug* in 1883 (II, 155). We have every reason to let this statement apply to *The Masterbuilder* (1892) as well as *The Epilogue*.

17. *Variété*, I, 69.

18. *Ibid.*, III, 280.

Goethe's *Faust*

JOHANNES PFEIFFER

Translated by *Vernon W. Gras*

Literature reveals something of the meaning of human existence not through abstract ideas but mediated through images; it poetizes the essence of life and world in a soaring vision which by its very nature is capable of innumerable interpretations. Just as the vision finds its realization in the image, so also does the image receive its life from the vision that supports it; each complements the other. If one looks behind the artistic expression into the depth of the lived experience which it concretely symbolizes, one must be eternally vigilant not to intellectualize and thereby dissipate poetic truth. One must perceive such truth from the whole representation as a figurative elicitation.

To this cautionary note must be added that Goethe's *Faust* over the decades has been interpreted from philosophic presuppositions that made insights into its underlying meaning impossible. Recapitulating this conventional interpretation with some rude simplifications, Goethe's *Faust* is said to deal with the growth and development of a man who progresses in restless discontent from one level to another until he finally reaches the summit of effective humanitarianism in his old age. That this development is framed within a supernatural action portraying a "wager" between God and the devil in accordance with which Faust's purification ends in a heavenly transfiguration is viewed merely as an opera-like dramatic device which makes free artistic use of mythological figures of a long out-worn superstition. In other words, one makes *Faust* into a symbol of a harmless, optimistic, secular piety according to which the destiny of man exhausts itself in this life and which believes that man saves himself. Or one makes the frame story symbolic of the fulfillment which culminates Faust's earthly progress, being its fitting result and last *Steigerung* (intensification). But that means that neither shame nor modesty hinders one from imputing to the greatest German-speaking poet an understanding of life that rests on complete illusions and could satisfy no one who experiences Dasein's authentic existence.[2]

I

Goethe's *Faust* carries the subtitle: "A Tragedy"; a circumstance anticipating that what we encounter here is not the ascension of a man to self-perfection, but rather a career which runs its course until the end in the ambiguous twilight of noble aspiration and tenacious obduracy. Even at the moment of his death, Faust remains entangled in outer mirage and inner delusion; and without the love that comes down to him, he would stay unredeemed. Of course it does say "Whoever aspires unweariedly/Is not above redeeming"; but one should not turn possibility into a "must" nor disregard that these words truly and earnestly presuppose the need for redemption.

Faust's exceptionality has quite definite stipulations, for he suffers in an extraordinary degree and manner from human finitude. Nevertheless, the fate of such a titan simultaneously reflects the fate of common man who, set apart and placed between world and upper world, must in the course of his life decide to be or not to be in the last and ultimate sense, i.e., whether to participate in Being or stray into Nothingness.

By original aim and predisposition, Faust is what one calls a seeker; he is oriented toward authentic being as the highest value. What drives him is passion for unconditional knowledge, a knowledge therefore that does not grope about externally on things but seeks to found and grasp them at their roots. To achieve this goal means submission to the fullness of Being; however, submission is genuine only if it isn't blind or coerced but flows voluntarily out of personal insight. For the sake of genuine submission, man opposes Authority with defiance, assured that he has been given cognitive power to free himself for the exploration of Being. However, for man to transmute his defiant wish for knowledge to submission to the ground of Being, patience is necessary. In view of infinity, patience must join itself to the immutable limitations of human knowledge and perceive the essential in the images of becoming and via the dark mirror of analogy. When patience, with believing surmise, reads finitude as the hieroglyphics of Being, the restless movement of time is brought to a halt by an eternity resting peacefully within itself; the now, this transient and unsubstantial moment, escaping any who seek to hold it, changes itself into that fulfilled moment lying open to time's atemporal depths. What Goethe in conjunction with Plato and Kant calls the "idea" now steps in place of the immediately perceived Ultimate as the latter's trace in the world of appearances. The "idea" is a totality never adequately objectified which orders a group of experiences in an illuminating way and finds an echo in human sentiment and in the active experience of love.

As Wilhelm Flitner explained so comprehensively, Faust's real problem is that he cannot make his way from a despairing impatience to a trusting patience but oscillates undecidedly between the two. As often as he begins to learn patience and with productive renunciation apprehends the eternal in the mundane just so often does he glide anew into criminal excess. His development is neither progress nor clarification but simply a maturing, i.e., he absorbs more of the world's experiences and meanings.[3]

The opening scenes reveal Faust in extreme despair. A scholar, indefatigable in pursuit of the science of his time, he has concluded painfully "that nothing can be known," at any rate no knowledge worthy to teach because it would improve and convert mankind. No common ordinary knowledge is meant here (the kind one heaps up in its factual correctness at will), but essential knowledge, the kind that brings a man to himself because it reveals genuine reality. Faust wishes to know "the inmost force which binds the world and guides its course"; he wants to penetrate to the source of things. Despairing of discursive thought which ever remains captive within the bonds of its own concepts, he has embraced magic—a form of secret knowledge whose signs and spells beat at the door separating man from the Ultimate. His goal is not merely an intuitive contact or presentiment of the world's germinating center, but—in Promethean extravagance—a direct participation in it. To see the world from God's point of view—yes, even to bring about the world with God's creative power—is, finally, Faust's dearest wish.

The first attempt to leap from the finite to the infinite, from things as we encounter them to things as they essentially are in themselves, fails; over against the macrocosm, the universe, the All, man remains an outsider, a mere distant spectator. "How grand a show! but Ah! a show alone." The second attempt expresses a self-limitation: Faust turns to the spirit of the Earth; but finite man is not equal to this encounter either: the face of reality is unbearable in its force and greatness. For the second time, only more deeply and irremediably, Faust is flung back from his superhuman pretensions into the human-all-too-human:

> I, image of the Godhead, who began—
> Deeming Eternal Truth secure in nearness—
> To sun myself in heavenly light and clearness,
> And laid aside the earthly man;—
> I, more than Cherub, whose free force had planned
> To flow through Nature's veins in glad pulsation,
> To reach beyond, enjoying in creation
> The life of Gods, behold my expiation!
> A thunder-word hath swept me from my stand.[4]

Horror fills him at our miserable human existence which raises itself to the eternal on the wings of fantasy but fails to maintain its achievement. Instead, retreating from this excess to a secure habitation, it consumes itself in trivial everyday cares.

Out of such boredom and discontent emerges a third attempt to burst the chains of finitude: Faust wishes to break out into the openness and freedom to true Being through suicide.

> Out on the open ocean speeds my dreaming;
> The glassy flood before my feet is gleaming,
> A new day beckons to a newer shore!
> A fiery chariot, borne on buoyant pinions,
> Sweeps near me now! I soon shall ready be
> To pierce the ether's high, unknown dominions,
> To reach new spheres of pure activity!

Though it may mean a drop into nothingness, Faust will undertake the leap. This alone proves his thoughts of suicide to be an expression of despairing impatience. While superior to the philistine who clutches at any worthless existence no matter how devoid of Being, Faust is just as deluded if he prefers to fall into nothingness rather than finitely surmising the hidden ground of Being in the reflection of appearances. But then the Easter choir recalls him to earthly existence. Not, however, because he has faith in any restoration through Christ's crucifixion and resurrection; rather, memory of the old customs which ripened his metaphysical consciousness, points toward the earth as the proving ground of what we have in trust.

If a titanlike discontent seeking God-status or nothingness preponderates in the opening scenes, Faust's oft-cited but little understood words about two souls cohabiting his breast (in the scene "Outside the City Gate") uncover the antagonism between his mighty upsurge toward limitless, superhuman freedom and the clinging restraint of simple, earthly, human existence:

> Two souls, alas! reside within my breast,
> And each withdraws from, and repels, its brother.
> One with tenacious organs holds in love
> And clinging lust the world in its embraces;
> The other strongly sweeps this dust above,
> Into the high ancestral spaces.

As Gerhard Storz illuminatingly demonstrated, this antithesis should not be interpreted by the Schillerian opposites of "sensual happiness" (*Sinnenglück*) and "spiritual peace" (*Seelenfrieden*); much more evident in the rebuffing of love's pleasures and the tentacles of sense is a desire to belittle and slander, to make finite necessities appear as weaknesses and all-too-human dependencies. Thus, the confirming background irony which closes the scene— namely, this hubridic upsurge finds its answer in a poodle snuffling along the ground, emissary from the demonic middle kingdom.[5]

When Faust returns from his Easter walk to his study, a mild resignation governs his mood; in verses of stirring warmth and ardor he expresses a feeling of piety and openness to holy influences:

> Behind me, field and meadow sleeping,
> I leave in deep, prophetic night,
> Within whose dread and holy keeping
> The better soul awakes to light.
> The wild desires no longer win us,
> The deeds of passion cease to chain;
> The love of Man revives within us,
> The love of God revives again.
> Ah, when, within our narrow chamber
> The lamp with friendly luster glows,
> Flames in the breast each faded ember,
> And in the heart, itself that knows.
> Then Hope again lends sweet assistance,
> And Reason then resumes her speech:
> One yearns, the rivers of existence,
> The very founts of Life, to reach.

Faith, love, and hope are entreated in these lines; defiance has un-
bent itself into submission; the heart to which reason speaks finds
its home in life's hidden center. Reason is more and other than understanding; in the midst of thought, it has concern for that Being
which remains superior to all thought. Neither discursive thinking nor magical revelation makes possible an approach to Being by
way of the idea. But when Mephisto, the growling, protesting
poodle, disturbs and scares away Faust's seeming contentment, leaving him once more "athirst," it should indicate that this embrace of
believing reasonableness is mere longing, an impulse, nonbinding
and incapable of withstanding realistic skepticism.[6] And when
Faust, trying to replace his painful deprivation, turns from irrational
magic to suprarational revelation, he does so from the start with
divided motive, not truly open and receptive to the enlightening,
healing influence of the Other. For, undoubtedly, the translation of
"Logos" with "deed" aims at the secret of divine creation, but in
such fashion that this aim becomes misconstrued and falsified
through the subjective projection of his own urge for self-realization.

The second scene in the study makes perfectly clear how hopelessly despondent Faust has remained at heart. In the discussion with Mephisto he confesses his detestation of life:

> What from the world have I to gain?
> Thou shalt abstain—renounce—refrain!

This does not signify the usual pursuit of fortune but that his life's inmost, dearest wish cannot be achieved, i.e., to feel existence as God would, to touch it with creative and authoritative power.

> The God that in my breast is owned
> Can deeply stir the inner sources;
> The God, above my powers enthroned,
> He cannot change external forces.
> So, by the burden of my days oppressed,
> Death is desired, and Life a thing unblest!

And when Mephisto with quiet scorn interposes that yet someone had failed to drink a brown juice on a certain night, Faust, angrily, tears himself loose from those very powers which in the previous scene had moved his sensibilities and calmed his soul:

> Though some familiar tone, retrieving
> My thoughts from torment, led me on,
> And sweet, clear echoes came, deceiving
> A faith bequeathed from Childhood's dawn,
> Yet now I curse whate'er entices
> And snares the soul with visions vain;
> With dazzling cheats and dear devices
> Confines it in this cave of pain!
> Cursed be, at once, the high ambition
> Wherewith the mind itself deludes!
> Cursed be the glare of apparition
> That on the finer sense intrudes!
> Cursed be the lying dream's impression
> Of name, and fame, and laurelled brow!
> Cursed, all that flatters as possession,

As wife and child, as knave and plow!
Cursed Mammon be, when he with treasures
To restless actions spurs our fate!
Cursed when, for soft, indulgent leisures,
He lays for us the pillows straight!
Cursed be the vine's transcendent nectar,
The highest favour Love lets fall!
Cursed, also, Hope!—cursed Faith, the spectre!
And cursed be Patience most of all!

Faith, love, hope, and that which interweaves and unifies them—
divine, heavenly patience—appear now to Faust, raging against his
better nature, as delusions holding men with snares and flattering
promises within this "cave of pain." The truth of our human existence is that it is futile and therefore not worth living; what hinders
truthful recognition and our opposition to life's shabby lusts is the
effectiveness of the so-called idols. Of these idols Faust names six:
self-esteem, the dazzle of appearances, fame, possessions, money,
and intoxication; they delude us with hope and fool us with a glitter
that hides the misery and emptiness of our true situation. While
Faust revolts against this demeaning constraint and imprisonment in
order to obtain a final independence vis-à-vis nothingness, yet
simultaneously he rages against that power which banishes mankind
to a thoroughly limited and conditioned existence and which grants
unconditioned Being only fragmentarily, mediated through living
experience.

Under such circumstances, what does Faust's pact with Mephisto
signify? Faust had learned that knowledge fails of its goal; as a finite
human, he remains excluded from nature's inner core. So what was
unreachable to thought and knowledge, he wishes now to uncover
by living and experiencing.

The Mighty Spirit deigns me no reply,
And Nature shuts on me her gate.
The thread of Thought at last is broken,
And Knowledge brings disgust unspoken.
Let us the sensual deeps explore,
To quench the fervours of glowing passion!

Let every marvel take form and fashion
Through the impervious veil it wore!
Plunge we in Time's tumultuous dance,
In the rush and roll of Circumstance!
Then may delight and distress,
And worry and success,
Alternately follow, as best they can:
Restless activity proves the man!

If it is a question of living fully, then expressly not in the usual superficial way. Faust does not wish to obtain pleasure but to measure every human possibility in order to arrive at a representative universal experience no longer limited to his single personal Dasein.

My bosom, of its thirst for knowledge sated,
Shall not, henceforth, from any pang be wrested
And all of life for all mankind created
Shall be within mine inmost being tested:
The highest, lowest forms my soul shall borrow,
Shall heap upon itself their bliss and sorrow,
And thus, my own sole self to all their selves expanded,
I too, at last, shall with them all be stranded!

However, Faust's decision aims at a breakdown; and he is so irrevocably certain of it that he stipulates in the pact with Mephisto that it should be all over with him as soon as he succumbs to the previously described deceitful, eternally vile pleasures of the moment:

Canst thou with lying flattery rule me,
Until, self-pleased, myself I see,
Canst thou with rich enjoyment fool me,
Let that day be the last for me!

and further;

When thus I hail the Moment flying:
"Ah, still delay—thou art so fair!"
Then bind me in thy bonds undying,

> My final ruin then declare!
> Then let the death-bell chime the token,
> Then art thou from thy service free!
> The clock may stop, the hand be broken,
> Then Time be finished unto me!

Paradoxically, Mephisto has no alternative but to object skeptically that a God may ponder the universe, not finite man in his narrowness and fragility; but if he finds himself compelled to witness for the truth, for the limits of finitude, this only because Faust in his nihilating urge for infinity threatens to overleap existence—one way, certainly, of handling the diversions of empty appearances.

The rejection of "reason and knowledge," the rejection thus of that prudential discretion which gives man his scale and direction, means that Faust has become susceptible to unlimited mirages; it is just this that Mephisto clearly perceives and which coincides with his plan:

> Reason and Knowledge only thou despise,
> The highest strength in man that lies!
> Let but the Lying Spirit bind thee
> With magic works and shows that blind thee,
> And I shall have thee fast and sure!
> Fate such a bold, untrammelled spirit gave him,
> As forwards, onwards, ever must endure;
> Whose over-hasty impulse drave him
> Past earthly joys he might secure.
> Dragged through the wildest life, will I enslave him,
> Through flat and stale indifference;
> With struggling, chilling, checking, so deprave him
> That, to his hot, insatiate sense,
> The dream of drink shall mock, but never lave him:
> Refreshment shall his lips in vain implore—
> Had he not made himself the Devil's, naught could save him,
> Still were he lost for evermore!

The stipulation, however, upon which Faust narrows his pact with Mephisto has an iridescence because the denial of every imaginable earthly satisfaction signifies both protection and curse. Protection because it preserves Faust from conclusively falling prey to empty appearances; curse because it makes impossible that the barren, empty present could ever be changed to a moment of fulfillment. Faust's conditional stipulation indicates he is confused about his life's fundamental concern; in back of his despairing decision to strive ever onward, restlessly, lies hidden a spark of receptivity toward Being which, in making time transparent, discovers cumulated eternity.

On three occasions this spark flares into a light, dominating the situation and illuminating the inner problematic in both a future and past direction: in the scene "Forest and Cavern"; in the opening scene of Part II; and in the scene that opens Act IV of Part II.

The "Forest and Cavern" scene pictures Faust in the solitude of the mountains.

> Spirit sublime, Thou gav'st me, gav'st me all
> For which I prayed. Not unto me in vain
> Hast Thou Thy countenance revealed in fire.
> Thou gav'st me Nature as a kingdom grand,
> With power to feel and to enjoy it. Thou
> Not only cold, amazed acquaintance yield'st,
> But grantest, that in her profoundest breast
> I gaze, as in the bosom of a friend.
> The ranks of living creatures Thou dost lead
> Before me, teaching me to know my brothers
> In air and water and the silent wood.
> And when the storm in forests roars and grinds,
> The giant firs, in falling, neighbour boughs
> And neighbour trunks with crushing weight bear down,
> And falling, fill the hills with hollow thunders,
> Then to the cave secure thou leadest me,
> Then show'st me mine own self, and in my breast
> The deep, mysterious miracles unfold.
> And when the perfect moon before my gaze
> Comes up with soothing light, around me float
> From every precipice and thicket damp
> The silvery phantoms of the ages past,

And temper the austere delight of thought.
That nothing can be perfect unto Man
I now am conscious. With this ecstasy,
Which brings me near and nearer to the Gods,
Thou gav'st the comrade whom I now no more
Can do without, though, cold and scornful, he
Demeans me to myself, and with a breath,
A word, transforms Thy gifts to nothingness.
Within my breast he fans a lawless fire,
Unwearied, for that fair and lovely form;
Thus in desire I hasten to enjoyment,
And in enjoyment pine to feel desire.

Mephisto began by leading Faust into what is called the world. But how could it be otherwise than that Faust was disappointed, even disgusted, with this vacuous, trivial reality? Accordingly, the trip to the witches' kitchen had the purpose to inflame in the hesitant, discontented Faust a glowing sexuality and in this manner make him receptive to Mephisto's ministrations. Because this sensual urge fastens itself onto a sweet innocent girl to whom heaven and earth seem equally close, this lust set upon "taking," turns into a love blessed and transformed by the other. In consequence, a feeling of responsibility for this other being is awakened in Faust, and this has driven him into solitude.

Of importance is that here again and in accentuated form, the monologue juxtaposes two different and opposed modes of behavior.[7] On one side is "pleasure," or put more exactly, "the pleasure of contemplation." Contemplation is more and other than a coldly perceptive observation (*der Betrachtung strenge Lust*); Faust no longer feels excluded from living nature but knows himself taken up as friend into her bosom secrets. In nature he comes to learn what is more than mere nature; whilst the natural forms speak brotherly to him, a depth becomes visible that finds reciprocation from the depth of his own heart. Objective forms become transparent to their actualizing powers and the ground of nature finds sympathetic response in the depth of the reflecting soul.

Apparently as a gift of redeeming love, Faust is allotted what time and again had been denied his overwrought search for the ultimate.

But if Mephisto can unsettle him by dragging his feelings for Gretchen into the mud and kindling in him unscrupulous lust, it is because the corrupter of that other soul lurks within Faust himself —not submissively open to the hieroglyphics of appearance but reeling from a consuming desire to live, though the world is sense-bereft. Sensuality in itself does not corrupt; what does is ego-imprisonment hindering a true encounter with the other, exploiting the other as substance and means for rankly self-glorifying dreams. When later in the scene Faust succumbs to the insinuations of desire, it means that his trustful submission to the hiddenness of Being was but again a contemplative mood unable to prevail against the stronger reality of an all-destructive despair; and so he sets out for Gretchen with a gloomy ruinous passion:

> She and her peace I yet must undermine:
> Thou, Hell, hast claimed this sacrifice as thine!
> Help, Devil! through the coming pangs to push me;
> What must be, let it quickly be!
> Let fall on me her fate, and also crush me,
> One ruin whelm both her and me!

The second part of the drama opens with a scene whose purpose is to reconcile Faust with himself and prepare him for new endeavors. What lies behind him can be summed up briefly. Mephisto as servant does not just carry out assignments but uses every one of them to guiltily ensnare Faust; he has made Faust into the murderer of Gretchen's mother and goaded him to kill her brother in a duel. The hopeless entanglement of someone fleeing from himself is mirrored in the confusion of the Walpurgisnight. But from the midst of that festive assembly headed for disintegration and nothingness the accusing apparition of the forsaken beloved tears the benumbed Faust away; his quickly awakened conscience recalls him to that person whom he has brought down into misery. In her helplessness, Gretchen, having murdered her child, awaits execution. Forcing his way into the prison with Mephisto's help, Faust vainly tries to help a deranged Gretchen escape her impending death. Gretchen now recognizes with visionary clairvoyance what she had only dimly felt before: that her beloved is in the bonds of

Satan and wishes to tear her away from God. Because she refuses to follow him and accepts her death as God-imposed, she becomes free of guilt. In a scene of decisive importance, the hesitating Faust stands between Mephisto urging departure and Gretchen, self-delivered unto God's judgment. For the sake of elucidation, one could imagine him stepping to her side in order to die in mutual atonement and thus extricating himself from Mephisto's power. But such an act would require an inner conversion for which all preparations are lacking in Faust. All the more illuminating then is the drama's contrasting actuality which banishes him anew to the earth as the realm of illusory and maturing experience.

But if he continues to live, then one must consider first of all that the total work, and particularly the second part, is not organized on a linear basis but—as Max Kommerell first pointed out [8]—appears as a series of interlaced concentric rings. It is not a matter of horizontal causal development but a variegated cross-section of alternating images whose meaning is properly grasped only when each individual scene and action is fitted together as immanent within the whole. Consider that such discontinuity supports Faust's fluctuating inconsistency; as long as he follows heedlessly each momentary attunement, the way to clarification remains closed.

The first scene of Part II symbolizes Faust's purification from the "experienced horror": a purification but not clarification. While something like rebirth certainly occurs, it doesn't happen through remorse and penance but through immersion in the healing powers of deep forgetfulness. Remorse and penance would demand a preparation, from which Faust is as far removed as ever, i.e., belief in God's forgiving grace. This grace is, nevertheless, present but disguised in the salutary goodwill of nature. Friendly nature-spirits hover over the sleep-needy one and return to him the holy light. Healed and facing a new future, he rises and greets the breaking day with fervent existential readiness:

> Life's pulses now with fresher force awaken
> To greet the mild ethereal twilight o'er me;
> This night, thou, Earth! hast also stood unshaken,
> And now thou breathest new-refreshed before me,
> And now beginnest, all thy gladness granting,

A vigorous resolution to restore me,
To seek that highest life for which I'm panting,
The world unfolded lies in twilight glimmer,
A thousand voices in the grove are chanting;
Vale in, vale out, the misty streaks grow dimmer;
The deeps with heavenly light are penetrated;
The boughs, refreshed, lift up their leafy shimmer
From gulfs of air where sleepily they waited;
Colour on colour from the background cleareth,
Where flower and leaf with trembling pearls are freighted:
And all around a Paradise appeareth.
Look up!—The mountain summits, grand, supernal,
Herald, e'en now, the solemn hour that neareth;
They earliest enjoy the light eternal
That later sinks, till here below we find it.
Now to the Alpine meadows, sloping vernal,
A newer beam descends ere we divined it,
And step by step unto the base hath bounded:
The sun comes forth! Alas, already blinded,
I turn away, with eyesight pierced and wounded!
'Tis thus, when, unto yearning hope's endeavour,
Its highest wish on sweet attainment grounded,
The portals of fulfilment widely sever:
But if there burst from those eternal spaces
A flood of flame, we stand confounded ever;
For Life's pure torch we sought the shining traces,
And seas of fire—and what a fire!—surprise us.
Is't Love? Is't Hate? that burningly embraces,
And that with pain and joy alternate tries us?
So that, our glances once more earthward throwing,
We seek in youthful drapery to disguise us.
Behind me, therefore, let the sun be glowing!
The cataract, between the crags deep-riven,
I thus behold with rapture ever-growing.
From plunge to plunge in thousand streams 'tis given,
And yet a thousand, to the valleys shaded,
While foam and spray in air are whirled and driven.
Yet how superb, across the tumult braided,

The painted rainbow's changeful life is bending,
Now clearly drawn, dissolving now and faded,
And evermore the showers of dew descending!
Of human striving there's no symbol fuller:
Consider, and 'tis easy comprehending—
Life is not light, but the refracted colour.

Faust has found himself again in his original striving: in the direction of the hiddenness of Being. What is new, however, in this monologue is that he anticipates the solution to his life-problem. Direct insight to the Absolute is forbidden us; we can grasp it only as reflected in appearances, in the fragments and mediations of our limited earthly existence. Renunciation of the titanlike demand to become one with the divine essence in knowledge and action and to renounce participating in God's creativity: such renunciation makes possible for Faust to walk in the way of the idea and to experience the eternal fullness of the primal Source in the image of the finite sensory world. Because the rainbow reconciles darkness with light and change with permanence, it clearly articulates that out of transient multiplicity emanates the everlasting One.[9]

This climactic moment harks back to the scene "Forest and Cavern" with its reverential submersion in the hidden meaning of appearances; again despite intensified awareness, Faust cannot hold onto this fundamental mood and the possibilities now available of productive renunciation. So after the sojourn in the "little world" of human desire and suffering, the way now leads into the "great world" of statecraft and culture—with its political and aesthetic concerns. Faust will throw himself with renewed impatience into the intoxication of time and events, remaining entangled in delusion and mirage until the end in his magical attempts to coerce the power of Being from out his earthly estate.

The first scene of the fourth Act, once again a turning point, reveals the structure of the work both retrospectively and prospectively:

Strong, serrated rocky peaks. A cloud approaches, pauses, and settles down upon a projecting ledge. It then divides.

FAUST (*steps forth*).

Down-gazing on the deepest solitudes below,
I tread deliberately this summit's lonely edge,
Relinquishing my cloudy car, which hither bore
Me softly through the shining day o'er land and sea.
Unscattered, slowly moved, it separates from me.
Off eastward strives the mass with rounded, rolling march:
And strives the eye, amazed, admiring, after it.
In motion it divides, in wave-like, changeful guise;
Yet seems to shape a figure.—Yes! mine eyes not err!—
On sun-illumined pillows beauteously reclined,
Colossal, truly, but a godlike woman-form,
I see! The like of Juno, Leda, Helena,
Majestically lovely, floats before my sight!
Ah, now 't is broken! Towering broad and formlessly,
It rests along the east like distant icy hills,
And shapes the grand significance of fleeting days.
Yet still there clings a light and delicate band of mist
Around my breast and brow, caressing, cheering me.
Now light, delayingly, it soars and higher soars,
And folds together.—Cheats me an ecstatic form,
As early-youthful, long-foregone and highest bliss?
The first glad treasures of my deepest heart break forth;
Aurora's love, so light of pinion, is its type,
The swiftly-felt, the first, scarce-comprehended glance,
Outshining every treasure, when retained and held.
Like Spiritual Beauty mounts the gracious Form,
Dissolving not, but lifts itself through ether far,
And from my inner being bears the best away.

Faust had sought access to politics and society at the Emperor's court and under Mephisto's influence had hit upon the invention of paper money to solve the frivolous and pleasure-seeking ruler's financial crisis, thus ingratiating himself. Since magic had reestablished his bankrupt power, the Emperor now wants it to provide more spiritual entertainment: the experience of beauty in its paragon,

Helen of Troy. Because Faust journeys down to the mothers, that dark primal source of all earthly appearances, he becomes capable of conjuring Helen as a poet. But the vision objectified in such manner awakens in him an enthusiastic desire to possess it in the flesh. Faust's spiritual craving is directed toward archetypal beauty itself; the marriage with Helen draws him again to that fulfilled moment in which transient existence becomes transparent to imperishable Being and man participates in an essential reality withdrawn from the power of nothingness. Thus may we transpose the vision which in the opening scene of Act Four "towering(ly) . . . shapes the grand significance of fleeting days."

That experience rests only indirectly on magic and much more essentially on inner transformation or release. Had Faust wished to come to rest in this insular halfway house, he would have been out of Mephisto's reach but at the price of sublimating his responsible and decision-making life in time. Accordingly, it is the task of Euphorion to break through this completely detached self-sufficiency and, with his infinite yearning to grow, to loosen the tie between Faust and Helena from within.

Yet the monologue conjures up another vision which illuminates past and future. If the first cloud appeared mighty in outline, the second slowly ascends as a light haze reflected in the ether. In turn, it becomes a vision of the soul's beauty on which the memory of Gretchen's love catalyzes. Faust addresses this cloud symbol as the highest good, the good welling up from the deepest springs of the heart. Softly, it draws the best and inmost part of him upward and indicates the path toward freedom.

When Mephisto rejoins him, he greets Faust's nobly aspiring soul with the old incomprehension of what human existence actually demands and needs. Mephisto's element is the skeptical and deleterious worldly wisdom which exhausts itself in allures and excitations. With artful dexterity, he extols but one thing: the raw, stale joys of sensual pleasure. But Faust disdains not only pleasure, he also brushes fame aside as worthless. "The Deed is everything; the Glory naught."

While his mood turns to action, his passion to rule remains dependent as ever on Mephisto's magic arts. Also, the motive for his action is not public-spirited, to seek ordered justice for the human community, but is rather heightened egotism seeking aggrandizement of power for its own sake. Faust has had the idea to force the infertile sea into fruitfulness by diking up the shoreland: in itself symbolic of the unceasing effort required of the community to maintain itself against the elements. The tone of his utterance leaves no doubt that his motives, again, are self-serving: i.e., consisting in the enjoyment of the superhuman power granted by his pact and in the deadening of his inner unrest through pacification of his illimitable urge for world consumption and possession.

> The Sea sweeps on, in thousand quarters flowing,
> Itself unfruitful, barrenness bestowing;
> It breaks and swells, and rolls, and overwhelms
> The desert stretch of desolated realms.
>
> There endless waves hold sway, in strength erected
> And then withdrawn,—and nothing is effected.
> If aught could drive me to despair, 't were, truly
> The aimless force of elements unruly.
> Then dared my mind its dreams to over-soar:
> Here would I fight,—subdue this fierce uproar!

The fifth Act shows Faust at the projected labor; after Gretchen's tragedy and Helen's tragedy now comes the statesman's tragedy. Through renewed initiative in state affairs, Faust has placed the beleaguered Emperor so in his debt that the latter has gifted Faust with the shoreland he wishes to reclaim. But just as the wartime assistance given to the Emperor against his rival was demonic and magical, so also is the work on the land reclamation:

> Knaves in vain by day were storming,
> Plying pick and spade alike;
> Where the fires at night were swarming,
> Stood, the following day, a dike.
> Nightly rose the sounds of sorrow,
> Human victims there must bleed:
> Lines of torches, on the morrow,
> Were canals that seaward lead.

The work of Faust's old age rests on shady foundations—as do all his undertakings since his renunciation of faith, love, hope, and patience. One must be blind or have blinded himself not to admit how faded and pale are the mood of these last scenes. True enough, Lynkeus the watchman paints a grand, well-rounded landscape of Faust's performance and luck:

> The sun goes down, the ships are veering
> To reach the port, with song and cheer:
> A heavy galley, now appearing
> On the canal, will soon be here.
> The gaudy pennons merrily flutter,
> The masts and rigging upward climb:
> Blessings on thee the seamen utter,
> And Fortune greets thee at thy prime.

But Mephisto knows better: the imposing facade deceives; that which gives the impression of permanent excavation is in truth but transient mirage and empty appearance.

> And yet, thou 'rt laboring for us alone,
> With all thy dikes and bulwarks daring;
> Since thou for Neptune art preparing—
> The Ocean-Devil—carousal great.
> In every way shall ye be stranded;
> The elements with us are banded,
> And ruin is the certain fate.

And Faust himself: he is so little changed that the tolling bell infuriates him to be reminded that his estate lacks the hillock upon which in a hut next to a chapel Philemon and Baucis are living out their last days. Annoyedly reacting to the bell as that "damned ringing," he wishes: "Oh, were I far away from here!"—a word which is then repeated to Mephisto in a vehement outburst:

> Still that accursed *Here!*
> To me a burden most severe.
> To thee, so clever, I declare it,—

It gives my very heart a sting;
It is impossible to bear it!
Yet shamed am I, to say the thing.
The old ones, there, should make concession;
A shady seat would I create:
The lindens, not my own possession,
Disturb my joy in mine estate.

At bottom it is once more the old despairing impatience which envelops and snatches to itself, while raging against every boundary to its egotism. The improbable life of the elderly pair who trust in God and with believing obedience authenticate the spirit of love acts as a quiet reproach to the ego-imprisoned Faust who still lives in that schism between titanlike world domination and all-nihilating despair because in his relationship to finitude he has surrendered the contrary possibility from which alone comes fulfillment, security, and direction.

The command to remove the obstacle motivated by an ungovernable will to possess is carried out in the usual manner by Mephisto so that Faust's conscience accrues another heavy burden. Whereas Faust had in mind a generous relocation, Mephisto with his cohorts perpetrate destruction and murder.

Late at night Lynkeus, the watchman on the tower of Faust's palace, sings those gently cradling, softly ardent verses whose blessed purview confesses to an eternal world harmony:

For seeing intended,
Employed for my sight,
The tower's my dwelling,
The world my delight.
I gaze on the Distant,
I look on the Near,—
The moon and the planets,
The forest and deer.
So see I in all things
The grace without end,
And even as they please me,
Myself I commend.

> Thou fortunate Vision,
> Of all thou wast 'ware,
> Whatever it might be,
> Yet still it was fair!

This confession, however, should not be taken out of context. Lynkeus (i.e., lynx-eyed) has the function to proclaim with spontaneous cheerfulness the lovely appearance of things open to direct observation. But this beautiful vista rests on a hidden strata of guilt-entangled commerce, and it is put into question immediately after by the watchman's extreme horror over the violent deed taking place in the darkness.

Faust greets the cynical report of Mephisto and his three cohorts with revulsion and a curse; he wishes to have nothing to do with their crime and contemptuously leaves them the booty. While trying thus to free himself from the clutch of the demons, he is overtaken by Care and Death. With death imminent, however, clear insight into his situation breaks in on him:

> Not yet have I my liberty made good:
> If I could banish Magic's fell creations,
> And totally unlearn the incantations,—
> Stood I, O Nature! Man alone in thee,
> Then were it worth one's while a man to be!
> Ere in the Obscure I sought it, such was I,—
> Ere I had cursed the world so wickedly.

The drama curves back to its point of origin; what lies between proves absolutely to be lifelong error. Yet this labyrinth has ripened in Faust the consciousness of the human task. Thrown into this mysterious existence and surrounded by the mundane, man's destiny in his encounter with nature is to await God, intuiting the essential ground within transient appearances. For nature in *Faust* is not formularized but a speaking reality, whose forms in speaking to us reveal the hidden primal source. Naked and unpretentious, no longer superhuman but a man among men, Faust would like to stand before this reality which is neither acquiescent to discursive knowledge nor open to magic but comes halfway to meet that reason which alone experiences, patiently and laboriously, the infinite in the finite.

This newly acquired insight into the virtue of patience is tested by the shaken Faust in his discussion with Care. When the latter relentlessly tarries, the angry Faust recovers himself with the warning: "Take care, and speak no word of sorcery!" What follows, however, remains ambiguous self-assertion which may appear equally as stubbornness or justification. Because frail and subject to finite conditions, Faust cannot escape Care. But what he sets against it to neutralize its paralyzing litany is mostly a summation of that prior frenetic life into which he had thrown himself in despair of any and all fulfillment:

> I only through the world have flown:
> Each appetite I seized as by the hair;
> What not sufficed me, forth I let it fare,
> And what escaped me, I let go.

Yet in this extreme situation, he is also right not to be subjugated nor deluded but in high-minded consciousness of man's direction of the world to affirm his readiness to stand up for Dasein's concentrated self-realization:

> The sphere of Earth is known enough to me;
> The view beyond is barred immutably:
> A fool, who there his blinking eyes directeth,
> And o'er his clouds of peers a place expecteth!
> Firm let him stand, and look around him well!
> This World means something to the Capable.
> Why needs he through Eternity to wend?
> He here acquires what he can apprehend.
> Thus let him wander down his earthly day;
> When spirits haunt, go quietly his way;
> In marching onwards, bliss and torment find,
> Though, every moment, with unsated mind!

However situationally just it may be that Faust with resolute unerringness deflects Care and, even though blinded, holds fast to his masterful self-assurance, one must not overlook the limiting context of these words nor their specific presuppositions at the time Faust uttered them.[10]

How inextricably ambiguous that clear light shines within the "inmost heart" is indicated in the following scene, when Faust steps out of his palace to exhort his servants to complete the work begun. Not only does he totally mistake his situation because—a tragic irony—he believes the clatter of spades preparing his own grave are signs of work progressing; even beyond this, the whole death scene is submerged in the obscure twilight of a fettered, schismatic consciousness. Granted that Faust elevates and obligates himself to that image of a free human community daily struggling to survive through mutual help against the elements—yet his own behavior thoroughly contradicts this vision. If "one mind suffices for a thousand hands" then that mind originates outside the community in him who plans, commands, and leads; accordingly, Faust here also glorifies himself in will-to-power and unscrupulous exploitation:

> It is the crowd, for me in service moiling,

and further:

> However possible,
> Collect a crowd of men with vigour,
> Spur by indulgence, praise, or rigour,
> Reward, allure, conscript, compel!

Indeed, to the extent that Faust intoxicates himself by imagining that his ego finds replication thousandfold in the swarming folk and that traces of his earthly presence will remain for aeons, the vision itself is in no way free from self-seeking and self-indulgence. Finally, the actual foundation for this anticipated life-goal would still have been laid by Mephisto's demonic arts whose assistance must be repudiated by any work successfully given over to plain humanity and voluntary submission.

Thus, it is a matter neither of a new message which capstones the whole drama nor even of Faust's ultimate access to freedom; but, once again it is a contradictory mixture of noble yearning and botched deeds, of large-souled endeavor and turbid delusion. And when the dying Faust enjoys the highest moment by anticipating it —to which he could say, "Ah, still delay; thou art so fair!" because transient time had insouled itself with permanent significance—this very restricted and frail anticipation so little abolishes the comprehensive denial of every possible fulfillment that Mephisto contrariwise to his expectation is robbed of any hold upon Faust's soul. Behind this paradoxical outcome, the decisive question concerning Faust's salvation and purification admittedly now raises itself as problem.

NOTES

1. The Bayard Taylor translation of Goethe's *Faust* is used throughout (Ed.).

2. Wilhelm Böhm in his book *Faust der Nichtfaustische* (Halle, 1933) undertook the first energetic attack against this conventional interpretation; however, because Böhm separates poetic truth from its "aesthetic language," limiting it to what is clearly understandable, he misses the configurated meaning of Faust as much as does the opposed "perfectibility" convention.

3. Cf. Wilhelm Flitner's discussion of "Faust's Läuterung and Rettung" (in the *Festschrift für Eduard Spranger*, Leipzig, 1942) as well as Chapter 8 in his book *Goethe im Spätwerk* (Hamburg, 1947).

4. For the new edition of this introduction, all the text citations were compared with the meritorious edition of Erich Trunz (Hamburg, 1949) whose remarks—truly building stones of a comprehensive commentary—I, moreover, thank for a series of important insights.

5. Gerhard Storz "Einführung in Goethe's Faust, beschränkt auf den ersten Teil von Faust I" in *Goethe-Vigilien oder Versuche in der Kunst, Dichtung zu verstehen* (Stuttgart, 1953).

6. The insight comes from Wilhelm Michel. Cf. the remarks about the "Hausteufel" in the section "Gestalten der Angst" in his book *Das Leiden am Ich* (Bremen, 1930).

7. How to interpret the "exalted Spirit" whom Faust addresses in the monologue has been deliberately left aside.

8. "The relation of cause and effect is replaced by the relation of spiritual cohesiveness." "Faust II takes place in a symbolic time. The form demands consecutive ordering but actually this drama is a spatial expansion of what belongs together." "The passage of time becomes a poetic illusion. According to the oppositions and multeity of life, space is divided into spaces and time into the various chronologies of these spaces. Everything serves only to fully develop one idea through a series of appearances. The happenings do not constitute a necessary temporal sequence but a spatialized total picture of those events creating a self identity." Max Kommerell, "Faust Zweiter Teil—zum Verständins der Form," in *Geist und Buchstabe der Dichtung*. (Revised ed., Frankfurt a. Main, 1942), pp. 32–40.

9. For explanation of these verses, cf. also: Emil Staiger, "Faust's Heilschlaf" (*Hamburger Akademische Rundschau*, December, 1947).

10. For interpretation of this scene compare also Paul Stöcklein, "Die Begegnung mit der Sorge" in *Wege zum späten Goethe: Dichtung, Gedanke, Zeichnung, Interpretationen* (Hamburg, 1949).

Saint Genet: "My Victory Is Verbal"

JEAN-PAUL SARTRE

Translated by *Bernard Frechtman*

He aimed first at making himself the most irreplaceable of *beings*, thus at giving himself the particularity of an object; he tried in vain to be in himself and for himself the goldsmith and the jewel; then, realizing that he was an object through and for Others, he decided to engrave his particularity on the freedom of Others. Thereupon, this particularity as a defined thing falls away from him; a third Genet springs up, one who is neither the poor tramp nor the legendary hero of the poems, but the synthetic activity that turns the former into the latter; this activity, which effects the regulated transformation of one objective reality into another objective reality, cannot belong to the world of objectivity. Genet's particularity shifts: it now lies in his will to create *this* particular work. And this particularity which is no longer an object for anyone, not even for himself, which is not, which is in the making, is situated beyond being and language: anyone wishing to describe and name it would always find himself naming the operation or describing the work. But it is more than that and something else, since it produces the work and is a consciousness of the operation. We know what this creative consciousness is: it is *existence*. The original will to Evil appeared to us as an existential tension, but we immediately saw all the contradictions of the situation oblige it to submit to essence: so long as Genet wanted to be a "Thief-in-itself," he hid his deeper existence behind his essentialist passion. But now, leaving to the minds of others the job of realizing his being, he frees himself from it: he is now only a faceless freedom that sets fascinating traps for other freedoms.

By technical means, this freedom dissolves the darkness that clouded it: it is a pure consciousness of itself and of its objective ends. In fulfilling its ends, it transcends them. Let us bear in mind what Hegel says of the artist and his work in the "Animal Kingdom of the Spirit": the work is the limited reality which consciousness gives itself, but which it immediately overflows. "The work, like the original nature which it expresses, is something determined, but in the presence of the work the consciousness is determined as that which had within itself determinability by virtue of negativity in general. Thus, the consciousness is the universal with respect to this precise determinability of the work. The consciousness withdrawing from its work is in actual fact the universal consciousness because it becomes, in this opposition, absolute negativity . . . whereas its work is the defined consciousness." In determining himself *in his work* as the Thief, Genet escapes this determination; he stands opposed to it as a free creative consciousness which can be defined only in terms of undetermined free activity; in creating himself in the other, he empties himself of himself and becomes the absolute void as an unconditioned power to create. In making himself the Thief for the Other, he makes himself a creator for himself. A moment ago, he found Being at the end of nothingness; at present, in affirming his being to the very end, in endowing it, by means of words, with a new reality, in depositing it as filth in the other, he frees himself from it and finds himself in that pure negativity, that presence of nothingness to itself, that perpetual transcending of the given, namely consciousness. In carrying commitment to an extreme, he again becomes available. He has put himself entirely into his poems, with his heavy past, his murdered childhood, his present life of crime and dreams, and his destiny, already determined, which is to lead him, from prison to prison, lower and lower until he is taken by death. But by the same token he wrests himself from the past by giving himself an entirely new past as a creator, by substituting for his childhood memories the memory of the words that sing it; he frees himself from the present by transforming his gestures into acts and his dreams into literary motifs; while his passive future as a thief, which has been prophesied, settles in his work as a future-which-is-an-object, and thereby changes into a past, the work which is in progress or which is being planned offers the creator a free future of creation. Even his feelings are modified: he "communciates emotions which he does not experience" and all of which enter words. No sooner does he feel an incipient excitement than he makes of it a means of moving others: he feels the upheaval caused by love or hatred, but he feels it *over there*, in the Other, insofar as the other becomes Genet. As for the creator himself, he experiences a kind of ataraxia because he no longer undergoes anything: Genet has finally succeeded in introducing activity even into pure affectivity. "Pretexts for my iridescence, then for my transparence, and finally for my absence." What he said about young boys applies to his books. They are pretexts for his absence, for the absence whereby Valéry defined *the man of mind* and which he reduced to the refusal to be anything whatever: "All phenomena, stricken thereby with a kind of equal repulsion and, as it were, successively rejected by an identical gesture, appear in a kind of equivalence. The feelings and thoughts are enveloped in this uniform condemnation which extends to everything perceptible." [1] But Valéry, who is intellectualistic, refers to the knowing and observing consciousness: Genet's consciousness, which, like beauty, is voracious, unfeeling, and absent, is in active relationship with the universe: it keeps the universe at a distance and covers it with a veil, but its aim is not so much to know the universe as to draw from it the subject of a work whose purpose, like the poems of Mallarmé, is to *make the world useless*. [2] His consciousness has at last come to terms with itself: the little thief was eager to *will* Being as a whole, whereas it can be accepted only in detail. The cold, solitary consciousness of the rebel now *accepts* large parts of the universe that it hated; with greedy indifference it draws from the universe the materials of its work; everything interests it; it seizes upon raw events and works on them, "interprets" them in order to give them at last a symbolic meaning, to force them to speak of sexuality, murder, or poetry. The world was the thorn in his flesh; by *willing* it, Genet was fleeing from it, was producing an imaginary world. When, by a slight shifting of his intention, he decides to *realize* this imaginary world, to make of it, with the cooperation of others, a fictive object, a network of signs and figures whose sole purpose is to indicate Genet himself, the real world belongs to him: simply because it becomes *usable*. Starting with *Miracle of the Rose*, the attentive reader finds a shade of optimism in his works. To be sure, the object of his thinking remains despair, but the sentence itself, with its noble vivacity and its boldness, leaves us with a less desperate impression. The man who writes: "I give the name violence to a boldness lying idle and hankering for danger" is certainly not a "*misérabiliste*." For him the ogress Beauty gives meaning to the universe, despite her dreadful rigor: she uses it as a pretext for language. The poet's ambiguous situation lies in his taking God's creation in reverse: he puts the Word at the end. To absorb the universe into language is to destroy the universe, but it is to create the poet. What exactly happens? Is the real annihilated in significations? Does the contingency of being give way to necessity? Both. For language, as Blanchot has observed, is both the flight of being into significations and the evaporation of significations, in short, annihilation—and it is also *being*, whipped air, written, engraved words. Engaged, like the surrealists, in a process of demolition, Genet must, like them, construct a war machine in order to achieve his ends; and this machine has two faces, one of shadow and the other of light: it is the evil sacrifice of being to nothing, but it is also the inclusion of nothingness in being. It attempts to dissolve reality, but it salvages nonbeing. Genet's optimism comes from his presenting Evil, in the imaginary, as being produced in Being by freedom. And in the last analysis it matters little that being means this or that: it is enough that it means something. Optimism is the affirmation not that man is or can be happy but simply that he does not suffer for nothing. Even if the world has been created only to be annihilated in a cone of cold light, ultimate resplendence of an eye whose optic nerve is cut, this annihilation would still have a meaning. In wanting to dissolve being in nonbeing, Genet reconquers nonbeing on behalf of being; he confines it in his books like the devil in a bottle. His works are, in one respect, repeated suicides and, in another, the renewed affirmation of human grandeur. We find here, once again, the game of loser wins. But this time Genet knows the rules: he wins every single time. Masturbation and homosexual intercourse gave him nightmarish joys: ever since he has been *telling* about his masturbation and intercourse Genet has known happiness.

Sooner or later it will have to be recognized that he is a moralist.
—COCTEAU

He is much too lucid to be unaware of this aspect of his under-taking; he knows that it is liberating him. Whatever progress he makes as a result of it, one can be sure that he is the first to know about it. But as he has been refusing since childhood to submit to anything, as he wants to get nothing from Providence or fortune, he cannot accept passively, as if it were a simple return shock, the moral benefits of his literary activity: pleasure and pain must come from him. Moreover, his poetry is voluntary: to write is to explore systematically the situation into which he is thrown; he is a poet as a result of becoming completely aware of what it means for him to be a thief; poetry will withdraw into itself if he becomes aware of what it means for him to be a poet. His books are born of what I have called cathartic crises; since the poet must become a full consciousness of himself and of the world, he must provoke these crises, must direct and observe them; and since the book is nothing other than this consciousness as expressed in words, it must return to the latter in order to relate his deliverance. These monstrous and perfect works want to be *consciousness through and through*, with-out the slightest zone of darkness, ignorance, or inertia. They will contain both the story and the story of the story, the thoughts and the history of the thoughts, the spiritual procedure, its method and the progress report, in short a poem and a journal of a poem which, unlike that of Gide, will accompany the creation by ethical com-ments. Whence the Jansenistic austerity and moral pedantry which combines so strangely with the shocking portrayals. It is this will to edify that is least forgiven him; the high-minded reader would, if need be, overlook his obscenities but does not tolerate his moralizing about them. We would be less indignant if we first realized that this display of moralism does not concern us. No doubt Genet knows that he shocks us; no doubt he secretly enjoys doing so; but he has never dreamed of making us better and he does not want us to profit from his instruction; the one he wants to edify is himself. "It is with good sentiments," said Gide, "that one writes bad books." Genet wants to write good books with bad sentiments: he thinks that a gratuitous art would not be worth bothering about, and this ought not to surprise us since ethical values have always been his chief concern. No doubt he was chiefly interested in profaning them, but that is a way of recognizing them. And besides, as one can imagine, his edifying discourses bear little resemblance to those of the average clergyman. They are moral because the comments which they attach to the characters' acts remain in the sphere of the might-be. But this moral art is not a moralizing art: Genet upholds no thesis, does not want to demonstrate anything; though his works are criminal assaults upon his readers, they are, at the same time, presented as systematically conducted ethical experiments which are their own comments upon themselves. Furthermore, he defines his creative activity as follows: "Creation is not a somewhat frivolous game. The creator has committed himself to the fearful adventure of taking upon himself, to the very end, the perils risked by his creatures. . . . But then the creator will charge himself with the weight of his characters' sins. . . . He must take upon himself—the expression seems feeble—must make his own to the point of knowing it to be his own substance, circulating in his arteries, the evil given by him, which his heroes choose freely."

Thus, creation is a passion. Not content with producing characters from his own flesh, the author embodies himself in them and suffers with their suffering: each of them provides him with an opportunity to explore a humiliation, a despair, an anger. Having entered Querelle, he will feel the anguish that follows murder; with Green Eyes he will writhe in an effort to escape the consequences of his crime, then will decide to face them; as Divine he will have the experience of aging; as Erik, that of beauty; with the executioner, that of ugliness; once, lost in the dense darkness of Lysiane, he will be a woman.

What is the purpose of these Passions? Suffering? Yes, of course, and, besides, he tells us so himself. He needs, as he informs us, the rule and sorrows of a penal colony: "I shall wear myself away with slow, minute patience, I shall perform the painful gestures of the punished. . . . I shall become as polished as they, pumiced." But the penal colony no longer exists. That does not matter. Genet will install his penal colony in himself, he will live the colony through the convicts whom he invents: "But I am speaking of a colony that has been abolished. Let me therefore restore it in secret and live there in spirit as in spirit the Christian suffers the Passion." We know about his fake masochism, his sham dolorism, we know that Christianity has left its mark on him and that he was able to bear his wretched lot only by aspiring to be the Iphigenia of a pure sacrifice offered to all and to nothing. But, when all is said and done, we must not lose sight of the fact that these sufferings are imaginary: he does not feel them. We know him well enough not to be taken in by these appearances: the beautiful word Passion is hollow when Genet uses it. Moreover, we have never seen him really seek suffering: when he does experience it, he carries it to an extreme in order to master it; he magnifies it or tries to utilize it. But it offers him nothing in itself. One has only to compare Genet's spiritual exercises with those of Bataille, who is a godless mystic. The latter tells us, in *The Inner Experience*, that he is sometimes entranced by the photograph of an executed criminal, as the Christian is by the Crucifixion. I regard this meditation as a fake. At least the photograph is a real object, at least the person whose picture we see really lived, really suffered: the ghastly ecstasy of his smile and the wounds on his chest inspire real horror; perhaps it is possible to intensify this horror to the point of "execution," to realize for a moment, by means of it, the suffering state of man, his abandonment in Nothingness. But that is not and never has been Genet's purpose. Can one imagine him meditating on the face of the Chinese who has been flayed alive? He doesn't give a damn about the pain of others; as for suffering humanity, he detests it: if everybody suffers, suffering is devaluated. You will not find any mournful suffering or meditation on "agony" in Genet. Far from proclaiming the absurdity of universal suffering, he tries to give meaning to his own. His dolorism is mainly sexual, and we have seen his reveries on Divine's woes end peacefully with masturbation. No: we have discovered the trap, we are not taken in. Let us see whether he has not specified, in other passages, the moral value he attaches to his works.

Such passages are not wanting. I quote the following at random: "I liberate myself by declaiming poems that leave my mind clarified," he says in *Our Lady of the Flowers*. "And with Divine dead, what is left for me to do, to say? . . . I have given up my desires. I too am 'already way beyond that.'" "I can keep dying until my death. . . . Have I said all that ought to have been said about this adventure? If I leave this book, I leave what can be related. The rest is beyond words. The rest is silence. I remain silent and walk barefoot." He does the same at the end of *Funeral Rites*, which was likewise an ascesis; it is now finished: "I belonged to the tribe . . . by the grace of an adoption. . . . In short, I belonged to the France which I cursed and so desired." And in *The Thief's Journal:* "This journal is not a mere literary diversion. The further I progress, reducing to order what my past life suggests, and the more I persist in the rigor of composition—of the chapters, of the sentences, of the book itself—the more do I feel myself hardening in my will to utilize . . . my former hardships."

These passages—and a dozen others—all have the same intention: they make of his work an ascetic experience which is achieved by the Word and whose fulfillment is to dissolve language into silence. Let us follow this lead.

In his cell, Genet produced images in order to heighten or maintain his excitement, thus, in order to act upon himself. The function of the story that he told himself was to bring him to orgasm, after which it dissolved. When the masturbator changes into an artist, he likewise does so in order to act upon himself; let us recall that he throws himself into writing as into stealing, as into lovemaking, frenziedly, doped by Dexedrine tables, and that he does not put down his pen until he has finished. This verbal frenzy ends with the breaking-up of the word as does the onanistic imagery with the breaking-up of the images. He hastens toward the moment when he will write "THE END" at the bottom of the last page and when he will have *nothing more to say* because he will have *said everything*. Nothing more to say: the words are there, but there is no further need to use them; if he tried, he would start, despite himself, to write sentences he had already written. But how can he be sure of having said everything? By systematically developing in the realm of the imaginary all the possibilities contained in the situation itself, particularly those which have not been realized.

The operation takes place in two stages: his heroes, who are products of masturbation, were at first only the transparent film that separated him from himself. He was then "mean, like all creators," and prolonged his excitement by torturing his creatures as children torture flies. But as his heroes are, in another sense, himself as Other and as he has assigned to each of them the function of embodying what he wants to become or is afraid of becoming, he inflicts imaginary tortures upon himself by making them suffer. A shifting of intention is enough for these sadistic games to become spiritual exercises. Genet, who is passive, full of hatred, a prisoner and an onanist, will humiliate Darling in order to take revenge on the toughs or to satisfy an old sexual dream; when he is free and active and lives with a handsome boy, his sadistic will fades away. However, the themes remain, because they are the major motifs of his sensibility. Every mishap of his heroes then reflects to him an aspect of his situation, a possibility of suffering that has been denied him, a conclusion that destiny has not drawn. In developing these adventures, Genet achieves what logicians call a *mental experience*. Does he not have that wonderful instrument of investigation, the gesture? "One has the momentary soul of one's gesture." In order to know what a particular beggar or princess is thinking, he has only to install his or her gestures in himself. He borrows the fatal movements of one, the gait of the other, copies the bodily movements that he has observed, with the aim of discovering the mental movements that correspond to them. Thus, "he will possess" Erik, Darling and the executioner, as he formerly possessed Stilitano. Before long the word will be a substitute for the gesture; the experience will take place in and through language. What exactly is this "mental experience"? An inquiry by Genet as to his potentialities, nothing else. It is, if need be, a valid method of investigation. You've never committed a crime? Then imagine that you are going to commit one. Choose the victim, ponder the motive, try to feel your fear before and after the murder, ask yourself whether you would experience remorse, etc. At the end of the exercise you will have certainly learned something about yourself. Of course, you will still not know how you would really kill. Besides, you will never kill, or if you have not already done so it is because you do not have the vocation. But you will have explored certain feelings which you tend to hide from yourself, and by reviewing your story in your mind you will be able to discover the real difficulties and desires that it reveals. If you go further, if you carry out the investigation systematically, if you make it your duty to rework the story of your life, to bring forth, in thought, what might have been, if your aim is to group about you all your possibilities in order to escape the niggardly contingency that realizes only a few of them and in order to be able to make contact with yourself as a *totality*, you will begin to understand Jean Genet. But, you may say, all novelists do that. They do not: to begin with, most of them want to know the others as much as and more than they want to know themselves. It is not true that all the characters in *War and Peace* are Tolstoy: we know the models he used; and if he depicts himself, in spite of everything, by his way of describing them, by his choice of their characteristics, he does so unwittingly and in spite of himself.[3] And, in addition, a novelist invents in order to write; Genet writes in order to invent. Art, style, and composition enable him to impart to the experience its full rigor; they fix it.

The content of these figments of the imagination is *moral*, as are the comments attached to them. In this respect, the most striking passage is the account of the sexual relations between Paulo and Hitler. Nothing is spared us. Genet uses every possible means of shocking us. But at the same time this sexual play is described in terms of ethical voluntarism. Every gesture reveals a moral concern, an intention that relates to value and being more than to pleasure: "This single and shy evidence of graciousness *heightened my grati-tude*. . . . Having . . . with *sovereign and self-confident authority* made him turn around, I covered the back of his neck with kisses. . . . His mother's presence, rapid and *sacred*, flashed through his mind. But he felt *the disadvantage of such a posture for meditat-ing on a mother*.[4] . . . His right hand, that big, thick, broad hand, became very tiny, docile, quiet, and murmured, 'Thank you.' My hand and I understood this language. . . . He suffered in the pres-ence of his regained *wholeness*, in the presence of his free, lonely personality whose *solitude was suddenly revealed to him by the detachment of a God*. . . . By the grace of an *unequaled generosity* the fabulous emblem of Satan's chosen people went down to live in that simple dwelling. . . . I was about to—I mean that no part of the gesture was revealed overtly, but its intention had already given me greater self-control by describing it from its beginning to its end, inside myself, who thereby felt a lightening capable of making time go backward—I was about, as I was saying. to jump on the bed, but I quickly pulled myself together and very deliberately lay down beside Paulo. By this sharp gesture which remained internal and of which *I had and had not been master, my soul meant to place itself on the level of Paulo's soul* and my gestures to have the gestures of his age. . . . With Paulo I was able to make natural gestures. . . . It was the great disorder—or rather *the systematic labor* —in which *I sought, by every possible means,* to reassume the larval form thanks to which one returns to Limbo," etc.

Where it not for the context—which context I spare you—who the devil would ever think that the passage deals with anal intercourse? You will not find this moral preciosity in *Our Lady of the Flowers.* The reason is that Genet was trying to be excited; his descriptions were meant to be erotic. But I do not think that the relating of this act of intercourse excited him for a single moment. Yet he does more than imagine it: he substitutes for Hitler in order to take part in it and suddenly says "I," although in the preceding line he used the third person singular. But since he does not really and truly feel the crushing weight of another body, since he supports a pure appearance by an effort of will, since he must, while imagining the scene, find the right words and accurate phrase, these fleshless shadows arouse in him only a shadow of excitement: the movement of his hands to caress a naked thigh would have been caused in reality by the insolent blooming of a young body. Even if the moral signification and intention had existed, they would have been drowned in desire. When systematically imagined with the purpose of being written about, the same movement loses its massive inertia; its substance is will and, if it is thus *willed,* it cannot be willed for itself but for its signification. The latter, in turn, instead of being painfully extracted from a memory by means of retrospective analysis, is given to us in the account itself as the goal of the gesture. The gesture is performed because Genet's soul "means to place itself on the level of Paulo's soul." But the ends which are posed by an act of freedom are characterized by the fact that they are *values.* Thus, the sexual act becomes, in the realm of the imaginary, a dramatization of the values: the very slight opacity of being melts; being becomes a dialectic of sexual communication. Hitler the war lord humiliates himself before Paulo, whom he terrorizes, and the latter affirms his superiority during the act without even wanting to do so, by the mere force of the dominating gesture. These shadows disappear; there remains a pure movement. The moral values surrender and humiliate themselves before vital values; transcendence yields to the massiveness of being; communication must take place through the bodies and first by the submission of the weaker to the stronger. But the supremacy of the ethical is reaffirmed immediately thereafter; transcendence aims at new ends beyond being. This dialectical connection between ethical domination and sexual domination, the latter being only a generously accepted reversal of the former and the former disappearing after the orgasm for the benefit of the latter, is the transcription, on a moral level, of the sexual problem of the virilified ex-fairy Genet [5] and at the same time the effort to find a solution: Divine wanted to take Our Lady and then slid under him in a swoon—that is the fact. How is she to give herself to an adolescent without losing all authority over him?—that is the problem. Let the gift be an act of generosity on the part of the superior, let the latter affirm his superiority even in his momentary submission—that is the solution. Genet carries out the experiment via Hitler and Paulo, then, immediately thereafter, goes beyond it; he classifies it and integrates it into his knowledge.

For Genet has only one purpose in setting up these moral experiments: *to go beyond them*. He makes of these situations, of these problems and their solutions, the skeleton of an event which is invented so that the ethical dramas *have already taken place, in order for him to have already experienced it* and to find himself beyond the conflict as one wakes up one day and finds oneself cured of an illness or an unhappy passion: he wants to establish for himself an imaginary past, with its unfulfilled possibilities, its dramas, its abortive undertakings. All this *has already been*, the story of it *has been written* in a book, there is no point in going back to it. The function of Genet's imaginative conceptions is to enable him to progress in the realm of the imaginary. Each experience is an inventory followed by liquidation. We have seen the example of this in *Funeral Rites:* the entire book is only the exercise of an exaggerated, heightened, and thus imaginary suffering. To suffer becomes a *duty:* Genet will become the source of his pain in order to deny the contingent reason for his mourning, the "anecdotic" death of Jean; he will transform his grief into a perfect and absolute essence of pain and will thereby do away with its particularity, its humble reality, as a feeling that has been experienced; he will aim at incorporating into himself the actual person of Jean and will thereby destroy at one and the same time both the dead person and the mourning. At the end of the book he is again free, empty, ready for something new. The mechanism of the ethical experience is thus as follows: one carries a real experience to the point of changing it into an *appearance;* one dissolves the appearance in the might-be; one makes of the *contingent accident* a pure movement and of the latter an idea of movement, that is, a word. The moral experience is, at bottom, only a verbal experience. The creator produces his characters in order to live through them, to the very dregs, his own possibilities and thereby to divest himself of the latter; he will deliver himself from his desires, his astonishments, his last illusions, and also of his obsessions. *In the book* he will submit to the Pimps, then will betray them, then will betray betrayal: in the book he will, by a verbal ascesis, experience all the stages of *Saintliness.* And Saintliness becomes "the most beautiful word in the French language." The moral world is *in the words;* one sacrifices the words to each other; the ethical events are events of language. In the end, all the words are sacrificed to the one word Beauty, which in turn disappears. The book is finished: the verbal divesting ends in silence; Genet, delivered from the poem, perceives himself as a pure abstract form of thought. Saintliness was that which was beyond nothingness; but since it becomes a language and *speaks,* Genet makes contact with himself as something beyond Saintliness, as a freedom. The moral experience produces the same result as the artistic experience; it *is* the artistic experience of which Genet becomes conscious and which he translates into another language. He has delivered himself from the Word by the "full employment" of the terms; he has delivered himself from Beauty by making it enter language: being the pure organization of the verbal world, Beauty sinks into silence along with this world. Above all, he has succeeded in what he did not plan to undertake: *he has freed himself from Good and Evil,* both of which have crept into the work and no longer have meaning except through the work. Evil is a certain sophistical order that is imposed upon words and that gives rise to unrealizable significations; Good, which is the logical order of the words that designate Being, exists only to be violated by the magnifying judgments. When the work grows silent, when, dragged down by its own weight, it sinks to the depths of darkness, Good and Evil sink into the same nothingness: Juve and Fantomas, the enemy brothers, perish in the same shipwreck. The deeper meaning of Genet's moralism is finally disclosed: he has put the moral element into words in order to get rid of it.

"My victory is verbal and I owe it to the sumptuousness of the terms." In point of fact, he has won on all the boards: he escapes from poverty, from prison, from horror; the decent folk support him in style, seek him out, admire him; even those who still censure him have to accept him since he has filled their minds with obsessive images. What does he give in return? Nothing. A moment of horror, a suspect beauty that disappears: he has spoken at length about a sinister and iniquitous world and yet has managed to say nothing about it. His extraordinary books are their own rebuttal: they contain both the myth and its dissolution, the appearance and the exposure of the appearance, language and the exposure of language. When we finish them, the reading leaves a taste of ashes since their content cancels itself. The good conscience dreamed of fullness, of being; Genet disturbs it by giving it "the notion of an escaping object that is missing." This happens because he has not called anything into question nor created new values. He has entered the readers' hearts and imparted to them his infernal lightness. He will henceforth be in them this sudden, suspicious lightness, this void; he has restored *negativity* to them.[6] *Verbal* victory: what Blanchot aptly says about Mallarmé can be applied word for word to Genet: "It is the singularity and wonder of language to give creative value, lightninglike power, to nothing, to pure emptiness, to the nothingness which it approaches—but does not attain —as its limit. . . . Let us note that in this endeavor to detach us from being, poetry is a hoax and a game. It necessarily deceives us: dishonesty and lying are its virtues. Like the hero of Igitur, it says: 'I cannot do this seriously. . . .' One would think that, owing to the fact that man speaks and by means of speech gives new meaning to the world, man is already dead . . . and, by the silence that enables him to speak, he attempts at every moment, to be missing from himself and from everything." Indeed, it was Genet who said: "The poet is a dead man." His victory is his being able "to be missing from himself and from everything": at the end of each poem he has said everything, and this was nothing. The book has closed upon itself and upon the universe; it sinks into the reader's mind; a phantom Genet installs himself in the reader's soul; but the real Genet has delivered himself from this character, that is, from his empirical self: he remains a pure absence in which creation and negation coincide; he is both this extraordinarily living emptiness that can produce fantasies by the thousand, that can distribute them among us, and the "corrosive," voracious nothing that absorbs and dissolves everything. He has, one by one, in a vacuum, gone through his experiences of progressive "destitution": he has said nothing and yet has nothing more to say; he has identified himself with all the passions, all the creatures, so as the better to escape them; instead of acquiring a new quality with each embodiment, he abandoned a little of himself. But at the end of the divesting, he retains eminently the Goods which he rejects, as do St. Theresa and the real saints, for he carries within himself, in the transparency of his consciousness, the world which he has, with one and the same movement, created and dissolved. Outside, in the midst of the world, he triumphs: in people's minds, in newspapers, in books, he is Genet the Thief; during this time he is, within himself, a quiet and total absence. He has delivered himself from himself: he can no longer will Evil or even Good; at the moment when the hoodwinked society of the Just *accepts* him, he metamorphoses himself, by the very act that obliges us to install him within us, and places himself above our subjugated minds. What would the little tramp who was pushed around by the police not have given for a show of tenderness? Our Lady so needs love that he loves his judges. But the poet would have to make only a gesture for us to give him our friendship, and he despises it. A word, a smile, would be enough. It would be enough if he recognized our good will, our efforts, if he were grateful to us for becoming his accomplices. He does not deign to make the gesture or utter the word. Rather, it is we who need his tenderness since we do not want to have damned ourselves for nothing, and it is he who refuses to let us have it since he despises us for having let ourselves be taken in.

And now here is a story for an Anthology of Grim Humor: "An abandoned child manifests evil instincts in his early childhood. He robs the poor peasants who adopted him. Though reprimanded, he persists. He escapes from the reformatory into which he had to be put, steals and plunders more than ever and, in addition, prostitutes himself. He lives in squalor, committing petty thefts and begging. He sleeps with everybody and betrays everyone. Nothing can discourage his zeal. This is the moment he chooses for devoting himself deliberately to evil. He decides that he will do the worst in every circumstance and, as he has come to realize that the greatest crime was not the doing of evil but the manifesting of evil, he writes, in prison, abominable books which stand up for crime and which fall within the provisions of the law. Precisely for that reason he will cease to be abject and squalid and will get out of prison. His books are printed and read. A stage director who has been decorated by the Legion of Honor mounts one of his plays which incites to murder. The President of the Republic nullifies the sentence he was supposed to serve for his latest offenses, precisely because he boasted in his books of having committed them. And when he is introduced to one of his former victims, she says to him: 'Delighted to meet you, sir. Please continue.' "

You will say that this story lacks verisimilitude. And yet that is what happened to Genet. "Rubbish," I was told by a pretentious idiot. "Stop looking for complicated explanations. Genet wasn't saved by his persisting in evil. If he succeeded, it's because he had talent." Very well: and if you're a failure, it's because you haven't any. But Genet's case isn't as clear as yours. *Precisely* because he has talent. What do you think talent is? Mildew of the brain? A supernumerary bone? I have shown that his work is the imaginary aspect of his life and that his genius is one with his unswerving will to live his condition to the very end. It was one and the same for him to will failure and to be a poet. He has never gone back on his pledges, he has never given in, has never abdicated, and if he has won, it is because he has steadily played loser wins.

For he has won. He comes and goes. He is free. It is almost eight years since he was last in prison. He has money, "honorable friends." This common-law criminal lives part of the time in Paris and part in Cannes, leading the life of a well-to-do bourgeois. He is "received." He is taken up by followers of fashion, is admired by others, but as he has not stopped associating with burglars and queers, he goes from drawing rooms to Montmartre bars, plays *The*

Mysteries of Paris all by himself and, because he comes from no-where, feels at home everywhere. The finest proof of his victory: two letters which he has received, one from a cop and the other from a turnkey, both requesting that he use his influence on their behalf.

What then? He has won. No doubt about it. But the game of loser wins has reversals that are to be expected: he has lost, there-fore has won; but if he wins, then he loses. The secret failure of every triumph is that the winner is changed by his victory and the loser by his defeat: when Genet put out his hand to sweep the board, the stake had disappeared. When the enemy is at the height of his power, it would be sweet to humiliate him; the day after the victory, when he is in chains, miserable and trembling, he is a mere man, and, whatever the victor may decide to do, there lurks in his decision a profound disenchantment: to be eager to punish out of fidelity to oneself is to want to cling to a dead past, to prefer what one was to what one has become; magnanimity, on the other hand, repudiates past sufferings, rises above years of struggle and hope. Genet's enemies are the Just. When he was an underdog, he dreamed of a Day of Glory when they would be forced to accept him while continuing to reject him. This contradiction reflected his own con-flict: society had to welcome him *as he was*, that is, *as an evildoer*. But is not the evildoer the man whom all society rejects? It therefore had to glorify him precisely to the extent that it condemned him. Whence those strange inventions, those fancied impostures: the son of a fake prince, received with open arms by a family that would throw him out if it suspected his real origin. But these fictions cannot fulfill his desire: the noble family welcomes him because it does not know the truth, whereas the Just would, in order to satisfy him, have to accept him while condemning him as unjust and to love him without ceasing to hate him. And as that is not possible, both Genet and the Just are transformed as they approach each other. The thief decided to write in order to know the glory of the criminal; society, in its shrewdness, accords him that of the poet. In the privacy of our home each of us damns himself in read-ing Genet; each of us experiences, while reading, a deep inner con-flict. The love we feel for the good writer is thwarted by the horror aroused by the evildoer. But as soon as the reader is back among his fellows, he regains his assurance: they decide together to honor

Genet *for his talent* and *in spite of* his crimes. They admire the art while condemning the subject, as if form and content could ever be separated. He keeps screaming at them: My talent is my crime. But to no avail. They persist in regarding him as a freakish poet who has devoted his genius to glorifying vice, or else they see him as an unhappy man whose hostility is forgivable because he has suffered so much. In a sense, they are not wrong, and we have said much the same thing: it was the impossibility of living that made Genet. However, we have shown that he decided to do Evil, that he willed himself unequivocally and that he defined himself, in his own eyes, by this decision. He does not want readers to pity him or to tolerate him as a singing derelict, but to recognize his dignity, the dignity of a self-made man. There are others who deliberately close their eyes to the obscenities, sophisms, and provocations in his books and pretend to see him not as the infernal Saint that he wants to be but as a Saint purely and simply, a *veritable* oblate personifying all human suffering. And, once again, there is an element of truth in this attitude: *in a sense*, any suffering is always all suffering. But that is a bit hasty: for Genet's misfortune has a particular aspect that these high-minded souls fail to recognize. His is the horrible and grating misfortune of the damned. Thus, he has the bitter experience of never being taken *for what he is*.

NOTES

1. *Variety I:* Leonardo da Vinci.
2. After the crisis of 1865–1867, Mallarmé, too, discovered, by following a quite different path, the "universal determinability" and "absolute negativity" of consciousness. He, too, was to extend this "uniform condemnation to everything perceptible": "My Mind, that habitual solitary of its own Purity, which is no longer dimmed even by the reflection of Time" (letter to Cazalis, May 14, 1867).
3. A feeble fashion perfectly in keeping with present-day complacency. It is claimed that the novelist depicts himself in his characters and the critic in his criticism. If Blanchot writes about Mallarmé, we are told that he reveals much more about himself than about the author he is examining. This is the residue of nineteenth-century bourgeois idealism, that inane subjectivism which is responsible for a great deal of the nonsense written (even by Proust) about love. See what it leads to: Blanchot has seen, in Mallarmé, only Blanchot; very well: then you see, in Blanchot, only yourself. In that case, how can you know whether Blanchot is talking about Mallarmé, or about himself? That is the vicious circle of all skepticism. So let us drop this outmoded cleverness. To be sure—I am ashamed to repeat these truisms, but our sophisticates are so shallow and silly that it has to be said—to be sure, Blanchot's point of view is personal to him. In like manner, whatever the instruments that the experimenter employs, he perceives the result of the experiment with his own eyes. But although objectivity is, to a certain extent, distorted, it is also *revealed*. Blanchot's passions, sensibility, and turn of mind incline him to make one conjecture rather than another, but it is Mallarmé who will verify Blanchot's conjecture. A critic's mental attitude and emotional makeup serve as "revealers," prepare the intuition. The conjecture, whether true or false, helps to reveal. If it is true, it is confirmed by the evidence; if false, it indicates other paths. No doubt the critic can "force" Mallarmé, can use him for his own purposes; that is precisely proof that he can also shed light on his objective reality. But, you may answer, the critic is a historical creature and his judgments are related to the age. That is true, but it would be wrong to confuse the historicism of our sophisticates with their idealistic subjectivism. For, if it is true (I say "if it is true," for I believe in the existence of trans-historical truths. There is nothing sublime about these truths. But if I say, for example: "Descartes wrote the *Discourse on Method*," that is true for all ages. This truth is not

"eternal," since its content is historical and dated. But it is trans-historical, for it does not depend on the economic, social, or religious evolution of mankind. It will be as true in a hundred years as it is today.) that the critic, who is a historical creature, reveals only Mallarmé's significance *for our age*, it is also true that this significance is objective. In short, we must return to very simple and very vulgar verities: in a *good* critical work, we will find a good deal of information about the author who is being criticized and some information about the critic. The latter information, moreover, is so obscure and blurred that it has to be interpreted in the light of all that we know about him. Furthermore, not everyone is capable of this kind of insight. One has only to read the nonsense that is written every day. Man is an object for man; the value of objectivity must be restored in order to dispose of the subjectivist banalities that always try to beg the question.

(You can see what they are driving at. I am reminded of the bourgeois salons where the hostess knows how to avoid quarrels because she has the art of reducing objective value judgments [that play is *bad*, that political operation is *blameworthy*] to purely subjective opinions [I *don't like* that play, etc.]. If it is taken for granted that you are merely depicting yourself in condemning police repression of a miners' strike, you will not be disturbing anyone. "I disapprove of the death penalty," said Clemenceau. To which Barrès, who was fond of the guillotine, replied: "Of course. Monsieur Clemenceau can't bear the sight of blood.")

4. The sentence is, of course, ironic. Again the theme of the "humiliated mother." But the very irony masks a sacrilegious will, including a recourse to antivalues, far removed from abandonment to sensuality.

5. And, of course, you will find in the background the dialectic of the Criminal and the Saint.

6. Mallarmé, too, wanted "his future poems to be [for people] . . . poisonous phials, frightful drops." We know that the phial of Igitur contains: "The drop of nothingness which is lacking to the sea."

The Phenomenology of Roundness

GASTON BACHELARD

TRANSLATED BY *Maria Jolas*

When metaphysicians speak briefly, they can reach immediate truth,
a truth that, in due course, would yield to proof. Metaphysicians,
then, may be compared and associated with poets who, in a single
verse, can lay bare a truth concerning inner man. The following con-
cise statement is taken from Karl Jaspers' thick volume entitled *Von
der Wahrheit* (p. 50): "Jedes Dasein scheint in sich rund" (Every
being seems in itself round). In support of this unsubstantiated
metaphysician's truth, I should like to present several texts formulated
in schools of thought that are all oriented differently from metaphysical thought.

Thus, without commentary, Van Gogh wrote: "Life is probably
round."

And Joë Bousquet, with no knowledge of Van Gogh's sentence,
wrote: "He had been told that life was beautiful. No! Life is
round." [1]

Lastly, I should like to know where La Fontaine said: "A walnut
makes me quite round."

With these four texts of such different origin, it seems to me that
here we have the phenomenological problem very clearly posed. It
should be solved by enriching it with further examples to which we
should add other data, taking care to conserve their nature of intimate data, independent of all knowledge of the outside world. Such
data as these can receive nothing from the outside world but *illustrations*. We must even be careful lest the too vivid colors of the
illustration make the *being of the image* lose its original light. Here
the average psychologist can do nothing but abstain from action,
since the perspective of psychological research must be reversed.
Such images cannot be justified by perception. Nor can they be taken
for metaphors as, for instance, when we say of a man who is simple
and frank, that he is: "*tout rond*." [2] This roundness of a being, or of

being, that Jaspers speaks of, cannot appear in its direct truth otherwise than in the purest sort of phenomenological meditation.

Nor can such images as these be transported into just any consciousness. No doubt there are those who will want to "understand," whereas the image must first be taken at its inception. Others will declare ostentatiously that they do not understand, and will object that life itself is certainly not spherical. They will express surprise that this being we seek to characterize in its intimate truth should be so ingenuously handed over to geometricians, whose thinking is exterior thinking. From every side, objections accumulate to put a quick end to the discussion. And yet the expressions I have just noted are there. They are there, in relief, in everyday language, implying meanings of their own. They do not come from immoderateness of language, any more than they do from linguistic clumsiness. They are not born of a desire to astonish others. In fact, despite their extraordinary nature, they bear the mark of primitivity. They suddenly appear and, in a twinkling, they are completed. This is why, from my standpoint, these expressions are marvels of phenomenology. In order to judge them, and to like and make them our own, they oblige us to take a phenomenological attitude.

These images blot out the world, and they have no past. They do not stem from any earlier experience. We can be quite sure that they are metapsychological. They give us a lesson in solitude. For a brief instant we must take them for ourselves alone. If we take them in their suddenness, we realize that we think of nothing else, that we are entirely in the being of this expression. If we submit to the hypnotic power of such expressions, suddenly we find ourselves entirely in the roundness of this being, we live in the roundness of life, like a walnut that becomes round in its shell. A philosopher, a painter, a poet, and an inventor of fables have given us documents of pure phenomenology. It is up to us now to use them in order to learn how to gather being together in its center. It is our task, too, to sensitize the document by multiplying its variations.

II

Before giving additional examples, I believe that it would be advisable to reduce Jaspers' formula by one word, in order to make it phenomenologically purer. I should say, therefore: *das Dasein ist rund*, being is round. Because to add that it *seems round* is to keep a doublet of being and appearance, when we mean the entire being in its roundness. In fact, it is not a question of observing, but of experiencing being in its immediacy. Full contemplation would divide into the observing being and being observed. In the limited domain in which we are working, phenomenology must do away with all intermediaries, all additional functions. Consequently, in order to obtain maximum phenomenological purity, we must divest Jaspers' formula of everything that could conceal its ontological value. This condition is necessary if the formula "being is round" is to become an instrument that will allow us to recognize the primitivity of certain images of being. I repeat, images of *full roundness* help us to collect ourselves, permit us to confer an initial constitution on ourselves, and to confirm our being intimately, inside. For when it is experienced from the inside, devoid of all exterior features, being cannot be otherwise than round.

Is this the moment to recall pre-Socratic philosophy, to refer to Parmenidian being and the "sphere" of Parmenides? Or, to speak more generally, can philosophical culture be the propaedeutics to phenomenology? It does not seem so. Philosophy introduces us to ideas that are too well coordinated for us to examine and reexamine them, detail after detail, as the phenomenologist must from the beginning. If a phenomenology of the logical sequence of ideas is possible, it must be acknowledged that this could not be an elementary phenomenology. In a phenomenology of the imagination, however, we receive a benefit of elementariness. An image that is worked over loses its initial virtues. Parmenides' "sphere" has played too important a role for his image to have retained its primitivity. Consequently, it could not be the tool required for our research on the subject of the primitivity of images of being. It would be hard to resist the temptation to enrich the image of Parmenidian being by means of the perfections of the geometrical being of the sphere.

But why speak of enriching an image, when we crystallize it in geometrical perfection? Examples could be furnished in which the value of perfection attributed to the sphere is entirely verbal. Here is one that we can use as a counter-example, in which, quite evidently, the author has failed to recognize all the values of images.

One of Alfred de Vigny's characters, a young lawyer, is educating himself by reading Descartes' *Méditations*: [3] "Sometimes," writes Vigny, "he would take up a sphere set near him, and after turning it between his fingers for a long time, would sink into the most profound daydreams of science." One would love to know which ones. The author doesn't say. Does he imagine that the reading of Descartes' *Méditations* is helped if the reader begins to roll a marble between his fingers? Scientific thought develops on another horizon and Descartes' philosophy cannot be learned from an object, even a sphere. Used by Alfred de Vigny, the word *profound*, as is often the case, is a negation of profundity.

Moreover, it is evident that when a geometrician speaks of volumes, he is only dealing with the surfaces that limit them. The geometrician's sphere is an empty one, essentially empty. Therefore it cannot be a good symbol for our phenomenological study of roundness.

III

There is no doubt that these preliminary remarks are heavy with implicit philosophy. I have nevertheless felt obliged to give them brief mention because they have served me personally, and because, too, a phenomenologist must tell everything. They have helped me to "dephilosophize," to shun the allures of culture and to place myself on the margin of convictions acquired through long philosophical inquiry on the subject of scientific thinking. Philosophy makes us ripen quickly, and crystallizes us in a state of maturity. How, then, without "dephilosophizing" ourselves, may we hope to experience the shocks that being receives from new images, shocks which are always the phenomena of youthful being? When we are at an age to imagine, we cannot say how or why we imagine. Then, when we could say how we imagine, we cease to imagine. We should therefore dematurize ourselves.

But since I seem to have been seized—quite accidentally—with a neological fit, let me say again, by way of introduction to the phenomenological examination of images of solid roundness, that I have sensed the necessity here, as on many other occasions, of "depsychoanalyzing" ourselves.

In fact, some five or ten years ago,[4] in any psychological examination of images of roundness, but especially of solid roundness, we should have laid stress on psychoanalytical explanations, for which we could have collected an enormous amount of documentation, since everything round invites a caress. Such psychoanalytical explanations are, no doubt, largely sound. But they do not tell everything, and above all, they cannot be put in the direct line of ontological determinations. When a metaphysician tells us that being is round, he displaces all psychological determinations at one time. He rids us of a past of dreams and thoughts, at the same time that he invites us to actuality of being. It is not likely that a psychoanalyst would become attached to this actuality enclosed in the very being of an expression. From his standpoint such an expression is humanly insignificant because of the very fact of its rarity. But it is this rarity that attracts the attention of the phenomenologist and encourages him to look with fresh eyes, with the perspective of being that is suggested by metaphysicians and poets.

IV

I should like to give an example of an image that is outside all realistic meaning, either psychological or psychoanalytical.

Without preparing us, precisely as regards the absolute nature of the image, Michelet says that "a bird is almost completely spherical." If we drop the "almost," which moderates the formula uselessly, and is a concession to a viewpoint that would judge from the form, we have an obvious participation in Jaspers' principle of "round being." A bird, for Michelet, is solid roundness, it is round life, and in a few lines, his commentary gives it its meaning of *model of being*.[5] "The bird, which is almost completely spherical, is certainly the sublime and divine summit of living concentration. One can neither see, nor even imagine, a higher degree of unity. Excess of concentration, which constitutes the great personal force of the bird, but which implies its extreme individuality, its isolation, its social weakness."

In the book, these lines also appear totally isolated from the rest. One feels that the author, too, followed an image of "concentration" and acceded to a plane of meditation on which he has taken cognizance of the "sources" of life. Of course, he is above being concerned with description. Once again, a geometrician may wonder, all the more so since here the bird is considered on the wing, in its out-of-doors aspect, consequently, the arrow figures could accord here with an imagined dynamics. But Michelet seized the bird's being in its cosmic situation, as a centralization of life guarded on every side, enclosed in a live ball, and consequently, at the maximum of its *unity*. All the other images, whether of form, color, or movement, are stricken with relativism in the face of what we shall have to call the absolute bird, the being of round life.

The image of being—because it is an image of being—that appears in this fragment by Michelet is extraordinary for the very reason that it was considered of no significance. Literary criticism has attached no more importance to it than has psychoanalysis. And yet, it was written, and it exists in an important book. It would take on both interest and meaning if a philosophy of the cosmic imagination could be instituted that would look for centers of cosmicity.

Seized in its center and brevity, the mere designation of this roundness is astonishingly complete. The poets who mention it, unaware that others have done the same, reply to one another. Thus Rilke, who undoubtedly did not recall what Michelet had written on the subject, wrote: [6]

> . . . *Ce rond cri d'oiseau*
> *Repose dans l'instant qui l'engendre*
> *Grand comme un ciel sur la forêt fanée*
> *Tout vient docilement se ranger dans ce cri*
> *Tout le paysage y semble reposer.*

> (. . . This round bird-call
> Rests in the instant that engenders it
> Huge as the sky above the withered forest
> Docilely things take their place in this call
> In it the entire landscape seems to rest.)

To anyone who is receptive to the cosmicity of images, the essentially central image of the bird is the same in Rilke's poem as in the fragment by Michelet, only expressed in another register. The round cry of round being makes the sky round like a cupola. And in this rounded landscape, everything seems to be in repose. The round being propagates its roundness, together with the calm of all roundness.

And for a dreamer of words, what calm there is in the word round. How peacefully it makes one's mouth, lips, and the being of breath become round. Because this too should be spoken by a philosopher who believes in the poetic substance of speech. And for the professor who has broken with every kind of "being-there" (*être-là*), it is a joy to the ear to begin his course in metaphysics with the declaration: *Das Dasein ist rund.* Being is round. Then wait for the rumblings of this dogmatic thunders to die down, while his disciples beam with ecstasy.

But let us come back to a simpler, more tangible kind of roundness.

V

Sometimes we find ourselves in the presence of a form that guides and encloses our earliest dreams. For a painter, a tree is composed in its roundness. But a poet continues the dream from higher up. He knows that when a thing becomes isolated, it becomes round, assumes a figure of being that is concentrated upon itself. In Rilke's *Poèmes français*, this is how the walnut tree lives and commands attention. Here, again around a lone tree, which is the center of a world, the dome of the sky becomes round, in accordance with the rule of cosmic poetry. On p. 169 of this collection we read:

> *Arbre toujours au milieu*
> *De tout ce qui l'entoure*
> *Arbre qui savoure*
> *La voûte des cieux*

> (Tree always in the center
> Of all that surrounds it
> Tree feasting upon
> Heaven's great dome)

Needless to say, all the poet really sees is a tree in a meadow; he is not thinking of a legendary Yggdrasil that would concentrate the entire cosmos, uniting heaven and earth, within itself. But the imagination of round being follows its own law: since, as the poet says, the walnut tree is "proudly rounded," it can feast upon "heaven's great dome." The world is round around the round being.

And from verse to verse, the poem grows, increases its being. The tree is alive, reflective, straining toward God.

> *Dieu lui va apparaître*
> *Or, pour qu'il soit sûr*
> *Il développe en rond son être*
> *Et lui tend des bras mûrs.*
>
> *Arbre qui peut-être*
> *Pense au-dedans.*
> *Arbre qui se domine*
> *Se donnant lentement*
> *La forme qui élimine*
> *Les hasards du vent!*

(One day it will see God
And so, to be sure,
It develops its being in roundness
And holds out ripe arms to Him.

Tree that perhaps
Thinks innerly.
Tree that dominates self
Slowly giving itself
The form that eliminates
Hazards of wind!)

I shall never find a better document for a phenomenology of a being which is at once established in its roundness and developing in it. Rilke's tree propagates in green spheres a roundness that is a victory over accidents of form and the capricious events of mobility. Here becoming has countless forms, countless leaves, but being is subject to no dispersion: if I could ever succeed in grouping together all the images of being, all the multiple, changing images that, in spite of everything, illustrate permanence of being, Rilke's tree would open an important chapter in my album of concrete metaphysics.

NOTES

1. Joë Bousquet, *Le Meneur de lune*, p. 174.
2. Alas, in English, such a man is never "round" but "square." (Translator's note.)
3. Alfred de Vigny, *Cinq-Mars*, Chap. XVI.
4. This volume first appeared in 1958. (Translator's note.)
5. Jules Michelet, "L'oiseau," p. 291.
6. Rilke, *Poésie*, translated (into French) by Maurice Betz, under the title: *Inquiétude*, p. 95.

Notes on Racinian Time

GEORGES POULET

TRANSLATED BY *Elliott Coleman*

I

Racine's theater opens with *La Thébaïde*. But in the very first lines of it there is posed so urgent and so fundamental a problem that the entire Racinian theater will do nothing more than restate the question:

> O thou, Sun, thou that restorest light to the world,
> Why hast thou not abandoned it in the depths of night? [1]

It is the problem of existence, but posed with reference to the continuation of being, and not directly to its origin. The double reality which inbreathes and encloses these lines, the first in which the authentic Racinian accent vibrates, is that of a sun which restores light to the world, and of a world that has not deserved that light be returned to it. Why does the creative power consent to begin over again a work which has been confirmed to be defective and monstrous? Why does it consent to prolong for a single present day the series of past days which, of themselves, fell into "the depths of night"? The more inexplicable a problem, for the creation of a new day does not simply imply, like that of the first day, the creation of a being still pure and worthy of God; but this time the invention of a being who has already had an existence and who, by reason of this past existence, far from meriting a present existence, ought to be "abandoned to the night." Unless one can imagine this absurdity: the perpetual creation of a world radically new every time, and obliterated in each instant, in order to be "brought back" in the following instant to its first virginity; once evil has been acquired, and the worthlessness of the creature recognized, there is nothing at all for God to do except stop creating or create something that will be continuous, and which will continue precisely a past into which evil has been introduced. Before the fault and before the fall, God only continued to bring back to the light of day a being who was always the same, always equally worthy of the "light," and who therefore had no past. Now, on the contrary, the continued creation of the world implies the creation of a being which is prolonged backward, whose existence consists not only in living, but in having lived, and lived badly.

Such is the characteristic aspect which the problem of existence takes for Racine. Like Descartes and like the Jansenists, he poses in principle the *independence* of the parts of a duration in which God is obliged every day to bring back light to the world, instead of leaving the world to darkness; but on the other hand, he nonetheless feels the absolute *dependence* of each of the new moments upon a past out of which God is obliged to create them, to *co-create* them; so that in the Racinian, as in the Bergsonian universe, what one calls the present is not solely pure and ceaseless invention, but a preservation of the past and a continuation of the past into the present.

It is a continuation, however, which, for Racine, far from having as with Bergson the value of a progress and a promise, has on the contrary the most tragic significance; for it permits of no hope, except the hope that one day instead of being brought back to the light of day, we shall be abandoned to night and to nothingness. Even God is unable to make the past cease to exist and, therefore, also to make evil cease to continue and repeat itself; not even God can make hatreds cease to *persist* and prolong themselves from times elapsed to times not yet accomplished: "Sad and fatal effect of an incestuous blood," [2] the whole Racinian drama is presented as the intrusion of a fatal past, of a determining past, of a past of efficient cause, into a present that seeks desperately to become independent of it.

II

What is the subject of *La Thébaïde?* It is the story of a man who believes that he can free himself from the past. All the other characters are supremely conscious of continuing in their present a past which is consummated in their hatreds or their present terrors. What they are is made clear only by what they themselves or their fathers have been: "What, must I explain my thoughts any further?/One can discern them in the things of the past." [3] Creon alone dreams of a state in which, in the absolute actuality conferred by omnipotence, it would be possible to free oneself at one stroke from this fatal fidelity; of a state in which "A soul possessed of the pleasure of reigning,/Turns all his ideas away from time past"; [4] royal state which would be that of a being capable of having no remorse, no memories, no past; capable also of doing without a destiny; a state in which one could abandon himself to those transports of joy which the feeling of living in a naked present gives, cleansed of all blemish and so intensely real that past events would leave no more trace than a dream:

> Then speak to me only of subjects of joy,
> Allow me to leave myself only a prey to my transports;
> And, without ever reminding me of the shadows of hells,
> Tell me all that I gain, and not what I lose . . .
> All that is past is only a dream to me now,
> I was father and subject, I am lover and king, [5]

Strange transport which expresses a feeling believed to be joy, but which is unconscious despair; for the very motion by which the man-living-in-the-present had wished, so to speak, to fabricate himself and to consecrate his independence, his radical actuality, entails and forthwith completes his frightful, direct dependence upon the man he has been from his birth, the man he can never cease to be until death: "I am the last blood of the unhappy Laïus." [6]

The Racinian tragedy is the impossibility of limiting oneself to the present moment. Fidelity to hatred, as in *La Thébaïde;* fidelity to love, as in *Andromaque;* fidelity to custom, as in *Bérénice;* fidelity to blood, as in *Phèdre*—the subject of almost every tragedy of Racine consists in the repetition and the ineluctable continuation of the past into the present:

> He disguises himself in vain; I read upon his face—
> The sad and savage humor of the proud Domitian race. [7]

You belie not at all a deadly race,
Truly you are the blood of Atreus and Thyeste.[8]

Faithful to the blood of Achab. . . .[9]

III

Andromaque is, above all, the drama of beginning anew. Here passion is a "trail that one recognizes," [10] a "wound that one reopens"; [11] its objects are certain faces "which one remembers," [12] a vanished being which in a living being one begins again ceaselessly to love: "It is Hector. Behold his eyes, his mouth. . . ." [13]

Furthermore, *Andromaque* is a drama whose beings exist only insofar as they "represent" [14] certain beings who exist no longer but who, out of the depths of their past, must come "to be found again," [15] "to revive" [16] and be "recognized" [17] in living beings. And if, like Creon in *La Thébaïde,* Pyrrhus is of all the characters in *Andromaque* the most significant, it is because he is the living proof that it is impossible to escape from this *representation* of the past in the present, and that it is no less vain to want to seize in passion an instant that is without faith and without memories. For one would not know how to resist the double weight of an opinion and a conscience that see in the being that one is, only the prisoner and the executor of the past:

Ah! I recognize you . . .
It is no longer the play of a servile flame:
It is Pyrrhus, the son and the rival of Achilles
Who triumphs a second time over Troy.[18]

Thus the whole drama is only an immense and infinitely complex repetition of a more ancient drama. It is a drama played for the second time—a gigantic phenomenon of memory, in which not only feelings but existences are resuscitated. No work has expressed more completely the repetitive power of duration.

IV

Lengthening backward of the Racinian tragedy; also prolongation forward; immense spaces of duration between which it finds itself pressed. For if Racine likes to set his characters in faraway times, and against a remote background, it is doubtless first because "the respect the audience has for heroes grows in proportion the farther away they are withdrawn from us"; [19] but it is also because this very withdrawal, and the respect it inspires, have the effect of placing events and personages in a *historical* perspective and of preventing us from seeing in the action the bare, brutal image of the immediate.

Andromaque and *Iphigénie* both evoke the historic totality of an epoch, all the durational length of a great epic subject, and in both plays the subject is the same; but in the one it is situated just before the historic action commences, while in the other just after it ends. *Andromaque* begins where the *Iliad* finishes: "Do you no longer remember, my lord, what Hector was?/Our enfeebled people remember him still." [20] *Iphigénie* takes place just before the *Iliad* begins: "And one day my death, the source of your glory,/Shall start the recital of so beautiful a story." [21]

Opening or closing a recital, the moment of action thus almost entirely loses its proper value, its quality of the single "present" moment, its privilege of being the sole real part of moment. Its "reality" is not rich enough in itself to triumph over a past and over a future, unreal doubtless, but arrayed in all the opulence of history and poetry. And so the Racinian moment becomes the slave of an anterior or posterior duration which inspires it and sets its extremity. Extreme point of a past that is ending, of a future, of a monster "being born," it is as though it were stifled between two walls of events which draw together, which already touch each other. It hasn't the time to be time.

The Racinian moment is a point, but in the sense in which one says: It is here, at this point, that the drama took place. Point of fatal encounter between the line drawn from the past and the line drawn from the future—point where efficient cause and final cause collide and are confounded.

V

Situated at a point without duration, possessed by actual action, Racine's characters nevertheless seem to be endowed with the power of looking at themselves, as it were, historically, as if they were not only themselves but also our contemporaries; they are the prey of the immediate, but also they contemplate at the same time both the causes and the remote conclusion of the drama in which they are engaged. They view themselves *in the future* as we view them *in the past:*

> Then I had traversed so many seas, so many States,
> And come so far only to prepare his death? [22]

> I foresee that thy blows shall fall upon even thy mother.[23]

> . . . I foresee already everything necessary to foresee.
> My only hope is my despair.[24]

The Racinian character is like Calchas: "He knows all that was and all that still must be." [25]

His foresight does not differ at all from his memory. It is of the same nature. It holds, in Racine, to a conception of life which, although profoundly different from that of the Greeks, is no less fatalistic: a fatality no longer external, but internal, which situates the determining forces in the interior of the soul. They are in the being, they are of the being, and if at the same time they are hostile and deadly to the being, they are nonetheless a source of vital energy from which there springs what the being is in each one of its moments. Prescience, as well as memory, consists only in referring to this source, the creative influx of which may vary in intensity but never in its nature. Monster coming to birth or monster being completed; Nero in the past or in the future confirms Nero.

It is foreknowledge which informs the being not only of his actions but of the particular nuance of emotion which the future reserves for him. Racinian characters are not content to suffer from their present ills; they experience suffering in the future: "In a month, in a year, how shall we suffer?" [26] Eternal future, "frightful, inexhaustible cup" [27] from which the damned in the Racinian world know they will continue to imbibe in the future the bitter knowledge of their past:

> Thus with a plaintive voice
> Will express its remorse
> The tardy penitence
> Of the inconsolable dead.[28]

The extremity of emotion to which they thus attain, has for its complement the most poignant intensity of poetry: as if, in uniting certain states of mind which the order of the times separates, in distributing their passions over the vastest space of duration, they invested them with an absolute significance, no longer that of a fault or an actual misfortune, but of a despair that gives its name to all existence:

> One will know the roads by which I conducted him.[29]

> I shall turn back, alone and desperate,
> I shall see the roads all perfumed still
> With the flowers they had sown beneath her footsteps.[30]

VI

The *feeling of self* in the Racinian being: it is that of a man who falls over a precipice, is terrified, and yet looks at himself in a detached and extraordinarily lucid fashion, as if his future death were already accomplished, and he saw himself *in the past*.

The Racinian tragedy is an action *in the past*. We see it less in its actuality, in its immediacy, in the palpable shock of it, than in the reflective thought and in the affective echo it produces afterward, mediately and almost indirectly, in its victims and spectators. At the moment in which we have become conscious of it, it has already taken place. It fulminates, like the lightning one recognizes only when it is gone and has become part of the past. In that respect, the tragedy of Racine differs from all other tragedy, which by its nature renders the action in a time that is progressive, that is in the course of being. Here, it is a time realized that engages us, and the action which confronts us, being in each of its consecutive parts an action which has just taken place and which in each instant is only just past, it seems that we are witnessing the process by which things in the last analysis become "fatal" in our eyes and force us to recognize that indeed they could not have happened otherwise. The Racinian fatality is characterized by this *retardation* of thought upon action, which paints the latter the color of unchangeable lead, and which brings it about that each past contingency, even if it be only one second past, becomes as necessary as the most general law. The Racinian fatality is the "What have I said!" of Phèdre. It is the fatality of irreversibility.

VII

I know my frenzies, I recall them all.[31]

There is no light more intense or more cruel than that projected by the self-awareness of Racinian characters. The reflective consciousness which leads them to the discovery of their own being, reveals to them not only the kind of being they are, but the kind of continuity or progression in time which has more and more made them become what they are. The particular lucidity they bring to this knowledge reaches as far as their past extends. It makes rise up in their course and development all the thoughts and actions which have issued from their very depths to bring them to the extreme situation into which they are thrown and of which they become aware. It even goes back further and seems to search the original shadows for a primary principle, a prenatal tendency, which, from before their existence, contained its germ and waited to enfold it in frenzies and passions. Thus the tragic consciousness is here found invested with the power of contemplating itself through the whole field of its duration: it everywhere recognizes itself as monstrously similar.

But it happens also, in Racinian humanity, that a human being finds himself provisionally saved from this fatal knowledge. He is then mysteriously allowed to remain ignorant of what he is and what he has been. He lives for a time in a present which has yet no past. And because of this fact, neither has it yet any destiny; for what is truly fatal for a human being is the clear-sightedness by which, in discovering what he has been, he finds out what he is going to be; ready to consummate his ruin and his doom:

> I ignore who I am; and to crown the horror,
> A dreadful oracle binds me to my error,
> And when I search for the blood that brought me to birth,
> I am told that without perishing I cannot know myself.[32]

Or again it may happen in the Racinian drama that sudden forgetfulness follows the recognition of self. There is occasionally a vivid moment in which, in the very shock of catastrophe, everything is effaced and collapses; a moment in which there no longer remains anything in thought except a sort of blind consciousness of the present instant. The past is swallowed up, and the being, face to face with the brutality of the actual, feels the sense of his identity vacillate:

> "Is it Pyrrhus who is dying, or am I finally Orestes?" [33]
> "Who am I? Is it Monima, and am I Mithridates?" [34]

Instantaneous testimonials of the being reduced to the instant, torn out of duration, which reveals how essentially the Racinian character differs from the Corneilian character. The latter exists only in and for the moment. It is realized there. The instantaneous makes rise from his lips, not a question, not a *Who am I?* but an affirmation: *I know what I am and what I ought to be.* With Corneille we are in a universe in which God has given a part to the human will. It thrills with the joy of feeling within it the perfect identity of the moment in which it wills and of the moment in which it feels itself will: I will, therefore I am. This unique moment encloses it, completes it, assures it, and gives it fullness of life. But the Racinian moment, as soon as it finds itself stripped of duration, is then no more than a shred of existence, a discontinuous being, a sort of fragment, as if in losing the feeling of being victim and prey, man lost at the same time the consciousness of the profound unity which, in binding together the different moments of his temporal life, creates the sense of his existence and his true self.

VIII

"Racine," says Thierry Maulnier, "goes straight to what is hardest and purest in life and death—to destiny." How is it that one can speak of the *purity* of Racinian destiny, since nothing is less pure or more horrible than the successive visages it seems to present? "What wilt thou say, my father, of this horrible spectacle?" [35]

Let us be careful, however, not to confound with destiny the *horrible spectacle* which makes the consciousness of Phèdre, like the shade of Minos, shudder; for it is the spectacle offered to Phèdre by Phèdre, the light under which she sees herself in the horrible and incessant revolutions of the life of her senses: "I feel my whole body shiver and burn";[36] experience of the self by the self, situated in the contact and contrast of the successive moments, but which immediately another presence replaces: "I recognized Venus and her terrible fires,/Inevitable torments of a blood she pursues." [37]

Upon the horrible, instantaneous spectacle of sensory experience there is superimposed the consciousness of an eternal, continuous, supersensible reality which Phèdre *recognizes:* a reality which, as much by its nature as by the extent of the field of duration upon which its action is performed, inspires no longer the horror that one has over impure things, but the awe engendered by the presence and perseverance of the divine. Immediately the tracked-down consciousness is lifted up to a zone more tragic still, but more serene, in which it even acquires a sort of grandeur; as if in the midst of feeling itself entangled in the miserable web of impassioned intermittences, of remorse and premonitions in which "each moment kills it," it saw itself endowed and arrayed, on the other hand— not indeed as in the romantic poets with the prestige of the rebel Titan, but rather with the dignity of a sacrificial victim, in the fulfillment of the rites by which his destiny is wrought. On the one hand it is a being stricken with the palpitation and rendings of a discontinuous time; on the other, it is a person whose destiny is inscribed above the eddies of duration, in the eternal zone of celestial wills—whose destiny is fulfilled in still another zone, in the order of providential temporality, unfolding regularly, inevitably, and serenely the arcanae of those wills. Hence the existence of three parallel durations in Racine as in the medieval thinkers: the discontinuous time of actual passions; the continuous time of the fulfillment of the divine will; and finally this will itself in its pure nontemporality.

IX

Close as Racine's superimposition of times comes to the medieval conception, there is a point of difference; and this point is so important that, despite everything, it forces us to place Racine at the very antipodes of the scholastic spirit. Racine's three times are indeed disposed in the stages of the scholastic order; but in the Racinian tragedy there is the constant impression that these stages brush against each other; that in some way these planes of existence are liable to unite or to be confused. The triple existence of things does not stand out with the clearness of design which, in a Saint Thomas or a Dante, allows a distinction to be made, then and there, between eternity and time proper. In Racine, on the contrary, there is something indecisive and turbid which makes the human drama a long, anguished meditation and almost a religious mystery, in which it is no longer a question whether passion is passion, or evil is evil, but whether or not the gods themselves are malevolent, or infected by evil; whether, finally, the fatal discontinuity of human realities does not end by extending and even encroaching in some manner upon eternity; so that this eternal world whose image ideally transpires through the ferocity of human duration, far from having the serenity and the purity one fancied, far from assuring us, as we would wish to believe, of the continuity of a purpose and design in an existence which of itself is torn to pieces and perverted, this eternal world would seem in its turn contaminated and corrupted, becoming a mere reflection of our tragic condition, projected into the clouds: "Halt, barbarians:/It is the pure blood of the God that hurls the thunderbolt." [38]

This cry breathes forth the most authentic religious anguish.

Suddenly it is no longer the question of a mother who fears for her daughter, but of a soul that fears for its God. We are in the presence here of one of the most undefinable and most profound of the fears which are at the base of all religions; the fear that in the contact between the divine and the human, which is religion itself, there may be something perilous, not only for the creature but for the divine itself; the fear lest the intangible become tangible, the light become dark, and the purity become corrupted. Let the thunderbolt split and destroy a sacrilegious creation; this is not the most terrible risk. The risk is that the thunder clap may be the signal for an annihilation of Heaven as well.

x

At the extreme opposite of this terror, and as if Racine had had to traverse the deepest shadows to emerge into the light, there is at the very end of that long tunnel which is the tragedy of *Phèdre*, the sudden restoration of day: "And death, robbing my eyes of their brightness,/Restores to the day all the purity they defiled."

The extraordinary beauty of these lines is owing to the double image of the dawn which they evoke: a dawn, on the one hand, so cruel to the dying; a dawn, on the other hand, so sweet to the eyes of those who will continue to live. For the former, the brightness of day is darkened; for the latter, its purity is restored. In the consciousness of Phèdre the reality of peace and of purity is perceived only at the moment when she must bid them good bye forever. She is brought to the farthest limit of despair. She *is* that limit. The consciousness of the pure, of the bright, of the light of day, is achieved by her, as something *interior to her*, only at the moment it leaves her forever. Until then, the world of daylight and purity had existed only by implication, as the reverse side of the world of shadows constituting her mind. And now at the moment of death she *sees* this purity and this brightness, she knows them to be true, but she has lost them.

Farthest limit of despair, but a despair that implies, though certainly not a hope, at least a discovery and a belief, let us even say a faith: faith in transcendence, in a being by which she has held on to being, in a brightness which makes her shadow be shadow, in a purity that, through an anguish from which she is delivered, she had come to fear that she had irremediably contaminated the nature. This is a purgation by which the consciousness of eternity is attained and which ends in an act of faith: I recognize the eternal; dying, and by my death, I pay homage.

From this eternity she is doubtless excluded. She knows that fact. She thinks of it only in passing. Her final lot, her eternal destiny is suddenly of very little concern compared with the immense reality in the face of which her humiliation overwhelms her. There is something here that is analogous to the pure love of François de Sales and of Fénelon: "O my God," said a mystic of that period, "I would choose not to be at all, rather than that you should cease to be." [39] "O my God," says Phèdre, "my being matters nothing, since you will not cease to be, and to be the one who washes away the stains of the world, but whom the stains of the world do not soil." An entire disinterestedness of self in the perception of the Being who is *light* and supreme purity. Perhaps one can see in this the action of a saving grace; perhaps, after all, Phèdre is a Christian in whom *grace has not failed;* perhaps she dies saved, without knowing it; because she has rejoined, in a transport of absolute humility, the same state of loving self-annihilation at which the great contemplatives arrive. Did not Fénelon say that pure love consists in loving God in indifference to one's own salvation, even if one knows he is going to be damned? Phèdre dies, doubtless not in the divine love, not in *caritas*, but she dies *in renunciation*, in total resignation to the divine will. Her supreme, unique act is an act of perfect abandonment; she dies "a willing slave" of God and not "a slave of death." [40]

XI

In all the plays of Racine, up until the conclusion of *Phèdre*, the dominating idea is that of a world which reveals itself as radically evil, whose very survival seems for that reason to compromise or obscure the notion of a God of Light and a God of Purity. By dint of seeing the continuation of the world only as a repetition of the same crimes and the same passions, the mind ends by perceiving in the dark unfolding of things, only their interdependence. The entire duration of a being is no more in his own eyes than the ceaseless beginning again of what stains and destroys him—thus the more and more desperate tone of the earlier Racinian theater. But in *Phèdre* and after *Phèdre* a roundabout face is accomplished. Suddenly the accent is no longer on the ceaseless continuation of being, but on the ceaseless act by which it is continued, and on the dependence of the creature on the act by which it exists. Over and above the endless chain of causes and effects which seem to engender duration, there is distinguished the presence of a first cause that mercifully joins its eternity to the instant; and beyond the despair which indefinite perpetuity of evil engenders, the soul suddenly discovers in its infinite dependence upon God, a peace which lifts the instant to eternity: "The soul happily captive/Under thy yoke finds peace. . . ." [41] And in the same *Cantique* these lines, in which once more the creature is astonished to see the sun restore light to the world: "And who am I that thou deignest/To condescend even to me?" Identical question to that of those lines of *La Thébaïde* quoted at the beginning of this chapter; but here, without losing its urgency, it is robbed of the venom. The question is concluded in supplication, in prayer; for what shows through the most intense feeling of human indignity is the feeling, no less intense, of the prodigious dignity which in every instant the eternal act of creation confers upon and restores to this unworthy being. Thus the fatality of past cause and past evil is exorcised by the recognition of a cause which transcends all duration, and which is found immediately and almost miraculously, even in the moment of death— of the death of Phèdre, since this moment, like all moments, is the gift of God.

After that, no more remains than to set forth the divine acts of this Providence in human durations. That is what Racine will do in *Esther* and *Athalie*.

NOTES

1. Act I, scene 1.
2. Act IV, scene 1.
3. *Ibid.*, scene 3.
4. Act III, scene 6.
5. Act V, scene 4.
6. Act V, scene 6.
7. *Britannicus*, Act I, scene 1.
8. *Iphigénie*, Act IV, scene 4.
9. *Athalie*, Act V, scene 6.
10. Act I, scene 1.
11. Act II, scene 2.
12. Act I, scene I; Act II, scene 1; Act III, scene 8.
13. Act II, scene 5.
14. *Ibid.*, scene 4.
15. Act III, scene 8.
16. Act II, scene 4.
17. Act V, scene 3.
18. Act II, scene 5.
19. *Bajazet*, preface.
20. *Andromaque*, Act I, scene 2.
21. *Iphigénie*, Act V, scene 2.
22. *Andromaque*, Act V, scene 1.
23. *Britannicus*, Act V, scene 6.
24. *Bajazet*, Act I, scene 4.
25. *Iphigénie*, Act II, scene 1.
26. *Bérénice*, Act IV, scene 5.
27. *Athalie*, Act II, scene 9.
28. *Cantiques spirituels*, 2.
29. *Britannicus*, Act III, scene 3.
30. *Iphigénie*, Act IV, scene 4.
31. *Phèdre*, Act III, scene 3.
32. *Iphigénie*, Act II, scene 1.
33. *Andromaque*, Act V, scene 4.
34. *Mithridate*, Act IV, scene 5.
35. *Phèdre*, Act IV, scene 6.
36. *Ibid.*, Act I, scene 3.
37. *Ibid.*
38. *Iphigénie*, Act V, scene 4.

39. Quoted by H. Bremond, *Histoire du sentiment religieux*, VIII, 418.
40. *Cantiques spirituels*, 3.
41. *Ibid.*, 4.

Structuralism

The Structural Study of Myth

CLAUDE LEVI-STRAUSS

TRANSLATED BY *Claire Jacobson*

> *It would seem that mythological worlds have been built up only to be shattered again, and that new worlds were built from the fragments.*
>
> —FRANZ BOAS [1]

Despite some recent attempts to renew them, it seems that during the past twenty years anthropology has increasingly turned from studies in the field of religion. At the same time, and precisely because the interest of professional anthropologists has withdrawn from primitive religion, all kinds of amateurs who claim to belong to other disciplines have seized this opportunity to move in, thereby turning into their private playground what we had left as a wasteland. The prospects for the scientific study of religion have thus been undermined in two ways.

The explanation for this situation lies to some extent in the fact that the anthropological study of religion was started by men like Tylor, Frazer, and Durkheim, who were psychologically oriented although not in a position to keep up with the progress of psychological research and theory. Their interpretations, therefore, soon became vitiated by the outmoded psychological approach which they used as their basis. Although they were undoubtedly right in giving their attention to intellectual processes, the way they handled these remained so crude that it discredited them altogether. This is much to be regretted, since, as Hocart so profoundly noted in his introduction to a posthumous book recently published,[2] psychological interpretations were withdrawn from the intellectual field only to be introduced again in the field of affectivity, thus adding to "the inherent defects of the psychological school . . . the mistake of deriving clear-cut ideas . . . from vague emotions." Instead of trying to enlarge the framework of our logic to include processes which, whatever their apparent differences, belong to the same kind of intellectual operation, a naïve attempt was made to reduce them to inarticulate emotional drives, which resulted only in hampering our studies.

Of all the chapters of religious anthropology probably none has tarried to the same extent as studies in the field of mythology. From a theoretical point of view the situation remains very much the same as it was fifty years ago, namely, chaotic. Myths are still widely interpreted in conflicting ways: as collective dreams, as the outcome of a kind of esthetic play, or as the basis of ritual. Mythological figures are considered as personified abstractions, divinized heroes, or fallen gods. Whatever the hypothesis, the choice amounts to reducing mythology either to idle play or to a crude kind of philosophic speculation.

In order to understand what a myth really is, must we choose between platitude and sophism? Some claim that human societies merely express, through their mythology, fundamental feelings common to the whole of mankind, such as love, hate, or revenge; or that they try to provide some kind of explanations for phenomena which they cannot otherwise understand—astronomical, meteorological, and the like. But why should these societies do it in such elaborate and devious ways, when all of them are also acquainted with empirical explanations? On the other hand, psychoanalysts and many anthropologists have shifted the problems away from the natural or cosmological toward the sociological and psychological fields. But then the interpretation becomes too easy: If a given mythology confers prominence on a certain figure, let us say an evil grandmother, it will be claimed that in such a society grandmothers are actually evil and that mythology reflects the social structure and the social relations; but should the actual data be conflicting, it would be as readily claimed that the purpose of mythology is to provide an outlet for repressed feelings. Whatever the situation, a clever dialectic will always find a way to pretend that a meaning has been found.

Mythology confronts the student with a situation which at first sight appears contradictory. On the one hand it would seem that in the course of a myth anything is likely to happen. There is no logic, no continuity. Any characteristic can be attributed to any subject; every conceivable relation can be found. With myth, everything becomes possible. But on the other hand, this apparent arbitrariness is belied by the astounding similarity between myths collected in widely different regions. Therefore the problem: If the content of a myth is contingent, how are we going to explain the fact that myths throughout the world are so similar?

It is precisely this awareness of a basic antinomy pertaining to the nature of myth that may lead us toward its solution. For the contradiction which we face is very similar to that which in earlier times brought considerable worry to the first philosophers concerned with linguistic problems; linguistics could only begin to evolve as a science after this contradiction had been overcome. Ancient philosophers reasoned about language the way we do about mythology. On the one hand, they did notice that in a given language certain sequences of sounds were associated with definite meanings, and they earnestly aimed at discovering a reason for the linkage between those *sounds* and that *meaning*. Their attempt, however, was thwarted from the very beginning by the fact that the same sounds were equally present in other languages although the meaning they conveyed was entirely different. The contradiction was surmounted only by the discovery that it is the combination of sounds, not the sounds themselves, which provides the significant data.

It is easy to see, moreover, that some of the more recent interpretations of mythological thought originated from the same kind of misconception under which those early linguists were laboring. Let us consider, for instance, Jung's idea that a given mythological pattern—the so-called archetype—possesses a certain meaning. This is comparable to the long-supported error that a sound may possess a certain affinity with a meaning: for instance, the "liquid" semivowels with water, the open vowels with things that are big, large, loud, or heavy, etc., a theory which still has its supporters.[3] Whatever emendations the original formulation may now call for,[4] everybody will agree that the Saussurean principle of the *arbitrary character of linguistic signs* was a prerequisite for the accession of linguistics to the scientific level.

To invite the mythologist to compare his precarious situation with that of the linguist in the prescientific stage is not enough. As a matter of fact we may thus be led only from one difficulty to another. There is a very good reason why myth cannot simply be treated as language if its specific problems are to be solved; myth *is* language: to be known, myth has to be told; it is a part of human speech. In order to preserve its specificity we must be able to show that it is both the same thing as language, and also something different from it. Here, too, the past experience of linguists may help us. For language itself can be analyzed into things which are at the same time similar and yet different. This is precisely what is expressed in Saussure's distinction between *langue* and *parole*, one being the structural side of language, the other the statistical aspect of it, *langue* belonging to a reversible time, *parole* being nonreversible. If those two levels already exist in language, then a third one can conceivably be isolated.

We have distinguished *langue* and *parole* by the different time referents which they use. Keeping this in mind, we may notice that myth uses a third referent which combines the properties of the first two. On the one hand, a myth always refers to events alleged to have taken place long ago. But what gives the myth an operational value is that the specific pattern described is timeless; it explains the present and the past as well as the future. This can be made clear through a comparison between myth and what appears to have largely replaced it in modern societies, namely, politics. When the historian refers to the French Revolution, it is always as a sequence of past happenings, a nonreversible series of events the remote consequences of which may still be felt at present. But to the French politician, as well as to his followers, the French Revolution is both a sequence belonging to the past—as to the historian—and a timeless pattern which can be detected in the contemporary French social structure and which provides a clue for its interpretation, a lead from which to infer future developments. Michelet, for instance, was a politically minded historian. He describes the French Revolution thus: "That day . . . everything was possible. . . . Future became present . . . that is, no more time, a glimpse of eternity." [5] It is that double structure, altogether historical and ahistorical, which explains how myth, while pertaining to the realm of *parole* and calling for an explanation as such, as well as to that of *langue* in which it is expressed, can also be an absolute entity on a third level which, though it remains linguistic by nature, is nevertheless distinct from the other two.

A remark can be introduced at this point which will help to show the originality of myth in relation to other linguistic phenomena. Myth is the part of language where the formula *traduttore, tradittore* reaches its lowest truth value. From that point of view it should be placed in the gamut of linguistic expressions at the end opposite to that of poetry, in spite of all the claims which have been made to prove the contrary. Poetry is a kind of speech which cannot be translated except at the cost of serious distortions; whereas the mythical value of the myth is preserved even through the worst translation. Whatever our ignorance of the language and the culture of the people where it originated, a myth is still felt as a myth by any reader anywhere in the world. Its substance does not lie in its style, its original music, or its syntax, but in the *story* which it tells. Myth is language, functioning on an especially high level where meaning succeeds practically at "taking off" from the linguistic ground on which it keeps on rolling.

To sum up the discussion at this point, we have so far made the following claims: (1) If there is a meaning to be found in mythology, it cannot reside in the isolated elements which enter into the composition of a myth, but only in the way those elements are combined. (2) Although myth belongs to the same category as language, being, as a matter of fact, only part of it, language in myth exhibits specific properties. (3) Those properties are only to be found *above* the ordinary linguistic level, that is, they exhibit more complex features than those which are to be found in any other kind of linguistic expression.

If the above three points are granted, at least as a working hypothesis, two consequences will follow: (1) Myth, like the rest of language, is made up of constituent units. (2) These constituent units presuppose the constituent units present in language when analyzed on other levels—namely, phonemes, morphemes, and sememes—but they, nevertheless, differ from the latter in the same way as the latter differ among themselves; they belong to a higher and more complex order. For this reason, we shall call them *gross constituent units*.

How shall we proceed in order to identify and isolate these gross constituent units or mythemes? We know that they cannot be found among phonemes, morphemes, or sememes, but only on a higher level; otherwise myth would become confused with any other kind of speech. Therefore, we should look for them on the sentence level. The only method we can suggest at this stage is to proceed tentatively, by trial and error, using as a check the principles which serve as a basis for any kind of structural analysis: economy of explanation; unity of solution; and ability to reconstruct the whole from a fragment, as well as later stages from previous ones.

The technique which has been applied so far by this writer consists in analyzing each myth individually, breaking down its story into the shortest possible sentences, and writing each sentence on an index card bearing a number corresponding to the unfolding of the story.

Practically each card will thus show that a certain function is, at a given time, linked to a given subject. Or, to put it otherwise, each gross constituent unit will consist of a *relation*.

However, the above definition remains highly unsatisfactory for two different reasons. First, it is well known to structural linguists that constituent units on all levels are made up of relations, and the true difference between our *gross* units and the others remains unexplained; second, we still find ourselves in the realm of a nonreversible time, since the numbers of the cards correspond to the unfolding of the narrative. Thus the specific character of mythological time, which as we have seen is both reversible and nonreversible, synchronic and diachronic, remains unaccounted for. From this springs a new hypothesis, which constitutes the very core of our argument: The true constituent units of a myth are not the isolated relations but *bundles of such relations*, and it is only as bundles that these relations can be put to use and combined so as to produce a meaning. Relations pertaining to the same bundle may appear diachronically at remote intervals, but when we have succeeded in grouping them together we have reorganized our myth according to a time referent of a new nature, corresponding to the prerequisite of the initial hypothesis, namely a two-dimensional time referent which is simultaneously diachronic and synchronic, and which accordingly integrates the characteristics of *langue* on the one hand, and those of *parole* on the other. To put it in even more linguistic terms, it is as though a phoneme were always made up of all its variants.

Two comparisons may help to explain what we have in mind.

Let us first suppose that archaeologists of the future coming from another planet would one day, when all human life had disappeared from the earth, excavate one of our libraries. Even if they were at first ignorant of our writing, they might succeed in deciphering it—an undertaking which would require, at some early stage, the discovery that the alphabet, as we are in the habit of printing it, should be read from left to right and from top to bottom. However, they would soon discover that a whole category of books did not fit the usual pattern—these would be the orchestra scores on the shelves of the music division. But after trying, without success, to decipher staffs one after the other, from the upper down to the lower, they would probably notice that the same patterns of notes recurred at intervals, either in full or in part, or that some patterns were strongly reminiscent of earlier ones. Hence the hypothesis: What if patterns showing affinity, instead of being considered in succession, were to be treated as one complex pattern and read as a whole? By getting at what we call *harmony*, they would then see that an orchestra score, to be meaningful, must be read diachronically along one axis—that is, page after page, and from left to right— and synchronically along the other axis, all the notes written vertically making up one gross constituent unit, that is, one bundle of relations.

The other comparison is somewhat different. Let us take an observer ignorant of our playing cards, sitting for a long time with a fortune-teller. He would know something of the visitors: sex, age, physical appearance, social situation, etc., in the same way as we know something of the different cultures whose myths we try to study. He would also listen to the séances and record them so as to be able to go over them and make comparisons—as we do when we listen to myth-telling and record it. Mathematicians to whom I have put the problem agree that if the man is bright and if the material available to him is sufficient, he may be able to reconstruct the nature of the deck of cards being used, that is, fifty-two or thirty-two cards according to the case, made up of four homologous sets consisting of the same units (the individual cards) with only one varying feature, the suit.

Now for a concrete example of the method we propose. We shall use the Oedipus myth, which is well known to everyone. I am well aware that the Oedipus myth has only reached us under late forms and through literary transmutations concerned more with esthetic and moral preoccupations than with religious or ritual ones, whatever these may have been. But we shall not interpret the Oedipus myth in literal terms, much less offer an explanation acceptable to the specialist. We simply wish to illustrate—and without reaching any conclusions with respect to it—a certain technique, whose use is probably not legitimate in this particular instance, owing to the problematic elements indicated above. The "demonstration" should therefore be conceived, not in terms of what the scientist means by this term, but at best in terms of what is meant by the street peddler, whose aim is not to achieve a concrete result, but to explain, as succinctly as possible, the functioning of the mechanical toy which he is trying to sell to the onlookers.

The myth will be treated as an orchestra score would be if it were unwittingly considered as a unilinear series; our task is to re-establish the correct arrangement. Say, for instance, we were confronted with a sequence of the type: 1,2,4,7,8,2,3,4,6,8,1,4,5,7,8,1, 2,5,7,3,4,5,6,8 . . . , the assignment being to put all the 1's together, all the 2's, the 3's, etc.; the result is a chart:

1	2		4			7	8
	2	3	4		6		8
1			4	5		7	8
1	2			5		7	
		3	4	5	6		8

We shall attempt to perform the same kind of operation on the Oedipus myth, trying out several arrangements of the mythemes until we find one which is in harmony with the principles enumerated above. Let us suppose, for the sake of argument, that the best arrangement is the following (although it might certainly be improved with the help of a specialist in Greek mythology):

Cadmos seeks his sister Europa, ravished by Zeus		
		Cadmos kills the dragon
	The Spartoi kill one another	
		Labdacos (Laïos' father) = *lame* (?)
	Oedipus kills his father, Laïos	Laïos (Oedipus' father) = *left-sided* (?)
		Oedipus kills the Sphinx
		Oedipus = *swollen-foot* (?)
Oedipus marries his mother, Jocasta		
	Eteocles kills his brother, Polynices	
Antigone buries her brother, Polynices, despite prohibition		

We thus find ourselves confronted with four vertical columns, each of which includes several relations belonging to the same bundle. Were we to *tell* the myth, we would disregard the columns and read the rows from left to right and from top to bottom. But if we want to *understand* the myth, then we will have to disregard one half of the diachronic dimension (top to bottom) and read from left to right, column after column, each one being considered as a unit.

All the relations belonging to the same column exhibit one common feature which it is our task to discover. For instance, all the events grouped in the first column on the left have something to do with blood relations which are overemphasized, that is, are more intimate than they should be. Let us say, then, that the first column has as its common feature the *overrating of blood relations*. It is obvious that the second column expresses the same thing, but inverted: *underrating of blood relations*. The third column refers to monsters being slain. As to the fourth, a few words of clarification are needed. The remarkable connotation of the surnames in Oedipus' father-line has often been noticed. However, linguists usually disregard it, since to them the only way to define the meaning of a term is to investigate all the contexts in which it appears, and personal names, precisely because they are used as such, are not accompanied by any context. With the method we propose to follow, the objection disappears, since the myth itself provides its own context. The significance is no longer to be sought in the eventual meaning of each name, but in the fact that all the names have a common feature: All the hypothetical meanings (which may well remain hypothetical) refer to *difficulties in walking straight and standing upright*.

What then is the relationship between the two columns on the right? Column three refers to monsters. The dragon is a chthonian being which has to be killed in order that mankind be born from the Earth; the Sphinx is a monster unwilling to permit men to live. The last unit reproduces the first one, which has to do with the *autochthonous origin* of mankind. Since the monsters are overcome by men, we may thus say that the common feature of the third column is *denial of the autochthonous origin of man*.[6]

This immediately helps us to understand the meaning of the

fourth column. In mythology it is a universal characteristic of men born from the Earth that at the moment they emerge from the depth they either cannot walk or they walk clumsily. This is the case of the chthonian beings in the mythology of the Pueblo: Muyingwu, who leads the emergence, and the chthonian Shumaikoli are lame ("bleeding-foot," "sore-foot"). The same happens to the Koskimo of the Kwakiutl after they have been swallowed by the chthonian monster, Tsiakish: When they returned to the surface of the earth "they limped forward or tripped sideways." Thus the common feature of the fourth column is *the persistence of the auto-chthonous origin of man.* It follows that column four is to column three as column one is to column two. The inability to connect two kinds of relationships is overcome (or rather replaced) by the assertion that contradictory relationships are identical inasmuch as they are both self-contradictory in a similar way. Although this is still a provisional formulation of the structure of mythical thought, it is sufficient at this stage.

Turning back to the Oedipus myth, we may now see what it means. The myth has to do with the inability, for a culture which holds the belief that mankind is autochthonous (see, for instance, Pausanias, VIII, xxix, 4: plants provide a *model* for humans), to find a satisfactory transition between this theory and the knowledge that human beings are actually born from the union of man and woman. Although the problem obviously cannot be solved, the Oedipus myth provides a kind of logical tool which relates the original problem—born from one or born from two?—to the derivative problem: born from different or born from same? By a correlation of this type, the overrating of blood relations is to the underrating of blood relations as the attempt to escape autochthony is to the impossibility to succeed in it. Although experience contradicts theory, social life validates cosmology by its similarity of structure. Hence cosmology is true.

Two remarks should be made at this stage.

In order to interpret the myth, we left aside a point which has worried the specialists until now, namely, that in the earlier (Homeric) versions of the Oedipus myth, some basic elements are lacking, such as Jocasta killing herself and Oedipus piercing his own eyes. These events do not alter the substance of the myth although they can easily be integrated, the first one as a new case of auto-destruction (column three) and the second as another case of crip-pledness (column four). At the same time there is something significant in these additions, since the shift from foot to head is to be correlated with the shift from autochthonous origin to self-destruction.

Our method thus eliminates a problem which has, so far, been one of the main obstacles to the progress of mythological studies, namely, the quest for the *true* version, or the *earlier* one. On the contrary, we define the myth as consisting of all its versions; or to put it otherwise, a myth remains the same as long as it is felt as such. A striking example is offered by the fact that our interpretation may take into account the Freudian use of the Oedipus myth and is cer-tainly applicable to it. Although the Freudian problem has ceased to be that of autochthony *versus* bisexual reproduction, it is still the problem of understanding how *one* can be born from *two:* How is it that we do not have only one procreator, but a mother plus a father? Therefore, not only Sophocles, but Freud himself, should be included among the recorded versions of the Oedipus myth on a par with earlier or seemingly more "authentic" versions.

An important consequence follows. If a myth is made up of all its variants, structural analysis should take all of them into ac-count. After analyzing all the known variants of the Theban ver-sion, we should thus treat the others in the same way: first, the tales about Labdacos' collateral line including Agave, Pentheus, and Jocasta herself; the Theban variant about Lycos with Amphion and Zetos as the city founders; more remote variants concerning Dionysus (Oedipus' matrilateral cousin); and Athenian legends where Cecrops takes the place of Cadmos, etc. For each of them a similar chart should be drawn and then compared and reorganized accord-ing to the findings: Cecrops killing the serpent with the parallel episode of Cadmos; abandonment of Dionysus with abandonment of Oedipus; "Swollen Foot" with Dionysus' *loxias*, that is, walking obliquely; Europa's quest with Antiope's; the founding of Thebes by the Spartoi or by the brothers Amphion and Zetos; Zeus kid-napping Europa and Antiope and the same with Semele; the Theban Oedipus and the Argian Perseus, etc. We shall then have several two-dimensional charts, each dealing with a variant, to be organized in

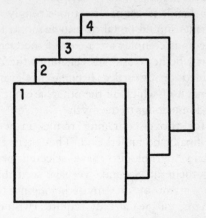

a three-dimensional order, as shown in Figure 1, so that three different readings become possible: left to right, top to bottom, front to back (or vice versa). All of these charts cannot be expected to be identical; but experience shows that any difference to be observed may be correlated with other differences, so that a logical treatment of the whole will allow simplifications, the final outcome being the structural law of the myth.

At this point the objection may be raised that the task is impossible to perform, since we can only work with known versions. Is it not possible that a new version might alter the picture? This is true enough if only one or two versions are available, but the objection becomes theoretical as soon as a reasonably large number have been recorded. Let us make this point clear by a comparison. If the furniture of a room and its arrangement were known to us only through its reflection in two mirrors placed on opposite walls, we should theoretically dispose of an almost infinite number of mirror images which would provide us with a complete knowledge. However, should the two mirrors be obliquely set, the number of mirror images would become very small; nevertheless, four or five such images would very likely give us, if not complete information, at least a sufficient coverage so that we would feel sure that no large piece of furniture is missing in our description.

On the other hand, it cannot be too strongly emphasized that all available variants should be taken into account. If Freudian comments on the Oedipus complex are a part of the Oedipus myth, then questions such as whether Cushing's version of the Zuñi origin myth should be retained or discarded become irrelevant. There is no single "true" version of which all the others are but copies or distortions. Every version belongs to the myth.

The reason for the discouraging results in works on general mythology can finally be understood. They stem from two causes. First, comparative mythologists have selected preferred versions instead of using them all. Second, we have seen that the structural analysis of *one* variant of *one* myth belonging to *one* tribe (in some cases, even *one* village) already requires two dimensions. When we use several variants of the same myth for the same tribe or village, the frame of reference becomes three-dimensional, and as soon as we try to enlarge the comparison, the number of dimensions required increases until it appears quite impossible to handle them intuitively. The confusions and platitudes which are the outcome of comparative mythology can be explained by the fact that multidimensional frames of reference are often ignored or are naïvely replaced by two- or three-dimensional ones. Indeed, progress in comparative mythology depends largely on the cooperation of mathematicians who would undertake to express in symbols multidimensional relations which cannot be handled otherwise.

To check this theory,[7] an attempt was made from 1952 to 1954 toward an exhaustive analysis of all the known versions of the Zuñi origin and emergence myth: Cushing, 1883 and 1896; Stevenson, 1904; Parsons, 1923; Bunzel, 1932; Benedict, 1934. Furthermore, a preliminary attempt was made at a comparison of the results with similar myths in other Pueblo tribes, Western and Eastern. Finally, a test was undertaken with Plains mythology. In all cases, it was found that the theory was sound; light was thrown, not only on North American mythology, but also on a previously unnoticed kind of logical operation, or one known so far only in a wholly different context. The bulk of material which needs to be handled practically at the outset of the work makes it impossible to enter into details, and we shall have to limit ourselves here to a few illustrations.

A simplified chart of the Zuñi emergence myth would read:

CHANGE			DEATH
mechanical value of plants (used as ladders to emerge from lower world)	emergence led by Beloved Twins	sibling incest (origin of water)	gods kill children of men (by drowning)
food value of wild plants	migration led by the two Newekwe (ceremonial clowns)		magical contest with People of the Dew (collecting wild food *versus* cultivation)
		brother and sister sacrificed (to gain victory)	
food value of cultivated plants			
		brother and sister adopted (in exchange for corn)	
periodical character of agricultural work			
			war against the Kyanakwe (gardeners *versus* hunters)

CHANGE   DEATH

food value
of game
(hunting)

        war led by
        the two
        War-Gods

inevitability of   salvation of the
warfare   tribe (center of
                              the World found)

                  brother and
                  sister sacri-
                  ficed (to
                  avoid the
                  Flood)

DEATH   PERMANENCE

As the chart indicates, the problem is the discovery of a life-death mediation. For the Pueblo, this is especially difficult; they understand the origin of human life in terms of the model of plant life (emergence from the earth). They share that belief with the ancient Greeks, and it is not without reason that we chose the Oedipus myth as our first example. But in the American Indian case, the highest form of plant life is to be found in agriculture which is periodical in nature, that is, which consists in an alternation between life and death. If this is disregarded, the contradiction appears elsewhere: Agriculture provides food, therefore life; but hunting provides food and is similar to warfare which means death. Hence there are three different ways of handling the problem. In the Cushing version, the difficulty revolves around an opposition between activities yielding an immediate result (collecting wild food) and activities yielding a delayed result—death has to become integrated so that agriculture can exist. Parsons' version shifts from hunting to agriculture, while Stevenson's version operates the other way around. It can be shown that all the differences between these versions can be rigorously correlated with these basic structures.

Thus the three versions described the great war waged by the ancestors of the Zuñi against a mythical population, the Kyanakwe, by introducing into the narrative significant variations which consist (1) in the friendship or hostility of the gods; (2) in the granting of final victory to one camp or the other; (3) in the attribution of the symbolic function to the Kyanakwe, described sometimes as hunters (whose bows are strung with animal sinews) and sometimes as gardeners (whose bows are strung with plant fibers).

	CUSHING	PARSONS	STEVENSON
Gods, Kyanakwe	allied, use fiber string on their bows (gardeners)	Kyanakwe, alone, use fiber string	Gods, Men — allied, use fiber string

VICTORIOUS OVER	VICTORIOUS OVER	VICTORIOUS OVER
Men, alone, use sinew (until they shift to fiber)	Gods, Men — allied, use sinew string	Kyanakwe, alone, use sinew string

Since fiber string (agriculture) is always superior to sinew string (hunting), and since (to a lesser extent) the gods' alliance is preferable to their antagonism, it follows that in Cushing's version, men are seen as doubly underprivileged (hostile gods, sinew string); in the Stevenson version, doubly privileged (friendly gods, fiber string); while Parsons' version confronts us with an intermediary situation (friendly gods, but sinew strings, since men begin by being hunters). Hence:

OPPOSITIONS	CUSHING	PARSONS	STEVENSON
gods/men	—	+	+
fiber/sinew	—	—	+

Bunzel's version is of the same type as Cushing's from a structural point of view. However, it differs from both Cushing's and Stevenson's, inasmuch as the latter two explain the emergence as the result of man's need to evade his pitiful condition, while Bunzel's version makes it the consequence of a call from the higher powers—hence the inverted sequences of the means resorted to for the emergence: In both Cushing and Stevenson, they go from plants to animals; in Bunzel, from mammals to insects, and from insects to plants.

Among the Western Pueblo the logical approach always remains the same; the starting point and the point of arrival are simplest, whereas the intermediate stage is characterized by ambiguity:

LIFE (= INCREASE)

(Mechanical) value of the plant kingdom, taking growth alone into account		ORIGINS
Food value of the plant kingdom, limited to wild plants		FOOD-GATHERING
Food value of the plant kingdom, including wild and cultivated plants		AGRICULTURE
Food value of the animal kingdom, limited to animals	*(but there is a contradiction here, owing to the negation of life = destruction, hence:)*	
		HUNTING
Destruction of the animal kingdom, extended to human beings		
		WARFARE

DEATH (= DECREASE)

The fact that contradiction appears in the middle of the dialectical process results in a double set of dioscuric pairs, the purpose of which is to mediate between conflicting terms:

1. 2 divine messengers	2 ceremonial clowns		2-war-gods
2. homogeneous pair: dioscuri (2 brothers)	siblings (brother and sister)	couple (husband and wife)	heterogeneous pair: (grandmother and grandchild)

We have here combinational variants of the same function in different contexts (hence the war attribute of the clowns, which has given rise to so many queries).

The problem, often regarded as insoluble, vanishes when it is shown that the clowns—gluttons who may with impunity make excessive use of agricultural products—have the same function in relation to food production as the war-gods. (This function appears, in the dialectical process, as *overstepping the boundaries* of hunting, that is, hunting for men instead of for animals for human consumption.)

Some Central and Eastern Pueblos proceed the other way around. They begin by stating the identity of hunting and cultivation (first corn obtained by Game-Father sowing deer-dewclaws), and they try to derive both life and death from that central notion. Then, instead of extreme terms being simple and intermediary ones duplicated as among the Western groups, the extreme terms become duplicated (i.e., the two sisters of the Eastern Pueblo) while a simple mediating term comes to the foreground (for instance, the Poshaiyanne of the Zia), but endowed with equivocal attributes. Hence the attributes of this "messiah" can be deduced from the place it occupies in the time sequence: good when at the beginning (Zuñi, Cushing), equivocal in the middle (Central Pueblo), bad at the end (Zia), except in Bunzel's version, where the sequence is reversed as has been shown.

By systematically using this kind of structural analysis it becomes possible to organize all the known variants of a myth into a set forming a kind of permutation group, the two variants placed at the far ends being in a symmetrical, though inverted, relationship to each other.

Our method not only has the advantage of bringing some kind of order to what was previously chaos; it also enables us to perceive some basic logical processes which are at the root of mythical thought.[8] Three main processes should be distinguished.

The trickster of American mythology has remained so far a problematic figure. Why is it that throughout North America his role is assigned practically everywhere to either coyote or raven? If we keep in mind that mythical thought always progresses from the awareness of oppositions toward their resolution, the reason for these choices becomes clearer. We need only assume that two opposite terms with no intermediary always tend to be replaced by two equivalent terms which admit of a third one as a mediator; then one of the polar terms and the mediator become replaced by a new triad, and so on. Thus we have a mediating structure of the following type:

INITIAL PAIR	FIRST TRIAD	SECOND TRIAD
Life		
	Agriculture	
		Herbivorous animals
		Carrion-eating animals
		(raven; coyote)
	Hunting	
		Beasts of prey
	Warfare	
Death		

The unformulated argument is as follows: carrion-eating animals are like beasts of prey (they eat animal food), but they are also like food-plant producers (they do not kill what they eat). Or to put it otherwise, Pueblo style (for Pueblo agriculture is more "meaningful" than hunting): ravens are to gardens as beasts of prey are to herbivorous animals. But it is also clear that herbivorous animals may be called first to act as mediators on the assumption that they are like collectors and gatherers (plant-food eaters), while they can be used as animal food though they are not themselves hunters. Thus we may have mediators of the first order, of the second order, and so on, where each term generates the next by a double process of opposition and correlation.

This kind of process can be followed in the mythology of the Plains, where we may order the data according to the set:

Unsuccessful mediator between Earth and Sky
(Star-Husband's wife)

Heterogeneous pair of mediators
(grandmother and grandchild)

Semi-homogeneous pair of mediators
(Lodge-Boy and Thrown-away)

While among the Pueblo (Zuñi) we have the corresponding set:

> Successful mediator between Earth and Sky
> (Poshaiyanki)
>
> Semi-homogeneous pair of mediators
> (Uyuyewi and Matsailema)
>
> Homogeneous pair of mediators
> (the two Ahaiyuta)

On the other hand, correlations may appear on a horizontal axis (this is true even on the linguistic level; see the manifold connotation of the root *pose* in Tewa according to Parsons: coyote, mist, scalp, etc.). Coyote (a carrion-eater) is intermediary between herbivorous and carnivorous just as mist between Sky and Earth; as scalp between war and agriculture (scalp is a war crop); as corn smut between wild and cultivated plants; as garments between "nature" and "culture"; as refuse between village and outside; and as ashes (or soot) between roof (sky vault) and hearth (in the ground). This chain of mediators, if one may call them so, not only throws light on entire parts of North American mythology—why the Dew-God may be at the same time the Game-Master and the giver of raiments and be personified as an "Ash-Boy"; or why scalps are mist-producing; or why the Game-Mother is associated with corn smut; etc.—but it also probably corresponds to a universal way of organizing daily experience. See, for instance, the French for plant smut (*nielle*, from Latin *nebula*); the luck-bringing power attributed in Europe to refuse (old shoe) and ashes (kissing chimney sweeps); and compare the American Ash-Boy cycle with the Indo-European Cinderella: Both are phallic figures (mediators between male and female); masters of the dew and the game; owners of fine raiments; and social mediators (low class marrying into high class); but they are impossible to interpret through recent diffusion, as has been contended, since Ash-Boy and Cinderella are symmetrical but inverted in every detail (while the borrowed Cinderella tale in America—Zuñi Turkey-Girl—is parallel to the prototype). Hence the chart:

	EUROPE	AMERICA
Sex	female	male
Family Status	double family (remarried father)	no family (orphan)
Appearance	pretty girl	ugly boy
Sentimental status	nobody likes her	unrequited love for girl
Transformation	luxuriously clothed with supernatural help	stripped of ugliness with supernatural help

Thus, like Ash-Boy and Cinderella, the trickster is a mediator. Since his mediating function occupies a position halfway between two polar terms, he must retain something of that duality—namely an ambiguous and equivocal character. But the trickster figure is not the only conceivable form of mediation; some myths seem to be entirely devoted to the task of exhausting all the possible solutions to the problem of bridging the gap between *two* and *one*. For instance, a comparison between all the variants of the Zuñi emergence myth provides us with a series of mediating devices, each of which generates the next one by a process of opposition and correlation:

messiah > dioscuri > trickster > bisexual being > sibling pair > married couple > grandmother-grandchild > four-term group > triad

In Cushing's version, this dialectic is associated with a change from a spatial dimension (mediation between Sky and Earth) to a temporal dimension (mediation between summer and winter, that is, between birth and death). But while the shift is being made from space to time, the final solution (triad) re-introduces space, since a triad consists of a dioscuric pair *plus* a messiah, present simultaneously; and while the point of departure was ostensibly formulated in terms of a space referent (Sky and Earth), this was nevertheless implicitly conceived in terms of a time referent (first the messiah calls, *then* the dioscuri descend). Therefore the logic of myth confronts us with a double, reciprocal exchange of functions to which we shall return shortly.

Not only can we account for the ambiguous character of the trickster, but we can also understand another property of mythical figures the world over, namely, that the same god is endowed with contradictory attributes—for instance, he may be *good* and *bad* at the same time. If we compare the variants of the Hopi myth of the origin of Shalako, we may order them in terms of the following structure:

$$(\text{Masauwu}: x) \simeq (\text{Muyingwu}: \text{Masauwu}) \simeq (\text{Shalako}:\text{Muyingwu})$$
$$\simeq (y: \text{Masauwu})$$

where x and y represent arbitrary values corresponding to the fact that in the two "extreme" variants the god Masauwu, while appearing alone rather than associated with another god, as in variant two, or being absent, as in variant three, still retains intrinsically a relative value. In variant one, Masauwu (alone) is depicted as helpful to mankind (though not as helpful as he could be), and in version four, harmful to mankind (though not as harmful as he could be). His role is thus defined—at least implicitly—in contrast with another role which is possible but not specified and which is represented here by the values x and y. In version two, on the other hand, Muyingwu is relatively more helpful than Masauwu, and in version three, Shalako more helpful than Muyingwu. We find an identical series when ordering the Keresan variants:

$$(\text{Poshaiyanki}: x) \simeq (\text{Lea}: \text{Poshaiyanki}) \simeq (\text{Poshaiyanki}: \text{Tiamoni})$$
$$\simeq (y: \text{Poshaiyanki})$$

This logical framework is particularly interesting, since anthropologists are already acquainted with it on two other levels—first, in regard to the problem of the pecking order among hens, and second, to what this writer has called *generalized exchange* in the field of kinship. By recognizing it also on the level of mythical thought, we may find ourselves in a better position to appraise its basic importance in anthropological studies and to give it a more inclusive theoretical interpretation.

Finally, when we have succeeded in organizing a whole series of variants into a kind of permutation group, we are in a position to formulate the law of that group. Although it is not possible at the present stage to come closer than an approximate formulation which will certainly need to be refined in the future, it seems that every myth (considered as the aggregate of all its variants) corresponds to a formula of the following type:

$$F_x(a): F_y(b) \simeq F_x(b): F_{a\text{-}1}(y)$$

Here, with two terms, *a* and *b*, being given as well as two functions, *x* and *y*, of these terms, it is assumed that a relation of equivalence exists between two situations defined respectively by an inversion of *terms* and *relations*, under two conditions: (1) that one term be replaced by its opposite (in the above formula, *a* and *a-1*); (2) that an inversion be made between the *function value* and the *term value* of two elements (above, *y* and *a*).

This formula becomes highly significant when we recall that Freud considered that *two traumas* (and not one, as is so commonly said) are necessary in order to generate the individual myth in which a neurosis consists. By trying to apply the formula to the analysis of these traumas (and assuming that they correspond to conditions 1 and 2 respectively) we should not only be able to provide a more precise and rigorous formulation of the genetic law of the myth, but we would find ourselves in the much desired position of developing side by side the anthropological and the psychological aspects of the theory; we might also take it to the laboratory and subject it to experimental verification.

At this point it seems unfortunate that with the limited means at the disposal of French anthropological research no further advance can be made. It should be emphasized that the task of analyzing mythological literature, which is extremely bulky, and of breaking it down into its constituent units, requires teamwork and technical help. A variant of average length requires several hundred cards to be properly analyzed. To discover a suitable pattern of rows and columns for those cards, special devices are needed, consisting of vertical boards about six feet long and four and a half feet high, where cards can be pigeonholed and moved at will. In order to build up three-dimensional models enabling one to compare the variants, several such boards are necessary, and this in turn requires a spacious workshop, a commodity particularly unavailable in Western Europe nowadays. Futhermore, as soon as the frame of reference becomes multi-dimensional (which occurs at an early stage, as has been shown above) the board system has to be replaced by perforated cards, which in turn require IBM equipment, etc.

Three final remarks may serve as conclusion.

First, the question has often been raised why myths, and more generally oral literature, are so much addicted to duplication, triplication, or quadruplication of the same sequence. If our hypotheses are accepted, the answer is obvious: The function of repetition is to render the structure of the myth apparent. For we have seen that the synchronic-diachronic structure of the myth permits us to organize it into diachronic sequences (the rows in our tables) which should be read synchronically (the columns). Thus, a myth exhibits a "slated" structure, which comes to the surface, so to speak, through the process of repetition.

However, the slates are not absolutely identical. And since the purpose of myth is to provide a logical model capable of overcoming a contradiction (an impossible achievement if, as it happens, the contradiction is real), a theoretically infinite number of slates will be generated, each one slightly different from the others. Thus, myth grows spiral-wise until the intellectual impulse which has produced it is exhausted. Its *growth* is a continuous process, whereas its *structure* remains discontinuous. If this is the case, we should assume that it closely corresponds, in the realm of the spoken word, to a crystal in the realm of physical matter. This analogy may help us to better understand the relationship of myth to both *langue* on the one hand and *parole* on the other. Myth is an intermediary entity between a statistical aggregate of molecules and the molecular structure itself.

Prevalent attempts to explain alleged differences between the so-called primitive mind and scientific thought have resorted to qualitative differences between the working processes of the mind in both cases, while assuming that the entities which they were studying remained very much the same. If our interpretation is correct, we are led toward a completely different view—namely, that the kind of logic in mythical thought is as rigorous as that of modern science, and that the difference lies, not in the quality of the intellectual process, but in the nature of the things to which it is applied. This is well in agreement with the situation known to prevail in the field of technology: What makes a steel axe superior to a stone axe is not that the first one is better made than the second. They are equally well made, but steel is quite different from stone. In the same way we may be able to show that the same logical processes operate in myth as in science, and that man has always been thinking equally well; the improvement lies, not in an alleged progress of man's mind, but in the discovery of new areas to which it may apply its unchanged and unchanging powers.

NOTES

1. In Boas' Introduction to James Teit, "Traditions of the Thompson River Indians of British Columbia," *Memoirs of the American Folklore Society*, VI (1898), p. 18.
2. A. M. Hocart, *Social Origins* (London, 1954), p. 7.
3. See, for instance, Sir R. A. Paget, "The Origin of Language," *Journal of World History*, I, No. 2 (UNESCO, 1953).
4. See Émile Benveniste, "Nature du signe linguistique," *Acta Linguistica*, I, No. 1 (1939), and Claude Levi-Strauss, *Structural Anthropology* (New York, 1963), Chap. V.
5. Jules Michelet, *Histoire de la Révolution française*, IV, 1. I took this quotation from M. Merleau-Ponty, *Les Aventures de la dialectique* (Paris, 1955), p. 273.
6. We are not trying to become involved with specialists in an argument; this would be presumptuous and even meaningless on our part. Since the Oedipus myth is taken here merely as an example treated in arbitrary fashion, the chthonian nature ascribed to the Sphinx might seem surprising; we shall refer to the testimony of Marie Delcourt: "In the archaic legends, [she is] certainly born of the Earth itself" (*Oedipe ou la légende du conquérant* [Liège, 1944], p. 108). No matter how remote from Delcourt's our method may be (and our conclusions would be, no doubt, if we were competent to deal with the problem in depth), it seems to us that she has convincingly established the nature of the Sphinx in the archaic tradition, namely, that of a female monster who attacks and rapes young men; in other words, the personification of a female being with an inversion of the sign. This explains why, in the handsome iconography compiled by Delcourt at the end of her work, men and women are always found in an inverted "sky/earth" relationship.

As we shall point out below, we selected the Oedipus myth as our first example because of the striking analogies that seem to exist between certain aspects of archaic Greek thought and that of the Pueblo Indians, from whom we have borrowed the examples that follow. In this respect it should be noted that the figure of the Sphinx, as reconstructed by Delcourt, coincides with two figures of North American mythology (who probably merge into one). We are referring, on the one hand, to "the old hag," a repulsive witch whose physical appearance presents a "problem" to the young hero. If he "solves" this problem—that is, if he responds to the advances of the abject creature

—he will find in his bed, upon awakening, a beautiful young woman who will confer power upon him (this is also a Celtic theme). The Sphinx, on the other hand, recalls even more "the child-protruding woman" of the Hopi Indians, that is, a phallic mother par excellence. This young woman was abandoned by her group in the course of a difficult migration, just as she was about to give birth. Hencefore she wanders in the desert as the "Mother of Animals," which she withholds from hunters. He who meets her in her bloody clothes "is so frightened that he has an erection," of which she takes advantage to rape him, after which she rewards him with unfailing success in hunting. See H. R. Voth, "The Oraibi Summer Snake Ceremony," *Field Columbian Museum*, Publication No. 83, Anthropological Series, Vol. III, No. 4 (Chicago, 1903), pp. 352–353 and p. 353, *n* 1.

7. See *Annuaire de l'École pratique des Hautes Études*, Section des Sciences religieuses, 1952–1953, pp. 19–21, and 1953–1954, pp. 27–29. Thanks are due here to an unrequested but deeply appreciated grant from the Ford Foundation.

8. For another application of this method, see our study "Four Winnebago Myths: A Structural Sketch," in Stanley Diamond (ed.), *Culture in History: Essays in Honor of Paul Radin* (New York, 1960), pp. 351–362.

Genesis as Myth [1]

EDMUND R. LEACH

A distinguished German theologian has defined myth as "the expression of unobservable realities in terms of observable phenomena" (Bartsch, 1953). All stories which occur in the Bible are myths for the devout Christian, whether they correspond to historical fact or not. All human societies have myths in this sense, and normally the myths to which the greatest importance is attached are those which are the least probable. The nonrationality of myth is its very essence, for religion requires a demonstration of faith by the suspension of critical doubt.

But if myths do not mean what they appear to mean, how do they come to mean anything at all? What is the nature of the esoteric mode of communication by which myth is felt to give "expression to unobservable realities"?

This is an old problem which has lately taken on a new shape because, if myth be a mode of communication, then a part of the theory which is embodied in digital computer systems ought to be relevant. The merit of this approach is that it draws special attention to precisely those features of myth which have formerly been regarded as accidental defects. It is common to all mythological systems that all important stories recur in several different versions. Man is created in Genesis (I, 27) [2] and then he is created all over again (II, 7). And, as if two first men were not enough, we also have Noah in Chapter VIII. Likewise in the New Testament, why must there be four gospels each telling "the same" story yet sometimes flatly contradictory on details of fact? Another noticeable characteristic of mythical stories is their markedly binary aspect; myth is constantly setting up opposing categories: "In the beginning God created the heaven and the earth," "they crucified Him and two others with him, on either side one, and Jesus in the midst," "I am

the Alpha and the Omega, the beginning and the end, saith the Lord."
So always it is in myth—God against the world and the world itself
for ever dividing into opposites on either side—male and female,
living and dead, good and evil, first and last . . .

Now, in the language of communication engineers, the first of
these common characteristics of myth is called *redundancy* while
the second is strongly reminiscent of the unit of information—the
bit. "Information" in this technical sense is a measure of the freedom of choice in selecting a message. If there are only two messages
and it is arbitrary which you choose then "information is unity,"
that is $= 1$ bit (*bit* stands for "binary digit") (Shannon and Weaver,
1949).

Communication engineers employ these concepts for the analysis
of problems which arise when a particular individual (the sender)
wishes to transmit a coded message correctly to another individual
(the receiver) against a background of interference (noise). "Information" refers on the one hand to the degrees of choice open to
the sender in encoding his transmission and on the other to the
degrees of choice open to the receiver in interpreting what he
receives (which will include noise in addition to the original transmitted signal). In this situation a high level of redundancy makes it
easy to correct errors introduced by noise.

Now in the mind of the believer, myth does indeed convey
messages which are the Word of God. To such a man the redundancy of myth is a very reassuring fact. Any particular myth in
isolation is like a coded message badly snarled up with noisy interference. Even the most confident devotee might feel a little uncertain as to what precisely is being said. But, as a result of redundancy,
the believer can feel that, even when the details vary, each alternative
version of a myth confirms his understanding and reinforces the
essential meaning of all the others.

BINARY STRUCTURE OF MYTH

The anthropologist's viewpoint is different. He rejects the idea of
a supernatural sender. He observes only a variety of possible re-
ceivers. Redundancy increases information—that is the uncertainty
of the possible means of decoding the message. This explains what

is surely the most striking of all religious phenomena—the passionate adherence to sectarian belief. The whole of Christendom shares a single corpus of mythology so it is surely very remarkable that the members of each particular Christian sect are able to convince themselves that they alone possess the secret of revealed truth. The abstract propositions of communication theory help us to understand this paradox.

But if the true believer can interpret his own mythology in almost any way he chooses, what principle governs the formation of the original myth? Is it random chance that a myth assumes one pattern rather than another? The binary structure of myth suggests otherwise.

Binary oppositions are intrinsic to the process of human thought. Any description of the world must discriminate categories in the form "p is what not-p is not." An object is alive or not alive and one could not formulate the concept "alive" except as the converse of its partner "dead." So also human beings are male or not male, and persons of the opposite sex are either available as sexual partners or not available. Universally these are the most fundamentally important oppositions in all human experience.

Religion everywhere is preoccupied with the first, the antinomy of life and death. Religion seeks to deny the binary link between the two words; it does this by creating the mystical idea of "another world," a land of the dead where life is perpetual. The attributes of this other world are necessarily those which are not of this world; imperfection here is balanced by perfection there. But this logical ordering of ideas has a disconcerting consequence—God comes to belong to the other world. The central "problem" of religion is then to reestablish some kind of bridge between Man and God.

This pattern is built into the structure of every mythical system; the myth first discriminates between gods and men and then becomes preoccupied with the relations and intermediaries which link men and gods together. This much is already implicit in our initial definition.

So too with sex relations. Every human society has rules of incest and exogamy. Though the rules vary they always have the implication that for any particular male individual all women are divided by at least one binary distinction, there are women of *our kind* with whom sex relations would be incestuous and there are women of the *other kind* with whom sex relations are allowed. But here again we are immediately led into paradox. How was it in the beginning? If our first parents were persons of two kinds, what was that other kind? But if they were both of our kind, then their relations must have been incestuous and we are all born in sin. The myths of the world offer many different solutions to this childish intellectual puzzle, but the prominence which it receives shows that it entails the most profound moral issues. The crux is as before. If the logic of our thought leads us to distinguish *we* from *they*, how can we bridge the gap and establish social and sexual relations with "the others" without throwing our categories into confusion?

So, despite all variations of theology, this aspect of myth is a constant. In every myth system we will find a persistent sequence of binary discriminations as between human/superhuman, mortal/immortal, male/female, legitimate/illegitimate, good/bad . . . followed by a "mediation" of the paired categories thus distinguished.

"Mediation" (in this sense) is always achieved by introducing a third category which is "abnormal" or "anomalous" in terms of ordinary "rational" categories. Thus myths are full of fabulous monsters, incarnate gods, virgin mothers. This middle ground is abnormal, non-natural, holy. It is typically the focus of all taboo and ritual observance.

This approach to myth analysis derives originally from the techniques of structural linguistics associated with the name of Roman Jakobson (Jakobson and Halle, 1956) but is more immediately due to C. Levi-Strauss, one of whose examples may serve to illustrate the general principle.

Certain Pueblo Indian myths focus on the opposition between life and death. In these myths we find a threefold category distinction: agriculture (means to life), war (means to death), and hunting (a mediating category since it is means to life for men but means to death for animals). Other myths of the same cluster deploy a different triad: grass-eating animals (which live without killing), predators (which live by killing), and carrion-eating creatures (mediators, since they eat meat but do not kill in order to eat). In accumulation this total set of associated symbols serves to imply that life and death are *not* just the back and front of the same penny, that death is *not* the necessary consequence of life (Levi-Strauss, 1955).

My Figure 1 has been designed to display an analogous structure for the case of the first four chapters of Genesis. The three horizontal bands of the diagram correspond to (i) the story of the seven-day creation, (ii) the story of the Garden of Eden, and (iii) the story of Cain and Abel. The diagram can also be read vertically: column 1 in band (ii) corresponds to column 1 in band (i) and so on. The detailed analysis is as follows:—

Upper Band
First Day (I, 1–5; not on diagram). Heaven distinguished from Earth; Light from Darkness; Day from Night; Evening from Morning.

Second Day (I, 6–8; col. 1 of diagram). (Fertile) water (rain) above; (infertile) water (sea) below. Mediated by firmament (sky).

Third Day (I, 9–10; col. 2 and I, 11–12; col. 3). Sea opposed to dry land. Mediated by "grass, herb yielding seed (cereals), fruit trees." These grow on dry land but need water. They are classed as things "whose seed is in itself" and thereby contrasted with bisexual animals, birds, etc.

The creation of the world as a static (that is, dead) entity is now complete and this whole phase of the creation is opposed to the creation of moving (that is, living) things.

Fourth Day (I, 13–18; col. 4). Mobile sun and moon are placed in the fixed firmament of col. 1. Light and darkness become alternations (life and death become alternates).

Fifth Day (I, 20–23; col. 5). Fish and birds are living things corresponding to the sea/land opposition of col. 2 but they also mediate the col. 1 oppositions between sky and earth and between salt water and fresh water.

Sixth Day (I, 24–25; col. 6). Cattle (domestic animals), beasts (wild animals), creeping things. These correspond to the static triad of col. 3. But only the grass is allocated to the animals. Everything else, including the meat of the animals, is for Man's use (I, 29–30). Later, at Leviticus XI, creatures which do not fit this exact ordering of the world—for instance, water creatures with no fins, animals and birds which eat meat or fish, etc.—are classed as "abominations."

Creeping Things are anomalous with respect to the major categories, Fowl, Fish, Cattle, Beast and are thus abominations *ab initio* (Leviticus XI, 41–42). This classification in turn leads to an anomalous contradiction. In order to allow the Israelites to eat locusts the author of Leviticus XI had to introduce a special qualification to the prohibition against eating creeping things: "Yet these ye *may* eat: of every flying creeping thing that goeth on all four which have legs above their feet, to leap withal upon the earth" (v. 21). The procedures of binary discrimination could scarcely be carried further!

(I, 26–27; col. 7), Man and Woman are created simultaneously.

The whole system of living creatures is instructed to "be fruitful and multiply" but the problems of Life versus Death, and Incest versus Procreation are not faced at all.

Center Band

The Garden of Eden story which now follows tackles from the start these very problems which have been evaded in the first version. We start again with the opposition Heaven versus Earth, but this is mediated by a fertilizing mist drawn from the dry infertile earth (II, 4–6). This theme, which blurs the distinction life/death, is repeated. Living Adam is formed from the dead dust of the ground (II, 7); so are the animals (II, 19); the garden is fertilized by a river which "went out of Eden" (II, 10); finally fertile Eve is formed from a rib of infertile Adam (II, 22–23).

The opposition Heaven/Earth is followed by further oppositions —Man/Garden (II, 15); Tree of Life/Tree of Death (II, 9, 17); the latter is called the tree of the "knowledge of good and evil" which means the knowledge of sexual difference.

Recurrent also is the theme that unity in the other world (Eden, Paradise) becomes duality in this world. Outside Eden the river splits into four and divides the world into separate lands (II, 10–14). In Eden, Adam can exist by himself, Life can exist by itself; in this world, there are men and women, life and death. This repeats the contrast between monosexual plants and bisexual animals which is stressed in the first story.

The other living creatures are now created specifically because of the loneliness of Man in Eden (II, 18). The categories are

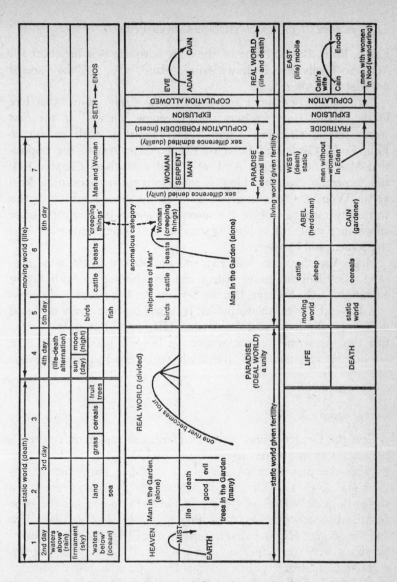

Figure 1. The first four chapters of Genesis contain three separate creation stories. Horizontal bands correspond to (a) 7-day creation; (b) Garden of Eden; and (c) Cain and Abel. Each story sets up opposition of Death versus Life, God versus Man. World is "made alive" by using categories of "woman" and "creeping thing" to mediate this opposition.

Cattle, Birds, Beasts. None of these are adequate as a helpmeet for Man. So finally Eve is drawn from Adam's rib . . . "they are of one flesh" (II, 18–24).

Comparision of Band 1 and Band 2 at this stage shows that Eve in the second story replaces the "Creeping Things" of the first story. Just as Creeping Things were anomalous with respect to Fish, Fowl, Cattle and Beast so Eve is anomalous to the opposition Man versus Animal. And, as a final mediation (Chapter III), the Serpent, a creeping thing, is anomalous to the opposition Man versus Woman. Christian artists have always been sensitive to this fact; they manage to give the monster a somewhat hermaphrodite appearance while still indicating some kind of identification between the Serpent and Eve herself.

Hugo Van der Goes puts Eve and the Serpent in the same posture; Michelangelo makes Adam and Eve both gaze with loving adoration on the Serpent, but the Serpent has Eve's face.

Adam and Eve eat the forbidden fruit and become aware of sexual difference, death becomes inevitable (III, 3–8). But now for the first time pregnancy and reproduction become possible. Eve does not become pregnant until after she has been expelled from Paradise (IV, 1).

Lower Band

Cain the Gardener and Abel the Herdsman repeat the antithesis between the first three days of the creation and the last three days in the first story. Abel's living world is more pleasing to God (IV, 4–5). Cain's fratricide compares with Adam's incest and so God's questioning and cursing of Cain (IV, 9–12) has the same form and sequence as God's questioning and cursing of Adam, Eve and the Serpent (III, 9–19). The latter part of III, 16 is later repeated exactly (IV, 7) so Cain's sin was not only fratricide but also incestuous homosexuality. In order that immortal monosexual existence in Paradise may be exchanged for fertile heterosexual existence in reality, Cain, like Adam, must acquire a wife (IV, 17). To this end Adam must eliminate a sister; Cain a brother. The symmetry is complete.

CROSS-CULTURAL COMPARISON

The issue here is the logical basis of incest categories, and closely analogous patterns must occur in all mythologies regardless of this superficial content. Cross-cultural comparison becomes easier if we represent the analysis as a systematic pattern of binary discriminations as in Figure 2.

Adam/Eve and Cain/Abel are then seen to be variants of a theme which can also occur in other forms as in the well known myth of Oedipus. The actual symbolism in these two cases is nearly identical. Oedipus, like Adam and Cain, is initially earthbound and immobile. The conclusion of the Athenian version of the Oedipus story is that he is an exiled wanderer, protected by the gods. So also is Cain (IV, 14–15). The Bible also includes the converse of this pattern. In Genesis XXVIII Jacob is a lonely exile and wanderer under God's protection but (XXXII, 24–32) he is renamed Israel and thus given the status of a first ancestor with a territorial autochthonous base, and he is lamed by God. Although Jacob dies abroad in Egypt he is buried on his own ancestral soil in Israel (XL, 29–32; L, 5–7).

In the Oedipus story, in place of Eve's Serpent we have Jocasta's Sphinx. Like Jocasta the Sphinx is female, like Jocasta the Sphinx commits suicide, like the Serpent the Sphinx leads men to their doom by verbal cunning, like the Serpent the Sphinx is an anomalous monster. Eve listens to the Serpent's words and betrays Adam into incest; Oedipus solves the Sphinx riddle and is led into incest. Again, Oedipus' patricide replaces Cain's fratricide—Oedipus, incidentally, meets Laïus "at a crossroads."

Parallels of this kind seem too close to be accidental but this kind of algebra is unfamiliar and more evidence will be needed to convince the skeptical. Genesis contains several further examples of first ancestors.

Firstly, Noah survived the destruction of the world by flood together with three sons and their wives. Prior to this the population of the world had included three kinds of being—"sons of God," "daughters of men" and "giants" who were the offspring of the union of the other two (VI, 1–4). Since the forbears of Noah's daughters-in-law have all been destroyed in the Flood, Noah becomes a unique ancestor of all mankind without the implication of incest. Chapter IX, 1–7 addressed to Noah is almost the duplicate of I, 27–30 addressed to Adam.

Though heterosexual incest is evaded, the theme of homosexual incest in the Cain and Abel story recurs in the Noah saga when drunken Noah is seduced by his own son Ham (IX, 21–25). The Canaanites, descendants of Ham, are for this reason accursed. (That a homosexual act is intended is evident from the language "Ham saw the nakedness of his father." Compare Leviticus XVIII, 6–19, where "to uncover the nakedness of" consistently means to have sexual relations with.)

In the second place, Lot survives the destruction of the world by fire together with two nubile daughters. Drunken Lot is seduced by his own daughters (XIX, 30–38). The Moabites and the Ammonites, descendants of these daughters, are for this reason accursed. In Chapter XIX the men of Sodom endeavor to have homosexual relations with two angels who are visiting Lot. Lot offers his nubile daughters instead but they escape unscathed. The implication is that Lot's incest is less grave than heterosexual relations with a foreigner, and still less grave than homosexual relations.

Thirdly, the affair of the Sodomites and the Angels contains echoes of "the sons of God" and "the daughters of men" but links specifically with Chapter XVIII where Abraham receives a visit from God and two Angels who promise that his aging and barren wife Sarah shall bear a son. Sarah is Abraham's half-sister by the same father (XX, 12) and his relations with her are unambiguously incestuous (Leviticus XVIII, 9). Abraham loans Sarah to Pharaoh saying that she is his sister (XII, 19). He does the same with King Abimelech (XX, 2). Isaac repeats the game with Abimelech (XXVI, 9–11) but with a difference. Isaac's wife Rebekah is his father's brother's son's daughter (second cousin) and the relation is *not* in fact incestuous. The barrenness of Sarah is an aspect of her incest. The supernatural intervention which ultimately ensures that she shall bear a child is evidence that the incest is condoned. Pharaoh and Abimelech both suffer supernatural penalties for the lesser offense of adultery, but Abraham, the incestuous husband, survives unscathed.

There are other stories in the same set. Hagar, Sarah's Egyptian slave, bears a son Ishmael to Abraham whose descendants are wanderers of low status. Sarah's son Isaac is marked out as of higher status than the sons of Abraham's concubines who are sent away to "the east country" (cf. wandering Cain who made his home in Nod "eastward of Eden"). Isaac marries a kinswoman in preference to a Canaanite woman. Esau's marriage to a Hittite woman is marked as a sin. In contrast his younger and favored twin brother Jacob marries two daughters of his mother's brother who is in turn Jacob's father's father's brother's son's son.

All in all, this long series of repetitive and inverted tales asserts:

a. the overriding virtue of close kin endogamy;

b. that the sacred hero ancestor Abraham can carry this so far that he marries his paternal half-sister (an incestuous relationship). Abraham is thus likened to Pharaoh, for the Pharaohs of Egypt regularly married their paternal half-sisters; and

c. that a rank order is established which places the tribal neighbors of the Israelites in varying degrees of inferior status depending upon the nature of the defect in their original ancestry as compared with the pure descent of Jacob (Israel).

The myth requires that the Israelites be descended unambiguously from Terah the father of Abraham. This is achieved only at the cost of a breach of the incest rule; but by reciting a large number of similar stories which entail even greater breaches of sexual morality the relations of Abraham and Sarah finally stand out as uniquely virtuous. Just as Adam and Eve are virtuous as compared to Cain and Abel, so Abraham's incest can pass unnoticed in the context of such outrageous characters as Ham, Lot's daughters, and the men of Sodom.

I have concentrated here upon the issue of sexual rules and transgressions so as to show how a multiplicity of repetitions, inversions, and variations can add up to a consistent "message." I do not wish to imply that this is the only structural pattern which these myths contain.

The novelty of the analysis which I have presented does not lie in the facts but in the procedure. Instead of taking each myth

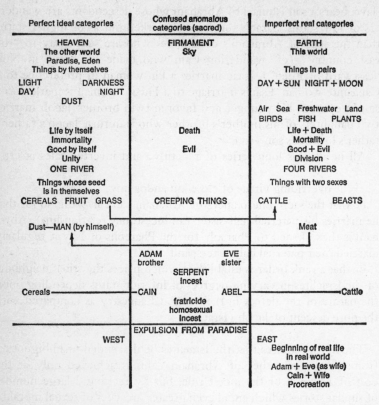

Perfect ideal categories	Confused anomalous categories (sacred)	Imperfect real categories
HEAVEN The other world Paradise, Eden Things by themselves	FIRMAMENT Sky	EARTH This world Things in pairs
LIGHT DARKNESS DAY NIGHT DUST		DAY + SUN NIGHT + MOON Air Sea Freshwater Land BIRDS FISH PLANTS
Life by itself Immortality Good by itself Unity ONE RIVER	Death Evil	Life + Death Mortality Good + Evil Division FOUR RIVERS
Things whose seed is in themselves CEREALS FRUIT GRASS	CREEPING THINGS	Things with two sexes CATTLE BEASTS
Dust—MAN (by himself)		Meat

	ADAM EVE
	brother sister
	        SERPENT
	        Incest	

Cereals————————————	—CAIN ABEL—	————————Cattle
	fratricide homosexual Incest	
	EXPULSION FROM PARADISE	
WEST		EAST Beginning of real life in real world Adam + Eve (as wife) Cain + Wife Procreation

Figure 2. Incest categories have a logical basis in all myths. Similarity between myths is seen most clearly if they are analyzed in a binary form as shown in this table.

as a thing in itself with a "meaning" peculiar to itself, it is assumed from the start that every myth is one of a complex and that any pattern which occurs in one myth will recur, in the same or other variations, in other parts of the complex. The structure that is common to all variations becomes apparent when different versions are "superimposed" one upon the other.

Whenever a corpus of mythology is recited in its religious setting such structural patterns are "felt" to be present, and convey meaning much as poetry conveys meaning. Even though the ordinary listener is not fully conscious of what has been communicated, the "message" is there in a quite objective sense. If the labor of programming could be performed the actual analysis could be done by a computer far better than by any human. Furthermore it seems evident that much the same patterns exist in the most diverse kinds of mythology. This seems to me to be a fact of great psychological, sociological and scientific significance. Here truly are observable phenomena which are the expression of unobservable realities.

NOTES

1. Readers should consult E. R. Leach, "Levi-Strauss in the Garden of Eden," *Transactions of the New York Academy of Sciences* 23 (4), 1961; p. 386–396, for an earlier verson of this paper.
2. References such as (IV, 3) refer to the third verse of the fourth chapter of the book of Genesis (English Authorized Version) unless otherwise stated.

Racinian Man

ROLAND BARTHES

TRANSLATED BY *Richard Howard*

DIVISION

We must remember that division is the fundamental structure of
the tragic universe. It is even its distinctive sign and privilege. For
example, only the tragic hero is divided; confidants and counselors
never debate; they calculate actions, not alternatives. Racinian division is rigorously binary, the possible is never anything but the
contrary. This elementary partition doubtless reproduces a Christian
idea; [1] but in the profane Racine, there is no Manicheism, division is
pure form: it is the dual function that counts, not its terms. Racinian
man does not debate between Good and Evil: he debates, that is all;
his problem is on the level of structure, not of character. [2]

In its most explicit form, cleavage seizes first on the *je* that feels
in perpetual conflict with itself. Love here is a kind of catalytic
power accelerating the crystallization of the two sides. Soliloquy
is the proper expression of division. The Racinian soliloquy is necessarily articulated into two contrary members (*Mais non* . . . , *Hé
quoi* . . . , etc.); it is a spoken consciousness of division, and not a
true deliberation. [3] This is because the hero always feels driven by a
force external to himself, by a very remote and terrible otherness,
of which he feels himself to be the plaything, which can even divide
time from his own person, which can cheat him of his own memory, [4]
and which is strong enough to *reverse* him, causing him to shift, for
instance, from love to hate. [5] We must add that division is the normal
state of the Racinian hero; he recovers his unity only in certain
ecstatic moments, precisely and paradoxically when he is *beside
himself:* rage deliciously solidifies this lacerated ego. [6]

Naturally division involves not only the ego, but also the figure,
in the mythical sense in which this term has already been defined;
the Racinian theater is full of doubles, which continually raise divi-

sion to the level of the play itself: Eteocles and Polynices, Taxiles and Cleofile, Hector and Pyrrhus,[7] Burrhus and Narcissus, Titus and Antiochus, Xiphares and Pharnaces, Nero and Britannicus, and so on. As we shall see in a moment, division, whatever suffering it entails, permits the hero to solve his essential problem, loyalty. Divided, the Racinian being is in a sense deported from his personal past into an external past that he has not made. His disease is to be disloyal to himself and too loyal to the Other. One might say that he himself suffers the cleavage that he has not the courage to impose upon his partner: fused with his tormentor, the victim partly detaches himself from himself. This is why division also permits him to live: it is the price paid in order to *survive:* schism is the ambiguous expression of the disease and the remedy.

THE FATHER

Who is this Other from whom the hero cannot detach himself? First of all—that is, most explicitly—it is the Father. There is no tragedy in which he is not actually or virtually present.[8] It is not necessarily Blood or sex [9] that constitutes him, nor even Power; his being is his anteriority: what comes after him is descended from him, ineluctably committed to a problematics of loyalty. The Father is the Past. And it is because his definition lies far behind his attributes (Blood, authority, age, sex) that he is actually and always a total Father; transcending Nature, he is a primordial, irreversible fact: what has been *is*, that is the code of Racinian time.[10] Naturally for Racine this identity is the ultimate disaster, ineffaceable, inexpiable. It is in this sense that the Father is immortal: his immortality is marked much more by return than by survival. Mithridates, Theseus, Amurath (under the features of the black Orcan) return from death, remind the son (or the younger brother, which is the same thing) that the Father can never be killed. To say that the Father is immortal means that the Anterior is motionless: when the Father is (temporarily) absent, everything falls apart; when he returns, everything is alienated. The Father's absence constitutes disorder; his return institutes the transgression.

Blood, which is granted an eminent position in Racinian metaphysics, is an extensive substitute for the Father. In either case, what is in question is not a biological reality, but a form: Blood is a more diffuse and consequently more terrible anteriority than the Father: it is a trans-temporal being that *abides* like a tree: it subsists integrally and possesses, retains, ensnares. Thus Blood is literally a law, which means a bond and a legality. The only movement permitted to the son is to break, not to detach himself. Here, too, we find the constitutive impasse of the authoritarian relation, the catastrophic alternative of the Racinian theater; either the son kills the Father, or the Father destroys the son: in Racine, infanticides are as numerous as parricides.[11]

The inexpiable struggle between Father and son is that between God and His creature. God or the gods? In the Racinian theater the two fables exist side by side, classical and Jewish. But actually Racine retains only the oppressive and grace-wielding nature of the pagan gods: by the curse they attach to the Blood, the gods merely guarantee the inexpiable character of the Past; their plurality conceals a unique function, which is also that of the Jewish God: vengeance and retribution, but a retribution that always exceeds the transgression,[12] so that we are always concerned with a God somehow anterior to the restrictive law of retaliation. The only true Racinian God is neither Greek nor Christian, but the God of the Old Testament, in His literary and, indeed, epic form: Yahweh. All the Racinian conflicts are based on a single model, that of the couple formed by Yahweh and His people. For both, the relation consists of a *reciprocal* alienation: the omnipotent Being is *personally* attached to His creature, protects and punishes him capriciously, maintains him, by repeated onslaughts, as the chosen term of an indissoluble couple (divine election and tragic election are both terrible). In his turn, the creature feels toward his Creator a panic sentiment of attachment and terror, and of guile as well. In short, son and Father, slave and master, victim and tyrant, lover and beloved, creature and divinity are linked by a dialogue without issue and without mediation. Every case is one of an *immediate* relation, which is denied escape, transcendence, forgiveness, and even victory. The language in which the Racinian hero speaks to Heaven is always a language of combat, and of personal combat. It is either irony (*Voilà de ces grands dieux la suprême justice!* [Such is the ultimate justice of these great gods!]) or chicanery (*Un oracle dit-il tout ce qu'il semble dire?* [Does an oracle say all it seems to say?]) or blasphemy (*Dieu des Juifs, tu l'emportes!* [God of the Jews, you have won!]). The Racinian God exists in proportion to His malignity; devourer of men, like the earliest divinities,[13] His habitual attributes are injustice, frustration,[14] contradiction.[15] But His very Being is Wickedness.

REVERSAL

We must recall here that the mainspring of tragedy-as-spectacle is the same as that of any providential metaphysics: reversal. To change all things into their opposite is both the formula of divine power and the very recipe of tragedy.[16] Reversal is, in fact, the fundamental figure of all Racinian theater either on the level of minor situations, or on the level of an entire play (*Esther*, for example). Here again, we find the obsession of a two-dimensional universe: the world consists of pure contraries that are never mediated. God raises up or casts down—that is the monotonous movement of creation. Examples of these inversions are countless. It is as if Racine constructed his entire theater on this model, which is, etymologically speaking, the peripeteia, and only afterwards invested it with what is called psychology. This is evidently a very old theme, that of the captive crowned, or the tyrant deposed, but in Racine this theme is not a "story," it has no epic density; it is in fact a form, an obsessive image that is adapted to a varying content. The reversal affects a totality: the hero has the feeling that *everything* is caught up in this rocking motion: the whole world oscillates, there is no alloy in the minting of Destiny, precisely because Destiny always seizes on a situation already organized, provided with a meaning, a figure (a *face*).[17] The reversal affects a universe already created by an intelligence. The direction of the reversal is always depressive (except in the "sacred" tragedies): it casts things down from their height, and its image is the fall [18] (Racine's is probably a *descensional* imagination, as the *Cantique spirituel* no. 3 suggests: [19] the reader will recall the analysis of the Racinian *tenebroso*). As pure act, reversal has no duration, it is a point, an explosion (what in classical language is called a *coup*), one might almost say a simultaneity: [20] the hero, struck down, holds in a single lacerating perception the former state of which he is dispossessed and the new state that is assigned to him. As a matter of fact, as in division, the awareness of life is nothing but the awareness of reversal: to be is not only to be divided, but to be reversed.

Now what constitutes the special nature of the tragic reversal is that it is exact and, so to speak, measured. Its fundamental design is symmetry. Destiny turns each thing into its contrary as though in a mirror: inverted, the world continues, only the *direction* of its elements is switched. It is the awareness of this symmetry that terrifies the stricken hero; what he calls the *comble*, the crowning blow of a change, is the very intelligence that always seems to lead fortune *precisely* to its opposite; with terror he sees the universe subject to an *exact* power: for him, tragedy is the art of *precision* (the Latin *ipse*, the essence of the thing).[21]

TRANSGRESSION

Thus tragedy is essentially an action against God, but an action infinitely suspended and reversed. All of Racine lies in that paradoxical moment when the child discovers that his father is wicked, yet wants to remain his child. This contradiction admits of only one solution (and this is the tragedy itself: that the son assume the Father's transgression, that the creature's guilt exempt the Creator). The Father overwhelms unjustly: it will suffice to deserve his onslaughts retroactively for them to become just. Blood is precisely the vehicle of this retroaction. We might say that every tragic hero is born innocent: he becomes guilty in order to save God.[22] Racinian theology is an inverted redemption: it is man who atones for God. Thus we see what is the function of Blood (or of Destiny): it gives man the right to be guilty. The hero's guilt is a functional necessity: if man is pure, then God is impure, and the world falls apart. Hence man must *cling* to his transgression as his most precious belonging: and what surer means of being guilty than making oneself responsible for what is outside oneself, previous to oneself? God, Blood, the Father, the Law—in short, anteriority becomes incriminating in essence. This form of absolute guilt suggests what in totalitarian politics is called objective guilt. The world is a tribunal: if the accused is innocent, the judge is guilty; hence the accused takes upon himself the judge's transgression.[23]

Here we see the exact nature of the relation of authority. A is not only powerful and B weak. A is guilty, B is innocent. But since it is *intolerable* that Power should be unjust, B takes A's transgression on himself: the oppressive relation is reversed into a punitive relation, though without ever halting a whole interplay of blasphemies, feints, breaks, and reconciliations between the two partners. For B's acknowledgment is not a generous oblation: it is the terror of opening his eyes and seeing the guilty Father.[24] This mechanism of guilt nourishes all Racinian conflicts, including the erotic ones: in Racine, there is only one relation, that between God and His creature.

THE "DOGMATISM" OF THE RACINIAN HERO

The liberating movement of Racinian man is purely intransitive, which is already the seed of failure: action has nothing on which it can fasten, since the world is alienated from the outset. The absolute division of the universe, the result of the couple's self-imprisonment, excludes all mediation; the Racinian world is a world of two terms, its status is paradoxical, not dialectical: the third term is missing. Nothing shows this intransitive nature better than the verbal expression of erotic feeling. Love is a state without a grammatical object: *j'aime, j'aimais, vous aimez, il faut que j'aime enfin* [I love, I loved, you love, at last I must love]—it seems that in Racine the verb "to love" is by nature intransitive; what is given is a force indifferent to its object and, in a word, the very essence of the act, as if the act exhausted itself outside of any goal.[25] Love is at its very outset dispossessed of its goal, it is *deceived*. Deprived of reality, it can only repeat, not develop itself. This is why the failure of the Racinian hero finally results from an inability to conceive of time except as a repetition: the alternative always tends to repetition, and repetition to failure. Racinian duration is never maturative, it is circular, it accumulates and harks back but never transforms anything (*Bérénice* is the purest example of this rotation, from which *nothing*, as Racine so perfectly puts it, emerges). In the grip of this motionless time, the act tends toward the rite. Thus, in a sense, nothing is more illusory than the notion of a tragic climax or crisis: it resolves nothing, it merely severs.[26] Such time-as-repetition is naturally the kind that defines the vendetta, the infinite and seemingly motionless generation of crimes. From *La Thébaïde* to *Athalie*, the failure of all the Racinian heroes is to be inexorably reinstated in this circular time.[27]

TENTATIVE SOLUTIONS

Reiterative time is to such a degree God's time that for Racine it is the time of Nature itself; so that to break with this time is to break with Nature, to tend to an anti*physis:* for example, it is to deny, in one way or another, the family and natural filiality. Some Racinian heroes attempt to perform this liberating movement. It must always be a question of accepting a third term in the conflict. For Bajazet, for example, this third term is time: he is the only tragic hero to follow a dilatory course of behavior, to *wait,* and thereby he threatens the tragedy in its essence;[28] it is Atalide who restores him to tragedy, to death, by rejecting any mediation in her love: despite her gentleness, she is an Erinys, she *retrieves* Bajazet. For Burrhus' Nero, the third term is the world, the Emperor's real task (this Nero is progressive); for Narcissus' Nero, it is crime erected into a system, "deliberate" tyranny (this Nero is regressive in relation to the other). For Agamemnon, it is the false Iphigenia, cunningly invented by the priest. For Pyrrhus, it is Astyanax, the child's real life, the construction of an open, new future as opposed to the vendettal law represented by the Erinys Hermione. The hope, in this hideously alternative world, is always to accede to a tertiary order, in which the duo of executioner and victim, Father and son, will finally be transcended. Such is perhaps the optative meaning of all those trios of lovers who pass through the tragedies, less like the classic elements of the adulterous triangle than like the utopian image of an exit from the sterility of the original couple.[29]

But the major solution, the one invented by Racine (and no longer by one or another of his figures), is *bad faith:* the hero is pacified by eluding the conflict without resolving it, by entirely deporting himself from the Father's shadow, by assimilating the Father to absolute Good. This is the conformist solution. Such bad faith inhabits all the Racinian tragedies, it touches a figure here and there, provides him with a moral language; it prevails explicitly in the four "happy" tragedies of Racine: *Alexandre, Mithridate, Iphigénie, Esther.* Here, the tragedy is in a sense transferred, like an abscess, to a black, apparently marginal character, who serves as an expiatory victim for the rest of the group (Taxiles, Pharnaces, Eriphyle, Aman). The tragic character is actually expelled as an undesirable. Once he has gone, the others can breathe, live, leave the tragedy, no one is there to look at them any longer: they can lie to each other and the world, celebrate the Father as a natural Law, enjoy the triumph of their good conscience. As a matter of fact, this elision of tragedy can only be accomplished at the cost of a final accommodation: the Father must be doubled, so that from him can be derived a transcendent, generous figure, detached from the vindictive Father by the distance of a great moral or social function. This is why, in all these tragedies, there is both a Father and a King, distinct from each other. Alexander can be generous, since the vendettal law is transferred to Porus; Mithridates is double: as Father, he returns from death, disturbs, punishes, but as King, he dies, forgives; Agamemnon wants to kill his daughter, but the Greeks, the Church (Calchas), the State (Ulysses) save her; Mordecai imposes the Law, *possesses* Esther, but Ahasuerus challenges the Law and exalts Esther. Perhaps we may see in this cunning division the very act by which Racine continually divided his life between his King (Louis XIV) and his Father (Port-Royal). It is Port-Royal that is in the background of all Racinian tragedy, generating the paradigmatic figures of fidelity and failure. But it is Louis XIV, the indulgence of the Father-as-King, who inspires all the *solutions* of the tragic impasse: it is always by the King that the tragedy is spoiled, and moreover it is to all these "rectified" tragedies that Louis XIV gave his warmest approval.

THE CONFIDANT

Between failure and bad faith, there is, however, one possible way out, that of dialectics. Tragedy does not ignore this possibility; but it has been able to admit it only by banalizing its functional figure: the confidant. In Racine's day, the role's popularity was waning, which perhaps increases its significance. The Racinian confidant (and this is in accord with his origin) is linked to the hero by a kind of feudal tie, a *devotion;* this liaison designates him as a true double, probably delegated to assume all the triviality of the conflict and of its solution, in short, to establish the nontragic part of the tragedy in a lateral zone where language is discredited, becomes *domestic*.[30] As we know, the hero's dogmatism is continually countered by the confidant's empiricism. Here we must recall what has already been observed apropos of the tragic enclosure. For the confidant, the world exists; leaving the stage, he can enter reality and then return from it: his insignificance authorizes his ubiquity. The first result of this *droit de sortie* is that for him the universe ceases to be absolutely antinomic: [31] essentially constituted by an alternative construction of the world, alienation yields once the world becomes multiple. The hero lives in the universe of forms, alternations, signs; the confidant in the world of content, causality, accident. Doubtless he is the voice of reason (an utterly stupid reason, yet with something of Reason all the same) against the voice of "passion"; but this means, in particular, that he voices the possible against the impossible. Failure constitutes the hero, it is transcendent to him; in the confidant's eyes, failure *touches* the hero, it is contingent to him. Whence the dialectical nature of the solutions he (unsuccessfully) proposes, which always consist in mediatizing the alternative.

For the hero, then, the confidant's medicine is therefore aperitive, it consists first of all in opening up the secret, defining the exact status of the hero's dilemma; the confidant tries to produce an illumination. His technique seems crude, but it is a tested one: he must provoke the hero by naïvely representing to him a hypothesis contrary to his impulse, in a word, the confidant must "blunder" [32] (in general, the hero "reacts" to the strategy, but rapidly conceals it under a flood of justifying words). As for the behavior which the confidant recommends for dealing with the conflict, it is always dialectical, that is, subordinates the end to the means. Here are the most frequent examples of such behavior: to *escape* (which is the nontragic expression of tragic death); to *wait* (which, again, is to oppose time-as-repetition by reality's time-as-maturation); [33] to *live* (*vivez!* this injunction, in the mouths of all confidants, stigmatizes the tragic dogmatism as a desire for failure and death: if only the hero would make life a value, he would be saved). In all three forms, the last one imperative, the viability recommended by the confidant is indeed the most antitragic value possible. The confidant's role is not only to represent it, but also to counter the alibis by which the hero masks his will to fail by a *ratio* external to the tragedy and in a sense explanatory of it. He *sympathizes* with the hero, in other words, attenuates his responsibility: he believes him free to escape but not to do wrong, forced into failure yet accessible to its outcome. This is quite the contrary of the tragic hero, who claims utter responsibility when it is a question of taking on himself an ancestral transgression he has not committed, but declares himself impotent when it is a question of transcending it; who seeks to be free, in a word, by being a slave, but not free by being free. Perhaps in the confidant, though he is clumsy and often utterly stupid, we already have a hint of that whole line of irreverent valets who will oppose the lord and master's psychological regression by a supple and happy mastery of reality.

LOGOS AND PRAXIS

What Racinian tragedy reveals is a veritable universality of language. Language here absorbs, in a kind of exaltation, all the functions elsewhere assigned to other forms of behavior; one might almost say that it is *polytechnical:* it is an organ, can take the place of sight, as if the ear looked; [34] it is a sentiment, for loving, suffering, dying are never anything here but speaking; it is a substance, it protects (to be *confounded* is to cease to speak, to be discovered); it is an order, it permits the hero to justify his aggressions or his failures, and from them to derive the illusion of an agreement with the world; it is a morality, it authorizes him to convert passion into a *privilege*. Here perhaps is the key to Racinian tragedy: to speak is to do, the *logos* takes over the functions of *praxis* and substitutes for it. All the disappointment of the world is gathered up and redeemed in speech, *praxis* is drained, language filled. It is not a question of verbalism; Racine's theater is not a garrulous one (much less, in a sense, than Corneille's), it is a theater where action and speech pursue each other and meet only to escape each other at once. One might say that speech here is never an action but a reaction. This may explain why Racine so readily accepted the formal unity of time—for him, spoken time has no difficulty coinciding with real time, since reality is speech—and also why he called *Bérénice* the model of his dramaturgy: here action tends to nullity, to the advantage of an excessive language. [35]

Thus the fundamental reality of tragedy is such speech-as-action. Its function is obvious: to mediatize the relation of force. In a world inexorably divided, tragic figures communicate only by the language of aggression: they *make* their language, they speak their division; that is the reality and the limit of their status. The *logos* functions here like a precious turnstile between hope and disappointment: it gives the original conflict the outlet of a third term (to speak is to endure), and in doing so is utterly a *praxis;* then it withdraws, becomes language again, leaves the relation without mediation, and plunges the hero back into the fundamental failure that protects him. This tragic *logos* is the very illusion of a dialectic, it is the form of an outlet, but only the form: a false door, against which the hero constantly flings himself, since it is alternately the image of a door and its reality.

This paradox explains the demented aspect of the Racinian *logos:* it is both agitation of words and fascination of silence, illusion of power and terror of cessation. Confined in speech, conflicts are obviously circular, for nothing keeps the Other from speaking again. Language reveals the delicious and terrible world of infinite and infinitely possible reversals; whence often, in Racine, a patient *marivaudage* of aggression: the hero becomes exaggeratedly stupid in order to maintain the contention, to postpone the dreadful time of silence. For silence is the invasion of the true *praxis*, the collapse of the entire tragic apparatus: to put an end to speech is to become part of an irreversible process. At this point, then, appears the true utopia of Racinian tragedy: that of a world in which speech would be a solution; but also its true limit: improbability. Language is never a proof. The Racinian hero can never prove himself: we never know who is speaking to whom.[36] Racinian tragedy is merely a failure that speaks itself.

But because the conflict between being and doing is here resolved in seeming, an art of spectacle is instituted. It is certain that Racinian tragedy is one of the most intelligent attempts ever made to give failure an esthetic profundity: it is really the art of failure, the admirably cunning construction of a spectacle of the impossible. In this it seems to contradict myth, since myth starts from contradictions and tends toward their mediation: [37] tragedy, on the contrary, immobilizes contradictions, refuses mediation, keeps the conflict open; and it is true that each time Racine seizes upon a myth to convert it into a tragedy, it is always in a sense to impugn it, to paralyze it, to make it a definitively closed fable. But precisely, subject to a profound esthetic reflection, confined in a form, systematized from play to play so that we can speak of a true Racinian tragedy, finally adopted by a whole posterity with admiration, this rejection of myth becomes itself mythic: *tragedy is the myth of the failure of myth*. Tragedy tends ultimately toward a dialectical function: out of the *spectacle* of failure it believes it can create a transcendence of failure, and out of the passion of the immediate, a mediation. When all things are destroyed, tragedy remains a *spectacle*, that is, a reconciliation with the world.

NOTES

1. See, for instance, the canticle Racine adapted from Saint Paul:
   Mon Dieu, quelle guerre cruelle!
   Je trouve deux hommes en moi . . . (*Cantique spirituel*, no. 3)
   My Lord, how fierce the struggle!
   I find two men within myself . . .

2. Need we recall that cleavage is the first characteristic of a neurotic state: every neurotic's ego is split, and consequently his relations with reality are limited. See Nunberg, *Principes de psychanalyse*, P.U.F., 1957.

3. We may oppose the sterile deliberation of the Racinian hero by the *real* deliberation of old King Danaos, in Aeschylus' *Suppliants*. It is true that Danaos must decide between peace or war—and that Aeschylus is regarded as an archaic poet!

4. Hermione forgets that she herself has ordered Orestes to murder Pyrrhus. (*And*. V,5)

5. *Ah, je l'ai trop aimé pour ne le point haïr.* (*And*. II,1)
   Oh, I have loved him too much not to hate him now.

6. *Ah! je vous reconnais; et ce juste courroux,*
   Ainsi qu'à tous les Grecs, seigneur, vous rend à vous. (*And*. II,5)
   Ah, I recognize you now, and that just wrath, my lord, restores you to yourself as to the Greeks.
   Ma colère revient, et je me reconnais. (*Mith*. IV,5)
   My rage returns, and I know myself once more.

7. Despite the disdain this interpretation has provoked, I am convinced that Hector and Pyrrhus share an ambivalence in Andromache's eyes.

8. The fathers of the Racinian theater: *La Thébaïde*—Oedipus (Blood). *Alexandre*—Alexander (Father-as-god). *Andromaque*—the Greeks, the Law (Hermione, Menelaus). *Britannicus*—Agrippina. *Bérénice*—Rome (Vespasian). *Bajazet*—Amurath, elder brothers (delegated to Roxanne). *Mithridate*—Mithridates. *Iphigénie*—the Greeks, the gods (Agamemnon). *Phèdre*—Theseus. *Esther*—Mordecai. *Athalie*—Jehoiada (God).

9. In addition to Agrippina, Mithridates and Mordecai are expressly father and mother simultaneously:
   Mais moi, qui dès l'enfance élevé dans son sein . . . (*Mith*. IV,2)
   But I, raised in his bosom from childhood . . .
   Mais lui, voyant en moi la fille de son frère,
   Me tint lieu, chère Elise, et de père et de mère. (*Es*. I,1)

But he, recognizing me as his brother's daughter, dear Elise, acted as both father and mother to me.

10. On Racinian time, see Georges Poulet, *Studies in Human Time*, The Johns Hopkins Press, Baltimore.

11. In the seventeenth century, the word "parricide" extended to every attack against authority (Father, Sovereign, State, the gods). As for infanticides, there is one in nearly every play:

Oedipus committing his sons to murderous hatred.
Hermione (the Greeks, the Past) causing the death of Pyrrhus.
Agrippina smothering Nero.
Vespasian (Rome) frustrating Titus.
Mithridates and his sons.
Agamemnon and Iphigenia.
Theseus and Hippolytus.
Athaliah and Joash.
Further, there are two curses from mother to son in Racine: Agrippina and Nero (V,7), Athaliah and Joash (V,6).

12. *Sa haine va toujours plus loin que son amour.* (*Mith.* I,5)
His hatred always reaches farther than his love.

13. *Et le sang d'un héros, auprès des Immortels,*
Vaut seul plus que celui de mille criminels. (*Théb.* III,3)
And a hero's blood is worth more to the Gods than that of a thousand criminals.
J'ai mendié la mort chez des peuples cruels
Qui n'apaisent leurs dieux que du sang des mortels. (*And.* II,2)
I have begged for death among cruel peoples who appease their gods only by human blood.

14. *Mais, hélas! quand sa main semble me secourir,*
C'est alors qu'il s'apprête à me faire périr. (*Théb.* III,3)
But alas, when Heaven seems to favor me is just when it is preparing my destruction.

15. *Voilà de ces grands Dieux la suprême justice!*
Jusques au bord du crime ils conduisent nos pas;
Ils nous le font commettre et ne l'excusent pas. (*Théb.* III,2)
Such is the ultimate justice of these great Gods! They lead us to the brink of crime, compel us to transgress, and do not fogive us for doing so.

16. The theory of the tragic reversal dates from Aristotle. A recent historian has attempted to express its sociological significance: the meaning of the reversal ("to change all things into their opposite," in Plato's phrase) is the expression of a society whose values are dis-

located and upset by the abrupt transition from feudalism to mercantilism, that is, by a sudden promotion of money (fifth-century Greece, Elizabethan England). But in this form, such an explanation cannot apply to French tragedy; a further ideological treatment is required, as in Lucien Goldman's *The Hidden God* and George Thomson's *Marxism and Poetry*.

17. This *solidification* of the experienced situation is expressed in such formulas as: *contre moi tout s'assemble* [everything unites against me]; *tout a changé de face* [everything has changed its aspect], etc.

18. The theory of the fall is given by Aman's wife, Zares:

Où tendez-vous plus haut? Je frémis quand je voi
Les abîmes profonds qui s'offrent devant moi:
La chute désormais ne peut être qu'horrible. (*Es.* III,1)

Why do you seek to rise still higher? I tremble, seeing the deep gulfs that yawn before me: henceforth, the fall can only be dreadful.

19. Referring to the two men in the self:

L'un tout esprit, et tout céleste,
Veut qu'au Ciel sans cesse attaché,
Et des biens éternels touché,
Je compte pour rien tout le reste
Et l'autre par son poids funeste
Me tient vers la terre penché. (*Cantique spirituel*, no. 3)

One, all spirit and celestial, bids me bind myself to Heaven, concerned with eternal things, and count the rest for nought, while the other by his mortal weight drags me down to earth below.

20. The *atemporality* of reversal is obviously emphasized by the unity of time (which proves once again to what a degree these rules are not mere conventions, but the living expression of a complete ideology):

Je me vois, dans le cours d'une même journée . . . (*Brit.* II,3)

I find myself, in the course of a single day . . .

21. The conjunction expressing the tragic *precision* is *lorsque* [just when]: *just when* . . . (statement of the *crowning blow*), *then* . . . (statement of the fall). It is the Latin *cum* . . . *tum* . . . , a complex that is both adversative and temporal (simultaneous). The examples are numberless, in other grammatical forms:

Je n'ai donc traversé tant de mers, tant d'États
Que pour venir si loin préparer son trépas. (*And.* V,1), etc.

Then I have crossed so many seas, so many nations, only to come so far to decide his death.

In the order of situations too, examples are very numerous; I list at random: it is *precisely* in Narcissus that Britannicus confides; it is *precisely* when Eriphyle knows about her birth that she must die; it is *precisely* when Agamemnon condemns his daughter that his daughter rejoices in his kindness; it is *precisely* when Aman supposes he is at the pinnacle of glory that he falls; it is *precisely* by trying to save her lover that Atalide destroys him, etc.

22. *Mon innocence enfin commence à me peser.*
    Je ne sais de tout temps quelle injuste puissance
    Laisse le crime en paix et poursuit l'innocence.
    De quelque part sur moi que je tourne les yeux,
    Je ne voix que malheurs qui condamnent les Dieux.
    Méritons leur courroux, justifions leur haine . . . (And. III,i)
    My innocence at last is beginning to weigh upon me. I do not know what unjust power always leaves crime in peace, and persecutes innocence. Wherever I look, I see nothing but miseries that condemn the gods. Let us deserve their wrath, let us justify their hatred . . .

23. Feudalism in ancient China: "One yields to a stranger only on condition that one commit a transgression; the feudal tie results from the transgression which "must" be committed and from the forgiveness which it is the *purpose* of this transgression to obtain." Granet, *Année sociologique,* 1952, p. 22.

24. In contrast to the famous Oedipus complex, we might call this movement the *Noah complex*: one son laughs at the Father's nakedness, the others look away and conceal it.

25. *J'aimais, Seigneur, j'aimais; je voulais être aimée. (Bér.,* final scene)
    I loved, my lord, I loved; I wanted to be loved.
    Another essentialized verb is "to fear" (*craindre*):
    Qu'est-ce que vous craignez? . . .
                            Je l'ignore moi-même,
    Mais je crains. (Brit. V,1)
    What is it you fear?
    I don't know myself, but I fear.

26. On the contrary, Aeschylean tragedy, for example, does not sever, it resolves (the *Oresteia* institutes the human tribunal): "The bonds are loosened, the remedy exists." (Aeschylus, *Agamemnon*)

27. Agrippina's curse on Nero:
    Ta fureur, s'irritant soi-même dans son cours,
    D'un sang toujours nouveau marquera tous tes jours. (Brit. V,6)
    Your frenzy, exasperating itself in its course, will mark all your days with forever new bloodshed.
    Athaliah's curse upon Joash:
                Je me flatte, j'espère

> Qu'indocile à ton joug, fatigué de ta loi,
> Fidèle au sang d'Achab qu'il a reçu de moi . . .
> On verra de David l'héritier détestable
> Abolir tes honneurs, profaner ton autel
> Et venger Athalie, Achab et Jézabel. (*Ath.* V,6)

I only hope and pray that, rebellious to your yoke, weary of your rule, loyal to the blood of Ahab he has received from me . . . this loathsome heir of David will soon abolish your honors, profane your altar, and revenge Athaliah, Ahab, and Jezebel.

28. Antitragic lines:
> Peut-être avec le temps j'oserai davantage.
> Ne précipitons rien . . . (*Baj.* II,1)

Perhaps with time I shall venture more. Let us not proceed too rashly . . .

29. Hermione says of Andromache, and Pyrrhus:
> Nous le verrions encore nous partager ses soins. (*And.* V,3)

We would still be seeing him divide his love between us.

Orestes, going mad:
> Réunissons trois cœurs qui n'ont pu s'accorder. (*And.* final scene)

Let us unite three hearts that have been unable to agree.

Junia, to Nero and Britannicus:
> Souffrez que de vos cœurs rapprochant les liens . . . (*Brit.* III,8)

Permit me to draw your hearts together once again . . .

Titus to Antiochus:
> Vous ne faites qu'un cœur et qu'une âme avec nous. (*Bér.* III,1)

You make, with us, but one heart and one soul.

Here and elsewhere, there is the trace of a curious Racinian Dostoevski-ism.

30. Phaedra makes Oenone responsible for ridding her of the *business* of the act, so that she retains, nobly, and childishly, only the tragic result:
> Pour le fléchir enfin tente tous les moyens. (*Phèd.* III,1)

To sway him, make use of every means.

31. "It is only in social existence that such antinomies as subjectivism objectivism, spiritualism/materialism, activity/passivity lose their antinomic character . . ." Marx, *Economic and Philosophic Manuscripts of 1844.*

32. Theramenes says to Hippolytus that it is precisely a matter of fulfilling the latter's love for Aricia:
> Quoi! vous-même, Seigneur, la persécutez-vous? (*Phèd.* I,1)

Then do you yourself, my lord, turn against her?

33. *Cédez, mon frère, à ce bouillant transport:*
    Alexandre et le temps vous rendront le plus fort. (Alex. III,3)
    Yield, brother, to this seething frenzy: Alexander and time will make
    you the stronger.
    Laissez à ce torrent le soin de s'écouler. (Ber. III,4)
    Give this torrent a chance to subside.
    Mais ce succès, Madame, est encore incertain.
    Attendez. (Baj. III,3)
    But this success, Lady, is still uncertain. Be patient.

34. The Seraglio makes it possible to turn the ear into a veritable organ of
    perception. (*Baj.* I,1)

35. "The hero and the heroine . . . who quite often suffer most and do
    least." (D'Aubignac, quoted by Schérer, *Dramaturgie française,* p.
    29.)

36. "Psychologically," the problem of the Racinian hero's authenticity is
    insoluble: it is impossible to define a *truth* of Titus' feelings toward
    Berenice! Titus becomes true only at the moment when he separates
    from Berenice, that is, when he shifts from *logos* to *praxis.*

37. C. Levi-Strauss, *Anthropologie structurale,* Chap. XI. (Plon.)

On Fairy Tales

MICHEL BUTOR

Translated by *Remy Hall*

The studies that have been made of French fairy tales are usually concerned with their origin, or their substructure, in folklore. To be sure, I would be the last person to contest the immense interest of such investigations. Yet to address oneself immediately to the peasant oral tradition is a way of evading the problem these tales raise for us.

As a matter of fact, these stories which have been told to us city children, schoolchildren, which we then tell to our own children—rediscovering them in the nick of time, choosing them without hesitation, but choosing them in the dark, without giving any reasons for our choice: "Puss in Boots," "The Blue Bird," "Beauty and the Beast" —were transmitted to us by the written as much as by the spoken word. They were read to us, we read them. The text is there to refresh our memory.

Perrault's tales and those of Mme. d'Aulnoy permit us to observe the precise moment when the transition occurs from folklore to book, when the oral tradition calls writing to its rescue in order to perpetuate itself. Perrault transcribed the *Contes de ma Mère l'Oye* because he was responsive to their beauty, but more particularly because he was aware of their usefulness, of their timeliness. He is in no way an excavator unearthing a buried treasure, an archaeologist of the fairy tale, like the brothers Grimm. He contrasts the "modern" French fantasy with the ancient fables. He does not propose new models, he firmly establishes a contemporary tradition. As for Mme. d'Aulnoy, she invents freely within the domain of fairyland, not concerned with respecting to the letter the stories she has heard.

The mechanism of transmitting the fairy tale is not fundamentally transformed by this intervention of the book. It always involves narratives told by adults to children who, when adults themselves, will tell them again, or read them, or listen to them being read by their

own children. But it is essential to remember that the entire tradition
of French fairy tales that has come down to us directly, which lives
within us, which is part of our very being, has passed, has been
filtered, through certain books, and a very small number of them.

Fairyland, as it is now experienced and transmitted, includes many
elements of foreign origin, like certain tales from the brothers
Grimm, from Andersen, or from *The Thousand and One Nights* in
Galland's translation; within this aggregate, the French tales form an
extremely solid and coherent group.

Innumerable collections have been published since the end of the
seventeenth century, but decantation has left only Perrault's tales,
those of Mme. d'Aulnoy, Mme. Leprince de Beaumont's *La Belle et
la bête*, lost in the dust of the silly moralities of her *Magasin des
enfants*, and the Comtesse de Ségur's *Nouveaux Contes de fées*,
which are the only nineteenth-century tales worthy of comparison
with their predecessors.

I   THE REALM OF THE IMAGINARY

The fairy tale is a narrative intended for children. The teller of the
tale is traditionally represented with the features of an old person.
All our writers have insisted on the usefulness of the tale, and a study
of its moral character indicates their awareness of the full significance
of what they were narrating. The old person, or the adult, is transmitting an experience, without necessarily representing it clearly to
himself.

The child has a limited apprehension of reality, a limited vocabulary. No matter what one discusses with him, one must transpose. In
order to make oneself understood, one must keep to familiar ideas, or
to others which are intelligible in relation to such ideas, by simple
links—the link of opposites, for example.

Veracious narratives, in which the child continually finds himself
immersed—what has been done when he was not present, what others
do—play a fundamental part in the widening, the consolidation, of
his immediate apprehension of reality. It is within this perpetual
story that the fairy tale or narrative of imaginary events intervenes.

It is essential for the child to be able to tell at once that he is in the
realm of the imaginary. The fairy tale is therefore necessarily fan-

tastic, in other words in flagrant opposition to everyday life. The child cannot start with a realistic "literature," particularly in French society where the adult notion of reality is so ossified.

In the sense of wonder which the fairy tale affords the child—and the child who continues to live in us beneath the rind of age—there is, certainly, a delight in novelty, in removal from our usual surroundings, a joy in the object never seen before. But we know very well that this joy is even greater if the object never seen before is presented as visible, as belonging to the world of reality. And most of all, to begin with, there is the pleasure of knowing that all this isn't true, the pleasure of not being taken in by a fiction, the pleasure of feeling in deep agreement with the adult about what is real and what is not. The fairy tale liberates one from the immediate by the possibility it offers of withdrawing from it with the utmost confidence. It is because of the fairy tale that reality presents itself as something certain and solid, something easily distinguished, something one masters and understands.

The stereotyped formulas—"once upon a time," "they lived happily ever after and had many children"—enclose the tale within their parenthesis, and mark, within the adult's perpetual narrative, the transition from the true to the fantastic and vice versa. But this is not enough; within the fairy tale itself the distance in relation to everyday life must be perpetually recalled, whence the constant use of the singularizing superlative: "She was the most beautiful girl ever seen," or "the ugliest dwarf there had ever been in all the history of dwarfs." The storyteller must keep the child's attention alert, put matters straight, assure him that it is really a story, by encounters with unexpected words, by astonishing events, by taking the opposite view, by lavishing the rare, by covering the walls with precious stones.

The fairy is the very incarnation of this improbability. She is what links the pumpkin and the coach. There is no question of believing in fairies, and the child runs no risk of a dangerous belief in fairies: they are there precisely so that he will not believe in fairy tales. To say that it is the fairy who changes the pumpkin into a coach is first of all a way of underlining that fact that, in reality, such an event has little likelihood of occurring.

I anticipate a major objection here. You will say: But the child does believe a little in fairies, we all believe a little in fairies, we want the fairies to appear; this is because we all want reality to be a little different from what grown-ups say about it, and because it is quite possible that reality really is different; it is because the isolation of fairyland is never completely effected, and because, as a consequence, reality never appears to be ossified for good and all.

Beneath Perrault's fairies, other fairies show through faintly, remotely—quite different ones, the fairies of folklore, in which survive the divinities of buried religions. They are the shadows of these shadows, and I am concerned to trace the meaning they have assumed from his time to ours, leaving to others more qualified than myself the task of sorting out their previous existences, to transform back into light the very faint reflection which reaches us here.

Finally, it is the very structure of the contents of fairyland which isolates it. It rests upon an architecture of inversions whose main features we shall explore. Fairyland is the world inverted, the other side of the mirror, the opposite.

II   THE REALM OF THE EXEMPLARY

Considered in its authentic situation—that is, as told or read within the family circle—the fairy tale is a relationship between the adult and the child which does not reduce itself to the fact that one listens to what the other says.

In fact, fairyland constitutes a realm of stable, well-determined consciousness which is indeed what adult and child have most in common. Their apprehensions of reality are very different, and that of the child changes without the adult's being able to follow its progress, but the child knows about fairyland only what the adult tells him. Fairyland is therefore common ground, a perfect center of references, the very realm of the exemplary.

Official, acknowledged morality is more likely to be expressed by direct precepts, and by examples taken from reality or claiming to be taken from reality (Plutarch's *Lives*—suitably edited for the young —lives of the saints, countless stories about good children). The instruction of fairy tales, without criticizing that morality too openly, will constitute a correction of it.

The special language of the fairy tale frees the adult's consciousness. By this ruse a moral experience is transmitted which transcends the acknowledged precepts.

This correction of official morality in no way represents an open rebellion. It fills its gaps, counterbalances its hypocrisy.

Only the useful fairy tales are transmitted, the others are forgotten.

The adult rediscovers only what has had a meaning for him, even if this meaning has remained obscure, only what has helped him. In telling the tale, he obeys the voice of the child he was, which murmurs to him that he is right, that this is what he must read or say, and which stirs and rejoices in the darkness.

Perrault makes an admirable statement in the preface to his verse tales: "They are seeds we sow, which at first produce no more than movements of joy and sadness, but which eventually flower into good inclinations," and under the pseudonym of his son, in the dedicatory epistle of the *Contes de ma Mère l'Oye:* "They encompass a highly judicious morality, one which is to be discovered more or less according to the degree of penetration in the reader."

A world inverted, an exemplary world, fairyland is a criticism of ossified reality. It does not remain side by side with the latter; it reacts upon it; it suggests that we transform it, that we reinstate what is out of place.

III   KINGS AND SHEPHERDS

Fairy tales offer a violently contrasted image of society. They do not speak only of kings and shepherds; they speak of kings who are greater, richer, more powerful, happier than any real kings, of laborers and woodcutters who are even poorer than any the child might encounter.

These superlatives isolate the characters as fictitious, make them into the very type, on the one hand, of the rich, the powerful, the superior person, and on the other, of the helpless, the underprivileged, the inferior in fact.

But the fairy tale does not restrict itself to stressing the inequality —it overcomes and recompenses it: the poor man becomes rich; the laborer becomes, or is revealed to be, a prince.

This reversal of a situation painted in such explicit colors is presented from the first as unlikely, contributes to the isolation of fairyland, and as a result stresses the weight and the rigidity of real social inequalities, the difficulty there is in overcoming them.

Furthermore, it provokes a resolution of the feeling of inferiority, furnishing the child the elements of compensatory waking dream. He can imagine himself the Marquis de Carabas.

But above all, it suggests that the child make this dream into a reality, that he overcome his situation, and shows him the means to do so.

The fairy tale therefore provides a group of more or less veiled practical suggestions, indicating in what way one may get on in the world. This advice may of course depart from official morality. One can scarcely claim that the Marquis de Carabas is scrupulously honest. The fundamental precept is this: the chief means of social elevation is an advantageous marriage.

This reversal, finally, this revelation of a prince disguised as a miller's son, constitutes a warning, an admonition. It exposes the lie of social appearances, and thereby denounces injustice. It assigns a contingent character to what passes itself off as a permanent, definitive, unalterable reality.

The realm of the imaginary, which is composed of the unlikely alongside the realm of reality, gradually applies itself to the latter, with an ever-larger degree of likelihood. In the end, fairyland appears to have covertly provided a deeper vision of that very reality to which at first it had been so contrary. In a sense, it begins to illuminate it from behind. It provides a new consciousness which, the moment it finds itself in dangerous conflict with the old one, acknowledges it, yields to it, and is thereby able to hide behind the mask of the pure fiction which it originally was.

This inequality between kings and shepherds concerns the society of adults or the relations between families. Within the family, in the society of children, of brothers and sisters, we shall find a homologous inequality, the one between older and younger siblings.

The fairy tale will amplify it, paint it in black and white, make it still more visible, and invert it.

Tom Thumb (Poucet) is not only the son of the poorest woodcutter who manages to become a great prince, he is also the youngest of seven brothers, the depised one, the smallest one, who ends by saving the whole family.

The two themes are linked: it is as a result of marriage and social elevation that the youngest becomes the protector, the elder of his elders.

The difference between oldest and youngest brothers, a difference of physical strength and of rank, finds clear illustration in the difference between animals, some strong and highly prized, others weak and despised, sometimes loved but not respected.

Thus the miller's youngest son laments that all he has received as his inheritance is the cat, whereas his elders were bequeathed the mill and the donkey. "My brothers," he said, "will be able to earn an honest living by joining forces; as for me, once I have eaten my cat and made a muff out of its fur, I shall die of hunger." The cat represents both the weakness and the cunning of the youngest son, the donkey the power and the boorishness of the oldest who lets himself be outwitted. If the youngest brother is clumsy, he could only dream that he is cunning as a cat, and if the oldest brother is cunning, he will keep his due.

Once again we find the despised animal who rescues the hero in the carp, the blackbird and the owl who enable Avenant, in Mme. d'Aulnoy's story, to carry out the tasks imposed upon him by the girl with the golden hair, and thus to supplant his king, and again in the blackbird, the cock and the frog who help good little Henri, in the Comtesse de Ségur's story, to climb the mountain.

We shall see that nearly all the themes in fairyland find an illustration in the animal world. It is a mirror within its mirror.

If we turn from the brothers to the sisters, the disadvantage of being the youngest will be translated by the fact that she stays at home. She is the one who is to be married off last, and who is denied fine clothes. Her inferiority is like that of the poorly dressed girl in relation to the elegantly dressed girl, hence like that of a girl who appears to be ugly.

Just as it reveals the hidden prince in the poor laborer, the fairy tale frees the ugly girl of her ass's skin or her cinders.

IV PARENTS AND CHILDREN

The inequalities we have just seen are horizontal; they concern individuals belonging to the same generation. They all appear against the background of vertical inequality between parents and children.

Unlike the preceding ones, this inequality is always surmounted in reality. Life will transform all children into adults. The overcoming of this inequality in the fairy tale therefore appears as an anticipation.

This is the fundamental theme of all the classic French fairy tales.

This transition always occurs, but more or less favorably. Through it, all the conquests of inequality we have already discussed can be made. Its essential moment is marriage, the nucleus around which the entire content of fairyland is organized.

The child becomes a man or a woman. The transition to adulthood has a different meaning for the girl and for the boy. Hence the tales are divided into two large groups, according to the sex of their principal hero.

This in no way implies that some are intended solely for boys, others solely for girls. Children are obviously interested in being informed about what will happen to those of the opposite sex.

The fairy tale, describing to the child his own future transformation, hence a reality which by definition he does not yet know, is obliged to proceed by transposition. The sexual symbolism in fairy tales may seem, after the fact, transparent, yet it is clear that the child is at first incapable of deciphering it. Only gradually will these figures be endowed with a second meaning; only gradually will they permit the child to identify, dimly, the novelties of experience, to make his way less dangerously along unknown paths.

If things were called by their names, the text would be totally unintellible to the child. They must therefore be designated through a story which possesses a patent meaning, beyond that latent meaning which will be desciphered later on. The symbolism of fairy tales corresponds to a necessity of expression.

But to this fundamental necessity is added the ban official morality places on the sexual realm in general. When the child becomes capable of deciphering the latent content, it strikes him as something he must not talk about openly, almost as something he must not decipher at all.

Thus the very fact that the tale possesses a sexual meaning is wrapped in mystery, hiding like a squid in its cloud of ink.

The central episode in "Tom Thumb" and in "Puss in Boots" is the killing of the ogre and the seizing of his possessions. It receives a very detailed treatment in *Le Bon Petit Henri*. A seven-year-old, in order to save his mother, must fetch the plant of life from the top of a mountain. He will reach his goal only after having shown that he is capable of putting the four principal labors of peasant civilization to good use: harvesting, grape gathering, hunting and fishing. These four tests are imposed upon him by four increasingly terrifying guardians: an old man, a giant, an enormous wolf, and a giant cat, each of which, once defeated, gives him a talisman: a snuffbox out of which will come little people, a thistle which gratifies every desire, a stick which one can climb astride for traveling, a talon which can cure and rejuvenate. The series ends with a doctor and a stalk of the plant of life which, pressed to the mother's mouth, will draw her from her sleep. In these three tales we are obviously witnessing a dramatization of the Oedipus complex, but this is only a particular aspect of a more general meaning.

The inequality between father and son receives the same treatment as the horizontal inequalities we have already discussed: it is amplified, then transcended. The ogre is far larger, far more terrifying, etc., than the real father. But the ogre is not only the father in superlatives, he is the masked father. Of course, the disguise is easily seen through, but it is always there. The father is never killed by name in the fairy tale. Opposition to the father, generally countered by love and respect, can be satisfied, even in a dream, only by a ruse. But murder above all is here the brutal image of the fact that the child who is given the rank of father will himself do without his father. In reality it is not the person of the father which will disappear, but his function. In the fairy tale, it is therefore not the father's person which is killed, but his aspect.

The killing of the ogre is linked to the acquisition of wealth and power. The victory over him permits the hero to marry the princess and become king; this elevation is the fulfillment of victory.

In a society of distinct strata, social elevation is sanctioned by marriage, and by marriage alone; this elevation can no longer occur once the transformation from child to father is complete. The child must make haste to seek his fortune, in other words must leave the family circle, must abolish his father's function. And when the grown child has succeeded in obtaining a rank superior to the original rank of his family, he then becomes the protector, the father of his father; he reverses the roles, he has really conquered.

The child reaching adulthood wrests his parents' secrets from them. The walls of their rooms become transparent, like those of the ogre's castle which Finette-Poucet perceives from the top of the tree she has planted, once it has reached its full growth.

The fairy tale sends boys out into the world, encourages them to adventure, but it admonishes girls. For them marriage is even more important than it is for their brothers, and the road leading to it is strewn with many more dangers.

The essential episode in the stories about girls is a catastrophe or a metamorphosis provoked by a symbolic enactment of the sexual act. It is always as a result of a public marriage that matters are set right again.

The anticipated description of the little girl's transformation into a woman is accompanied by the creation, within the child's mind, of a sort of alarm signal which will be set off—mysteriously—in the nick of time.

A spindle prick plunges Sleeping Beauty into a hundred-year sleep; she will awaken when the prince for whom she is destined has penetrated the forest.

In Mme. d'Aulnoy's story, for example, a princess is changed into a doe because a wicked companion has stuck a knife through the leather partition of the *barouche* in which she was imprisoned, causing her to see daylight before the prescribed day. She comments:

> *La princesse trop empressée*
> *De sortir de ces sombres lieux*
> *Oú voulait une sage fée*
> *Lui cacher la clarté des cieux,*
> *Ses malheurs, sa metamorphose,*
> *Font assez voir en quel danger*
> *Une jeune beauté s'expose*
> *Quand trop tôt dans le monde elle ose s'engager.*

> [The princess, being too eager
> To leave these dark places,
> Wherein a wise fairy

Sought to hide the light of heaven from her,
Her misfortunes, her metamorphosis
Clearly show the danger
To which a young beauty is exposed
When she dares face the world too soon.]

Metamorphosis, reduction to animal status, expulsion from society, collapse of every hope, afflict not only the imprudent girl but also the man she loves; the blue bird, *beau-minon*, the beast in "Beauty and the Beast."

These episodes designate what is forbidden. They cast a halo of danger around the sexual act officially despised, and thereby grant it a sacred character. It appears, in all fairy tales, as the most devastating of all things. The final marriage assumes all its glory from the fact that it is a victory over tremendous perils. The rose is so precious only because it blooms in a thornbush.

"Blondine, Blondine, do not ask me for that perfidious flower which pricks those who touch it. Never mention the rose to me, Blondine, you do not know the dangers which threaten you in this flower."

How flamboyant, how desirable, it is behind its iron bars.

The fairy tale protects the adolescent against that which society forbids by giving him the means of recognizing, however vaguely, what he must avoid, but the symbolism of the tale is a mask not only for sexuality, but also for its praise and celebration. Catastrophic images encircle a nucleus of tempting images. Disaster is so black only because it conceals a light, and the final light is so brilliant only because it disperses darkness.

At the end of one of the gardens, there stood a little rotunda filled with choice flowers; in the center was a box which seemed to contain a tree, but a cloth bag entirely covered it; through the cloth, one could see no more than a few specks shining with extraordinary brilliance. . . .

"This is the wedding present I shall give you, but you cannot see it before you are fifteen years old." . . .

She slipped her fingers into one of the holes, pulled lightly, and the cloth tore from top to bottom with a noise like that of thunder, and offered to Rosalie's astonished eyes the sight of a tree whose trunk was made of coral and the leaves of emeralds. . . . But no sooner had she looked upon this incomparable tree than a noise even louder than the first roused her out of her ecstasy: she felt herself being lifted up and transported to a plain, from which she saw the prince's palace collapsing . . . the prince himself climbing out of the ruins, bleeding, dressed in rags. . . .

"Rosalie, ungrateful Rosalie, see to what you have reduced me, me and all my court. . . ."

—Comtesse de Ségur, *La Souris grise*

V MEN AND WOMEN

The inequalities between kings and shepherds, older and younger siblings, can be diminished in reality. The child can advance himself socially and supplant his elders. But, whereas the difference between parents and children can be diminished, that between the sexes is accentuated. The same night consecrates the abolition of the first and the fulfillment of the second.

The difference between men and women is aggravated, in the society of the *ancien régime*, by a profound juridical inequality. The status of women is experienced as an inferiority, and this inferiority, contrary to the others, is definitive. There exists no means by which the child can effectively transcend it by passing into adulthood, since one of the fundamental characteristics of this age is the fact that this difference then appears in full force.

But the fairy tale, which stresses this difference by distinguishing, in general, very clearly between stories about girls and stories about boys, does however afford a certain compensation.

It is not enough to show that there is a sexual symbolism in the tales; we must examine their structure at close range. Then we notice that within the very legible general figuration, the language of the details is consistently ambivalent. In the secret chamber of the tale, the woman mimes the role of the man, as in the marriage ceremony of certain remote cultures.

In "Little Red Riding-Hood," we have a very good example of what we have called an alarm signal, and this is precisely the interpretation Perrault gives of it in his moral:

> *On voit ici que de jeunes enfants,*
> *Surtout de jeunes filles,*
> *Belles, bien faites et gentilles,*
> *Font très mal d'écouter toutes sortes de gens,*
> *Et que ce n'est pas chose étrange,*
> *S'il en est tant que le loup mange.*
> *Je dis le loup, car tous les loups*
> *Ne sont pas de la même sorte.*
> *Il en est d'une humeur accorte,*
> *Sans bruit, sans fiel et sans courroux,*
> *Qui, privés, complaisants et doux,*
> *Suivent les jeunes demoiselles*
> *Jusque dans les maisons, jusque dans les ruelles.*
> *Mais hélas qui ne sait que ces loups doucereux*
> *De tous les loups sont les plus dangereux.*

[We see here that young children,
Particularly young girls,
Beautiful, well-made and kind,
Make a great mistake in listening to all sorts of people,
And it is by no means strange
That the wolf should eat them.
I say the wolf, because not all wolves
Are of the same sort.
There are some of a gracious disposition,
Silent, never harsh, never angry,
Who, careful, compliant and gentle,
Follow young ladies
Even into their houses, even down the lanes.
But alas, we all know these charming wolves
Are the most dangerous wolves of all.]

Which is quite transparent. But if we examine the details, we perceive that a secondary, inverted symbolism is superimposed upon this primary symbolism.

Indeed, the little girl is designated not only by a masculine name, in French, but by a masculine symbol; she carries not only a cake, but also a pot of butter. At the moment indicated by the special formula —"draw the bolt and the latch will open"—it is she who enters the house. And the wolf has on the grandmother's clothes.

Let us note that this story is the only one of which the folk version has survived Perrault's transcription. Perrault stops at the words: "The wicked wolf leaped on Little Red Riding-Hood and ate her up." But everyone knows that this is not the real ending, that the fairy tale's parenthesis is not closed, that we must go on, that the villagers run in, open the wolf's belly, and take out Little Red Riding-Hood alive. I imagine that Perrault, who often gives several versions, deliberately eliminated this ending, which too flagrantly contradicts the moral he had drawn, since in it the wolf assumes an aspect too obviously feminine. But the logic of the tale has been more powerful.

Again, it is Cinderella who puts her foot in the slipper presented by the prince's envoy, it is Peau d'Âne who places his finger in the emerald ring which comes to him from the castle, it is Bluebeard's wife who thrusts the golden key into the lock, and Rosalie who puts her hand into the hole in the cloth. Within her own story, Mme. d'Aulnoy's Cinderella, Finette Cendron, lives through all the adventures of Tom Thumb. Riquet and his princess exchange their privileges, Ourson and Violette their skins.

One already finds in Perrault, as in Mme. d'Aulnoy, every one of the themes we have touched upon. The Comtesse de Ségur will recapitulate them all, organizing them in a remarkably clear manner. She is the twilight of the classic fairy tale.

Fairy tales are closely linked to the society which they helped counterpoise, and I believe it would no longer be possible today to write authentic "new fairy tales." The old ones live on, but, the difficulties of the growing child no longer being the same, we must complete them by new stories in which the fairies have so altered their faces that we must give them other names.

APPENDIX

The Mirror of Enigmas

JORGE LUIS BORGES

TRANSLATED BY *James E. Irby*

The idea that the Sacred Scriptures have (aside from their literal value) a symbolic value is ancient and not irrational: it is found in Philo of Alexandria, in the Cabalists, in Swedenborg. Since the events related in the Scriptures are true (God is Truth, Truth cannot lie, etc.), we should admit that men, in acting out those events, blindly represent a secret drama determined and premeditated by God. Going from this to the thought that the history of the universe —and in it our lives and the most tenuous detail of our lives—has an incalculable, symbolical value, is a reasonable step. Many have taken that step; no one so astonishingly as Léon Bloy. (In the psychological fragments by Novalis and in that volume of Machen's autobiography called *The London Adventure* there is a similar hypothesis: that the outer world—forms, temperatures, the moon— is a language we humans have forgotten or which we can scarcely distinguish . . . It is also declared by De Quincey:[1] "Even the articulate or brutal sounds of the globe must be all so many languages and ciphers that somewhere have their corresponding keys— have their own grammar and syntax; and thus the least things in the universe must be secret mirrors to the greatest.")

A verse from St. Paul (I Corinthians, 13:12) inspired Léon Bloy. *Videmus nunc per speculum in aenigmate: tunc autem facie ad faciem. Nunc cognosco ex parte: tunc autem cognoscam sicut et cognitus sum.* Torres Amat has miserably translated: "At present we do not see God except as in a mirror and beneath dark images; but later we shall see him face to face. I only know him now imperfectly; but later I shall know him in a clear vision, in the same way that I know myself." Forty-nine words do the work of 22; it is impossible to be more languid and verbose. Cipriano de Valera is more faithful: "Now we see in a mirror, in darkness; but later we shall see face to face. Now I know in part; but later I shall know as

I am known." Torres Amat opines that the verse refers to our vision of the divinity; Cipriano de Valera (and Léon Bloy), to our general vision of things.

So far as I know, Bloy never gave his conjecture a definitive form. Throughout his fragmentary work (in which there abound, as everyone knows, lamentations and insults) there are different versions and facets. Here are a few that I have rescued from the clamorous pages of *Le mendiant ingrat, Le Vieux de la Montagne* and *L'invendable*. I do not believe I have exhausted them: I hope that some specialist in Léon Bloy (I am not one) may complete and rectify them.

The first is from June, 1894. I translate it as follows: "The statement by St. Paul: *Videmus nunc per speculum in aenigmate* would be a skylight through which one might submerge himself in the true Abyss, which is the soul of man. The terrifying immensity of the firmament's abysses is an illusion, an external reflection of *our own* abysses, perceived 'in a mirror.' We should invert our eyes and practice a sublime astronomy in the infinitude of our hearts, for which God was willing to die . . . If we see the Milky Way, it is because it *actually exists in our souls.*"

The second is from November of the same year. "I recall one of my oldest ideas. The Czar is the leader and spiritual father of a hundred fifty million men. An atrocious responsibility which is only apparent. Perhaps he is not responsible to God, but rather to a few human beings. If the poor of his empire are oppressed during his reign, if immense catastrophies result from that reign, who knows if the servant charged with shining his boots is not the real and sole person guilty? In the mysterious dispositions of the Profundity, who is really Czar, who is king, who can boast of being a mere servant?"

The third is from a letter written in December. "Everything is a symbol, even the most piercing pain. We are dreamers who shout in our sleep. We do not know whether the things afflicting us are the secret beginning of our ulterior happiness or not. We now see, St. Paul maintains, *per speculum in aenigmate*, literally: 'in an enigma by means of a mirror' and we shall not see in any other way until the coming of the One who is all in flames and who must teach us all things."

The fourth is from May, 1904. "*Per speculum in aenigmate*, says St. Paul. We see everything backwards. When we believe we give, we receive, etc. Then (a beloved, anguished soul tells me) we are in Heaven and God suffers on earth."

The fifth is from May, 1908. "A terrifying idea of Jeanne's, about the text *Per speculum*. The pleasures of this world would be the torments of Hell, seen backwards, in a mirror."

The sixth is from 1912. It is each of the pages of *L'Âme de Napoléon*, a book whose purpose is to decipher the symbol Napoleon, considered as the precursor of another hero—man and symbol as well—who is hidden in the future. It is sufficient for me to cite two passages. One: "Every man is on earth to symbolize something he is ignorant of and to realize a particle or a mountain of the invisible materials that will serve to build the City of God." The other: "There is no human being on earth capable of declaring with certitude who he is. No one knows what he has come into this world to do, what his acts correspond to, his sentiments, his ideas, or what his real name is, his enduring Name in the register of Light . . . History is an immense liturgical text where the iotas and the dots are worth no less than the entire verses or chapters, but the importance of one and the other is indeterminable and profoundly hidden."

The foregoing paragraphs will perhaps seem to the reader mere gratuities by Bloy. So far as I know, he never took care to reason them out. I venture to judge them verisimilar and perhaps inevitable within the Christian doctrine. Bloy (I repeat) did no more than apply to the whole of Creation the method which the Jewish Cabalists applied to the Scriptures. They thought that a work dictated by the Holy Spirit was an absolute text: in other words, a text in which the collaboration of chance was calculable as zero. This portentous premise of a book impenetrable to contingency, of a book which is a mechanism of infinite purposes, moved them to permute the scriptural words, add up the numerical value of the letters, consider their form, observe the small letters and capitals, seek acrostics and anagrams and perform other exegetical rigors which it is not difficult to ridicule. Their excuse is that nothing can be contingent in the work of an infinite mind.[2] Léon Bloy postulates this hieroglyphical character—this character of a divine writing, of an angelic cryptography—at all moments and in all beings on earth.

The superstitious person believes he can decipher this organic writing: thirteen guests form the symbol of death; a yellow opal, that of misfortune.

It is doubtful that the world has a meaning; it is even more doubtful that it has a double or triple meaning, the unbeliever will observe. I understand that this is so; but I understand that the hieroglyphical world postulated by Bloy is the one which best befits the dignity of the theologian's intellectual God.

No man knows who he is, affirmed Léon Bloy. No one could illustrate that intimate ignorance better than he. He believed himself a rigorous Catholic and he was a continuer of the Cabalists, a secret brother of Swedenborg and Blake: heresiarchs.

NOTES

1. *Writings*, 1896, Vol. 1, p. 129.
2. What is a divine mind? the reader will perhaps inquire. There is not a theologian who does not define it; I prefer an example. The steps a man takes from the day of his birth until that of his death trace in time an inconceivable figure. The Divine Mind intuitively grasps that form immediately, as men do a triangle. This figure (perhaps) has its given function in the economy of the universe.